The Best American
Travel Writing 2014

The Best American Travel Writing™ 2014

Edited and with an Introduction
by **Paul Theroux**

Jason Wilson, Series Editor

A Mariner Original

HOUGHTON MIFFLIN HARCOURT

BOSTON • NEW YORK 2014

ISSN 1530-1516
ISBN 978-0-544-33015-3

Printed in the United States of America
DOC 10 9 8 7 6 5 4 3 2 1

"Poisoned Land" by Elif Batuman. First published in *The New Yorker*, August 12, 2013. Copyright © 2013 by Elif Batuman. Reprinted by permission of The Wylie Agency, LLC.

"Amigos" by Julia Cooke. First published in *Virginia Quarterly Review*, Spring 2013. Copyright © 2013 by Julia Cooke. Reprinted by permission of Julia Cooke.

"Life During Wartime" by Janine di Giovanni. First published in *Harper's Magazine*, April 2013. Copyright © 2013 by Janine di Giovanni. Reprinted by permission of Janine di Giovanni.

"America the Marvelous" by A. A. Gill. First published in *Vanity Fair*, July 2013. Extracted from chapter 2 of *To America with Love* by A. A. Gill. Copyright © 2011 by A. A. Gill. Originally published in Great Britain by Weidenfeld and Nicholson. Reprinted with permission of Simon and Schuster, Inc. All rights reserved.

"Christmas in Thessaloniki" by Arnon Grunberg. Translated from the Dutch by Sam Garrett. First published in *The Believer*, September 2013. Copyright © 2013 by Arnon Grunberg. Reprinted by permission of Arnon Grunberg.

"Fifty Shades of Greyhound" by Harrison Scott Key. First published in *Oxford American*, Summer 2013. Copyright © 2013 by Harrison Scott Key. Reprinted by permission of *Oxford American*.

"Au Train de Vie" by Peter LaSalle. First published in the *Missouri Review*, Sum-

Contents

Foreword

TAPED TO MY DESKTOP computer monitor is a yellowing *New Yorker* cartoon from about a decade ago: a chic-looking man and woman sit at a table and gaze at each other over glasses of wine; the woman, her hand clutching at her bosom, says to the man, "Do wine writers suffer and all that?"

I keep this cartoon at my desk because, for years, alongside my work shepherding this travel writing anthology through 15 editions, I have also been writing about wine. Wine writing should, or could, be an adjunct to travel writing: at its most basic level, wine writing takes me on amazing trips around the world. But I'm always surprised how dissimilar the two genres have become.

Part of it has to do with the lack of immediate, visceral drama that happens on my wine itineraries. When I travel to write about wine, I go to some of the most beautiful places on earth, where I drink amazing bottles from some of the world's best winemakers and dine in some of the world's finest restaurants. While all this is fantastic and a lovely way to earn money, it does not exactly offer the gripping, universal, ripped-from-experience conflict that is the linchpin of compelling narrative nonfiction. (Please, do not cry for me.)

"Hmmmmm," says the wine writer, swirling, sipping, and spitting in the tasting room overlooking the gorgeous vineyards. "The tannins on the '06 are a little bit green and aggressive right now. How disappointing. Perhaps it needs a few more years in the cellar. What a pity."

As the woman in the cartoon asks, "Do wine writers suffer and all that?"

Travel writing, as we've come to know, is all about travail. We've been told that travel without suffering makes for a lousy story. As Camus once wrote, "What gives value to travel is fear." Whatever I feel about the ripeness of last autumn's Gewürztraminer in Alsace, it is far from fear.

Now, I am certainly not complaining that I do not suffer sufficiently. I can't think of anything worse than a whining wine or travel writer. But when I sat down to write my first wine book last year, I thought a lot about what made my wine writing so different from my travel writing.

All genre writing has certain generic conventions. Travel writing, for instance, has a convention called the "why I went." I saw the "why I went" defined in L. Peat O'Neil's book *Travel Writing: A Guide to Research, Writing, and Selling:* "The writer's 'I' has one specific place to appear after the reader is grounded and gives the 'why I went' signal for the trip's purpose . . . Explaining why you are there may give readers their own motivations to travel to the same place and certainly a reason to continue reading. Share your travel motivation to heighten identification and gain reader sympathy." The "why I went" that O'Neil describes is well established, almost strictly enforced within travel publishing: "Since I have been nomadic my whole life, I decided to go on my very own Australian walkabout." Or: "My marriage ended, so I bought a farmhouse in Tuscany." Most loyal readers of travel books know the drill.

Wine writing has generic conventions similar to the "why I went." Wine books, for instance, almost always begin with a light-hearted tale of the author's initiation into the world of wine via some crappy bottle of plonk. This is where you'll normally read an anecdote of misguided youth involving, say, Thunderbird, Sutter Home white zinfandel, Boone's Farm, Lancers, Mateus, Korbel, Bartles & Jaymes wine coolers, or—for the generation of wine books soon to be written by millennials—boxes of Franzia. It's sort of an immutable law.

I began my own book by describing a period during my senior year of high school when I was very enthusiastic about Mogen David's flavored and fortified wine MD 20/20, otherwise known as

"Mad Dog." MD 20/20's Orange Jubilee was my particular tipple of choice, and the reason had more to do with how much easier it was to hide in the woods than a six-pack of beer. I vaguely remember it tasting like a mix of chalky, watered-down SunnyD and grain alcohol, but I've mostly tried to cleanse that memory from my mind, along with numerous other suburban New Jersey public school rites of passage.

My MD 20/20 connoisseurship ended soon after I left for college in the big city. During the first week of college, I professed my enthusiasm for Mad Dog and shared some Orange Jubilee with the new friends on my floor. After gagging and spitting out the MD 20/20, they laughed and gave me the ironic nickname "Mad Dog," which stuck until I transferred to a new school at the end of my freshman year. It was an early lesson in how fraught it can be to express a wine preference. It was also a lesson in how it feels to have one's taste disapprovingly assessed.

In reality, there was no reason my first "wine" had to be MD 20/20 Orange Jubilee. My father was of the generation that, in the late 1970s and 1980s, leapt headlong into an appreciation of Napa and Sonoma Cabernet Sauvignon and Chardonnay. There were often bottles of Kendall Jackson, Robert Mondavi, Grgich Hills, or Beringer opened at dinners and parties. I occasionally had a taste, but back then I had little interest in drinking what my parents drank.

So it wouldn't be until the summer after my sophomore year, when I was 19, that I first truly *experienced* wine. I was studying abroad in Italy, living with a family in a village called Pieve San Giacomo, near the Po River in the province of Cremona. Every night, Paolo, the father, sliced a plateful of prosciutto and cut a hunk from a wheel of Grana Padano. Then he uncorked and poured a fizzy red, chilled, from an unlabeled liter bottle he'd fetched from a dark corner of the barn—the same barn I'd wandered into one morning and there saw him butchering a cow. Paolo didn't go for fancy wineglasses, but rather used what we would have called juice glasses back home in Jersey. Beyond retrieving the sliced meat, cheese, and wine, men were otherwise forbidden in his wife's kitchen, so while Anna busily made us dinner and the television blared a soccer game, Paolo and I would sip our cool, fizzy red wine from our juice glasses on those hot evenings.

I had never tasted or witnessed a wine like this. The liquid was bright purple, with a thick pink foam that formed as it was poured. I knew enough to know that the Napa Cabs on my parents' table back home didn't foam. Paolo's wine certainly tasted fruity, though it was more tangy than sweet, and what made it strange to me was the aroma. Whereas my father's wines smelled like identifiable fruits—plums, cherries, berries—this fizzy wine was a little stinky, to be honest, but in a pleasant way. I didn't have the language back then, but in my memory the aroma is earthy, rustic, fertile, alive, almost like the essence of the farm and the dusty streets of the village. Back then, it simply smelled and tasted like the Old World I had hoped to find.

Of course, being young and naive, I never bothered to ask Paolo anything about his wine—the grapes, where it was made, who made it. I kept in touch with the family, but Paolo died a decade ago, and since neither Anna nor his daughter, Daniela, drink wine, I never did learn the fizzy red's provenance. Over the years, though, as my wine knowledge grew, I hypothesized that what I'd been imbibing on those summer evenings long ago had been Lambrusco, mainly since Pieve San Giacomo is just over an hour's drive from Modena, Lambrusco's spiritual home.

As I moved further into drinking and writing about wine, I occasionally told Wine People I met at trade tastings and industry events about enjoying this fizzy red wine as a 19-year-old, and it never failed to draw a chuckle. "Lambrusco!" they'd say. "Riunite!" Cheap, sweet Lambrusco had, of course, had its heyday in the 1970s, just like the leisure suit and swingers and fern bars, and I can remember seeing those cheesy "Riunite on ice. That's nice!" commercials when the babysitter let us stay up late to watch *The Love Boat* and *Fantasy Island*. But as Americans' knowledge increased during the 1980s and 1990s, budding wine connoisseurs didn't want to hear about fizzy red wine anymore.

So even though the stuff I used to drink back in Pieve San Giacomo was neither sweet nor cheap, I just stopped talking about it, or even thinking about it. Like so many other aspirational Wine People my age, I dutifully learned to appreciate Serious Red Wines, which in the early 21st century mainly meant Cabernet Sauvignon and Pinot Noir from various pricey bottlings. I studiously pursued an education in Bordeaux and Burgundy and all those big California reds that my father appreciated. Instead of rustic Italian wine, I delved deeply into Barolo and Brunello di Montalcino.

I filed my old "unserious" fizzy red alongside my youthful Orange Jubilee. I was being schooled by wine educators and sommeliers and wine critics that, as a knowledgeable wine drinker, a Wine Person, I should be moving beyond things like fizzy reds. That is, after all, what usually happens next in a traditional wine education. You're told that wine is a ladder, with the student constantly reaching upward, leaving behind so-called lesser wines and climbing toward greatness, toward the profound, toward—inevitably—the expensive.

This is why, two decades after my summer abroad, I found myself in Italy's Langhe region, in Piedmont, visiting a bunch of producers of Barolo, the complex, elegant wine made from Nebbiolo grapes—the epitome of a Serious Wine. I tasted dozens of amazing, and often profound and transcendent, Barolos, which convinced me, once again, that Nebbiolo grapes grown in this corner of northwestern Italy create one of the world's greatest wines.

My visit culminated on a sunny Sunday afternoon with an auction called the Asta del Barolo, inside the famous castle in the town of Barolo. Collectors—some from as far away as China, Singapore, and Dubai—purchased bottles from prized vintages for thousands of dollars. One acquaintance, an Austrian banker living in Hong Kong, paid 3,000 euros (about $4,100) for three magnums dating from the mid-1980s. I sat next to a charming producer, whose family's elegant, silky Barolos annually receive high scores from critics, who call them "genius" and "breathtaking." During lunch, we tasted about 15 examples of the 2009 vintage. Later, there was talk among the younger winemakers about Jay-Z's recent visit to Barolo, where he supposedly dropped $50,000 on wine and truffles.

I won't lie: it is sexy and exciting to be part of an afternoon crowd like that. And I cannot state clearly enough how much I enjoy Barolo. Perhaps it is geeky to say, but sipping it can be like listening to a beautiful, challenging piece of music or standing before a grand, moving work of art. I love it so much that when people ask what my favorite wine is, I often exclaim, "Barolo!" And they nod and say, "Ah, yes. Barolo, of course."

But that afternoon at the castle was total fantasyland. When I returned home, would I be drinking very much Barolo? Um, no, not so much. Saying that Barolo is my "favorite" is very much a misrepresentation of my everyday drinking habits. How often do I drink it? Outside of professional tastings, when I'm buying wine to serve at home or when I order it in restaurants, I probably drink Barolo three or four times a year. Maybe five if I'm particularly flush. That's because the price of a decent Barolo at a wine shop starts at around $60 a bottle and quickly climbs to well over $100. Double or triple that price on a restaurant wine list. Even though I love Barolo, it will always be a special-occasion wine.

I was thinking deeply about greatness in wines when I decided to make a quick side trip to visit my old exchange family in Pieve San Giacomo. On a whim, I'd asked Daniela, Paolo's daughter, to do a little research to see where her father used to buy his fizzy red wine, and with some effort we located the winemaker. To my surprise, the winemaker was not based in Modena, but rather a couple of hours in the other direction, in the Colli Piacentini—the Piacenza hills—a region I'd never heard of.

After getting lost, and refereeing an argument between Daniela and Anna, who was almost carsick in the back seat, we were finally welcomed into the garage of the winemaker, 80-year-old Antonio, and his daughter, who was roughly my age. Anna became emotional—the last time she'd visited the winemaker was in the early 1990s with Paolo. "I remember you had a goat, and it used to like eating the grapes!" she said. The goat, of course, was long dead.

From stainless steel tanks, we tasted his crisp Riesling and a strange, straw-yellow wine made from the local Ortrugo grapes. Antonio told me that most of his customers come to buy his wine in demijohns because they prefer to bottle it themselves, as Paolo did.

"What about the frizzante red?" I asked. "Do you still make it?"

He smiled broadly and retrieved a bottle from a corner of the garage. He grabbed a wide white bowl and splashed the purple wine into it as the wine formed a pink foam. "My customers insist on white bowls for the red," Antonio said, "to bring out the color and aromas."

I closed my eyes and took a sniff, then took a sip. Sharp, fresh, tangy, earthy. Wow! The aromas and flavors were like a time machine. I was again 19, dressed in a Grateful Dead T-shirt and Birkenstocks, experiencing wine for the first time. Holding the huge wide bowl to my face nearly brought me to tears in the dark garage. "Ah, Lambrusco," I said, with a satisfied smile.

Antonio laughed. "Lambrusco? No, no, no. This is Gutturnio!"

"Gutturnio?" I said. What the hell was Gutturnio? I must have said something wrong. Maybe I was having trouble understanding the dialect. "Is that the local name for Lambrusco?" I asked.

He laughed again. "No! It's Gutturnio. It's a blend of Barbera and Bonarda."

Um . . . what? For 20 years, I'd been telling myself that my seminal wine experience had been Lambrusco. Now I find out that it was a wine called Gutturnio? And how had I never even heard of this wine? It's not like it's new. I later learned that the Romans drank it from a round jug called a *gutturnium,* from which the wine's name is taken. Julius Caesar's father-in-law was famous for producing this wine.

We sat at Antonio's table and ate cheese and meat with the wine, and Anna and Antonio reminisced about the old days. Antonio said that he now sold about 4,000 bottles per year, about half what he had about 20 years ago. "Ah," he said, "a lot of my customers, they're dying." Meanwhile, the younger generation just isn't as interested in local wines like his anymore. "Nowadays, people want different tastes. There are a lot of other tastes that people seek." Antonio shrugged. "There is an end for everything. Everything ends."

Suddenly, this humble, fizzy, purple Gutturnio that I swirled around in a white bowl—which connected me to my own past, to ancient Rome, and yet at the same time was totally fresh knowledge—seemed more important than even the greatest Barolo. The strange experience I was having in a farmhouse in the Piacenza hills seemed to me to be the very essence of wine, the reason people spend their lives obsessed with it, an example of how wine becomes part of our lives.

As I thought about all this—about wine and Italy and youth and family and revisiting scenes of unadulterated happiness—it occurred to me that this wasn't so different from how one falls in love with travel in the first place. They might even go hand in hand. And telling this kind of story isn't so different from telling any other story that one might call travel writing.

Camus and others may have a point—that travel is about fear and suffering and travail. That has become an accepted truth of travel writing. But this truth is only partially correct. Travel is also very much about love and memory. I'm hoping that this anthology shows you that love—as well as fear and suffering and travail.

The stories included here were, as always, selected from among hundreds of pieces in hundreds of diverse publications—from mainstream and specialty magazines to Sunday newspaper travel sections to literary journals to travel websites. I've done my best to be fair and representative, and in my opinion the best travel stories from 2013 were forwarded to guest editor Paul Theroux, who made our final selections.

This is the second time I've worked with Paul on this anthology (the first was way back in 2001), and it was just as much of an honor today to work with a travel writing hero of mine and a master of the genre. The world has changed a great deal since 2001, but I think you'll find that the key characteristics of great travel writing never really change. I'd also like to thank Tim Mudie at Houghton Mifflin Harcourt for his help in producing this year's outstanding collection, our 15th. I hope you enjoy it.

I now begin anew by reading the hundreds of stories published in 2014. As I have for years, I am asking editors and writers to submit the best of whatever it is they define as travel writing. These submissions must be nonfiction, published in the United States during the 2014 calendar year. They must not be reprints or excerpts from published books. They must include the author's name, date of publication, and publication name, and they must be tear sheets, the complete publication, or a clear photocopy of the piece as it originally appeared. All submissions must be received by January 1, 2015, in order to ensure full consideration for the next collection.

Further, publications that want to make certain that their contributions will be considered for the next edition should be sure to include this anthology on their subscription list. Submissions or subscriptions should be sent to Jason Wilson, Best American Travel Writing, 228 Kings Highway, 1st floor, Suite 2, Haddonfield, NJ 08033.

Finally, I would like to dedicate this year's anthology to one of our contributors, Matthew Power, who died tragically in March of this year while on assignment in Uganda, reporting on an explorer walking the length of the Nile. Matt was 39, which made him a contemporary of mine, and he was a true adventurer and seeker of truth whom I admired tremendously. Those who are loyal readers of *The Best American Travel Writing* know Matt's work well, as it has been included here several times over the past decade. He will be greatly missed.

JASON WILSON

Introduction

TRAVEL WRITING TODAY is pretty much what travel writing has always been, a maddeningly hard-to-pin-down form—one traveler boasting of luxury and great meals, another making asinine lists ("Ten Best Waterslides on Cruise Ships"), yet another breathlessly recounting an itinerary of hardships and mishaps, and a fourth (and the most valuable, in my view) holding you like the wedding-guest with a skinny hand and fixing you with a glittering eye and saying, "There was a ship . . ."

If you're looking for a model, the greatest writer-traveler the world has known is the Moroccan Ibn Battutah, who set as his goal to travel the entire Islamic world, including China, India, Southeast Asia, and Africa, in the mid-14th century. This took him 29 years. He spent a year in the Maldives, that strange scattered archipelago of coral atolls, where he took a number of wives, and then moved on, leaving them behind. Unlike those other long sojourners Marco Polo and Sir John Mandeville (who might not have existed), Ibn Battutah wrote his book himself. In the words of one of his early Arab admirers:

> All master-works of travel, if you will but look
> Are merely tails that drag at Ibn-Battutah's heel,
> For he it was who hung the world, that turning wheel
> Of diverse parts, upon the axis of a book.

Ibn Battutah wrote about everything, great hospitality as well as catastrophes, miseries, wars, famines, plagues, pestilences, and xenophobia. Centuries later, what has changed? With—to speak only of Africa—the Ebola virus ravaging Guinea, the fanatical Boko Haram jihadists massacring thousands in northern Nigeria, tribal rioting and terrorist bombs in Kenya, and sprawling squatter camps in South Africa and Angola, travel in some of Africa is as much a challenge as it ever was. And yet in those same countries, there are still safari-goers, bird watchers, colorful dancers, and tarted-up tribal splendor. And there are travel writers reporting this somewhat hackneyed African experience, in pieces published in the glossier travel magazines extolling the spa experience and the cupcake culture in other pages. Some of these magazines are represented here, with more robust pieces, but in general what they call travel is in most cases a superior and safe holiday.

All countries crave tourism, because tourism creates employment, and the tourist makes a brief visit and leaves money behind. By contrast, the traveler is typically a budget-minded backpacker who lingers and is self-sufficient. India beckons tourists to its luxury hotels, but India is a wonderful example of a country full of contradictions, even old-fashioned adventures, if a traveler happens to be willing to take a few risks. The "Incredible India" ad campaign by the Indian Ministry of Tourism was claimed to be a success, but the most incredible aspect of it was that there was no mention of how dangerous India can be—in the so-called Red Corridor of the country, where Maoist guerrillas regularly massacre villagers or set off bombs, and other sporadically reported separatist movements, notably in Assam, cause some roads to be declared off-limits to travelers. Not long ago, I was discouraged from traveling a mere 80 miles by road from Silchar to Shillong in Assam because of "incidents." In a peaceable tea-growing area, I was warned of dacoits (bandits). It is the situation Kipling would have faced in the 1880s in the same place. In fact, there are 37 named terrorist/insurgent groups in Assam, with colorful names such as Adivasi Cobra Force, Black Widow, Liberation Tigers, and Rabha Viper Army. But, of course, bandits are out in force the world over. In many cases, the government in such places doesn't want you to know that.

I applied for an Indian visa two years ago, paid extra to have the visa approved quickly. When I did not receive my passport back on the given date or even two weeks later, I inquired about the reason for the delay. The Indian consular official explained that my application had to go to several other officials for approval, and this might take weeks more.

"What exactly is the problem?" I asked.

"On your application, under 'Occupation,' you have 'Writer.'"

"This is a problem?"

"Yes, one requiring higher authority."

So big, boasting, highly educated, literate, incredible India is as worried by the approach of a bespectacled senior with a ballpoint pen in his hand as a dacoit with a slasher.

China is no different. Write "journalist" or "travel writer" on your visa application at your peril, and good luck if you get the stamp. With its dazzling cities and booming factories, China is still a country governed by a repressive puritanical regime that has infuriated and displaced many minorities, among them the Uighur separatists of Xinjiang, who in March 2014 slit the throats of 29 travelers (and wounded 130 others) at the main railway station in Kunming.

And those bookish travelers hoping to find the literary and biographical landscape of Chekhov in the Crimea will find themselves in a turbulent place today and a potential war zone, poised for conflict, just as it was more than 150 years ago.

But if the traveler manages to breeze past such unpleasantness on tiny feet, he or she is able to return home to report, "I was there. I saw it all." The traveler's boast, sometimes couched as a complaint, is that of having been an eyewitness, and invariably this experience—shocking though it may seem at the time—is an enrichment, even a blessing, one of the trophies of travel, the life-altering journey.

Tourists have always taken vacations in tyrannies; Tunisia and Egypt are pretty good examples. The absurdist dictatorship gives such an illusion of stability, it is often a holiday destination. Myanmar is a classic example of a police state that is also a seemingly well-regulated country for sightseers, providing they don't look too closely. The Burmese guides are much too terrified to confide their fears to their clients. At a time when President Mugabe was starving and jailing his opponents in the 1990s, visitors to Zimbabwe were applying for licenses to shoot big game and having a swell time in the upscale game lodges. This is, to a degree, still the case.

By contrast, the free market–inspired, somewhat democratic, unregulated country can make for a bumpy trip, and a preponderance of rapacious locals. The old Soviet Union, with nannying guides, controlled and protected its tourists; the new Russia torments visitors with every scam available to rampant capitalism. But unless you are in delicate health and desire a serious rest, none of this is a reason to stay home

"You'd be a fool to take that ferry," people, both Scottish and English, said to me in the spring of 1982 when I set off at Stranraer in Scotland for Larne in Northern Ireland. I was making my clockwise trip around the British coast for the trip I later recounted in my book *The Kingdom by the Sea*. At the time and for more than 10 years, a particularly vicious sort of sectarian terror was general all over Ulster. It seemed from the outside to be Catholic versus Protestant, centuries old in its origins, harking back to King Billy (William of Orange) and the Battle of the Boyne in 1690, the decisive event still celebrated by marchers in silly hats every year on July 12. Ulster violence in the 1970s was pacified and then stirred by British troops, and the terror given material support by misguided enthusiasts in the United States.

How do I know this? I was there, keeping my head down, eating fish and chips, drinking beer, and making notes, while observing the effects of this confederacy of murderous dunces, the splinter groups, grudge bearers, and criminal hell-raisers of the purest ignorance.

The narcissism of minor differences was never more starkly illustrated than after that rainy night when I boarded the ferry from Scotland and made the short voyage into the 17th century, setting off to look at the rest of Northern Ireland. What I found—what I have usually found after hearing all those warnings—was that it was much more complicated and factional than it had been described to me. And there were unexpected pleasures. For one thing, the Irish of all sorts were grateful to have a listener. This is a trait of the aggrieved, and to be in the presence of talkers is a gift to a writer.

It was all a revelation that has become a rich and enlightening memory. Nor was it the only time I have been warned away from a place. "Don't—whatever you do—go to the Congo," I was told when I was a teacher in Uganda in the mid- and late 1960s. But the Congo was immense, and the parts I visited, Kivu in the east

and Katanga in the south, were full of life, in the way of belea-
guered places. In the mid-1970s, I was setting off from my hotel in
Berlin for the train to East Berlin when the writer Jerzy Kosinski
begged me not to go beyond the Brandenburg Gate. I might be
arrested, tortured, held in solitary confinement. "What did they
do to you?" he asked when he saw me reappear that evening. I
told him I had had a bad meal, taken a walk, seen a museum, and
generally gotten an unedited glimpse of the grim and threadbare
life of East Germany.

Not all warnings are frivolous or self-serving. I have mentioned
being cautioned about dacoits in Assam: it was good advice. Passing through Singapore in 1973, I was warned not to go to Khmer
Rouge–controlled Cambodia, and that was advice I heeded. There
is a difference between traveling in a country where there is a rule
of law and visiting one in a state of anarchy. Pol Pot had made
Cambodia uninhabitable. I traveled to Vietnam instead, aware of
the risks. This was just after the majority of American troops had
withdrawn and about 18 months before the fall of Saigon. My clear-
est memory is of the shattered Citadel and the muddy streets and
the stinking foreshore of the Pearl River in Hue, up the coast, the
terminus of the railway line. Now and then tracer fire, terror-struck
people, a collapsed economy, rundown hotels, and low spirits.

Thirty-three years later, I returned to Vietnam on my *Ghost Train
to the Eastern Star* journey, which was a revisiting of my *Great Railway
Bazaar*. I went back to the royal city of Hue and saw that there can
be life, even happiness, after war, and, almost unimaginably, there
can be forgiveness. Had I not seen the hellhole of Hue in wartime,
I would never have understood its achievement in a time of peace.

Just a few years ago, Sri Lanka emerged from a civil war, but
even as the Tamil north was embattled and fighting a rear-guard
action, there were tourists sunning themselves on the southern
coast and touring the Buddhist stupas in Kandy. Now the war is
over, and Sri Lanka can claim to be peaceful, except for the crow-
ing of its government over the vanquishing of the Tamils. Tourists
have returned in even greater numbers for the serenity and the
small population, and travel writers have begun to explore Jaffna
and the north of the island, which was for so long a war zone.

The pieces this year ably illustrate the defiance of the traveler
who, against the odds, sets off to find something new to write about.
I can imagine some chair-bound geek advising against going to

London or Venice or Las Vegas; but here is a refutation—strong, well-written accounts of London, Venice, and Las Vegas. Another warning finger might be wagged in the face of someone on his or her way to the remote parts of Brazil or the back alleys of Somalia, but here is an account of a confrontation in the Brazilian rain forest and an amazing experience in Somalia.

Around the time I was reading, with pleasure, Matthew Power's piece, marveling at yet another of his exploits, I learned of his premature death at age 39, apparently of heat stroke, in Uganda, on an assignment following a man who was walking the length of the Nile. I am delighted to include his story and regret that it is his last. He started young—he was a mere youth traveling in and writing about Afghanistan and the Philippines. This recent piece is in the nature of guerrilla travel, a portrait of disapproved and frequently arrested "space invaders"—the so-called urbex movement—who have a passion for infiltrating off-limits sites, gaining access to locked sewers and forbidden cathedrals. Matthew Power both observed and participated; his writing is vivid and memorable. He will be greatly missed.

In such a collection as this, the truly horrible experience can be found next to the mildly annoying incident: the kidnapping in Somalia of Amanda Lindhout (a joint credit with Sara Corbett), with—in sharp contrast and in another mood—Harrison Scott Key's reflections on riding by Greyhound bus, with his helpful observation, "Bus People are nothing like Airplane People." And in yet another paradoxical pairing, Alex Shoumatoff writes about one of my favorite subjects, the first contact between highly cultured, self-sufficient indigenous people in the Brazilian rain forest and desperate, rapacious savages—loggers in this case—from the outside world. Elsewhere, Michael Paterniti immerses himself in Guzmán, Spain, and Julia Cooke makes good friends in Havana. Some travelers are compelled by daring, others by dilettantism.

To see a familiar place in a new way is the mission of Sean Wilsey among the gondoliers of Venice, Peter LaSalle peregrinating Paris, Peter Selgin in New York, Colson Whitehead in Las Vegas, Stephen Rinella in the Alaska wilderness, Gary Shteyngart in a more-salubrious-than-usually-depicted Bombay, Andrew McCarthy negotiating Calcutta, and Bob Shacochis on a fishing trip in remote Argentina. Thomas Swick, in his shrewd essay on the nature of travel, suggests what motivates these travelers.

The earth is often perceived as a foolproof Google map, not very large, easily accessible, and knowable by any nerd drumming his fingers on a computer. In some respects, this is true. Distance is no longer a problem. You can nip over to Hong Kong or spend a weekend in Dubai or Rio. But as some countries open up, others shut down. Some countries have yet to earn their place on the traveler's map, such as Turkmenistan and Sudan, but I've been to both, and although I was the only sightseer at the time, I found hospitality, marvels, and a sense of discovery.

Distance was once the problem for the traveler to overcome. How to get to the Indies, or cross the Taklamakan Desert, or navigate the Sepik River? When Chekhov traveled to Sakhalin Island in 1887, it was as though he was heading for another planet. In my lifetime, Albania and Cuba were once forbidden and inaccessible countries, but these days you'll find them full of tourists sunning themselves on the beaches and windsurfers offshore.

The problem of distance has been solved. There are good trains through the Taklamakan Desert and tour boats up the Sepik. You can get yourself to the Highlands of New Guinea or the foothills of the Himalayas, or to Timbuktu, without much trouble. But access is still a problem in those, and in many other, places: in the fractured countries of Africa, in quarrelsome Pakistan, in the disputed parts of India, and in the nations that have emerged from the old Soviet Union—Dagestan, Chechnya, and now Ukraine. And there are the inner cities of the United States, many of which pose challenges to the curious visitor with probing questions. In writing this, I am betraying my love of reading about adventures and ordeals—the traveler's baptism of fire. These places that defy many travelers are opportunities for those who are willing to take a risk, for the reward of making a discovery and then writing about it brilliantly.

PAUL THEROUX

The Best American
Travel Writing 2014

Poisoned Land

FROM *The New Yorker*

LAST SEPTEMBER, at a hospital in eastern Croatia, my father and I visited a collection of some 400 human kidneys. Most had belonged to the victims of a mysterious, fatal kidney disease, which occurs in agrarian communities on the Danube River and its tributaries. Some villages have it; others, seemingly identical in every way, do not. The onset of the disease, which is known as Balkan endemic nephropathy (often abbreviated as BEN), takes place in middle to later life, after the patient has lived in an affected village for 15 or 20 years. The first symptoms include weakness, anemia, and a coppery skin discoloration. The kidneys begin to atrophy, and about half of patients also develop a rare cancer of the upper urinary tract. Without a kidney transplant or treatment by dialysis, death usually occurs within a year.

At the kidney collection, a pathologist took several formalin-filled jars out of a cabinet and lined them up on the counter. Inside were kidneys riddled with holes, misshapen kidneys with visible tumors, biopsied kidneys sliced in half, and atrophied kidneys, ghostly pale, some as small as walnuts. My father, a nephrologist, says that he has never seen kidneys as tiny as those removed from BEN patients.

BEN was first described in the 1950s. Over the years, many theories have been proposed to explain the disease, from cadmium poisoning and hantaviruses to toxic molds and chromosomal mutation. Uncertainty and controversy surround the most basic data, such as the number of people with the disease. One doctor I spoke to puts the figure at a hundred thousand. A recent Croatian study found that the incidence of the disease is declining, while a Serbian study found that it isn't.

Because BEN takes decades to develop, investigators are always following a cold trail, and this makes the disease a particularly intractable puzzle. Animals don't live long enough to get it, and respond to toxic substances differently from humans, which limits the possibilities of experimental research. The villages affected are in a demographically fragmented region, fraught with wars, revolutions, genocides, and totalitarianism—all of which have hampered research and medical record-keeping. Today, BEN is a budget-straitened side project for most scientists who study it. A disease that affects only middle-aged Balkan farmers isn't exactly a magnet for international funding.

My father began studying BEN in the 1980s, but his work was interrupted by the Yugoslav wars. Last fall, he returned to the Balkans for the first time in years, and I went with him. We began our trip in Timişoara, the largest city in western Romania, where we met Calin Tatu, a researcher who has been studying the disease with the U.S. Geological Survey for more than a decade. Tatu, who is in his 40s, and has a buzzcut and a close-trimmed beard, holds a medical degree in immunology but prefers working in the lab to seeing patients. He was wearing tinted glasses and a cargo vest, and had spent the previous week climbing Mont Blanc. At lunch, over two double espressos and two Coke Zeros, he told us about his research.

For the past 10 years, Tatu has been investigating the Pliocene lignite hypothesis—a theory developed by a geologist who noticed that the map of the endemic villages closely shadows the locations of Pliocene-era coal deposits. It isn't clear exactly how the coal would make people sick, but Tatu believes that toxic compounds may be leaching from the coal into the groundwater. At his lab, he showed us a machine capable of reducing 20 gallons of groundwater to a few teaspoons of brown sludge. He says that he has found unique organic compounds in water samples from the region, but he doesn't yet know whether they contribute to BEN.

In recent years, Tatu has been testing another theory as well: poisoning by aristolochic acid, a toxin found in plants of the *Aristolochia* genus. This theory, which has recently gained wide acceptance, was formulated thanks to one of those grievous human misfortunes described by scientists as "a natural experiment." In Brussels, in the 1990s, a number of otherwise healthy young women suffered end-stage kidney failure, requiring dialysis or transplants. It turned out that they all belonged to the same diet clinic, where they had taken a Chinese herbal slimming blend containing aristolochic acid. About half of them later developed the same rare upper-urinary-tract cancer found in BEN patients. Researchers soon made the connection with BEN, particularly since a species of aristolochia—*Aristolochia clematitis*, or European birthwort—is common throughout the Balkans.

In 2007, an American pharmacologist named Arthur Grollman analyzed kidneys from BEN patients and found molecules derived from aristolochic acid bound to the patients' DNA. In further studies, he identified aristolochic acid's mutational signature in DNA from patients' tumors. According to Grollman, these findings prove that the cancers were caused by aristolochic acid, which he suspects was ingested after seeds from the plant got mixed with wheat and ended up in the villagers' bread. Other researchers have built on these findings, and many now favor the term "aristolochic-acid nephropathy" over "Balkan endemic nephropathy." Grollman believes that the mystery has been solved.

Yet questions remain. Some researchers have been unable to find the same molecules, either in the Belgian women or in BEN patients. Others have drawn attention to the differences between the Belgian women's disease and BEN; notably, the Belgian women tended to become sick within 12 to 18 months, rather than 20 years. Perhaps the biggest puzzle is why aristolochic acid would make people sick only in certain areas, given that it grows throughout the Balkans, as well as in much of the rest of Europe and the Middle East.

The aristolochia theory is strong precisely where the Pliocene theory is weak, and vice versa. Pliocene coal is found throughout the endemic regions, but it has no known causal link to BEN symptoms. Aristolochia has been linked to the symptoms, but it grows all over the place. Tatu suggested that aristolochic acid and coal compounds might be working in combination. He agrees that aristolochic acid is a cause of BEN, and thinks that the biggest remaining question is how exposure to aristolochic acid occurs. He is skeptical about the idea that aristolochia seeds get ground into flour, having found no traces of the poison when he analyzed flour from mills in endemic regions of Romania.

We had met Tatu in downtown Timişoara, in the lobby of a vast rectangular Soviet-style hotel, and were joined by his collaborator, Nikola Pavlović, a Serbian nephrologist in his 60s, with mild blue eyes. Pavlović's speech was soft, hesitant yet relentless, each claim accompanied by a stream of qualifications. When the conversation turned to research, he spoke approvingly of almost all the hypotheses. He didn't seem bothered by the fact that a given risk factor could also be found in non-endemic regions, because maybe those regions weren't really non-endemic. "How do you know there aren't two or three cases there?" he asked. He even thought that a BEN-like disease might exist wherever there are lignite coal deposits. Showing us a lignite map of the United Kingdom, he observed that the areas with the most lignites also had the highest rates of undiagnosable renal disease. In the U.S., states with lignite deposits also have some of the highest death rates from certain kidney cancers.

My father objected that in 40 years of medical practice he had never seen an illness with quite the same profile as BEN, with kidneys so shrunken, fibrosis so severe, and such an advanced state of disease with no hypertension. His own hunch is that radiation is involved. He notes that the pattern of BEN distribution resembles that of radon distribution in the United States, and that radiation causes acute fibrosis in kidneys. If radioactive material were leaching into drinking water in the Balkans, the kidneys would process it in small amounts over the years. There is no hard evidence to support this theory, however. Two Michigan-based environmental scientists working on BEN told me that they think radiation is worth looking into—elevated levels of uranium have been found in the endemic regions—but they haven't raised the necessary funds.

Tatu, Pavlović, and my father exchanged news of BEN researchers past and present: who favored the aristolochic-acid theory and who didn't, who had retired, who had died, who was now producing minerals for laundry detergent. My father had last seen Pavlović in 1988. "I remember him a young man," he told me later. "I guess he thought the same thing about me."

*

That afternoon, we drove to the endemic region in Mehedinți County, 150 miles southeast of Timișoara. The trolley lines and the churches soon gave way to rolling countryside. Large haystacks stood in groups. Shaggy, hulking, almost shamanistic, they resembled animate huts. There was something mutable and alive about them, the way they absorbed the light. The leaves were starting to change, and the air was exceptionally clear. Tiny horses stood out against a distant hillside.

Along the way, Tatu pulled his car over next to a cornfield. It was overrun with aristolochia. In the golden afternoon light, I saw the famous plant for the first time, recognizing its heart-shaped leaves, narrow yellow tubular flowers, and the round brown pods that have given rise to one of its local names: priest's balls. Tatu broke open a pod. Inside, hundreds of seeds were lined up in two rows, like pupils in a schoolhouse.

I picked a leaf and smelled it. "If you taste it, it's very bitter," Tatu said, chewing on a leaf and immediately spitting it out. "Pah! This is actually not a good idea."

In Romania, as in many parts of the world, aristolochia leaves have been used in folk medicine for centuries. The leaves also contain aristolochic acid, but in a far lower concentration than the seeds. Tatu picked up a pod off the ground. "If you ate this, you would get really sick," he said. "You would have acute renal failure."

"If you want to eat it, go ahead," my father offered. "There are two nephrologists here." Nobody ate the pod.

As we drove through the Romanian countryside, Tatu frequently stopped to collect water and soil samples. Many villagers still don't have plumbing and get their water from natural springs. At one spring, two older women sat placidly on a bench. When Tatu asked them about nephropathy, their faces grew hard. Tatu told me that the villagers generally didn't like to be asked about the disease. They would say the other village had it, the one across the hill.

At an abandoned coal mine nearby, runoff water rushed noisily out of a pipe into a ditch. Tatu said that villagers collected the runoff and drank it. He pointed out where pieces of Pliocene coal lay scattered on the ground: 3-million-year-old chips of cypress. They still looked like wood. Being so young, the coal was of a terrible quality and hardly burned at all, especially since the mines were so waterlogged. "It was pretty much the worst coal you could get ever," Tatu said. Opened in the 1970s, the mine had been closed for some 20 years. A concrete barrier blocked the entrance. It had been erected after a boy and a cow wandered inside and drowned.

Two women came by with some cows. The women seemed excited to see us. It turned out that they thought we had come to reopen the mine and create jobs. The cows lowered their massive, beautiful heads to the water and drank.

"It's amazing how much you can observe just by watching," my father said, paraphrasing Yogi Berra. I was more amazed by how much you *couldn't* observe—how the things you saw seemed to withhold their meaning. The culprit wouldn't be the mold you saw in a granary today but the mold in a granary that had been torn down 20 years ago.

A drunk man arrived. He said that the mine was actually a tomb, and that you could tell this from the configuration of stones. He had been a miner for three years, and had seen many deaths, though from collapsing shafts and suffocation rather than from kidney disease. Twenty meters in, he said, the shaft was all water. The miners used to drink it. There had been a study of those miners. They didn't seem to get nephropathy any more frequently than anyone else.

The biggest dialysis clinic in Mehedinți County is housed in an old villa, with irregularly shaped rooms branching off a central staircase. Under the stairs stood several rows of 10-liter jugs of dialysate, a fluid that flows through the dialysis machine, separated from the patient's blood by a membrane.

The clinic serves 168 patients, more than half of whom have BEN. The BEN patients were instantly recognizable: frail, coppery-skinned peasants with haunted eyes, reclining on white chaises, as blood was pumped into and out of their bodies through tubes. The place where the two catheters punctured the forearm was marked on each patient by an irregular, discolored potato-size fistula, surgically created by connecting a vein and an artery. The fistula made me think for the first time about how much blood has to leave the body during dialysis: not a liter or two but *all* of it, several times over, to the extent that the blood vessels have to be hot-wired in order to get it in and out. Each patient's blood passed through a long plastic tube and around a slowly turning wheel, which pumped the blood through the machine. The machines turned slowly in unison, like mill wheels. A dialysis unit looks precise and powerful, but it can only approximate the intricate function of a human kidney. For patients with atrophying diseases like BEN, dialysis rarely buys more than 5 to 10 years.

"Dialysis creates essentially a new kind of human," Pavlović whispered.

In one room, we found two aged sisters, 79 and 80, delicate women wearing headscarves, pajamas, and thick woolen socks. The elder, tiny and emaciated, lay with her eyes closed, resembling a dead pharaoh. The younger was watching a television broadcast of Romanian folk dancing. She said that they had lived all their lives on a farm nearby, and that their father had died of BEN. She added that they knew what aristolochia was but had never taken it as medicine. The pigs, she said, wouldn't touch it, but goats ate it sometimes, and then the cheese came out bitter.

Outside, the sun shone through a white haze. Tatu was on his cell phone trying to set up a house visit, but everyone he could think of was dead.

When scientists started investigating BEN, they thought that it might be a gradual, cumulative form of lead poisoning. Researchers working in a Serbian endemic village found high levels of lead in patients' blood and hair, as well as in the local flour: the miller had been using a lead-based grout to repair his millstone. The government duly dismantled 36 water mills in Serbia. Further investigation, however, revealed that BEN patients in other villages didn't have high levels of lead in their blood, and many had never used water mills.

My father compares BEN research to the story of the blind men and the elephant: everyone noticed something different and built a theory around it, and nobody saw the whole picture. Data from one village, or the expertise of one specialist, or the aftereffects of one environmental trauma, would indicate a solution, only to crumble in light of other data. Virologists, studying a village where all the BEN patients had hidden in an oak forest during the Second World War, attributed the disease to a virus native to oak forests. A Serbian geochemist, citing the low selenium content of soil in Serbia, suggested that BEN was triggered by selenium deficiency. In five villages in Kosovo, Muslims, who made up half the population, were found to be 25 times less likely than Christians to get BEN. Virologists argued that the disease was a virus transmitted by pigs, and that Muslims were spared by their avoidance of pig husbandry. Geneticists, believing BEN to be hereditary, saw the same data and ascribed the lower incidence among Muslims to their ethnic makeup. Confusingly, the Muslims in Bulgaria, known as "white gypsies," often did get BEN, though actual Gypsies did not, and was that because of their genes or because they didn't work on farms? A Bulgarian researcher claimed that he had identified a chromosomal marker, but nobody else could find it.

In the 1950s, the Bulgarian village of Karash was hit particularly hard by the disease. The communist government, having decided that the problem lay in the village itself, shut Karash down and relocated the population to Sofia. Twenty years later, some of the Karash exiles began to develop BEN, but those who had moved as children never got the disease—only those who had lived in Karash for 15 years or more. BEN, it seemed, was a super-slow time bomb. Fifteen years of exposure would set the clock ticking.

A shift in BEN studies came in the 1970s. A charismatic Danish veterinarian named Palle Krogh had been studying a strange outbreak of kidney disease affecting pigs in Danish slaughterhouses. There were no obvious differences between the lives of the sick pigs and those of the healthy ones. The only clue was that the disease seemed to worsen after rainy summers. Krogh eventually determined that the pigs' grain had been contaminated by a fungal toxin called ochratoxin A, which produced effects not unlike BEN: the kidney damage was similar, and both were aggravated by wet weather. Sure enough, when tests were run in Yugoslavia, ochratoxin A was found in the blood and the urine of BEN patients, as well as in their grain supply.

Continued research, however, revealed that ochratoxin A was far more common than initially suspected: it appears in grains, coffee beans, wine, and other stored substances all over the world. Some of the highest levels of contamination have been recorded in countries with no known BEN-like disease. The story of ochratoxin illustrates the fundamental challenge in epidemiology: proof of exposure isn't the same thing as proof of causation. Every day, we're exposed to countless potential pathogens and toxins, most of which don't make us sick. Identifying the "right" toxin is particularly difficult when the disease affects the kidney, an organ whose main function is to clear the blood of toxins.

Oddly, or perhaps not so oddly, Palle Krogh himself died of kidney cancer, in 1990. Krogh's tumor was later dissected and analyzed by a group of his colleagues, including Tatu. Tatu suspected that the cancer had been caused by ochratoxin. My father pointed out that Krogh had been a chain smoker—smoking is a leading cause of renal carcinoma—and Tatu conceded that he could remember Krogh waving a cigarette in excitement at his latest findings. Nonetheless, it was difficult not to be struck by the death from kidney cancer of a scientist who had devoted many years to the study of nephrotoxic and possibly carcinogenic mold.

Two days later, in a high-ceilinged coffeehouse in Zagreb, my father and I met with Bojan Jelaković, a mild-mannered Croatian nephrologist who has worked closely with Grollman on the aristolochic-acid theory. He took us on a tour of an endemic region two hours southeast of Zagreb. We passed the towering grain silos of an industrial-looking mill. According to Jelaković and Grollman, such mills are eradicating BEN, because they combine wheat from so many different farms that the aristolochic acid is diluted. Patients we spoke to at a local dialysis clinic confirmed that they had once ground their own flour from their own wheat, but had switched to bigger communal mills after the war.

In the village of Kaniža, Jelaković showed us two churches standing face-to-face: one Croatian Catholic, with a white pointed steeple, and the other Ukrainian Orthodox, with an onion dome. These churches have come to stand for another famous "natural experiment" from the annals of BEN. Around 1905, a community of Ukrainian immigrants settled in Kaniža, having been offered free farmland by the Austro-Hungarian emperor. Although the Ukrainians kept their religion and did not intermarry with the Croats, they ended up getting sick just as frequently as the native villagers. The case proved that the disease isn't inherited in the classical Mendelian sense.

In a nearby village, Jelaković showed us a so-called black house—left empty and gone to ruin after its occupants were stricken with BEN. He told us that a household of around a dozen people had died here in the 1970s. Next door, a boy and a girl watched us through the front windows, then pulled the curtains closed.

Like most BEN regions, this one is prone to flooding, and we had parked our cars by a monument to a 19th-century deluge alongside the Sava River. Across the river was Bosnia. There had been a bridge here before the war. "A wooden bridge," Jelaković said. "A very beautiful one."

We parted with Jelaković and drove across the river into Bosnia. At a hospital in the city of Odžak, we were given the use of an ambulette and a driver, so that we could visit BEN patients in nearby villages. We sat in a sunny garden with an elderly husband and wife, both of whom had BEN. They had heard of aristolochia by one of its local names (wolf's paw), but they didn't know what it looked like. We showed them photographs, and they said they might have seen it around but they didn't pay much attention to weeds. When asked what they thought caused the disease, they immediately said water: more people got sick in the parts of the village that were prone to flooding, and fewer people were getting sick now, because of improvements to the water system. They noted that the disease didn't affect anyone who lived in the hills, with the exception of women who had grown up in the lowlands and had moved to the hills only after getting married. We heard something similar in another village, where a man with BEN, who had lost his father, his aunt, and three siblings to the disease, told us about a neighbor who had no BEN in his family. "You see, he comes from the other side of the street," the man said. It emerged that every house on one side of the street had one or several cases of BEN, but the other side, which was on slightly higher ground, was almost completely free of the disease. Annie Pfohl-Leszkowicz, a proponent of the ochratoxin theory, has cited similar patterns as evidence that BEN is caused by a fungal toxin: the healthy side of the street, she proposes, gets direct sunlight, which discourages the growth of mold.

In Odžak, my father and I met with Enisa Mesić, a nephrologist from nearby Tuzla. A magnetic presence, with a large head, copious dark hair, a deep voice, and piercing gray eyes, Mesić told us about the bureaucratic obstacles faced by BEN researchers. After the war, political power was decentralized in order to preserve equilibrium among different ethnic groups. As a result, Bosnia-Herzegovina now has no fewer than 13 ministries of health: one at the federal level, one for each of its 10 cantons, and one each for the self-governing Brčko District and the Republika Srpska. The two major centers for BEN research, in Tuzla and Sarajevo, are in cantons outside the endemic region, which means that before researchers can actually study any patients, they must submit requests to two different ministries.

Because of the war, nearly every patient's file is missing at least four years. There is no central BEN database, and establishing one would require the cooperation of all 13 ministers of health. The municipalities used to have local databases, but these were discontinued after the war. When asked what had happened to the databases, Mesić ticked off their fates: "In Bijeljina, the archive probably still exists, but it's difficult to access. In Šamac, it probably doesn't exist anymore. In Odžak, it was destroyed in 1992, together with the hospital."

Early in the 20th century, after the fall of the Ottoman Empire and the ensuing chaos in the Balkans, a new verb entered the English language: "Balkanize," defined by the OED as "to divide (a region) into a number of smaller and often mutually hostile units, as was done in the Balkan Peninsula in the late nineteenth and early twentieth centuries." Most European languages have an equivalent: the French *balkaniser,* the Italian *balkanizzare,* the German *balkanisieren,* and the Russian *balkanizirovat'*—attesting to the special relationship between the Balkan Peninsula and the human tendency toward division and faction. It's an apt word to describe the study of Balkan nephropathy, and its fragmentation along geopolitical, ethnic, religious, linguistic, and even disciplinary lines. Researching the disease requires expertise in a wide range of fields—nephrology, epidemiology, genetics, oncology, microbiology, hydrogeology, botany, toxicology, biochemistry—each of which can be as hermetic and insular as a tiny country, with its own language, customs, and sovereignty.

The basic philosophical question surrounding BEN is whether it's a big problem or a little one. For Arthur Grollman, BEN is part of a worldwide crisis of aristolochic-acid nephropathy: a story in which the true culprits are government agencies that fail to regulate herbal medications. When I met him later, at his apartment in Manhattan, he assured me that BEN was a closed case, and that a greater source of concern was the public health risk caused by the use of a variety of aristolochia in Chinese herbal medicine. He described his recent collaborations with researchers in Taiwan, where aristolochia is a commonly prescribed remedy, and where the reported incidence of upper-urinary-tract cancers is the highest in the world. Whereas a hundred women got sick in Belgium, Grollman says, millions of people may be at risk in Taiwan and China.

Researchers like Tatu, on the other hand, think that BEN is unique: although its causes may occur individually all over the world, their combined effect is specific to the endemic regions. For my father, too, the disease is defined by a set of particular locations. He thinks it's significant that patients speak of doomed houses—that they feel it's the places and not the people that are sick. He often quotes a remark by an old colleague, now deceased: "I could live in this town for twenty years, and I'd know which house to live in, to not get sick."

On our last afternoon in Bosnia, the driver drove my father and me around the countryside to look for aristolochia. We stopped at a swamp overgrown with creeping tendrils, trembling fronds, and strange, earlike formations. We did not find aristolochia. We stopped by a cornfield, and walked along the perimeter and down one of the rows. A sudden commotion broke out among the cornstalks, a violent rustling and shaking, as if from the thrashing of some hidden beast. A moment later, the source of the disturbance revealed itself: a glossy, compact pheasant, running through the corn.

We got back into the van. The sun hung low over the late-summer fields. The cornstalks seemed to be standing around chaotically, like skinny, crazy people, their arms flung in all directions. As we drove past, there was one magical moment when they arranged themselves into rows and it was possible to see clearly all the way to the end, before they dissolved back into disorder.

JULIA COOKE

Amigos

FROM *Virginia Quarterly Review*

IF THERE WAS ONE THING Sandra knew well, it was hair. She knew hair from root to split end. In beauty school, she had learned the shape of the human head and how the best thing to do when trimming its hair was to section the skull into eighths. Her long nails shone red as she held her soft hands in front of her to demonstrate on an imaginary client. Her gold rings glinted. When she tired of haircutting techniques, she waved her hands quickly and her fingers sparked through the thick night like fireworks.

Sandra, like other girls who hung out where we sat on Havana's waist-high seawall (*malecón*) where it hit Paseo, wore fashionable clothes of the barely there variety: diminutive shorts with interlocking *C*'s on back pockets, glittery heels, bras that peeked from tops, halters leaving midriffs bare. She dyed her own long, straight hair blue-black and lined her lips with the same dark pencil that she used around her eyes because shops hadn't carried red in months. Her plastic nails were thick and whispery along the tips; she grabbed my forearm as we crossed the street on our way to the bathroom at a nearby gas station, dodging the cars that sped around the curve at Paseo. We went the long way to avoid the police who hung in the shadows on the intersection's traffic island, keeping an eye on the strip. "The cars here, they'll hit you. And if it's him"—Sandra flicked her chin and pulled her hand down to mime a beard, the universal gesture for Fidel Castro—"they won't stop. They'll run you over and keep on going."

There were clubs and bars at the hotels that hulked over the crossroads—the mod Riviera, the shimmery Meliá Cohiba, the Jazz

Café—but since few locals could afford drinks there, the tourists who wanted to meet real Cubanos hung out by the sea. Everyone, Cuban and foreign, loved the *malecón,* to sit facing the ocean and Miami and feel the spray on bare shins, or to turn toward the city and watch old cars roar slowly by, or, after a long night at the bars, to see the brightening sky pull itself away from the sea. On nights when there was no moon, you could nod approvingly at the fish that men in mesh tank tops caught on sheer line stretched from coils on the sidewalk. On hot days, you watched kids who leapt from the wall into high tide, their arms pinwheeling past the rocks that cragged up from the ocean.

So young men toted bongo drums and guitars, imitating the Buena Vista Social Club for a few dollars' tip. Gentlemen in frayed straw fedoras asked tourists to pick up an extra beer at the gas station kiosk. Tired-looking women in Lycra shorts sang out the names of cones of roasted peanuts, *cucuruchos de maní,* and popcorn, *rositas de maíz.* Nonchalant girls cocked hips at the foreign men who walked past. Sandra had been taught the art of artifice to serve the Cuban Revolution through its beauty parlors, but she'd given up on hair. By the time she was 21, she'd been working as a prostitute for around five years. The dates changed every time I asked her. Either way, she made about three times in one night what she'd have been paid monthly at any of the government-owned salons.

In November 2011, when Cuban first daughter Mariela Castro Espín was in Amsterdam in her capacity as sexologist and director of Cuba's Center for Sexual Education, she was interviewed on Radio Netherlands Worldwide. Castro, prim and deliberate in a turtleneck and tweed blazer, sat in a room with draping red curtains and feather boas and effused about Amsterdam's red-light district. "I've enjoyed seeing how they do it," she said. "What I admire is that they've been able to dignify and value the work that they do—because yes, it is a job." She enunciated her Spanish so translators didn't miss a word for the televised interview. Castro went on to explain how, as she put it, the principles are the same in Cuba as in Amsterdam, but the circumstances are different. She talked about how the *malecón* is a place of pride for Havanans, and she smiled broadly until she mentioned the people who sell sex there. "Some people go there to practice prostitution in a way that is bothersome for, above all, the tourist or foreigner," and her agency is in close contact with the police to decrease the *malecón* prostitution, she said, without drawing too much attention from said tourist or foreigner.

This is what the Cuban government usually highlights when it talks about women and prostitution: Before Fidel Castro's revolution in 1959, women had represented only 13 percent of the workforce, and many were domestic servants. A large number were prostitutes, too—as a port city with a sexually liberal climate and a U.S.-backed puppet government, Havana was where *yanquis* had gone in search of louche, uninhibited nightlife from Prohibition on. In 1931, after the Volstead Act had tripled the numbers of tourists who visited the country in under 15 years, 7,400 women officially stated their professions as prostitutes. The city formerly known as "the Pearl of the Caribbean" was soon referred to as its brothel. Eradicating prostitution and increasing women's rights was one of Castro's stated goals. Forty years after the 1959 revolution, long after literacy drives had enabled the island's rural residents to read and prostitutes had been trained as seamstresses and given jobs and day care for their children, 51 percent of Cuba's scientists were women. Fifty percent of attorneys and 52 percent of medical doctors, too. Everyone was paid nearly equally—a doctor, male or female, made marginally more than a seamstress, around $20 a month in Cuban pesos.

Then, 20 years ago, the USSR fell and Soviet subsidies disappeared, and with them more than a third of Cuba's GDP. The value of the peso plummeted, and rations of food, clothing, and other necessities that removed pressure from monthly stipends dwindled. Increasingly, women, and some men, began to trade sexual favors for, say, the fish that a neighbor caught or the bread that only a well-placed state employee got very much of. When the government pushed to increase tourism and Cuba drew closer to the global capitalist marketplace, those activities again had cash value. By 1995, around the same time that studies on gender parity in the workforce came out, the Italian travel magazine *Viaggiare* had given the island the dubious honor of being the number one global "paradise of sexual tourism." The government, broke and desperate, did little to contradict this image. And though the economy lifted as Cuba rounded into the 21st century, and though the new decade saw police tossing the more obvious prostitutes into jail, sex was something that could be easily bought and sold in Havana.

But one key fact still sets Cuba apart today: there aren't many pimps or third-party intermediaries in the sex trade. A police state with tightly restricted access to weapons and severe penalties for drugs creates an underworld more seamy than overtly violent. And few romantic liaisons between locals and foreigners are deemed prostitution; rather, most fall under the banner of relationships with *amigos.* Any non-Cuban is eligible, and what locals want from *amigos,* foreigners like me, is neither finite nor clear, a mix of money, attention, and the possibility linked to anyone with a non-Cuban passport.

In the way that the language of a city fills in the blanks of what its people want to name, sometime between the early 1990s and today the word *jinetero/a* became the catchall to describe Cuba's hookers and hustlers, or any person who seeks foreign currency or CUC, the valuable tourist cash, rather than the pesos in which government salaries are paid, via foreigners. The word's provenance isn't clear. *Jinete* in Spanish is a horse jockey; whether this means that women hold the reins of the "horses" is unclear. Today, the masculine *jinetero* refers insultingly to a man who caters to tourists in any questionably legal, hustlerlike capacity. *Jinetera* means "a Cuban woman who trades sex for money." I'd avoided them whenever I'd visited Havana, until I met Sandra that night with a mutual acquaintance on the *malecón.*

The European and American media erupted into a mild frenzy in the weeks after Mariela Castro's remarks, given that the principles of prostitution in Cuba aren't at all like those in Amsterdam. But her comments pointed toward something that was still unsaid, something essential about the country that was both hers and Sandra's: *jineteras* are indicative of contemporary Havana's frustrations, opportunities, dreams, history, and ennui. Remittances and tourism are Cuba's top two sources of income, and the inevitable process of aging has shoved the country, with less fanfare than anticipated, into a post-Fidel era. The inheritance of the Castro revolution is hinted at every day in how Cuba interacts with an ever-encroaching world. Sandra, a small symbolic representative of communism's struggle for relevance, is both admired and reviled within her society.

Then again, that might be too much weight to put on her; she's also just a girl surviving Havana, using what's put in front of her to get by.

Sometimes it's hard to discern who's selling sex and who's just trying to wear as little fabric as possible in Havana's oppressive heat. The mainstays of *jinetera* fashion—miniskirts, transparent fabrics, cleavage- and shoulder-baring tops—appear on most women, including foreigners, who feel freer to be sexy in permissive Cuba than at home. At clubs, I saw foreign women with bikini-strap marks sunburned around their necks look left, right, then pull their necklines down before dancing with slim Cuban men in tight jeans and big silver belt buckles. These women lapped up the sensual aura, as if just breathing would send tiny cells of sexy through their bodies, the infusion pushing and pulling hips back and forth, transforming walks into sashays, planting dry one-liners in mouths.

Sandra had long since mastered these feminine tricks. Everything about her physical appearance was calibrated to entice: the tops that looked almost about to slip off, the hair that twisted around her neck, her long, soft, red nails. I had just five years on Sandra, but I felt large, clumsy, and dusty around her in my flats and loose dresses. I was a tattered stuffed animal next to her as we sat, the second time we met, in the back seat of a cab that took us from the *malecón* out to her house.

She'd met me downtown because she said I wouldn't find her place on my own. Sandra had recently moved from La Corea, one of Havana's few slumlike outlying neighborhoods, into a closer but smaller dwelling in San Miguel del Padrón. Her home was in a cluster of blocks between a fetid stream and the main road that linked downtown Havana with outer boroughs like San Francisco de Paula, where Ernest Hemingway lived. San Miguel was a place of contrasts: a street began with a few freshly painted houses near the road to San Francisco and faded into cinderblock shacks with stretched-out oil barrels for fences closer to the stream. Egg cartons, plastic bags, the rusted skeletons of metal chairs, and fruit rinds bobbed in the water.

The shiny taxi slowed as we pulled onto her street, dodging potholes. A couple on the corner stared at us, and Sandra waved. A few feet away, an old man in overalls, a burlap sack of oranges slung over his right shoulder, stood to attention and saluted. Sandra dissolved into giggles, slapping the vinyl seat. "What a *loco, loco loquito,"* she gasped. *"Viste?"* She jumped out as soon as we pulled up to her building and leaned against the car's trunk, picking at her nails as I paid the fare.

Years ago, Sandra's mother had kicked her out of the house. She now lived with her grandmother, Aboo, and her half-brother, Gallego, in a two-room apartment in what had once been a yard at the center of a block, down an alley and behind a single-story home with neoclassical columns and a street-side patio. Aboo didn't approve of Sandra staying out for days on end, but Sandra's father was in Florida and her mother had a new husband, a nice house in suburban La Lisa, and a set of twin toddlers. And the money Sandra brought home supported the household.

For every woman supported by foreign men, I'd heard it estimated that three more Cuban citizens got by on the money, whether directly or not. Sandra, Aboo, and Gallego, at least. The government didn't do much beyond tossing a too-blatant hooker into Villa Delicia, the nickname for the women's jail. Sandra had spent four days there when she was 19 and had eaten so little she'd come out "like this," she told me, holding up her pinkie. If men stopped coming to the island, tempted no longer by images of scantily clad mulattas on white-sand beaches and bodies pressed together in crowded bars, hotel rooms would languish unvisited, taxis would have fewer fares, and restaurants more empty tables. So policemen, Sandra said, were eminently bribable, for the right price.

Just inside Sandra's door, a small table and two matching chairs were piled high with folded clothes. The room also held a wooden armoire, a stereo, and a refrigerator near a small kitchenette. Sandra poked around for a box of photos. When she found it, we returned to the central patio, where we sat under the laundry lines that the three families who lived in the middle of the block used on alternating days. Sandra set the box on the ground and sorted through pictures. I pulled out a pack of cheap, unfiltered Criollo cigarettes, which I favored for their clean tobacco and sweet aftertaste. Sandra wrinkled her nose but took one anyway, and used it to point out the Spanish guy who'd asked her to marry him two years ago. He'd walked in on her a few weeks later with someone else. She still had the ring.

Sandra was 11 when she had sex for the first time (the average in Cuba is around 13), with a man whose name she'd tattooed across the small of her back, MUMÚA, above an image of two doves entwined with scrolls. He was 32 then, and even now he was "crazy for me," she said, waving her cigarette, though he was in jail for selling stolen motorcycle parts. What had begun as nights out slid quickly into prostitution; government salaries paled next to the $50 she could make on a night with a man, nearly always foreign, nearly always Spanish, Cuban American, or Italian. So she quit, never finished her certificate course.

The gate at the street end of the alley jingled as Gallego walked in. After introductions, I picked up my bag to leave. Sandra asked me where I was going. "To meet some friends downtown," I said. There weren't many decent restaurants in Havana then, and I had no kitchen in my rented room, so a generous cast of friends, Cubans and expats, regularly invited me around to eat during my three-week reporting trips. Sandra gave me a once-over and pushed me toward the floor-length mirror in her living room. If I'd just do my hair *like this,* she told me as she reached into my curls and flipped them into a messy, voluminous updo, I'd look way sexier. A red wash to make the dull brown more interesting would do me good. And my shorts could be shorter, too. I should also line my lips—you know, show off contours, make them inviting. I handed her bobby pins for my hair but liked my shorts the way they were, midthigh. She looked skeptical, the pins between her lips as she styled and then hands on her hips once she'd finished. It did look better.

I saw Sandra one last time on that trip to Cuba, a quick visit on the *malecón* again. She'd come up with a plan: when I went back to Mexico, I should get my company to write her a *carta de invitación,* an invitation letter that she'd use to get an exit visa. "You work at a newspaper or something, right?" she asked. "They wouldn't have to offer me a real job, just do the *carta oficial.* I can take care of myself once I get there."

I explained that I didn't really work for anyone, at least not like that, and some of the magazines I wrote for were actually based in Europe. She looked at me coyly. "Whatever," she said. "Wherever." I paused, uncomfortable, and then smiled a little and said that I could hardly get them to do favors for me, much less for an *amiga* in Cuba. Sandra shrugged. She began to gossip about a neighbor

of hers who'd come over the day I'd visited her house. There was
no change in her demeanor, as if the desire to go to Mexico or
anywhere else had dissipated as soon as her shoulders had moved.

The big turquoise Habana Riviera hotel was originally commis-
sioned by Meyer Lansky's men to be his mob's Havana gambling
hub, an extravagant high-rise with sophistication unrivaled in the
Caribbean—Manhattan on the Florida Strait. Architect Philip
Johnson did initial designs until he realized he'd be working for
the Mafia and passed the job along. The building opened in December 1957 with Ginger Rogers and her musical revue in the
hotel's Copa Cabaret. In the end, Lansky's henchmen and Hollywood hangers-on enjoyed only three years of ocean views before
Castro nationalized the hotel and casino in 1960.

Today, the wallpaper in many of the Riviera's rooms buckles
from the humidity. Only half of them have seen renovations after 50 years of use; most floors are partly habitable and some are
closed altogether. Viewed from the huge saltwater pool below, to
which $10 buys anyone a day pass, the broken curtain rods dan-
gling diagonally across the windows give the hotel the look of a
cross-eyed old man. What beds there are have been made up with
linens in sizes that don't fit the mattresses, and cockroaches skitter
around the hallways or lie belly-up in corners. But in the lobby,
the imagination sketches outlines of the three-piece suits and stiff
silk skirts of the past, ghostlike, conjured by the decor. Low-slung,
coral velvet couches and surfboard-shaped coffee tables with opal-
escent mosaic and gold inlay, all well preserved, invite time-travel
fantasies.

Lobbies were where one could forget the hotels and houses that
were crumbling for lack of maintenance, ignore the damp bubbles at the corners of walls. Lobbies were also where hotel security
could most easily identify the women in spandex and pleather hal-
ter tops. The Riviera was Sandra's beat. Some nights she'd stay out
on the *malecón* and other nights she'd slip one of the hotel workers
5 or 10 CUC to stay from around nine at night until she found a
client. The $50 she charged gave her a good profit margin. She'd
order a TuKola at the bar and proposition any man whose eyes
lingered on her. At the club, now called the Copa Room, she'd
shimmy up against a man and make him feel like he was the best
dancer in the room. She complained later about how embarrass-

ingly badly they danced, and sometimes even demonstrated for me in the middle of empty streets, but someone usually took her up to his room or whisked her off in a taxi to another hotel.

A tenuous confidence built between Sandra and me. That winter, we sat on her patio and watched the Brazilian *telenovela* on her neighbor's TV, which he dragged outside each night. He was supposed to be leaving for Panama soon, where he'd work as a physical therapist, always any day now. I watched Sandra untangle her 10-year-old neighbor's jump rope and tally scores from the *lotería*, the numbers racket that all of San Miguel played, on scraps of paper. Other days, we drank cheap coffees or beers in the cafés in San Miguel and ate the Toblerones I bought at Mexican airports and talked about not much and then hitchhiked downtown together. I got out of cars near my room in Centro Habana, and she continued on to the Riviera. I wore Birkenstocks to Sandra's heels and demurred when she asked me to buy her a cell phone or told me how great her half-brother was in bed. I rarely took cabs anymore.

One afternoon, we went for pizza at one of Habana Vieja's tourist-trap restaurants. Oil-stained white tablecloths hung limply atop red ones and pink-faced men sat with young women at the other two occupied tables. While I went to the bathroom, she flagged down the waiter and ordered a plate of olives.

"Ay, Julia," she sighed when I returned, stretching out the round vowels of my name in her hoarse voice, *"estoy en estado."* She shoveled the canned olives into her mouth, filling her cheeks. She'd been eating like a horse, she said, peeing four times an hour, had what looked like a spare tire though she could rarely buy the food she craved—she thought it was Mumúa's baby. He'd gotten out of jail recently and was the only man she didn't use a condom with. If she had any more abortions, she might not be able to have kids in the future, so she'd have a baby in seven months.

Mumúa wanted to make a family of them, but Sandra had a plan, she said as she dipped French fries in the olive brine. She'd tell Bong, the Italian who visited Havana every four months with a millionaire invalid boss, that he was the father. As Sandra told it, theirs was a torrid, Jane Austen–in–the–tropics tale, the hunt for an advantageous match. Bong, who had a wife and kid back in Italy, wanted to move to Cuba to be with her, but his boss, who had promised to leave his fortune to Bong, wouldn't hear of it, so they snuck around. Since he was crazy about Sandra, and he looked something like Mumúa, she'd tell him the baby was his. Then he'd support her until the old man died and Bong could divorce the wife, marry Sandra, and take her and "their" baby away from Cuba, or at least to a better house on the island. "If he asks for a genetic test, I'll just say no," she summed up, bobbing her head between bites of food.

She had never actually seen the invalid boss, though. One day Bong hailed from a town in Italy where everyone looked like they were Asian—Sandra wasn't sure which town, didn't care—and another day he was actually Filipino Italian. When I asked what she'd do for money if she did leave, how she'd pay rent or buy medicine, she was dismissive: "Aiouuuuuulia, I'll do anything, anything," she said with a wave of her hand.

Sandra's plans for the future were like clouds she thought she'd walk into; they'd envelop her and then everything would be different. She'd find a boyfriend who'd marry her and get her the hell out of Cuba, where the life she'd lived for 21 years bored her: the same ration food, the same lack of privacy, the same eternal wait for buses to get downtown, the gloom that rolled in when her days were occupied by sleeping and boredom. The languid sense of time—which I soaked up in Havana—suffocated Sandra. Foreigners opened up wormholes of opportunity: Sandra could have money, sleep in hotels, buy $1 H. Upmann cigarettes, eat her favorite dessert, Jell-O, every day. The dreams Sandra imagined were the size of all the rooms she'd ever been in.

A few weeks after we'd had dinner, Sandra stopped talking to Mumúa. She'd seen him zipping toward home on his motorcycle with a pretty little thing clinging to his back. He'd also slapped her once or twice, she told me flippantly. I was relieved that Mumúa was out of Sandra's life and hoped it stayed that way.

So she'd listed Gallego as the baby's father on her *carnet de embarazada*, the ID card with which a pregnant woman can claim state benefits. With her *carnet*, she was entitled to medical care throughout her pregnancy, including house calls if she couldn't make it to the clinic and enough sonogram pictures to show off to neighbors, plus, she said: "a cradle that never shows up, a roll of gauze to use as diapers, little bottles of perfume and cream, two baby outfits, and four cloth diapers." She had already bought an extra roll of gauze off a woman who would use disposables. In stores, disposables retailed for around $12 for a pack of 20, or, on the black market, $14 for 40. Sandra hoped that if Bong pulled through and decided to support "his" child, she'd use disposables once the baby came. It wasn't an exit visa, but it was progress.

I moved to Havana at the end of summer 2009, just a few months after I'd met Sandra. The more time I spent there, the more I understood that, in direct contradiction to the grand and lofty ideas that dominated the city's public discourse, the very small details of life were all that mattered in Havana. Since no one had any say in what happened anywhere else, or in the government, or in any larger way, the individual dramas of what one saw, heard, did, felt, or needed held weight. I would never understand how these details stitched together if I left after three or four weeks. And there was something of relief in the surrender that the country forced on its visitors: You couldn't eat what you wanted to eat, *porque no hay,* or visit a neighborhood with new buildings, because it didn't exist. Every car, townhouse, staircase, and avenue kept the patina of a city that had given itself to the passage of time and to which you were of no consequence.

By then, and since she was visibly pregnant that summer, Sandra had moved on to her second moneymaking plan. She and her neighbor Yessica had bought 200 cups of yogurt of the sort that retailed in the CUC supermarkets for 75 cents each. They paid a middleman 15 cents per cup and then walked the neighborhood to sell the yogurts at three for a dollar. I found them one afternoon near the main avenue, struggling to free a yogurt-filled stroller from one of the potholes that winked across the asphalt. Yessica and I took the stroller, while Sandra waddled along the sidewalk, whispering to people who sat on chairs outside their homes and sticking her head into open doorways and windows to advertise product. Someone emerged from every few doors, handed over cash, lifted the lacy blanket that covered the carriage, and pawed through its contents for the desired flavors.

Sandra was imminently due. Her pink-and-gray-striped T-shirt snuck up her belly, which protruded nearly a foot from her slight frame, to reveal thick purplish marks.

We snaked through the area. "Baby's still cooking, *china?*"

whistled the man who leaned against the counter of the near-bare corner bodega, where rations were dispensed. Sandra rolled her slightly slanty eyes.

"Child's coming out walking if she stays in much longer," muttered one woman as she sauntered by.

"When are you due?" asked a girl as she pressed Lilliputian hands against Sandra's swollen belly. "Today? Tomorrow?"

"If it were up to me," she said, "I'd go straight to the hospital right now and get this baby the hell out of me." The temperature stretched toward around a hundred degrees of mostly humidity.

When we reached the main avenue, Yessica and I stayed on the sidewalk with the stroller as Sandra advertised in shops—laundromat, cafeteria, Banco Nacional de Cuba. At the bank, the girls stopped to rest in the air-conditioned ATM cabin and sort out who wanted what inside. They ferried upwards of 40 cups of pineapple and strawberry while I stayed with the stroller. If a policeman came, Yessica said sternly, I was to invent an excuse or pretend not to speak Spanish and run. Sandra giggled: "The *yuma* comes to Cuba to sell yogurt. That's how bad the economy up north is." When one yogurt spilled open and the bitter smell of synthetic strawberry began to stink, Sandra whisked a towel embroidered with a yellow duckie out of her purse, which had at one point been my purse, a black faux-patent tote I'd given her on the last day of my last trip—she'd noted at our Habana Vieja pizza dinner what a good diaper bag it would make and I'd left it with her. She wiped up the yogurt and stuffed the damp towel in an interior zip compartment.

Once the stroller was empty, Yessica pointed it toward home and Sandra walked me toward the bus stop. The amber afternoon was dusty. As we paused at a corner to let a truck turn, she pivoted toward me. "I'd like to ask you something," she said. "Will you be the baby's godmother?"

I felt her at my side, gauging my response as she studied the ends of her long, layered hair for split ends. The truck passed, and we crossed the street. I needed to redraw the lines between us, I knew then, and if that meant she'd toss me aside, foreign and writer and all, I'd do it anyway. I wished that there was a part of me that wanted to say yes, or believe she'd asked me out of genuine sentiment, but there wasn't.

"The problem," I explained, "is that I'm still hoping to write something about you someday." If I was the godmother of her child, I could be seen as being too involved, I said, and my "bosses," hazy as they were, would find even our formal interviews suspect.

She nodded. We were on the main street among sweaty men in dago Ts, old ladies with shopping bags, and girls with hair in netted ballerina buns. We passed under shaded colonnades that had been painted, vandalized, and repainted darker shades, a mottled patchwork of scratched-out signatures, expletives encased in bubbles, and declarations of love, *PR+SN* and *Yoser y Lulu*.

Sandra shook her head and pursed her lips. "No," she said. She laughed and, after a beat, nodded. "Of course I'd rather maybe be famous. You just keep doing your job. Yessica wanted to be godmother anyway."

The day after Mia Jaqueline was born, yogurts were still stacked three-deep in Sandra's tepid freezer. All nonessential furniture had moved outside to the shared patio. A crib had been assembled in the windowless bedroom, and the two twin mattresses on which Aboo, Gallego, and Sandra slept were piled one atop another. Fourteen plastic bottles on which Winnie-the-Pooh licked honey from a jar sat atop the old washing machine that was the kitchen counter between cleaning days. Sandra's father had sent her a suitcase of baby goods from Florida, and she would sell the overstock.

I sat in a rocking chair next to Sandra. The baby squirmed on her knees. She had stuffed her bra full of tissue paper and stowed a lighter between her swollen breasts, and she waved to gesture that I should light a cigarette for her. I grabbed the packet off the table, lit the cigarette, and handed it over; she kept one hand on the baby's belly.

The Cuban government almost never granted exit papers for children. The consequences of this fact hadn't seemed real, I supposed, until Sandra had held Mia. This would be her life, she spat—these two rooms, these neighbors, motherhood. My presence in her home felt suddenly cruel. I sipped my coffee, nodded, and slipped away after 15 minutes or so.

It was a few weeks before I went to San Miguel again. There always seemed to be a reason to postpone: I was interviewing other people; dealing with the logistics of settling into living in Cuba; she had run out of phone minutes and didn't call me back when I left messages at her aunt's. The afternoon I returned, uninvited

but assuming she'd be home around two or three, tiny white baby
linens hung thick as curtains on the patio's laundry lines, one after
the other. Aboo waved me inside, cheerfully brushing off my offers
to help her hang the white gauze squares. She was nearly done
anyway. Sandra was out, the baby was asleep in her crib, and I sat
to wait. An army of ants carried thumbnail-size bread crumbs up
the lavender wall. The room smelled tangy. When Sandra arrived
a half-hour later, she bustled into the apartment with a *"Hooooooo-
lia!"* She pulled open her black patent purse and asked if I wanted
to buy air fresheners. I laughed.

"So that's what you're doing for money now," I said.

She shook her head and busied herself making coffee. "Nah,
not for long. An *amigo* comes out this weekend from Spain—he's
Cuban but he lives in Spain—and I ran into his daughter around
here last week. '*China,* he's crazy to see you,' she says, and I tell her
that I've just given birth, so she comes to see the baby. Of course
she said Mia was beautiful. Anyway, 'You call me as soon as the
cuarentena is done,' the girl says. 'You can see my dad as soon as
you're ready.' See, he knows no one can do the things I can do."
So, she continued, she was cutting short the 40 days of staying
sexually chaste. He wasn't technically a new partner.

Mia woke with a yowl, and Sandra asked me to grab her while
she prepared a bottle of formula. She was trying to stop breast-
feeding so she wouldn't sag too much, she said. The silence that
followed was swollen and barbed. I commented on how much Mia
had grown. She had huge, chubby cheeks, and milky-blue, barely
slanted eyes, like Sandra's, but *shhh,* she said—it was what made
her look like Bong.

"Any news from Bong?" I asked.

"Well, he called the other day," she said, "first time I'd spoken
to him since I told him I was having his baby, months ago, that
time when the call dropped. 'Sandra,' he says, 'how's the baby?'
Identical to you, I say. She's your carbon copy. 'Really,' he says. 'I
can't wait to meet her.' Then the call went dead. He said he was
coming next month, though."

State salons aren't the only ones allowed in Cuba anymore. Among
the 178 nonprofessional jobs that Raúl Castro signed into legality
last year is haircutting. Sandra could open a small business if she
wanted. She wouldn't, though, because a neighbor with a quicker

reaction time already had a monopoly on her block. We sat on the *malecón* again, in nearly the exact spot of our first meeting, a year and some after I'd moved away from Cuba in 2010.

Sandra dabbed her forehead with an orange washcloth so she looked dewy but never damp and introduced me to her new Cuban boyfriend. It had been tough to find clients lately, she said, and he nodded as she spoke. "I've been here last night, the night before, all last weekend, and nothing," she said. Sandra gestured toward the Riviera and the Meliá Cohiba on the opposite corner: "See how few lights are on?" She was brusque and stiff, as if her insides had puddled down and a shell kept her upright. "Not even worth paying to get in."

Gallego was in jail, seven years on charges Sandra wouldn't detail. Mia was two and back home with Aboo, same as always, doing fine. I could come over tomorrow. She'd call when she woke up. "That'd be great," I said. Before I left, she asked me for money. Just $5 or maybe $10 or whatever, just so she could get a cab home.

The second time I'd ever met Sandra, she'd asked to borrow 10 kilos, 10 cents, to buy cigarettes. I, misunderstanding her, had rustled through my pockets for bills. "Ay, no," she'd laughed, pushing at my forearm and holding out an incomplete palm full of coins. She wanted to buy a pack of cigarettes.

I understood slang now, sure, but also how Havana forced an acknowledgment of the shades that existed between people. *Jinetera* or *amiga,* self-sufficient or dependent, realistic or delusional. There were armies of young people around Havana whose private dramas unfolded in isolation in the vast stretch between the Castro estates in Siboney and San Miguel del Padrón, who were something like Sandra. Idlers, academics, Santería initiates, and punk rockers harbored poorly constructed skyscraper fantasies about the lives they'd lead beyond their island home. Some of them actually wound up elsewhere, whether with the help of an *amigo* or on their own, turning those dreamscapes into realities. The one binary that Havana tried to enforce was *Cubano* and *turista.* I would always be some unnamed in-between, neither *Cubano* nor *turista,* journalist nor friend. I would always be coming from somewhere else, always leaving, always able to leave.

I didn't have much cash on me but I handed Sandra a $5 bill and walked away, feeling like there was a fire at my back and I was gliding toward the air that fed it. I never heard from her again.

Life During Wartime

FROM *Harper's Magazine*

THERE WAS SPRING RAIN and pale fog in Sarajevo as my plane approached the city last April, veering over the green foothills of Mount Igman. Through the frosted window I could see the outline of the road we used to call Snipers' Alley, above which Serbian sharpshooters would perch and fire at anyone below. Twenty years had passed since I'd arrived in Sarajevo as a war reporter.

During the siege of the city, most foreign journalists had lived in the Holiday Inn, and it was in that grotty hotel that the man who was to become my husband and the father of my child professed undying love. I met some of my best friends in Sarajevo and lost several others—to alcoholism, drugs, insanity, and suicide. My own sense of compassion and integrity, I think, was shaped during those years.

Since then I had come back many times to report on Bosnia, on the genocide there, and to try to find people who had gone missing during the war. Now I was returning for a peculiar sort of reunion that would bring together reporters, photographers, and aid workers who, for one reason or another, had never forgotten the brutal and protracted siege, which lasted nearly four years. By the end of the war, in 1995, a city once renowned for its multiculturalism and industrial vigor had been reduced to medieval squalor.

Why was it that Sarajevo, and not Rwanda or Congo or Sierra Leone or Chechnya—wars that all of us went on to report—captured us the way this war did? One of us, I think it was Christiane Amanpour, called it "our generation's Vietnam." We were often accused of falling in love with Sarajevo because it was a European conflict—a war whose victims looked like us, who sat in cafés and loved Philip Roth and Susan Sontag. As reporters, we lived among the people of Sarajevo. We saw the West turn its back and felt helpless.

I had begun my career in journalism covering the First Intifada in the late 1980s. I came to Sarajevo because I wanted to experience firsthand the effect war had on civilians. My father had taught me to stick up for underdogs, to be on the right side of history. But I had no idea what it would feel like to stare into the open eyes of the recently dead; how to count bodies daily in a morgue; how to talk to a woman whose children had just been killed by shrapnel while they were building a snowman.

During my first ride into the city from the airport—past a blasted wall on which the words *Welcome to Hell* had been graffitied—it was clear that my wish to see war up close would be granted. I had gotten a lift from a photographer named Jon Jones, and as we careened down Snipers' Alley toward the city, he told me how many reporters had already been killed, how close the snipers were and how easily they could see us, and about the hundreds of mortar shells that fell on Sarajevo each day. He recounted in detail how a CNN camerawoman had been shot in the jaw, and told me that a bullet could rip through the metal of a car as easily as a needle pierces a piece of cloth.

"Think of being in a doll's house," he said, edging up to a hundred miles per hour on the straightaways. "We're the tiny dolls."

He dropped me off at the Holiday Inn, the only "functioning" hotel in the city, leaving me to lug inside my flak jacket, battery-operated Tandy computer, sleeping bag, and a duffel bag filled with protein bars, antibiotics, a flashlight, batteries, candles, waterproof matches, pens and notebooks, and a pair of silk long johns (which I never took off that entire first winter of the war). I had with me just a single book: a copy of *The Face of War*, by Martha Gellhorn, a journalist who had covered the Spanish Civil War, the Allies' invasion of Normandy, Vietnam, the Six-Day War, and almost every other major conflict of the 20th century. She settled in Paris in 1930, married a Frenchman, and began to write for *Collier's*, the *Saturday Evening Post*, and other publications. In 1936, in a bar in Key West (the Frenchman was long gone), she met

Ernest Hemingway, whom she married, and later moved with him to Spain. She was blond and beautiful and, above all, brave. She was also, as I would later find out, very ill-tempered and often not a "woman's woman."

I had gone to meet Gellhorn in Wales on a hot summer day in 1991, having been sent to interview her about a collection of her novels that was just being published. History had forgotten her to some extent, but she had a loyal cadre, mostly men, who adored her. She drank and smoked, but she had a rare femininity.

That day, I took a train, a bus, then finally hiked over hot fields to reach Catscradle, her remote cottage. I was keenly aware of my youth and inexperience, and felt embarrassed for all that I had not yet witnessed. She answered the door in tailored slacks with a long cigarette in her hand. She was in her 80s by then and still extremely good-looking. She invited me inside and together we watched the invasion of Slovenia on television while she made astute comments about the coming destruction of Yugoslavia. I listened intently, but, as she made clear, she had no interest in taking on a protégé.

"I hope you're not expecting lunch," she said rather sharply. She did bring me a glass of ice water, and had laid out a guest towel in her upstairs bathroom for me to use. But that was the limit of her hospitality and, by implication, her professional encouragement.

A few weeks later, I got a letter from her scolding me for having made mistakes in my article. I had reported that the light in the room was strong, when in fact it had been rather weak. What infuriated her most was that I had mentioned she had once been Hemingway's wife. You violated the rule of journalism, she wrote. You lied.

Some years later, shortly before she died (her close friends believed it was suicide), we served together on a panel about war reporting for Freedom House, and she called me "dear girl," and embraced me affectionately. By then, I had reported on many sieges and many wars. Someone took a photograph of us together, both speaking animatedly, our faces captured in heated emotion.

In the lobby of the Holiday Inn, I looked around and tried to be brave. To my surprise, there was an ordinary, if dark, reception area with cubbyholes for passports presided over by a rather elegant bespectacled man who took my documents, registered them, and handed me the keys to a room on the fourth floor.

"There's no elevator," he said matter-of-factly, "since there's no electricity. Take the stairs there." He gestured toward a cavernous hallway and told me the hours of the communal meals, which were served in a makeshift dining room lit by candles.

"And please, madame, don't walk on this side of the building." He pointed to a wall, through which you could see the sky and buildings outside, that looked as though a truck had run into it. "And don't go up on the seventh floor," he added cryptically. The seventh floor, I soon learned, was where the Bosnian snipers defending the city were positioned. And the forbidden side of the building faced the Serbian snipers and mortar emplacements. If you emerged from the hotel on that side and a sniper had you in his range, you got shot.

Walking into the dining room that first night, I felt I had made a terrible mistake. I knew no one in Sarajevo, it was a few weeks before Christmas, and it was bitterly cold. I had not seen the photographer since he'd dumped me at the hotel (declaring, in passing, that he hated all writers). Perhaps, I thought, staring at the blown-out windows and mortar-cracked walls, I should stay a few days and go home.

Around me, I heard many languages: Dutch, Flemish, French, German, Japanese, Spanish, as well as Serbo-Croatian (which is now often referred to as three separate but nearly identical tongues: Serbian, Croatian, and Bosnian). The huge room was full of grizzled reporters, everyone looking slightly dazed—a combination of exhaustion, hangover, and shock. In the distance I heard machine-gun fire and a mortar shell dropping somewhere in the city. No one paid attention to the noise, or to a newcomer like me.

But I soon encountered warmth and even fierce camaraderie. Over dinner—a plate of rice and canned meat from a humanitarian-aid box—an American cameraman of Armenian descent named Yervant Der Parthogh told me about the toilets. "Find an empty room and follow your nose," he said, passing me a bottle of Tabasco sauce, standard issue in war zones, where the bland diet of rice cried out for a little seasoning. (ABC, the BBC, and other TV-news organizations bought the condiment in bulk, and it was often shared.)

What exactly did he mean about the toilets? Yervant explained that certain rooms were always vacant, since their walls had been partially blown away, exposing the interior to sniper fire. But in the attached bathrooms, the toilets remained—unflushable, full, and stinking. "Find one and make it your own," he advised.

The window in my room had been destroyed by a rocket and replaced with plastic by the UN's refugee agency. The shelling was continuous. I unpacked my gear, propped my flashlight against a cup, brushed my teeth with the mineral water I had brought from Zagreb, laid out the St. Jude medallion my mother had given me, and unrolled my sleeping bag on top of an orange polyester blanket left over from the glory days of 1984, when Sarajevo was an Olympic city and the gruesome Soviet-style structure of the Holiday Inn had been built.

As I discovered the next day, the press corps consisted of a bunch of men with cameras or notebooks in a standard uniform: jeans, Timberland boots, and ugly zip-front fluorescent fleeces. The sole exception was a tall, thin Frenchman named Paul Marchand, a radio reporter, whose outfit consisted of a pressed white shirt, creased black trousers, and shiny dress shoes.

There were, I was relieved to see, other women. I recognized Amanpour, young, glamorous, and more visible than ever after her coverage two years earlier of the Gulf War. I also encountered a few French female reporters, all of whom violated the masculine dress code: a reporter from *Le Parisien* who wore cashmere sweaters; the petite radio reporter Ariane Quentier, who favored a Russian fur hat; and Alexandra Boulat, a photographer with a mane of long blond hair (she died after suffering a brain aneurysm in Ramallah, in 2007, at the age of 45).

I also met Kurt Schork, who had a room near mine on the fourth floor. He was a legendary Reuters correspondent who had become a war reporter at the age of 40 after working for New York City's Metropolitan Transportation Authority. Schork brought me to the Reuters office and showed me how to file my copy on a satellite phone for $50 a minute. There was a generator in the next room, which reeked of gasoline, and if it was running, one dialed the London office, then read the copy to a distant, frenetic typist, spelling out all the Serbo-Croatian words. It was very World War II. Carrier pigeons would have been faster.

Over the next few weeks, Schork patiently told me where and

where not to go. He showed me how to rig up a hose as a kind of makeshift shower. On Christmas Eve, we went to midnight mass together at St. Josip's Catholic church on Snipers' Alley (though not at midnight, since that would have been an invitation to the Serbs to shell us); Christian soldiers, who made up perhaps a quarter of Bosnia's largely Muslim defense force, came down from the frontline at the outskirts of the city to receive communion.

Room 437 would be my home, on and off, for the next three years: the mangy orange blanket, the plywood desk with cigarette burns, the empty minibar, the telephone on the bedside table that never rang because the lines were cut. And through the plastic sheeting of my window, I had a view of the city, with its 35,000 destroyed buildings and its courageous populace that refused to bend to its oppressors.

The 2012 reunion in Sarajevo was to take place over the first week of April, Holy Week. This had some resonance for me, since during the siege I often went to mass with other Catholic reporters in the battered Catholic church. It had given me solace, and seeing the old ladies bent over their rosary beads reassured me in some way that wherever I went in the world I could find a common community bound by religion.

Shortly after I arrived for the reunion, I ran into Emma Daly, who had been a reporter for the British *Independent* during the war and now worked for Human Rights Watch. She had married the war photographer Santiago Lyon, now a senior AP boss, and was the mother of two children. In those days, I don't think either one of us projected much into the future or could have imagined ourselves married, with children, living more or less normal lives.

"Have you seen the chairs yet?" she asked.

Emma explained that a kind of temporary memorial had been set up on Marshal Tito Street, in the center of the city: 11,541 empty red chairs, one for every resident killed during the siege. Walking downtown, we approached the Presidency Building, where we had risked sniper fire and stray mortar rounds during the war to interview President Alija Izetbegović or Vice President Ejup Ganić, who always let journalists into his office and sometimes offered us hot coffee. "If you're brave enough to come to this building," Ganić once told me, "then I am going to talk to you."

The rows of red chairs, some of them scaled down to represent children, stretched far into the distance. Later there would be some grumbling over the fact that the chairs had been made in a Serbian factory. Yet the amount of destruction they represented was overwhelming—every one of these people might still be alive if a sniper had failed to pull the trigger, if a mortar shell had landed 20 feet to the east or west.

That night, at the refurbished Holiday Inn, we all got horribly drunk. Then we started taking group pictures. All of us were a little rounder in the face, the men with less hair and bigger bellies. The women, though, looked remarkably good.

The Holiday Inn now offers Wi-Fi, working toilets, a few restaurants (the food still bad), and clean sheets. We gathered in the bar, a group of veteran reporters and photographers who hadn't seen one another in 20 years. There was Morten Hvaal, a Norwegian photographer who once had driven me around the city in the AP's armored car, pointing out landmarks; Shane ("Shaney") McDonald, an Australian cameraman who had sat in my room one night with Keith "Chuck" Tayman and Robbie Wright, watching falling stars from an open window; and there, in a corner, Jon Jones, the photographer who had scared me so on my first ride from the airport. Now he was nice. We had all grown up.

But some people were missing from the Holiday Inn lounge where we had spent years living on whiskey, cigarettes, and chocolate bars. Shouldn't Kurt Schork have been sitting on a barstool, drinking a cranberry juice? Kurt was killed by rebel soldiers in Sierra Leone in May 2000, the morning after we ate dinner together in a restaurant overlooking the sea. And where was Paul Marchand, with his black shoes and white shirt? (He had once called me in the middle of the night to shout, "The water is running and she is hot!") After the war he wrote novels, started drinking, and, one night in 2009, hanged himself. Juan Carlos Gumucio was gone, too. A bear of a man—and the second husband of *Sunday Times* reporter Marie Colvin, also gone, killed in Homs, Syria, in February 2012—he had introduced himself to me in central Bosnia by exclaiming, "Call me JC! Like Jesus Christ. Or like King Juan Carlos." We used to go to Sunday mass together in Sarajevo—and in London, too, but then out afterward for bloody marys. In 2002 he shot himself in the heart after, in Colvin's words, "seeing too much war." I was in Somalia at the time, on a hotel rooftop, and someone phoned to tell me. There were gunshots all around me, and over that din I began to cry for my friend.

The morning after our reunion, we all had hangovers. Gradually, we pulled ourselves together, and shortly after noon, we went to a vineyard owned by a local former employee of the AP. There we spent the afternoon drinking wine and looking out over the hills at Sarajevo. It was almost unthinkable, but we were sipping wine and eating slow-cooked lamb in the exact spot where snipers had set up 20 years before.

Our return to our homes in Auckland, Beirut, Boston, London, Milan, New York, Nicosia, Paris, and Vienna was followed by a flurry of comradely e-mails and pictures posted on Facebook. There was much talk of getting together again, which we all knew would never happen. Then we all plunged into depression. A few days later I received a letter from Edward Serotta, who had gone to Sarajevo to document its Jewish population during the Bosnian war and now works in Vienna reconstructing family histories that were lost during the Holocaust. Serotta said that he remembered coming back to his Berlin apartment after weeks in Sarajevo and putting on a pair of trousers that slid off him. At first he thought they belonged to someone else. Then he realized that they were his—and that he was still himself—but physically and emotionally, he was not the same person who first went to Sarajevo.

Serotta told me he remembered a night he walked through the city, in November 1993, thinking, "If mankind is going to destroy itself, I feel honored and privileged to be here to see how it is done."

After I put his letter away, I gathered up all my Sarajevo mementos—the tiny bits of shrapnel, a photograph of me and Ariane in helmets on the frontline, a copper coffeepot, a love note that Bruno, my husband, had left me in Room 437 after our first meeting, his English then imperfect: "I won't loose you."

At the airport, a group of us had gathered for coffee: Serotta; the Pulitzer Prize–winning journalist Roy Gutman; Ariane; Peter Kessler (a UN refugee worker) and his wife, Lisa; and Anna Cataldi, an Italian writer and UN ambassador. Ariane and I soon boarded the plane to Paris, and she—always the astute little reporter in the fur hat—caught my mood.

"Don't be sad," she said. "There are many places to go." She fiddled with her handbag and read *Paris Match*.

But I was sad. My experience in Sarajevo was the last time I thought I could change something. The city was passing below my eyes from the plane window, forever broken, resting on a long flowing river.

America the Marvelous

FROM *Vanity Fair*

"STUPID, STUPID. Americans are stupid. America is stupid. A stupid, stupid country made stupid by stupid, stupid people." I particularly remember that because of the nine stupids. It was said over a dinner table by a professional woman, a clever, clever, clever woman. Hardback educated, bespokely traveled, liberally humane, worked in the arts. I can't remember specifically why she said it, what evidence of New World idiocy triggered the trope. Nor do I remember what the reaction was, but I don't need to remember. It would have been a nodded and muttered agreement. Even from me. I've heard this cock crow so often I don't even feel guilt for not wringing its neck.

Among the educated, enlightened, expensive middle classes of Europe, this is a received wisdom. A given. Stronger in some countries, like France, less so somewhere like Germany, but overall the Old World patronizes America for being a big, dumb, fat, belligerent child. The intellectuals, the movers and the makers and the creators, the dinner-party establishments of people who count, are united in the belief—no, the knowledge—that Americans are stupid, crass, ignorant, soulless, naive oafs without attention, irony, or intellect. These same people will use every comforting, clever, and ingenious American invention, will demand America's medicine, wear its clothes, eat its food, drink its drink, go to its cinema, love its music, thank God for its expertise in a hundred disciplines, and will all adore New York. More than that, more shaming and hypocritical than that, these are people who collectively owe their nations' and their personal freedom to American intervention and protection in wars, both hot and cold. Who, whether they credit it or not, also owe their concepts of freedom, equality, and civil rights in no small part to America. Of course, they will also sign collective letters accusing America of being a fascist, totalitarian, racist state.

Enough. Enough, enough, enough of this convivial rant, this collectively confirming bigotry. The nasty laugh of little togetherness, or Euro-liberal insecurity. It's embarrassing, infectious, and belittling. Look at that European snapshot of America. It is so unlike the country I have known for 30 years. Not just a caricature but a travesty, an invention. Even on the most cursory observation, the intellectual European view of the New World is a homemade, Old World effigy that suits some internal purpose. The belittling, the discounting, the mocking of Americans is not about them at all. It's about us, back here on the ancient, classical, civilized Continent. Well, how stupid can America actually be? On the international list of the world's best universities, 14 of the top 20 are American. Four are British. Of the top 100, only 4 are French, and Heidelberg is one of 4 that creeps in for the Germans. America has won 338 Nobel Prizes. The UK, 119. France, 59. America has more Nobel Prizes than Britain, France, Germany, Japan, and Russia combined. Of course, Nobel Prizes aren't everything, and America's aren't all for inventing Prozac or refining oil. It has 22 Peace Prizes, 12 for literature. (T. S. Eliot is shared with the Brits.)

And are Americans emotionally dim, naive, irony-free? Do you imagine the society that produced Dorothy Parker and Lenny Bruce doesn't understand irony? It was an American who said that political satire died when they awarded the Nobel Peace Prize to Henry Kissinger. It's not irony that America lacks; it's cynicism. In Europe, that arid sneer out of which nothing is grown or made is often mistaken for the creative scalpel of irony. And what about vulgarity? Americans are innately, sniggeringly vulgar. What, vulgar like Henry James or Eleanor Roosevelt or Cole Porter, or the Mormons? Again, it's a question of definitions. What Americans value and strive for is straight talking, plain saying. They don't go in for ambiguity or dissembling, the etiquette of hidden meaning, the skill of the socially polite lie. The French in particular confuse unadorned direct language with a lack of culture or intellectual elegance. It was Camus who sniffily said that only in America could you be a novelist without being an intellectual. There is a belief that America has no cultural depth or critical seriousness. Well, you only have to walk into an American bookshop to realize that is wildly wrong and willfully blind. What about Mark Twain, or jazz, or abstract expressionism?

What is so contrary about Europe's liberal antipathy to America is that any visiting Venusian anthropologist would see with the merest cursory glance that America and Europe are far more similar than they are different. The threads of the Old World are woven into the New. America is Europe's greatest invention. That's not to exclude the contribution to America that has come from around the globe, but it is built out of Europe's ideas, Europe's understanding, aesthetic, morality, assumptions, and laws. From the way it sets a table to the chairs it sits on, to the rhythms of its poetry and the scales of its music, the meter of its aspirations and its laws, its markets, its prejudices and neuroses. The conventions and the breadth of America's reason are European.

This isn't a claim for ownership, or for credit. But America didn't arrive by chance. It wasn't a ship that lost its way. It wasn't coincidence or happenstance. America grew tall out of the cramping ache of old Europe.

When I was a child, there was a lot of talk of a "brain drain"—commentators, professors, directors, politicians would worry at the seeping of gray matter across the Atlantic. Brains were being lured to California by mere money. Mere money and space, and sun, and steak, and Hollywood, and more money and opportunity and optimism and openness. People who took the dollar in exchange for their brains were unpatriotic in much the same way that tax exiles were. The unfair luring of indigenous British thought would, it was darkly said, lead to Britain falling behind, ceasing to be the preeminently brilliant and inventive nation that had produced the Morris Minor and the hovercraft. You may have little idea how lauded and revered Sir Christopher Cockerell, the inventor of the hovercraft, was, and you may well not be aware of what a noisy, unstable waste of effort the hovercraft turned out to be, but we were very proud of it for a moment.

The underlying motif of the brain drain was that for real cleverness you needed years of careful breeding. Cold bedrooms, tinned tomatoes on toast, a temperament and a heritage that led to invention and discovery. And that was really available only in Europe and, to the greatest extent, in Britain. The brain drain was symbolic of a postwar self-pity. The handing back of Empire, the slow, Kiplingesque watch as the things you gave your life to are broken, and you have to stoop to build them up with worn-out tools. There was resentment and envy—whereas in the first half of the 20th century Britain had spent the last of Grandfather's inherited capital, leaving it exhausted and depressed, for America the war had been the engine that geared up industry and pulled it out of the Depression, capitalizing it for a half century of plenty. It seemed so unfair.

The real brain drain was already 300 years old. The idea of America attracted the brightest and most idealistic, and the best from all over Europe. European civilization had reached a stasis. By its own accounting, it had grown from classical Greece to become an identifiable, homogeneous place, thanks to the Roman Empire and the spread of Christianity. Following the Dark Ages, there was the Renaissance and the Reformation, and then the Age of Reason, from which grew a series of ideas and discoveries, philosophies and visions, that became preeminent. But at the moment of their creation here comes the United States—just as Europe was reaching a point where the ideas that moved it were outgrowing the conventions and the hierarchies that governed it. Democracy, free economy, free trade, free speech, and social mobility were stifled by the vested interests and competing stresses of a crowded and class-bound continent. Migration to America may have been primarily economic, but it also created the space where the ideas that in Europe had grown too root-bound to flourish might be transplanted. Over 200 years the flame that had been lit in Athens and fanned in Rome, Paris, London, Edinburgh, Berlin, Stockholm, Prague, and Vienna was passed, a spark at a time, to the New World.

In 1776 the white and indentured population of America was 2.5 million. A hundred years later it was nearly 50 million. In 1890, America overtook Britain in manufacturing output to become the biggest industrial economy in the world. No economy in the history of commerce has grown that precipitously, and this was 25 years after the most murderous, expensive, and desperate civil war. Indeed, America may have reached parity with Britain as early as 1830. Right from its inception it had faster growth than old Europe. It now accounts for a quarter of the world's economy. It wasn't individual brains that made this happen. It wasn't a man with a better mousetrap. It was a million families who wanted a better mousetrap and were willing to work making mousetraps. It was banks that would finance the manufacture of better mousetraps, and it was a big nation with lots of mice.

One of the most embarrassing things I've ever done in public was to appear—against all judgment—in a debate at the Hay Literary Festival in the mid-'90s, speaking in defense of the motion that American culture should be resisted. Along with me on this cretin's errand was the historian Norman Stone. I can't remember what I said—I've erased it. It had no weight or consequence. On the other side, the right side, were Adam Gopnik, from *The New Yorker,* and Salman Rushdie. After we'd proposed the damn motion, Rushdie leaned in to the microphone, paused for a moment, regarding the packed theater from those half-closed eyes, and said, soft and clear, "Be-bop-a-lula, she's my baby . . . Be-bop-a-lula, she's my baby love."

It was the triumph of the sublime. The bookish audience burst into applause and cheered. It was all over, bar some dry coughing. America didn't bypass or escape civilization. It did something far more profound, far cleverer: it simply changed what civilization could be. It set aside the canon of rote, the long chain letter of drawing-room, bon-mot received aesthetics. It was offered a new, neoclassical, reconditioned, reupholstered start, a second verse to an old song, and it just took a look at the view and felt the beat of this vast nation and went for the sublime.

There is in Europe another popular snobbery, about the parochialism of America, the unsophistication of its taste, the limit of its inquiry. This, we're told, is proved by "how few Americans travel abroad." Apparently, so we're told, only 35 percent of Americans have passports. Whenever I hear this, I always think, My good golly gosh, really? That many? Why would you go anywhere else? There is so much of America to wonder at. So much that is the miracle of a newly minted civilization. And anyway, European kids only get passports because they all want to go to New York.

Christmas in Thessaloniki

FROM *The Believer*

Translated from the Dutch by Sam Garrett

UNTIL RECENTLY, wars had a venue. They had a front. Wars had a beginning, and often came to a clear end. Then the war against terrorism came along. This war was everywhere and nowhere; it could pop up anyplace. And although the war was more manifest in some places than others—Afghanistan and Iraq, for example—it remained elusive. Then the financial crisis hit, and proved every bit as elusive as the "real" wars at the start of the 21st century. The crisis, too, was everywhere and nowhere, but it did have a single nation at its epicenter: Greece.

Not at Lehman Brothers, which collapsed in 2008, and not on Wall Street; Greece was where the fire broke out. One heard the word *contamination* again and again, but this time it was no imperial cultural contamination, no creeping process of civilization. This time the crisis was a contagion: debts and obligations that would never be repaid, a gradual deterioration of the financial immune system.

And so, in the darkest days of winter, I decided to set off for Thessaloniki, Greece's second-largest city. Cities like that are often at least as interesting as the capital, and if God is in the details, then the truth is going to be revealed at the periphery. In conversations with people working in various capacities to regenerate Greek social and economic life, I would try to assess the collateral damage from this newest international conflagration. But I also went to Thessaloniki to meet its mayor, Yiannis Boutaris, who had recently rocketed to international stardom. In newspaper articles he was portrayed as a "good Greek," a man who wanted to combat corruption, who did not compare Angela Merkel to Hitler, who did not blame everything on capitalism, and who had no desire to defend in veiled terms the country's nepotism and status quo. In those articles one detected an unmistakable relief at the fact that a good Greek had been found.

I would spend Christmas in Thessaloniki—the light in the darkened world of the crisis.

I. Kostas

About a 15-minute walk uphill from the sea—Thessaloniki has an upper city and a lower city—is the RentRooms Thessaloniki youth hostel. In the cafeteria there I meet with Kostas Terzopoulos. He has a little beard and kindly, not-quite-shy eyes. Kostas is wearing a gray sweater that looks like it's been washed too often. I've been told that he organizes the Totally Naked Bike Ride in Thessaloniki. Why wear clothes in a climate like this? Clothes, too, are something on which one can economize.

We both order tea. "To start with, it's an ecological thing," Kostas says. "I'm a member of the Green Ecological Party. It's a small party. In the last elections we just made our quorum—we ended up with 2.93 percent. And in the second round of the elections we only made 0.88 percent. People had no more confidence in us then. It's a pleasant party. We have a representative in the European Parliament, and there's also someone on the municipal council in Thessaloniki; he's been misbehaving lately, though, so we're trying to drum him out of the party." Kostas talks to me as though I'm his friend, or at least as though I'm rapidly becoming his friend.

"I'm unemployed these days, but it all started back when I still had a job. I did the IT for a radio station, and I was a part-time DJ. At school, all the cool guys had scooters, and later on—like lots of Greeks—my car was one of the most important things in my life. I did all the things you're not supposed to do: I parked wherever I found a spot. My car meant everything to me. Like a lot of Greeks, I had the idea that I didn't have to do anything and that the government had to do everything for me. The change in my mentality started when I became a nudist."

"How did that go?" I ask.

"I was always very shy, especially in the bodily sense. But a few years ago I was with a few friends at a lovely, quiet beach. One of them said: 'Let's go skinny-dipping.' I hesitated, but I finally took off my clothes, too, even though I didn't really enjoy that yet. A few weeks later I actually started as a practicing nudist. At first only at home, where I walked around naked as much as possible, but later also outdoors, in natural surroundings. I didn't do any nudism in an urban setting, not yet.

"Then, I guess that was in 2007, a colleague said to me: 'Why don't you ever come to work on a bike? It would make it a lot easier to find a parking spot.' I bought my first bike, an Ideal Megisto, something between a mountain bike and a regular bicycle. At first, biking was an experiment, like nudism.

"I haven't eaten all day; would you mind if I ordered a sandwich?"

"Go right ahead," I say.

"I wanted to combine my two great passions," Kostas tells me, "nudism and cycling. That's how I stumbled on the Totally Naked Bike Ride. I called some friends and I got a lot of help. People liked the idea. Thessaloniki's first Totally Naked Bike Ride was held on June 27, 2008. There were about a hundred participants; ten of them were women. The police said they were going to arrest us, and they actually did arrest a couple of participants who were totally naked, but we kept protesting until they let them go. Not everyone, by the way, has to be totally naked. Some of the participants wear strings, others wear body paint. Each year, more and more people take part in the Totally Naked Bike Ride. In 2009 there were 350 riders, in 2010 there were 700, in 2011 there were 1,300, and in 2012 we had 2,000 participants. The Totally Naked Bide Ride originally started in Vancouver, but it's spread all over the world."

Kostas takes a few bites of his sandwich.

"It's a social movement," he says. "We have three objectives: to promote cycling, to increase environmental awareness, and to promote bodily freedom. I always have to explain to people that nudity has nothing to do with sex. Nudity isn't at all sexy. I've gone through four phases myself. It started with nudism, then I discovered the bike, after that I became a vegetarian, and in 2013 I'm going to go vegan. But the Totally Naked Bike Ride isn't the only thing I do. I also organize the bicycle carnival. Thessaloniki has no carnival tradition, which is how I hit on the idea. The floats will all be pulled by bicycles. This year's theme is 'anti-gold'; there are plans to give a Canadian company permission to start a gold mine near here, and we're against that. The new mayor likes us, but the church doesn't."

"And what about the crisis?" I ask.

"I'm thirty-eight," Kostas says. "And like I said, I'm unemployed. I live alone, but in a house that belongs to my parents, so I just get by. But I'm going to stay here. Ever since 1974"—the year the Greek military junta collapsed—"we've been stuck with politicians who keep on failing. But the crisis also brings out good things in people. They do more things together; sometimes they even do things for each other. They talk to each other more, because that doesn't cost anything either. Soon I'm going to organize a totally naked event where people come in and take off all their clothes."

"That doesn't cost anything either," I say.

Kostas nods.

I feel sympathy for him.

Walking back to my hotel, I realize that I forgot to ask him if it hurts when you sit on a bike naked. I e-mail the question to him and receive a reply almost immediately: "It depends on the seat. My seat is very soft, and therefore very comfortable."

II. Debbie

At the Social Clinic of Solidarity, located in a rather dilapidated building, I have an appointment with Debbie Litsa.

Behind her glasses, her eyes are inquisitive; she looks to be in her mid-30s. We sit down in the waiting room. Beside her is a man who I figure at first is one of the doctors who works here, but he turns out to be her boyfriend, waiting for an appointment with the dentist—beside the doctor's office is a little room with a dentist's office.

"It started two years ago," Debbie says. "Illegal immigrants who had been here for years but had never been legalized were holding a big hunger strike. There were two hundred and fifty hunger strikers in Athens and fifty in Thessaloniki. They received support from local activists. The hunger strikers came from northern Africa, most of them from Morocco, Tunisia, and Algeria. The strike ended after forty-four days, when the strikers received a temporary residence permit that had to be extended every six months. Some people considered that a victory, others a defeat. We figured: We can't stop now. We have to do something for the community."

A woman comes in with her husband and child.

"In Greece, everyone with a job has health insurance," Debbie Litsa continues. "But there are lots of self-employed people who can't afford it. Private health insurance is not at all common in Greece. We asked the mayor to give us an office, but he didn't want to do that. This building was where the trade unions used to meet to decide whether or not to go on strike. We fixed it up into a health center for people who are uninsured: the Social Clinic of Solidarity."

More patients are coming into the waiting room now. Debbie Litsa's friend gets up and goes into the dentist's office.

"This project is greater than the sum of the people who work here," she says. "We're not hierarchical. Here, there's no difference between the secretary and the physician. We don't provide charity, because charity assumes a relationship based on power. Patients are welcome at our meetings, too."

"How many patients have shown up at meetings so far?"

"None," she says. "That's disappointing, I admit. But changes in mentality take time."

"And during those meetings, do you vote?"

"No," Debbie says. "A vote implies that the minority is not heard. We discuss things until we reach a consensus. Everyone has the right of veto."

"That's not very efficient," I remark.

"*Efficiency* is a capitalist term that assumes one has the goal of achieving a certain level of productivity. That's not the way we think. Capitalism, of course, is what sired this crisis. But the crisis is also an opportunity to ask the right questions. We want to teach people that they have the power to fight back. No one can take away your dignity; that's what I tell them. No one has to be embarrassed by the fact that the system can't guarantee that everyone has health insurance. The power of capitalism lies in how it presents itself as the sole alternative. I don't have any illusions about ever seeing it disappear, but we can create little fissures in it."

Debbie's boyfriend comes back from the dentist.

"How did the clinic get dental equipment?" I ask.

"It was donated by a dentist who was retiring."

She doesn't want to have her picture taken, but she encourages me to take pictures of the patients. A black man refuses to have his picture taken and one woman gets up and walks away, but the other patients meekly allow themselves to be photographed.

"Don't forget the secretary," Debbie says.

III. Dora

Nothing drives out melancholy better than music, as Spinoza knew. Orfanidou 5 is the address I was given, along with instructions to take the elevator to the sixth floor. Here I am going to meet Dora Seitanidou; I've heard that she leads a percussion group.

Dora is in her late 30s, with dark shoulder-length hair. Her boyfriend, Nick, is there, too, but Nick leaves the talking to Dora.

"This neighborhood we're in," Dora says as she makes coffee for me, "used to have a lot of small industry. Shoemakers, for example, but they've all closed down. Not so much because of the crisis; the process started long before that. The Chinese have taken over. Nick is my boyfriend. He's a musician, a teacher, and an educator. This space is used to give dance, music, and drama lessons. Nick does the percussion group. We call ourselves Ektos, which means 'outside.' As in 'outside myself' or 'outside of town,' but also as in 'out of fashion.' The crisis has changed a lot, of course. The person living in times of crisis needs to express himself, and money is important, but if you don't have it, you have to find some other way. We're a nonprofit organization, and the course fees are low. Some courses, like percussion, cost forty euros a month. Others, like modern dance, cost thirty euros, and students and the unemployed get a five-euro discount. We made all this ourselves—almost everything you see here was found on the street. We don't do all the lessons ourselves, though; we also have teachers. But the money we make on courses isn't enough to pay the rent."

We drink our coffee at a makeshift bar. Dora sits across from me; Nick is sitting beside me.

"Most people feel betrayed by the state, and their attitude is like: If you don't help me then I won't help you," Dora says. "Look at the garbage. Look at obesity, and you'll see that the problem is education. That's the big problem here in Greece. You have to teach yourself; there's no other way. All the parties have tried to push reforms in the Greek educational system, but it hasn't gotten any better. For example, now there's a law that allows the police to go onto campus. That wasn't legal for a while; it led to lots of rioting, but better education? Roughly speaking, you can say that Greek education is aimed at making children and students learn a lot of things by rote, but no attention is paid to teaching them to think."

She sips her coffee.

"If we become increasingly fascist—and Greek society *is* becoming increasingly fascist—you have to put the blame not only on the crisis but also on the educational system. The whole system is sick. Until recently everyone wanted to work for the government in Athens, because working for the government meant security, and it also meant you didn't have to really work—it meant you could just set up a business for yourself on the side. Security is an obsession that was passed down from grandfather to father to son; maybe it can be explained by the fact that here in Thessaloniki, we're almost all the descendants of refugees." (Many of the inhabitants of Thessaloniki are the descendants of Greeks who were run out of Turkey.) "Take my uncle and aunt, for example; they're not incredibly rich people, but they have five houses. They have the house that they live in, three houses they rent out, and they also have a vacation home. The Greek is obsessed with property because he sees property ownership as security. My uncle and aunt have a son who's confined to a wheelchair; they think that those houses are going to guarantee his financial security.

"Or take Fena, the department store, where you can buy the most expensive brand clothing on credit. People from the lower classes were suddenly walking around in Armani suits because the down payment was so low and they didn't ask any bothersome questions. Everyone could buy fancy clothes on credit. They took out loans for everything.

"You could get a loan to go on vacation, a loan for Christmas, a loan for your own funeral—there was a loan for everything. We were taught to borrow money; we weren't taught to be productive. But you've seen it already: at Christmas the department stores are packed. Life on the installment plan has never stopped; maybe it never will. It just moves from one place to the next. But Athens is meaner and bigger than Thessaloniki. We have the sun; we have family; we don't need much."

I decide to take the plunge and ask: "How much do you earn?"

"I work for the university," Dora says. "One of the things I do is teach classes in Greek culture to foreign students. I gross eight hundred euros a month. The university holds back twenty percent of that, and twenty-three percent goes to taxes. If I had to pay rent I could never get by, but we live in a house that belongs to Nick's parents. Like I said, we wouldn't be able to pay the rent for this place from the money we get from courses, but we also have to pay municipal taxes that are included along with the electric bill, and we can pay those taxes only because we sell coffee and tea to our students, and drinks under the counter. Otherwise it would be impossible."

"Have you two ever thought about going away?" I ask.

"Of course. Lots of our friends have left. They live in Wales or in Sweden now. They have more money, they have a better life, but the Greeks there aren't happy. We have friends who went to Sweden. Financially they're doing well, but they tell us: 'The Swedes are as cold as the weather. If you laugh out loud on the street in Sweden, they think you're out of your mind.'"

Dora is quiet for a moment. She seems to be thinking about Sweden, where she doesn't want to live.

"I know a lot of Greeks," she says, "who drive to Bulgaria to go to the dentist. The dentist in Bulgaria is five times cheaper than in Greece. Coca-Cola just closed down a big plant here and is going to open a new one in Bulgaria. Bulgaria is going to be the new Greece."

"But don't you think Bulgaria will learn from the recent history of Greece?" I ask cautiously.

"No one learns from history. We don't even learn from our own history. Before the war there were almost fifty thousand Jews living here. Who remembers that these days? The university is built on the old Jewish cemetery. You can still see the gravestones in some of the walls, because the marble was recycled."

IV. George

At nine o'clock the next morning I find George Kastanis waiting in front of my hotel. George is a young, energetic man with a quiet voice. We stop in at a nearby café to pick up his girlfriend, another

Dora. She is wearing a gray wool cap and matching scarf. We go to an old military base, about half an hour's drive from the hotel. This is where the PERKA project is being carried out. PERKA stands for "Peri-Urban Cultivation Team," a gardeners' collective. Where soldiers once marched, PERKA now plants vegetable gardens.

"We started in January 2011 with forty people," George says. "Now there are one hundred and fifty people active in the collective. This is what we call 'suburban farming.' You don't pay for it. You cultivate your own garden."

We walk past the gardens. Some plots are neater than others.

"There's no electricity here," George says, "and no fences. We accept the fact that some people in the neighborhood come and steal our vegetables. The only fence you see here is to keep the dogs out. In fact, the army wants to build here. But now we're working on a proposal to preserve this place as a park, maybe as a campground, too. We're going to present the plan to the mayor. You've probably noticed that there aren't any parks in Thessaloniki. Experts say that if this green lung disappears, the temperature in Thessaloniki in the summer will go up a few degrees. Along with another army base a little farther up that way, the ground here is worth one billion euros. So, as you can imagine, there are big interests at stake."

We walk on.

"I'd like to show you the room we made from one of the soldiers' dormitories—that's where we hold our meetings now," George says.

Everywhere around the green lung there are dormitories, more or less in ruins.

"I'm thirty-two," George says when we stop at a spot with a view of this part of the city. "Dora is twenty-nine. I'm unemployed, but the important thing is not to leave solidarity to the fascists. The extreme right-wing parties go into the working-class neighborhoods and hand out food. You can't combat fascism with weapons, only with education, but the schools in Greece produce people with no political awareness. That's why you have to be self-taught. Anarchism is creativity; anarchism is democracy in the true sense of the word. At PERKA, we don't vote; we reach a consensus. There are days when we're not ready to reach a consensus. But another day always comes along."

"Things weren't any better before," Dora says. "But now people are less motivated, because they have so many problems. They're depressed. But there is a small, dynamic minority that really does do something. We meet two times a month."

"And what about the EU?" I ask.

"Being in the EU or not being in the EU is actually not the real issue," George says. "The issue is: IMF or no IMF. We want to keep this spot green. We want to protect our seeds. Everything we grow here is organic and for our own use. It's a struggle for freedom, and for the country."

The man with the key shows up. They show me around the renovated dormitory.

"We built a kitchen over here," Dora says.

The kitchen is simple, almost Spartan, but they are proud of it.

As we head for the door, Dora says: "The people in northern Europe who say we're lazy don't realize that one day people will say that they're lazy, too."

V. Yiannis

You can walk right into Thessaloniki's city hall; there's no security at the door. One of the mayor's assistants, whom I've contacted by e-mail, says the mayor is running a little late because of a wedding.

I take a seat. The people walking around, all of whom work for the mayor, are young and hip. The atmosphere seems more like that of an Internet start-up than a city hall.

The mayor makes me wait for an hour and a half. He has the air of a rock star, and for a rock star an hour and a half is nothing.

In *One Step Ahead*, Dimitris Athyridis's documentary on the 2010 municipal elections in Thessaloniki, the then mayoral candidate, Yiannis Boutaris, talks frankly about his alcohol dependency, his marital problems, and his conflict with Anthimos, the archbishop of the city, whom he accuses of hatemongering because of Anthimos's outspokenly nationalistic speeches. It's hard not to feel sympathy for Boutaris after watching the documentary, even though it's clear that the mayor, after the electoral close call, has not been able to solve all the problems before him. Garbage continues to pile up on street corners.

The mayor is not a career politician; he's a vintner. He got his first diploma in chemistry in 1965 from the Aristotle University of Thessaloniki, and another—in oenology—in 1969 from the Athens Wine Institute. I recognize the tattoos on his fingers from other articles I've read about him.

Boutaris is now 71, his voice smoky.

"We were opposed to this building," Boutaris begins. "But we weren't able to keep them from building it. This used to be a military base. The law specified that a new city hall had to be built here. There's going to be a square built outside, and all the roads you see will be going underground."

"But that's a long-term project," adds his assistant, who is sitting beside us, taking notes.

"I'm afraid that maybe it's not a very original question," I say, "but why did you wait so long to go into politics?"

"I'm a political animal. I have political convictions. I have ideals. I'm a social democrat, even though I don't know exactly what that means anymore in this day and age: neoliberal, social democrat—what does that mean? But anyway. When I was chairman of the vintners' association, I said: 'It's not about wangling a little market share away from each other; it's about boosting the total market for Greek wine; we have to do this together.' Besides, I have three children: one daughter and two sons. If we all went into the wine business, there would be too many of us. So I went into politics."

Boutaris laughs self-deprecatingly.

I ask him: "Were you prepared for this office? Is being a political animal enough of a preparation?"

"You can't live without politics. Well, not unless you're very egotistical or very blasé. That's why I told the citizens of Thessaloniki: 'Whatever we do about the garbage problem, if you don't help, it's not going to go away. If you don't help out, the city will stay dirty; if you throw garbage all over the place, there's not much I can do.' We're not going through an economic crisis; we're going through a social crisis. The economic crisis will be over in five years, but the social crisis won't just go away, and it's been going on for a lot longer. To find the beginning you have to go back to 'seventy-four, to the end of the dictatorship.

"In actual practice, there is no law. That's the problem. The people relate to the law in the sense that they place themselves above it. That starts with the politicians. We're supposed to implement the law. I get attacked because I implement the law. I've had to call the police in order to enforce the law, even right here in this building. The Greeks' relationship with the state is problematic—maybe there's also a historical reason for that. We had the German occupation, the civil war. We haven't learned to respect the decisions made by a majority. There is no natural relationship between the Greek citizen and the Greek state. The most natural relationship that exists is the Greek citizens' suspicion that the state is lying. But we've become arrogant. We do everything we can to not pay taxes, but at the same time we want social facilities, good roads, good schools. We have no respect for wealth.

"The Stavros Niarchos Foundation was set up by a rich Greek; it has given more than five hundred million euros to good causes. But people despise it because they say that Niarchos lived from the lifeblood of workers. Don't forget that as recently as 1952 there was a political execution in Greece." (In 1952, the Greek government executed Nikos Beloyannis, a communist leader and resistance fighter in World War II, after accusing him of spying for the Soviet Union.)

"What people praise you for most often," I point out, "is having promoted tourism."

"That's right," Boutaris says. "I've brought Turks and Israelis to Thessaloniki. Because of our history. For five hundred years, this was part of the Ottoman Empire. Before the war, Thessaloniki had one of the largest Jewish communities in Europe. The Jews from Spain fled to Thessaloniki. We're working on a subway system, and during the excavations we keep finding things from the Roman and Byzantine Empires. Coexistence is a part of Thessaloniki's identity. The Ottomans were clever enough to invite the Jews driven out of Spain to settle here. After the city was liberated, in 1912, it was no longer an Ottoman town. There were three or four Jewish newspapers here at the time, four Turkish newspapers, two or three Greek newspapers, an English paper, a French one, and a German paper. That was Thessaloniki.

"In the 1920s, the Turks disappeared." (Both the Greeks and the Turks at that time carried out pogroms and programs of ethnic cleansing.) "The Nazis exterminated the Jews. And that's how Thessaloniki lost its identity. Not so long ago there were three hundred thousand people living here. Now there are a million. I want to remind the people of Thessaloniki of their history."

"What can a mayor like you do during a crisis," I ask, "when the Greek presence in the EU, and certainly in the Eurozone, no longer seems like something we can take for granted?"

"One of the pillars of the EU is solidarity; you can't have an EU without solidarity. What's more, it would be wrong to pretend that the German and Dutch companies were not overjoyed to sell Greece military equipment and consumer goods. Some German politicians have made it sound as though they are prepared to start the Third World War. Now Merkel has adopted a different attitude toward Greece, but in principle nothing has changed. I'm in direct contact with my fellow mayors in Germany. In that modest way, I try to influence national politics there."

I ask: "And what exactly does that mean for Thessaloniki?"

"All over Greece there has been a huge trek from the countryside to the city. Except for South Korea, in Seoul, there is no other place where a country's population is so proportionally concentrated as it is in Athens. But the people haven't become urbanites. A rural mentality still prevails. That's why I want to point out the city's history to the inhabitants of Thessaloniki. The big question is whether we can become a central European city again. The question is whether we can take the farmer out of the city dweller. That's my job."

As I get up to leave, I ask Boutaris whether he will run again, in 2014. For the first time, a huge smile appears on his face. "Oh sure," he says. "This is lots of fun."

Fifty Shades of Greyhound

FROM *Oxford American*

ON FRIDAY, MAY 12, 1995, I stepped onto a bus in Jackson, Mississippi, bound for West Yellowstone, Montana. The journey would take four days, with no stops for anything but gas and cigarettes and the occasional disemboweling of one passenger by another. When I said goodbye, my father, who only embraces things when he is trying to kill them, hugged me. It was his way of saying: Your mother thinks you might die.

When I tell this story, sometimes people ask why, given my general state of mental health and fiscal stability, I would choose to ride to the other side of the North American landmass in the world's fastest portable toilet, passing through a gauntlet of unholy downtowns where I would likely be accosted by psychotic barnacles who desired to rape and eat my carcass behind an Americas Best Value Inn.

The answer is simple: I wanted to see a mountain, a topological feature I had often read about in books. In Rankin County, Mississippi, we had many books, but no mountains. When it was all over, when I peeled myself from the back seat of the bus two months and 4,200 miles later, carrying a box of Hostess Chocodiles that had constituted my only foodstuffs in three days, having lost all of my underwear and much of my mind, I found my mother waiting for me at the bottom of the steps, weeping.

"Promise you won't do this again," she said.

I promised.

And 18 years later, I broke that promise. Because I wanted to see another mountain.

*

One of the most surprising qualities of the Greyhound station in Savannah is its lack of parking. How did they expect people to get to the station? Given the clientele I noted in the predawn darkness, the answer appeared to be: on crutches.

I was excited to meet them. Bus People are nothing like Airplane People, who are boring and have "luggage" and enjoy "skiing." Bus People, on the other hand, enjoy "talking about grenades" and "screaming." In '95, I met a woman in Wichita Falls who said she was the first person to taste Dr Pepper, when she was five, which would have made her 115 years old, which made her a liar. In Billings, I met a Crow Indian who wore a stovepipe hat and either wanted to hug or stab me, it was unclear. Would such people be on my bus in Savannah? And was it wrong to want them to be?

These were my thoughts as I looked at the other passengers and noted a woman wearing a bologna sandwich on her head. Was there really a bologna sandwich on her head? Yes, unmistakably. Also, she wore a blue Snuggie.

On the wall, a poster: THE BUS OF THE FUTURE HAS ARRIVED.

The Future-Bus was depicted in new colors: silver, blue, and black. The message was clear. This is not your grandmother's Greyhound, which was silver, blue, and red. I was eager to experience this futuristic bus. Things were looking up. What I was experiencing, of course, was Greyhound Stage One: Hope.

Early in one's journey, one begins to appreciate the candor of the Greyhound operation. Nobody here is trying to act like this is fun. And one begins to realize: that's okay. For example, nobody "invites" people to board. Rather, a designated staff member stands on a chair and shouts the names of nearby villages, whether or not they have any relation to actual destinations of the bus. If a PA system is available, staff members will use it both to inform and disorient passengers, eliminating every few words.

"All passengers going to KSHHHH at this time please KSHHHH, otherwise, it's very likely that KSHHHH until you bleed to death."

The terminal signage is refreshingly honest, too, eschewing the sophistry of advertising for plain American. PHONE, read one sign, hanging over a pay phone. Was this for the youth, who perhaps did not understand? DO YOU WANT TO GO HOME? read another sign, which seemed more of a threat. In the Atlanta terminal, a poster:

PAY WITH CASH. For what, it didn't say. Underneath was a picture of $20 and a hand. Was someone buying a human hand? The human hand looked pretty clean and healthy. Good deal for a hand!

Even the overheard conversations have the ring of unvarnished truth, as in this exchange between two young women:

"Man, if I die at a Greyhound station, nobody will know."

"I will know."

"Yeah, but then you be dead, too."

"Yeah, I guess so."

One thing was for sure, this Bus of the Future was equipped with Truth.

The transition was quick to Greyhound Stage Two: Concern. "Charleston! Going to Charleston! Load it up! Argh!" Was he our driver? Possibly also a pirate? We hustled out through a tarpaulin into the dark, and boarded before sunrise. Our driver spoke in a velvety Barry White baritone that hushed us like babies, announcing stops in Charleston, Georgetown, Myrtle Beach, Florence, Camden, Fort Jackson, Columbia, Cartagena, Tierra del Fuego, Mos Eisley, Mordor, and the Spice Planet of Arrakis.

I woke up again in Charleston, a historic city where I hoped to espy some columned portico gaily festooned for that evening's cotillion, but was instead no less pleased to see across the street from the terminal a charming mercantile exchange called El Cheapo. My morning coffee beckoned for release, and I visited the onboard restroom. Best to do this when the bus is stopped, I deduced, for reasons that are immediately obvious to anyone who has straddled a bucket of someone else's feces at high speeds. I entered and beheld a horror. The Bus of the Future, it seemed, was covered in the gastrointestinal ailments of the past. What toilet paper remained appeared to have been ripped from the wall and attacked by a ferret.

One of the great things about Greyhound is that there are many toilets in which one can die. What to call this onboard bathroom? Not a restroom, for it is not restful. Not a water closet, for there is no water. Perhaps asphyxiation nook? Death slot? Concern flowers imperceptibly into Greyhound Stage Three: Fear.

It only seemed fair to wait and investigate the terminal toilet in Myrtle Beach, which was rumored to be clean, or at least anchored to the earth. After refusing a Gideon Bible upon exiting the bus,

on account of my having already read it, I stood in line for the
restroom. A woman exited, and I entered, locked the door, loos-
ened my garments, and was immediately clad in darkness. The
lights went out. Having failed to wear a headlamp and now surrounded by exposed wiring and unidentified pathogens on every
unseeable surface, I considered screaming for assistance. I regret-
ted not taking one of the free Bibles, for the comfort it might
provide in my final moments.

Having eventually freed myself, I walked outside and stood next
to a man who had stepped out of central casting on his way to
Thunderdome. His name was Barrel. You know how people named
Clark just "look" like a Clark? Well, Barrel just "looked" like a mur-
derer. He had the size and build of a grain silo wrapped in denim
and wore at least two pairs of jeans. Also, he carried an aluminum
grabber tool. It was his hair, though, that was most worthy of note,
for his large sunburned head was home to two quite opposing
hairstyles: the front hemisphere shorn to stubble, the rear running
wild in thick fields of ripe, silvery wheat, the two halves divided by
a perfect prime meridian of barbering, as though he had jumped
from the barber's chair mid-haircut, having been alerted of more
denim in the area. He looked like a sort of demented Hells Angel
Hobo Viking. "What do you call that kind of haircut?" is what I
would have asked, had I wanted to die.

Barrel was engaged in conversation with a smaller man who
rested an injured leg on a basket of laundry. Their conversation
concerned the nature of his wound and the universe.

"You got a rod there in your leg?" asked Barrel.

"Yeah," said Leg Boy.

"Does it take the place of your shinbone?"

"Sure."

"It'll be hellfire if there ever was."

"In Ohio at least."

"Might even get the old burning bush if you lucky."

"I'll tell you what it was—" said Leg Boy, preparing to drop on
us some Leg Wisdom. But what sort of dramatic zeniths such dialogue could reach, I shall never know, because Barrel stopped his
interlocutor to ask:

"Say, you ever listen to Bob Seger?"

On a bus, people speak as if they shared long histories. And I
suppose the bus becomes its own kind of long history. Eighteen

years before, I met a veteran from the first Gulf War who, standing outside the Cheyenne station, surveyed the vast plains before us and announced to me, "All women want to kill a man." I had met him 10, maybe 15 minutes before. At the time, I assumed he was mentally disturbed. But having now been married 10 years to a woman in whose eyes I have seen murder, I am not so sure.

One doesn't hear such truths on Delta. There's no time for it. And that's the one thing Greyhound has plenty of.

There comes a time in every Greyhound journey when the switch is flipped. Gone is the sanguine, tolerant liberal arts major who believes in the beauty of human frailty and the quiet dignity of poverty, replaced by a famished hobgoblin with scoliosis. The transformation is largely a result of the seats. They are not bad seats. They even recline, which is nice, although it's not really reclining, but more of an opportunity to continue to be uncomfortable while shattering the previously injured shinbones of those in one's immediate rear.

The problem with the seats is what happens when there's an empty one next to you. On an airplane, an empty seat is a small miracle, a sacred place to set one's book. On a bus, though, the empty seat invites lurid napping positions that resemble the attitudes of those who've been buried in lava and discovered many years later.

On an airplane, seats are reserved. When a flier approaches, especially when he is ovular in shape, one quietly prays that the Lord has predestined him to sit somewhere else, preferably near a small screaming child, whom the large person may by chance desire to eat. But if he sits next to you, you understand: it is not his fault. Not so on a bus, where seats are unreserved, where one's only recourse to keeping a seat open, short of detaching a limb and placing it there, is to appear insane.

There in Myrtle Beach, 20 of us had been invited to reboard while newer travelers pressed toward the door to menace the cabin. As they began to board, I looked around. Fifty seats. Twenty of us, sitting alone. That's 40 seats taken, leaving 10. Which is really 5. The five new passengers emerged, claimed these empty pairs of seats, and the cabin grew tense. Every new passenger shot up into the bus and began to search for a victim, someone with whom to mingle bodies and odors. Our open seats were our most valuable currency, and they were about to be taken from us. My only choice, I knew, was to look crazy.

But how does one look crazy? My wife had often told me to not look at her "all crazy like that." "Like what?" I would say. "With the dead eyes," she would say.

I made the dead eyes. Also, I set my baseball cap high on my head, so I looked like a farmer with dead eyes. But the eyeglasses, those professorial spectacles! They would undo me, make me look dependable and cogent. And so I turned them upside down, which made me look undependable and German. Then I slouched a little and bared my teeth, as though I had been dead for many days. A small, grandmotherly woman of what looked like Oceanic provenance shuffled toward me, surveying me like a large fruit she wished to purchase.

She moved on.

The bus exhaled, raised up, lurched forward. I held my pose of the German farmer corpse for a good 10 minutes, until everyone was settled. A girl in a Haverford sweatshirt eyeballed me over a seat. What was someone like *her* doing on this bus? Was she taking notes? What was she, some kind of journalism major? Stop taking notes about me! I am not an animal!

Greyhound Stage Four: I Am an Animal.

Had it really taken 10 hours to get to the capital of South Carolina? I hadn't eaten in a full day and hobbled off the bus in search of meats. In the terminal parking lot, I noted with delight an unfinished wiener that had been dropped onto the asphalt. Of course I wouldn't eat it. *Of course*. But then, there it was. Shouldn't I pick it up? To throw it away, or put it in my shoe?

My previous life as a homeowner and member of many benevolent societies had grown dim. Who was that man? He smelled of luxurious soaps and lotions. What relation was he to this old, stooped pilgrim, whose coy limbic system now believed it was operating inside a homeless man? I walked away from the terminal, over a hill, where I noted many fine eating establishments. Were they real? Dare I risk missing my connection for the procuring of their meats? Onward I walked, pausing at a gas station to purchase cigarettes, for I no longer feared death.

I found myself on the median, where my weariness overtook me and I sat down to smoke, which drew the attention of passing officers of law enforcement, who sent glad tidings to me through their loudspeakers. In time, I made my way onto the porch of a taco establishment that sold cans of beer, of which I consumed many. My jangled nerves calmed, and I noted the time was 5:25 P.M. Casually, I also noted the time of departure on my ticket was 5:30 P.M.

I ran.

Up the hill.

Past a craps game.

Past a man who wanted a quarter.

Running, sweating, backpack heaving to and fro, I ran. I ran so hard my crack was showing. When I finally made it to the queue, a cigarette behind my ear, gray with my athletic ministrations, beer in hand, tomatillo on my pants, vaporous abominations about my person, I realized my transformation was complete.

"What up?" a passenger said.

"Chilling," I said, panting.

"I get one dem smokes, homes?"

We smoked, there in the line, me and my homeskillet.

Four hours later, and with a crick in my neck that rendered me unusually susceptible to attack from my immediate right, I woke up on a mountain. It had taken us 14 hours to travel 300 miles, which is less than half the average running speed of the dog with the same name as the bus.

Had I really made it? Yes. Was I a changed man? Perhaps. What would my new life be like, with limited lumbosacral function? Interesting. But I no longer cared. I had achieved Greyhound Apotheosis, the strange, unbidden nirvana that comes after the hope and anxiety and fear and dementia blur like roadside trees. A certain peace overcomes one.

A funny thing happens when you tell people you're about to ride a Greyhound bus: They give you a look, like you asked them to smell a sock you found in the garbage.

"On purpose?" they ask.

"Yes," you say.

"But why?" And their voices will drop and they lean in. "Is everything okay?" What they are saying, of course, is that People Who Are Okay do not ride buses, unless those buses are going to Disney World. These people cannot handle the Truth of the Bus. And what do we learn from this Truth? Many things. How to carry one's clothes in an ice chest, or a bologna sandwich on the head. What a human hand costs, what a phone is. And what women want. And also what Bob Seger's fans want. And that perhaps more of us are one bad month from needing to ride Greyhound than we'd like to admit, and that some of us are already there.

These are not easy truths to learn. But there's another kind of reaction you get when you're about to ride a bus. What you get is a look. A look that remembers. "I did it once, when I was nineteen," they say, dreamily, as though speaking of an enchanted evening many moons ago filled with love and peyote and the cries of distant coyotes. And they will tell you where they went—Memphis to Cincinnati, Denver to Mobile, Jackson to Yellowstone—and they will not speak harshly of the seats, the stations, the toilets. They will remember only the people and the America it showed them and the wild and reckless reasons that drove them to it: to see a girl, or a headstone, or a mountain. And they will recall it fondly, as I do now.

And they will not want to do it again. But they will want to be able to do it again. It is a dream they have, you can see. To just leave. Deep urges they do not understand will drive them to go. One day, again, soon. And there is a bus waiting to take them there.

A Bus of the Future.

They say it has Wi-Fi and toilet paper.

PETER LaSALLE

Au Train de Vie

That Voice You Hear When Traveling

FROM *The Missouri Review*

I accepted with no other conscious prejudice on my walk than that of avoiding the wider avenues or streets, the most obscure invitations of chance. However, a kind of familiar gravitation led me farther on, in the direction of a certain neighborhood, the names of which I have every desire to recall and which dictate reverence to my heart.
— Borges, "A New Refutation of Time"

I don't know who I dream I am.
— Pessoa, from a poem

I'LL BE HONEST. I had a couple of large sadnesses to confront that summer in Paris. So I suppose it wasn't surprising that it repeatedly happened.

You see, I often found myself at this one spot at the end of my meandering walks through the balmy, traffic-empty streets of the early evening. The walks were in an everyday pocket of the Grands Boulevards, toward Place de la République — the outdoor cafés along the boulevards crowded but not noisy, if that makes any sense, the puzzle-barked plane trees even greener and leafier than the last time you noticed, if that makes any sense, too, everything in almost too-clear focus amid the thick honey sunlight that does linger till nearly 10 in July and August in Paris — and, yes, after an hour or so of rather aimless and surely comfortable walking, I usually seemed to end up there again. And the "there"

I'm referring to meant climbing the odd serpentine stone steps behind the stately Gare de l'Est train station; it meant continuing on along that decidedly shabby dead-end street, Rue d'Alsace, which overlooks the vast, cluttered railway yards, to sit down again in one of the big cushiony seats—old and salvaged from maybe a French Pullman car, set out right on the cracked sidewalk—for me to order a simple syrupy black coffee at the café called, tellingly and almost too appropriately, Au Train de Vie.

But even that doesn't get at it.

Or it isn't quite exact to say I repeatedly ended up there, because it was somehow beyond that. It was as if I had to go there, or more so, as if a voice was telling me to go there again because it was where I was *supposed* to be, where I, well, I *needed* to be right then and at that time of my own life in Paris.

And now, months later and back here in Austin, I've been thinking more about this—thinking *a lot* about it, in fact.

I've been thinking of it and specifically how it all reflects a feeling certainly metaphysical that many of us have experienced. And I realize it's something about which two writers I personally admire have had a good deal to say, not only that icon of French flâneurs, the surrealist Louis Aragon in his dreamily meditative volume *Le Paysan de Paris*, but also the acknowledged master of the metaphysical itself, the Argentine wizard Borges, with the same sort of experience often happening to him as well, probed in a poem like "Street with a Pink Corner Store" or the haunting essay that confronts the phenomenon head-on and analyzes it fully, "A New Refutation of Time."

All of which I'll get to in a bit, but first maybe at least some filling in is needed concerning my sadnesses that summer of 2011.

Truth of the matter is, I'd been outright lucky enough to receive from my university in Texas, where I teach creative writing, a grant to turn a short story of mine—a piece from a literary magazine and set in Paris—into something longer. The project would have me spending the summer in Paris. I would do the writing there and also research in more detail the actual setting of the scenes in the narrative.

Having taught in Paris on exchange several times over the years, I had a number of friends in the city, and they all contributed to

my e-mail–organized campaign that spring to check around for a
rental for me. One friend—a guy who was a lot of fun, formerly my
departmental chairman at one of the Paris universities where I'd
taught and the leading Saul Bellow scholar in France, now retired
from university teaching and always a quite dashing figure, married to a lovely opera singer—came up with a deal he jokingly pronounced I couldn't refuse. His wife's uncle had just refurbished
a very large apartment that had been in the family for years, and
this elderly "Oncle Robert"—living in Cannes now and seldom using the place—was willing to rent it out to an American writer in
need and at what turned out to be a truly bargain price that could
fit the modest budget of an academic grant. It was more than perfect, five stories up in a frilled, buff-stone 19th-century edifice of
the type that the controversial designer of the Grands Boulevards,
Baron Haussmann, would have heartily endorsed and, now that
I think of it, probably was directly responsible for when the area
had first been redeveloped, actually an upscale address for a residence back then; overlooking the handsome Porte Saint-Martin
ceremonial arch built by Louis XIV, it had a full four bedrooms.
And best was that there was nothing whatsoever touristy about the
location even in summer, when Paris can be overwhelmingly and
often discouragingly touristy. Far from chic nowadays, the neighborhood was a fine combination of the ready-to-wear boutiques
of the busy Sentier garment district and the epicenter of the sub-
Saharan African community today, working-class and colorful and
alive, offering a concentration of cubbyhole hairdressing salons
for wonderfully complicated African coiffures that I suspect has to
be denser than anywhere else on known earth. The first sadness
came after my teenage nephew visited for a week.

Of course, this shouldn't have entailed a sadness. And with me a
bachelor and used to having lived on my own for so long, it's always been good to have somebody around for a while, especially a
kid like my nephew.

We got along more like buddies than anything else, my assuming in the relationship the standard crazy-uncle role, I'd say. For
him I was the oddball writer who, maybe because I had spent a
lifetime around campuses teaching, had never really grown up
and seemed somebody often a little more tuned in on his interests
than his good, understandably concerned (but oh-so-parental)

mother and father, who did, also understandably, dote on him, an only child.

Tall, polite, bright, with an easy smile and longish hair in the Beatles mode rather than the buzzcut more favored by teenage guys today, he was captain of the hockey team at his prep school in Providence (mostly a benchwarmer and no star, who got elected captain only because his teammates liked him, he admitted) and also a budding playwright (he was intent on expanding the aspiration that summer and was in the midst of taking a screenwriting course at Brown U., very excited about it). He jumped at the idea I had proposed of coming over to spend time with me and practice his French, the two of us eventually convincing his parents to subsidize the trip as a year-too-early graduation present. During the day he would explore the city on his own, soon proud that with a little foldup map and the stack of Métro tickets I gave him, he was gradually mastering the underground system.

The kind of adventures expected to befall a 17-year-old ensued in the course of his trying to cover all of what he had decided were the big-time sights. At the Eiffel Tower he stood in the line for the elevator and met some kids from Australia, hooking up with them for all to make the ascent together. Finally as high up as you could go there, the second observation level, they took turns taking pictures of each other with their cell-phone cameras in poses as if they were falling over the retaining rail and into the full, wide expanse of Paris itself spreading out hazily soft blue and green in the background; he assured me it would be great to post on his Facebook page and his friends back home would get a real kick out of it. At the Arc de Triomphe he witnessed a police raid on a crew of those ragged guys—boys, really, African and only his age—who sell souvenir junk at the tourist hot spots, tiny key-chain trinkets cheaply plated and the like, the boys adept at fleeing fast from the cops with the stuff they spread out on blankets to peddle without a license. In the slapstick scenario of the particular raid he witnessed, the same blankets did become ready sacks to hastily wrap the trinkets in as they scattered in all directions across the traffic of L'Etoile. My nephew described how the burly cops in their military-serious uniforms—garrison caps low on the brow and combat boots—were left looking very stupid and standing in frustration with hands on their hips as the boys, running away, laughing, mocked them in what was surely a perpetual cat-and-mouse game. He said it was all wild, at first excited to tell me about the crazy episode, next admitting to me that he did feel somewhat bad because he had picked up one of the dropped little gold Eiffel Tower key chains during the mêlée (he showed it to me, I assured him he shouldn't have qualms, saying that I'd seen them offered at four for a euro, so it was no great loss to anybody); he then told me how he really would like to learn more about the boys and their lives. On another stay in Paris, while teaching at the university at Nanterre, I had dated a French woman who taught with me in the department, Études Anglo-Américaines, and also volunteered with programs for African émigrés, so I knew how the system worked from her explanations, the boys being sort of indentured to whomever had brought them to France. I filled my nephew in the best I could, as he listened to every word of it, intrigued and also concerned about those boys.

"But don't worry about that souvenir, man," I assured him again; "it's pretty much worthless."

Later at night, he usually headed over to the Kentucky Fried Chicken, a cavernous, weirdly illuminated place on Boulevard de Strasbourg emanating its greasy aroma for a couple of blocks in the warm bruised-blue evenings now that it would finally be dark. There he would buy a Coke to entitle him to go to a table in a quiet corner of the first floor for an hour or two and use the free Wi-Fi provided, seeing that there was no connection at Oncle Robert's sprawling apartment. Still, no matter where he was off to while I wrote during the day or in the evening, for me his return was always the best part of his being in Paris that week or so. Such return involved some complication because the ancient intercom buzzer system had been disabled and all but ripped out temporarily in the recent refurbishing, an exposed spaghetti of wires beside the apartment's entry door and not yet replaced. That meant my nephew and I would have to arrange beforehand when I should expect him and look down to Rue Saint-Martin, an approximate time for him to show up in front of a tiny Japanese restaurant across the street. I would go to one of the long French windows, and the two of us would exchange waves and smiles, then I would bound down the several flights of the spiral staircase—the small creaking elevator was slow, actually a rather dangerous affair—and unlatch the tall carved-wood door beyond the *rez-de-chaussée* with its potted palmettos at the street. Sometimes I lost track of time altogether as I worked on my writing at the clicking keyboard of my laptop set atop a vanity dresser, tortoiseshell veneer, that became my impromptu desk in the pale pink front bedroom, and then, checking my watch, realizing I was late and now going to the window in a bound—the apartment was too high for there to be any real vocal communication with the street below—I would see him patiently waiting, sitting down on the curb and contentedly watching the people and cars go by, smiling when he looked up and saw me again. I think I really liked how he would almost *materialize* there that way. After that we would sit around relaxing in the living room that could only be called vast (I once paced it off at 40 feet), complete with a grand piano and elegant, if badly faded and worn, Oriental carpets. There would be a can of Stella Artois beer for me and a big bottle of fruit juice for him, plus for both of us the paprika snack peanuts the French love; the long row of French windows all open to the summer night, an occasional Klaxon horn of an ambulance or gendarme squad car blaring loud, we'd talk more about what had happened to him during his day, laughing some in the course of it all, even discussing at length the screenplay he was working on for his summer-school class at Brown, the two of us bouncing back and forth ideas that he might blend into the plot and my soon getting as excited about it as he was.

Which meant that when he left, I drifted into a funk for a few days. I missed his company. The many rooms of the apartment seemed beyond empty, and then the all-too-predictable doubts and big questioning set in. You know, that kind of recurrent self-interrogation that perhaps many writers getting a bit older tend to conduct. And had I spent all too much of my own life sitting in a room alone and conjuring up in my fiction—with an endless flow of words and words and more words still—merely some phantom life, not real in the least and surely as incorporeal as the moonlight on the complicated slate mansard rooftops sprouting their ancient chimney pots I'd often stare at outside the apartment in Paris on those summer nights? It all brought up memories of past girlfriends I probably should have married along the way, starting a family of my own, that kind of dangerous thinking.

And more than once after writing all day, alone, I took long walks in the evening. And more than once I inevitably ended up there again, above the steps by the Gare de l'Est and at the café called Au Train de Vie.

The second large sadness was, of course, much more pronounced and certainly larger and heavier, if sadness itself can be quantitative, measured as a matter of sheer leaden emotional avoirdupois.

It just so happened that all that summer an old pal from Austin was in a hospital called Fernand-Widal in Paris, had been there for over a year, actually.

He was from Algeria, but with full dual citizenship in the U.S. I had known him for a long time, part of an international clique of guys in Austin who first gravitated together due to common interests and especially political world outlook. I guess that I myself was somebody who seemed to fit in with the group, being from a land far from Texas—New England—and therefore also a foreigner in Texas to begin with, which qualified me for at least pseudo-international standing; plus there was my track record of having logged a lot of time incessantly traveling in other parts of the world—Africa, India, plenty of Latin America, both the Spanish-speaking countries and marvelously (the only word for a place like that) Brazil. He was a stockily rugged, happy-go-lucky guy, seemingly always grinning. He'd never used his petroleum engineering degree from the University of Texas but had found a good lifestyle in cooking at a restaurant, a job balanced with working some import-export business deals over the Net with his brother in Algiers. A bachelor himself, my friend dated with about the same amount of pleasantly comical success and failure as I, the two of us often joking about that, dating at our age, and he was so athletically fit that, past 50, he still played soccer and refused to own a car, walking and bicycling everywhere.

Then it happened. Simply and suddenly, he suffered a debilitating massive stroke, which led to a bleak succession of failures that if looked at in any detail, or illustrative frankness, would sway the opinion, I suspect, of even the staunchest, most stingy-hearted Tea Partier robotically moaning about the alleged evils of American health care reform. After time in the ICU of Austin's municipal hospital, where he wasn't given the immediate physical therapy he needed because he lacked medical insurance, it only turned worse. My friend was moved to a supposedly state-accredited nursing home on an empty rural road out in the dry blond flatland

peppered with scrub mesquite and prickly pear just beyond the
city limits. It was a setup that looked like an abandoned and pa-
thetically lost motel in the middle of that sunbaked nowhere, a
packed-to-the-limit place surrounded by stark chainlink fence, and
within—and despite the best efforts of the friendly yet overworked
staff—about as clean as, and smelling much like, the restroom of
an interstate bus station; confused, disoriented patients in foam-
rubber slippers and untied hospital johnnies wandered aimlessly
in the linoleum corridors; frightening moans of the bedridden
could be heard from the open doors of some rooms as you passed.
Honestly. It didn't take long to realize that the patients were just
being stockpiled, the modus operandi of Texas's inept Medicaid
program, among the stingiest in the nation, according to published figures. When my friend's sister and her husband—originally from Algiers and now living in France—showed up to bring
him to Paris according to a long-standing treaty that existed between Algeria and its onetime colonizer, France, allowing an Algerian citizen to get medical assistance in France if the variety of
specific treatment needed wasn't available in Algeria, it was their
first time in the U.S.; both of them were amazed, if not silently appalled, that this was actually the *United States,* that something like
the nursing home was, in fact, to be found in a nation supposedly
so powerful and prosperous.

And so in Paris I'd go in the afternoon to visit him a couple of
times a week at L'Hôpital Fernand-Widal. It was an old yet entirely
immaculate operation, smallish and constructed in 1858, according to the plaque out front. Fernand-Widal catered to special services, including the kind of long-term rehab my friend needed,
and it was located up toward Montmartre and in a busy *quartier*
of Paris that was as vividly Indian as my own neighborhood was
vividly African. I'd pass the receptionist in his casual blazer sitting
at the hospital's little check-in desk—he'd gotten to recognize
me and simply waved me along—and then go first through the
outer courtyard, mostly parking, and then through the rear courtyard—some crisscrossing gravel walks and a long central arcade of
box-cut lime trees, parklike—where I'd enter the quiet building
and head up the stairs to "Secteur Bleu" and my friend's room,
104. I'd usually find him alone there and set up in a chair, often
dozing off with the TV flickering on a news station; my friend had
always been a news junkie, better versed than probably anybody I'd

ever known on the political situation of just about every country around the world. At the door, I'd maybe say his name, and he would wake with a smile as I entered the room, painted a fresh light blue and the same hue of everything else in Secteur Bleu, with the hospital gown and the crisp sheets on the neatly made bed all a matching light blue, too. Even if his speech was severely marred by the stroke, his dark eyes would widen, he would say only one word, breathy in his condition but the grin—showing two missing teeth pulled during his hospitalization—wider than ever:

"Pete."

Some French alternated with some English as I sat on the bed's edge and we talked. There was his filling me in on my questions about his condition: if he was getting nourishment (he had lost the ability to swallow, was fed through a stomach tube); and how he was being treated (the wife of a French writer acquaintance of mine was a nurse, and she told me that L'Hôpital Fernand-Widal was top-notch, with my Algerian friend himself now assuring me that the nurses were good, the doctor who was in charge of his case was especially good—also, several of the staff were Algerian, so he felt very comfortable with them); and if his therapy was going well (unlike the stockpiling of patients out in the bleak Texas flatland, here he was given a full morning of vigorous therapy every weekday, a real regimen where progress was monitored and assessed regularly). Yes, after the routine questions, everything slipped into casual, surprisingly mundane conversation. Talk concerning guys from our circle back in Austin, and always much talk about the upcoming election and Obama, whom he greatly admired. With such relaxed conversation, laughter, too, the whole idea of my friend being incapacitated could seem to me like nothing but a dream in itself that we both had inadvertently stumbled into. I mean, a couple of years before would I have foreseen anything like the scene of the two of us meeting in a hospital room in Paris like this, birds chirping in the lime trees outside the open window there in the courtyard where nurses wheeled patients this way and that to enjoy the afternoon sunshine, my friend writing words on a yellow legal pad when, as hard as we both tried to communicate, I sometimes couldn't understand the syllables he struggled to get out? And maybe as with a dream, I sometimes felt that all it would take would be a little jarring (hearing the phone in my bedroom ringing back where I *really* was, possibly, at home in Austin? or the

sound of a growling truck clankingly emptying the Dumpster below my apartment window when waking in the early morning back
in Austin?), yes, something to jar me out of it all, this odd dream,
with normalcy and life as it should be restored once more.

Some sadness, all right.

And that summer I thought about my friend so much. I continued to walk in the evening and, needless to add, ended up where
I did go repeatedly, climbing the winding stone steps again to that
place where I somehow definitely had to be, there behind the
Gare de l'Est.

Actually, maybe it's time now to turn to what I mentioned earlier,
the writers who have offered their own input on what I'm trying
to get at, this key idea of a voice calling you to a particular location, which probably often happens while traveling. And it seems I
should address Borges first.

The essential book of Borges in English translation is certainly
the popular miscellany of his work, *Labyrinths,* a paperback published in 1962 by New Directions and reprinted who knows how
many times. If you thumb toward the latter pages of the book, you
will come to, on page 217, what has always been for me Borges's
most powerful essay. Titled, as I said earlier, "A New Refutation of
Time," it's presented as a two-part affair (a tricky configuration,
with several textual reversals that in themselves challenge chro-
nology), and in it, through dazzling verbal legerdemain, Borges
examines many of those from the long string of philosophical
idealists who questioned the very reality of the supposed reality
of existence, all descended from dreamy-minded Father Plato
(who begat Berkeley, who begat Hume, who begat Schopenhauer,
etc.). Borges even includes a consideration of Twain's Huck, as
he, Borges, shows how time and also space are not the geometric,
rigidly enforced concepts we often too readily believe they are, recreating a scene from the Twain novel to reinforce how a strange
and inexplicable feeling is possibly more befitting than any reasonable understanding of time and space being what actually defines
experience:

> During one of his nights on the Mississippi, Huckleberry Finn awakens;
> the raft, lost in partial darkness, continues downstream; it is perhaps
> a bit cold. Huckleberry Finn recognizes the soft indefatigable sound

of the water; he negligently opens his eyes; he sees a vague number of stars, an indistinct line of trees; then, he sinks back into his immemorable sleep as into the dark waters.

With that reference and a pile of others, Borges eventually establishes the fragile nature of reality as we know it, just a glimpse of something fleeting and never clearly defined, there amid another more important psychic territory altogether. All the while, Borges is moving toward a detailed personal illustration of what he means. He describes how on an evening in 1928, while strolling in Buenos Aires, he found himself in a locale where he did seem to have gotten free of time and space as they are commonly accepted to be, had entered into that something larger, which, never being explained, possessed him with a quiet and true intimation of a state akin to maybe Huck's deeper sleep indeed. Listen to how Borges, again most beautifully, tells of it, a walk in the moonlight to the neighborhood of Barracas; it's an old and pleasantly leafy quarter of Buenos Aires (I once wandered around there myself) on the other side of the wide Plaza de Mayo esplanade and its aptly named and very pink presidential palace, the Casa Rosada:

The evening had no destiny at all; since it was clear, I went out to take a walk and to recollect after dinner. I did not want to determine a route for my stroll; I tried to attain a maximum of probabilities in order not to fatigue my expectation with the necessary foresight of any one of them. I managed, to the imperfect degree of possibility, to do what is called walking at random; I accepted with no other conscious prejudice on my walk than that of avoiding the wider avenues or streets, the most obscure invitations of chance. However, a kind of familiar gravitation led me farther on, in the direction of a certain neighborhood, the names of which I have every desire to recall and which dictate reverence to my heart. I do not mean by this my own neighborhood, the precise surroundings of my childhood, but rather its still mysterious environs: an area I have possessed often in words but seldom in reality, immediate and at the same time mythical . . . My progress brought me to a corner. I breathed in the night, in a most supreme holiday from thought. The view, not all that complex, seemed simplified by my tiredness. It was made unreal by its very typicality. The street was one of low houses and though its first meaning was one of poverty, its second was certainly one of contentment. It was humble and enchanting as anything could be. None of the houses dared open itself to the street; the fig tree darkened over the corner; the little arched doorways—higher than the walls—seemed wrought from the same infinite substance of the night.

And there he does find a certain sense of timelessness, unexplained because, again, it can't be explained. Nevertheless, this state of mind is very true, even to the point of being what he calls a "feeling in death," not in any frightening way but instead in some underlyingly perceptive way, revelatory, with a personal deliverance beyond the trivialities of the mundane; it's as if his own everyday life, like that of Huck on the raft, has been fragile and illusory, a mere glimpse, until he finds himself easing out of it and delivered back into a realm of those deeper waters, returning at last into an ultimate essence, if you will.

The other writer I spoke of earlier, Louis Aragon, builds on this kind of experience and explores it in depth with 200 pages of probing meditation in his 1926 *Le Paysan de Paris* (Paris peasant). For my own purposes here, *Le Paysan de Paris* might bring the argument into better focus, as it takes it back to the Paris that I myself have been thinking about. In fact, my time there that summer was spent mostly in the same part of the city that had provided a territory for considerable thoughtful exploration by the surrealists of the 1920s, including Aragon and also André Breton, the latter in what is today surely the best-known surrealist prose text of the period, *Nadja;* intensely autobiographical, Breton's novel has the protagonist, the author himself, repeatedly gravitating in his frequent long walks toward the Grands Boulevards and, more specifically (and a little spookily for me), to the very neighborhood where I was living: "Meanwhile, you can be sure of meeting me in Paris, of not spending more than three days without seeing me pass, toward the end of the afternoon, along the Boulevard de Bonne-Nouvelle between the *Matin* printing office and the Boulevard de Strasbourg."

Early on in his own thoroughly mesmerizing book, Aragon wonders if reality is but "a delirium of interpretation," and in the subsequent chapters he sets out on more or less a mission of exploring the Grands Boulevards that also attract Breton; he does so with a concentration on his favorite of the old *passages* (ancient shopping arcades) in the area, the Passage de l'Opéra, which, with its roof of cast iron and milky glass filtering the midafternoon sunlight, exists in an almost subaqueous glow for him, suitably oneiric. He approaches the whole project as if wandering through some foreign land, taking in everything with heightened perception at last, and in his repeated visits he responds to various enterprises housed within the mazelike and usually empty Passage de l'Opéra (a shop for ornate walking canes, another for trusses, a rundown café, even a "massage parlor" that appears to be only a ruse for outright hookerdom) with an awareness that declares transcendence is near, that he might eventually find himself at an exact place where it seems he was meant to be all along, perhaps has been all along, and valid insight almost beyond life — or better yet, an enhancement of life — is about to transpire; the impact of it all can render anything taken for granted in life suddenly in the category of the definitely mythic. Here's a borrowing from the original translation of *Le Paysan de Paris* by Simon Watson Taylor that the brave little publisher Exact Change used for its 2004 reprinting; Aragon's prose is appropriately lyrical as he senses a primal, even Edenic quality to it all:

> It is you, metaphysical entity of places, who lull children to sleep, it is you who people their dreams. These shores of the unknown, sands shivering with anguish and anticipation, are fringed by the substance of our minds . . . [It was] this sensation of strangeness which filled me when I was still a creature of pure wonder, in a setting where I first became aware of the presence of a coherence for which I could not account but which sent its roots deep into my heart.

Lovely stuff, no?

And it echoes Borges's feeling in Barracas. And in a way, both writers with their own aimless walking are travelers, too, granting that it is foot travel they speak of and in their own cities. And aren't we all travelers in our dreams, wandering alone and solitary, constantly being drawn to a place where we *should* be, for the larger perception we *should* have, a voice often urging us on, as described? In my case the voice was nearly a distinct whispering heard as my own 25-buck, black-and-white nylon Reeboks shuffled over the sidewalks of Paris in the warm evenings of summer 2011, where despite all that sadness and also, and often, too much time on my hands in Paris to think about everything I had messed up in my life over the years, I did what I did.

I inevitably ended up *there* again.

It would happen on any one of those evenings. And just to look up between the rows of mansard-roofed buildings, as Rue Saint-Martin became Rue du Faubourg Saint-Martin, was to see at the far-off top of the slope the imposing Gare de l'Est—very white and showing new red awnings for its many repeated rectangular windows flanking a massive fan-shaped window, airily delicate and almost as high as the building itself—which meant I knew again where I was going to, had my cue, so to speak. And I started up that slight hill of Rue du Faubourg Saint-Martin leading me to the place, heading that way.

Early evening in Paris.

Yes, early evening in Paris, and it's balmy summer, the daylight still remaining but softened.

A wide cobbled plaza with taxi stands spreads in front of the station. Right beside it is a narrow street, Rue d'Alsace, which offers still more taxi stands; there's a long line of double doors to the station here, always open in summer, so you can look within to see all those people, shadowy and with the many destinations they have, moving across the polished terrazzo floor, almost like a glassy lake they're magically walking on this way and that, the news kiosks and coffee counters busy. A dim street, Rue d'Alsace is an odd one, too, in that it abruptly dead-ends—or in this case is interrupted—at a stairway with a double set of steep white stone steps that must date back to the mid-19th century, when the station was built. The steps, with sculpted banister rails, ascend curvingly on each side of a *very* odd little platform enclave about halfway up of weeds and litter and an arched, rusty iron door; that door looks more like an entryway to a burial vault than anything else, even if it actually leads to maybe some kind of functional utilities tunnel. The individual slabs of the steps are as worn as old bars of soap, and in the steep climb you begin to feel it in your calves, agreeably so, while the stairway continues to take you higher, finally to another level altogether, quite far above the station.

At the top, a true other world altogether suddenly opens up, because as the narrow Rue d'Alsace resumes again now on this higher level, you're not only well above Paris, it seems, but in a wide-open space removed enough from everything else in the clutter of the city that it can feel as if you aren't even in the city of Paris below.

There are ramshackle shops and cafés along one side of Rue d'Alsace, and on the other open side, across the street's sticky summer asphalt, is a low stone wall, graffiti-splattered, that looks out over the sizable expanse of the railway yards below, leading into the rear of the station. Now deserted, the long platforms go on for probably a quarter mile, and the rails atop the rusted roadbed are as shiny as liquid mercury, the crisscrossing overhead wires for the electrified trains a complicated, uneven dark mesh; announcements from the station play on the speakers, soft and warbly at this distance, and the chime music repeating its little truncated song of a few notes—the trademark jingle in all Paris train stations to signal announcements—is even softer and more warbly, nice. Or it's all so nice, in fact, that it could be *rare,* in that this is one of the infrequent places in the city where, without the clutter of trees or buildings, you are in a space open enough that the sky itself seems to dominate. And to make it better in Paris in July and August, that huge sky at the end of a summer day can go all unheard-of shades of rich color, orange and purple and even full-fledged scarlet, sometimes big gilded clouds thrown into the panorama to render everything more striking still. Men in grimy clothes congregate in packs along the wall in the evening and drink tall cans of beer, talking low, laughing low, Indian or African and delivered at last, surely, from labor at the end of a long day. Across from the wall, back on the other side of the street, the very first shop in the row of marginal enterprises—those shabby cafés, a couple of cramped Internet and overseas-phoning nooks, a tiny old hotel with nothing more for identification than the standard blue-on-white plastic HOTEL sign glowing—is a bookshop called Librairie la Balustrade, which is wonderful and strangely intriguing in itself. Its façade is painted a bright cream color, hopeful among the surrounding sooty buildings, with a small hand-scrawled card hung behind the glass on the front door giving the limited hours each week the shop is open; the books displayed in the windows are usually left-wing fare (ecology manifestoes, political manifestoes) or philosophical fare (anything from Kant clear through to Derrida) or mysteriously spiritual fare (meditation texts, narratives on the visionary), entirely intriguing. The bookshop seems suitable indeed for the mood of this particular enclave of Paris, to the point

that you can't help but jot down in a pocket notebook every time
you go there the titles of some of the latest arrivals displayed; such
titles make for nearly little prayers in themselves and are often
metaphysical in intent, no doubt, sometimes directly so, to cause
you to linger on the sidewalk and, well, ponder:

> *La Vie des Océans, de Leur Naissance à Leur Disparition*
> par Yves Lancelot

and

> *Quand les Sciences Dialoguent avec la Métaphysique*
> par Pascal Charbonnat

*Oh, the lives of oceans, their births and their deaths! And—oh,
again—when the sciences do have their dreamy and extendedly spirited
dialogues with the metaphysical!*

The evening smells somehow sweetly of the summer warmth
cut by a tinge of thick, lingering exhaust, despite what the Parisian authorities claim to be their cleaning up of the city's air—a
good smell, nevertheless, because it *is* the smell of Paris and always
pleasant.

And where it all gets strangest, and best, is at that small café, the
one I previously spoke of, a block beyond the bookshop and at the
corner of Rue d'Alsace and Rue des Deux Gares. Rue des Deux
Gares is a nondescript little connecting street thick with more of
the blue-on-white lit plastic signs saying HOTEL, and it leads at
an angle to the nearby Gare du Nord, the other of the two railroad stations the street's name pays tribute to. In its own appel-
lation, the café is also perfectly suitable, because dull gold letters
on the tattered red awning out front do announce it as "Au Train
de Vie," meaning in this case not just the idiomatic French term
for "lifestyle" but nothing less than—with a crisp pun when taken
literally—"the train of life," all right. In some long-gone hope of
rendering it right for the location, probably back in the '60s or
'70s from the looks of it, somebody apparently decided to give this
everyday working-class café/brasserie a thoroughly railroad motif.
The doors at the corner remain open to the sidewalk, and with yellowing lace half curtains hung from tarnished brass rods in the row
of street-side windows, you're able to look above them and inside,
past a grimy flower-print tile floor, to see how the bar, short, is stud-
ded with the cluster of actual headlamps from a long-forgotten

streamlined train, all clear- or red-glass concentric lenses and polished chrome; on a high shelf on the far wall, above framed black-and-white photos of once-modern diesel locomotives and wagons-lits, is an extensive collection of moth-eaten conductor's caps, side by side. The finishing, and maybe most appreciated, touch of all is how the few tables for the dining area along the windows on the Rue des Deux Gares side use those salvaged Pullman-car seats, the artifacts also previously mentioned and lumpily upholstered in mustard-yellow faux leather trimmed with blue piping, the armrests the same dark blue. And to make everything even more right, on the narrow cracked sidewalk out front, instead of having the standard variety of café *terrasse* setup, small chairs and tables, they have arranged there—facing the low stone wall across the street and overlooking the open railway yards and with the huge, huge Paris sky beyond often igniting in such very unreal colors—more of the coach seats and wobbly low wooden tables set between them. Which means that in the early evening after so much walking, you *can* end up there, you *can* ease into one of the old oversize seats with the springs poking out here and there, you *can* sit down and order from the leathery-faced waiter—who doesn't wear any waiter's outfit and could be just another working-class guy doing this after a day on another job—a single strong black *café express* for a euro and a half, as brought to you in a white demitasse rattling on a white saucer, the waiter taking a little time to rearrange the couple of sugar cubes on the side of the saucer along with the single spoon after he sets the coffee down for you, "Monsieur," and you *can* sit there, for me that place where I had to be—almost comically named the "train of life," but, as emphasized, so appropriate for it, too—and take in the scene, enjoy the ride, if you will.

Or to put it another way, you do get on board again for a soothing and even transcendent silent excursion into the evening, as everything else seems to vanish—because remember Borges and Aragon and what happened to them when they found themselves in places where they needed to be, where a voice perhaps told them to go, also think of the general mind-set of another city wanderer, the poet Pessoa, a validly mysterious quotation from whom I attached to my writing here right at the start as an epigraph, which suggests the mood of this state as well—and in that seat, sipping the coffee, not even realizing how long it is you stay there, the many sadnesses you might have with you in the world seem to ease up, fall into proper perspective—like that of my friend paralyzed and perpetually watching CNN Europe in L'Hôpital Fernand-Widal, or that regarding my nephew, whom I didn't know well enough, and due to some drifting apart in our family, I had, rather stupidly, let time pass without getting to know him better, a sweet kid, so special that he actually worried if he had done the right thing in picking up a worthless souvenir trinket when the ragged boys peddling them fled the cops—and there you are above it all, flying along, traveling under the wide sky on a Pullman-car seat outdoors in the balmy evening of the 10th Arrondissement and at a café called—please don't laugh when I repeat it again—Au Train de Vie—entering into a calming state of mind deeper and more meaningful than life but still completely amazed at the whole very wonderful journey of it, life, too.

And that is where I would go, where I had to be on those many summer evenings. And there I seemed to encounter my own moment of timelessness, and there I wasn't fully sure where I was, but I realized I was somewhere that made me more sure of where I was than any other place I knew (something like this had happened to me other times in traveling, my returning, repeatedly and half somnambulistically, to a small whitewashed stone church on a high cliff beside the sparkling aqua ocean during a stay in Rio de Janeiro, also my returning again and again to get pleasantly lost in the maze of the old jewelry-market district of Hyderabad in India, with sacred cows grazing in the littered streets and the welcome full explosion of smells and color and noise that is any marketplace in India), and if maybe all of one's time on this planet does seem little more than an insubstantial dream, this experience offered transport into something larger, going beyond the dream and clear into what could be a dream about the dream itself, free of the ties of reality at last and laced with calm and understanding beyond understanding—truer than true.

On my last evening in Paris, before I was to fly out the next day, I had everything packed up back at the apartment and the place painstakingly cleaned, which I hoped the owner, my friend the Saul Bellow scholar's elderly Oncle Robert, would approve of if he ever showed up from Cannes. That done, I went to Rue d'Alsace again, or more exactly, ended up there yet again.

I knew had accomplished what I had to accomplish on the manuscript. I'd worked especially hard on it the past week or so, my overall performance ultimately not disappointing, I hoped, the taxpayers of the state of Texas, the people who funded my university and therefore my grant. I now sat outside at Au Train de Vie for close to an hour. I'm not sure that the sense of being beyond everything, almost in another, more significant realm entirely, quite set in on this final evening as I plunked a sugar cube into the coffee, stirred the rich black essence with the stubby spoon. And the sadness I experienced now was not in thinking about those troubling matters I had to face in Paris that summer, the large issues, because in truth most of that I had come to terms with the best I could; I did reach understanding. (My nephew, back in Rhode Island, wrote me excited e-mails about how great the trip had been for him, even said that he was tossing the original idea for the screenplay he'd been working on for his course and now was starting a completely different screenplay, less contrived, about a guy his age who plays prep school hockey, not very well, going to Paris to visit his screwy uncle and embarking on concocted adventures with some even screwier Australian kids; he wanted my input on the new scenario he had come up with, saying that the most valuable thing anybody had ever told him about writing was exactly what I had said to him, emphasizing that he should write about what he knew; his thanking me in the e-mails made me feel good. The sister and brother-in-law of my friend in the hospital finally had everything approved and in order, so that he could, in fact, be moved from Paris to Nantes, where they lived, and visiting him for a final time at Fernand-Widal a couple of days before, with the bed sheets and the hospital gown he was wearing now both a pale yellow, despite the room being off the quiet, empty corridor of Secteur Bleu, I entered to see him smiling in the sunshine pouring through that window he sat beside; he appeared nothing short of radiant amid so much yellow, telling me in his difficult speech, smiling more, how he looked forward to soon being near his relatives, who, as it currently stood, got to take the train to visit him here in Paris only once a month; I think I was taken by his optimism in the course of such personal disaster, our parting handshake eventually exchanged with both of us knowing we most likely would never see each other again, but still, there would always be for me this show of his sheer winning outlook, or unmitigated bravery—and that, too, made me feel good.) No, the current sadness now was more mildly mundane, and it existed,

predictably enough, in my realizing that I would miss this spot I
had often come to. I'd really miss being in Paris as well, where I
had spent much of my life over the last 25 years and where I had
many close friends to talk with about literature—good, enlightening conversation and definitely much more of that sort of thing
than I had with so-called academic colleagues at my supposed
home in Texas (where, if truth be known, I simply had moved for
a job years before, and to me Texas never felt anywhere near being
what one might call home). I had the pocket notebook with a red
marbleized cover and a Bic pen laid out on the wobbly table. In
between sips and looking up to that huge sky again—travelers with
roller luggage walking by now and then, heading to or coming
from the Gare de l'Est—I jotted some notes about the details of
the scene there on Rue d'Alsace, probably knowing already that I
would be writing an essay like the one you're reading now (several
days ago I was told in an e-mail that the café, thoroughly funky
and authentic when I had been there, has undergone some rather
clinical, and most unfortunate, extensive remodeling), and I guess
that I was just feeling a little lost suddenly and also pretty tired,
physically so.

I mean, I'd had only a few hours' sleep the night before due
to anxiousness, worry about getting the apartment cleaned and
making sure I had taken care of everything I had to take care of
in Paris (including a complicated session that day to close out a
French checking account I'd kept for years), and I knew that even
the walk back to Rue Saint-Martin would be somewhat of a chore
at this stage, seeing that I had to be up early to get out to the airport the next morning.

Leaving the café, I nodded to the wiry guy in a faded polo shirt
and jeans who was the waiter. He had come to expect me in the
evening, I suppose, and he nodded back to me, "Monsieur," then I
started back down one side of the twin sets of winding steps beside
the Gare de l'Est. I told myself that I shouldn't have lingered at the
café as long as I had: there were still some last phone calls to make
to French friends that evening, and it was already getting late, the
sun having set. But then—weary, as said, also pressed for time—I
remembered I had my trump card, and a literal card it was. You
see, in Austin a young French woman who was there for the summer doing research at the university's rare books and manuscript
library had lent me for the summer her card for those free bicycles

they have in Paris now. The system is called Vélib', a fabricated catchword more or less translating as, indeed, "free bicycles," and all over the city there are long racks of the matching things, sturdy beige-colored three-speeds, each with a generator light and a copious chrome basket on the front handlebars, waiting there for anybody who does subscribe to pay the deposit initially required and then the nominal annual fee to get a rider's card good for the year; the young woman—a genuinely brilliant professor of modern British lit at her French university, somebody I always greatly enjoyed discussing books with—certainly had subscribed, and I'd been using the handy mode of transport often that summer.

In front of the Gare de l'Est, at that cobblestone plaza, was a full supply of Vélib' bicycles, the little lights of the repeated stubby terminal stands for them in the long rack lit to make an extended row of green dots—jewel-like, intensely glowing—in the evening, which was a rich Wedgwood blue now and almost dark.

I walked up to the rack, felt the tires on one bicycle that didn't feel quite solid enough, then felt the tires on another, just right. I swiped my electronic card across the button-size green light at the low terminal post for the bicycle selected, to hear the buzz and clicking sound of the mechanism unlocking—I tugged the bike free. I put the card back in my wallet, slipped the wallet into the pocket of my black jeans, also pushed to the elbow the sleeves of the open-collar striped dress shirt I was wearing. I adjusted the saddle seat up a few notches for my height and swung my leg over it, squeezed the aluminum levers on the handle grips once or twice to test the brakes, too.

And then I got on and headed back down the slope of Rue du Faubourg Saint-Martin, aiming right toward the Porte Saint-Martin arch and my apartment there, the old buildings flickering by, my knowing maybe more than ever that it probably wouldn't be long before I would again hear that voice you do hear when traveling, in some other place, at some other time—again I would come close to understanding that particular something, which is so big and important because it *is* well beyond simple comprehension.

The bicycle glided along, the generator headlamp flickered bright in the warm August night, the wind was fresh against my face, the bicycle glided along some more.

Really nice.

AMANDA LINDHOUT with SARA CORBETT

460 Days

FROM *The New York Times Magazine*

WHEN I DESCRIBE what happened to me on August 23, 2008, I say that I was taken. On an empty stretch of road outside of Moga-dishu, the capital of Somalia, out of the back seat of a four-wheel-drive Mitsubishi by a dozen or so men whose faces were swaddled in checkered scarves. Each one of them carried an AK-47.

The truth of it dawned slowly on me, as the men seemed to rise up out of the sand, circling the car with their guns hefted, as they shouted a few words at our driver, as someone tugged open a door. We—me, my traveling companion Nigel Brennan, and the three Somali men helping us with our work—were headed that day to a sprawling settlement just outside the city to do some reporting. We were waved out from our air-conditioned vehicle into the swel-tering equatorial heat. I remember in that instant a narrow-shoul-dered woman dressed in a flowing hijab hurrying past on foot. She pointedly looked away, as if a couple of white Westerners getting pulled from a car and being forced to lie spread-eagle in the ditch at the side of the road were an everyday occurrence or, in any event, something she had no power to stop.

It was clear to me then that nobody was going to call for help. Nobody was going to punch some sort of reverse button so that we would be pulled to our feet, put back into our car, and sent spin-ning down the road to where we had started. No, with every sec-ond that passed, the way back was becoming more obscure. It was hot, the air tasting like cinder. We were lying on some sort of edge. I pressed my forehead into the dirt, closed my eyes, and waited for whatever was coming.

*

This is how one life ends and another one begins. In the eyes of my family and friends, in the eyes of the cheerful young waiter who served me coffee and an omelet that morning at our mostly empty hotel in Mogadishu, and from the point of view of anyone who would next try to piece together the story, I vanished. And so did Nigel, who was a photographer from Australia and an ex-boyfriend of mine—who decided at the last minute to come with me on the trip and who may well spend the rest of his life regretting that he did.

I was 27 years old. I had spent most of the last seven years traveling the world, often by myself, as a backpacker, financing extended low-budget trips with stints working as a waitress in a couple of fancy cocktail lounges at home in Canada, in the oil-rich city of Calgary. With my saved-up tip money, I went through Venezuela, then Burma, then Bangladesh. I saw Pakistan and Syria, Ethiopia and Sudan. Each trip bolstered my confidence, convincing me that even while strife and terror hogged the international headlines, there was always something more hopeful and humane to be found on the ground.

Before going to Somalia, I spent the last year or so trying to transition to more serious work, learning photography and teaching myself how to produce a television report, locating myself—as many aspiring journalists did—strategically in the world's hot spots. I did a six-month stint in Kabul, followed by seven months in Baghdad. As a freelancer, I filed stories for a couple of English-language cable networks, taking whatever work I could get, and was writing a regular column for my small hometown paper in Alberta. I was getting by, but just barely. My plan was to spend a week in Somalia, which, with its civil war and what seemed to be an impending famine, had no shortage of potential stories to cover. Knowing it was risky, I took what felt like the necessary precautions—hiring a local fixer to arrange our logistics, paying for a pair of armed government guards to escort us around Mogadishu. For me, going to Somalia felt like a steppingstone, though I recognized it was a dangerous one.

Later, our captors would tell us they had been watching our hotel. What happened was planned, to the extent anything like this can be planned. Guns were marshaled; a place to take us afterward was secured. As we headed northwest out of the city that day, they somehow knew Westerners were coming. Maybe it was a cousin's cousin who tipped them off. Maybe it was the sight of our freshly washed SUV rental ripping around the battle-worn Old City, with its collapsed buildings and bullet-pocked walls. Most assuredly, there had been cash promised to somebody—a driver, a hotel employee, a guard—in exchange for information about where the foreigners were headed. We were ambushed just outside the city limits, at a precisely vulnerable moment, right after our government guards climbed out at a checkpoint and just before we were to meet two replacement guards a few kilometers down the road. Somebody—we don't know who—sold us out.

After our car was searched that day, we were pulled from the ditch and then driven about 45 minutes through the desert, swerving off the paved road and into a brushy wilderness. My heart pounded loudly in my ears. The car—piloted by one of the masked men—dodged thorn trees and ran right over bushes, not following any sort of path. With every passing minute, I knew we were moving farther off the grid.

One of the three men sitting in the front seat was unmasked. He turned back, smiling in a way that gave me some hope.

"Sister," he said, "don't worry, nothing will happen to you. There is no problem here. *Inshallah*." God willing, it meant. He added: "Our commander would like to ask you some questions. We are taking you to our base. We think maybe you are spies."

I could feel the fear spike in my throat. I tried to keep talking. I started babbling, listing off every Islamic country I had been to, as if that made me more of an insider.

The man ignored me. We drove on. Eventually, we pulled into a walled compound and were put in a darkened room inside a low, tin-roofed building. The Somali men with whom we were traveling—our cameraman, driver, and a representative from the displaced-persons camp we were hoping to visit—arrived in a different vehicle and were installed in a nearby room.

Nigel and I sat glumly on two foul-smelling foam mattresses on the floor, our shoulders pressed against the dirty walls. We whispered in low voices, wondering what was happening: Was this a robbery? Did they really think we were spies? Some part of me believed that we had just overstepped our boundaries as foreigners, that we would receive some sort of militiaman reprimand and be sent back down the road. Outside, I could see a cooking area underneath a lean-to made from scrap wood and a thick tree whose branches hung heavily over the yard. In front of the house was a small out-house. The sun radiated across the metal roof above, heating the room like an oven. Beyond our door, men were murmuring.

A man who had earlier told us his name was Ali came into the room and demanded our money. "Where is it?" he screamed. I fumbled with my backpack and produced $211—U.S. dollars being the currency of choice in Somalia. It was all I'd brought for the day, having left the rest of my cash under lock and key at the Shamo Hotel (sometimes spelled Shamow), where we were staying in Mogadishu. Nigel was carrying a few coins and a folded-up hundred-dollar bill he had stashed in his front pocket.

The men had already confiscated our cell phones, and now Ali grabbed my bag and dumped out its contents. He inspected everything disdainfully. My camera, my notebook, my water bottle. He took the cap off my lip balm. He examined both sides of my hairbrush. He handled each item delicately, as if it might explode.

It wasn't until later that day, when a new man arrived, introducing himself as Adam, that it became clear they were after more money than we had in our pockets. Adam looked to be in his mid-20s, thin and serene. He wore an orange-striped polo shirt and Ben Franklin eyeglasses. He asked for the phone numbers for our families and told us that he no longer believed we were spies. "Allah," he said, "has put it into my heart to ask for a ransom."

The thought was crushing. My parents were divorced. My father had chronic health issues and lived on disability checks. My mother had a low-paying job in a bakery. My bank account was just about empty. I'm not sure anybody I knew back home could even find Somalia on a map.

Nigel and I were allowed out of the room that evening, to use the bathroom and to get some air. Ali ushered us to a straw mat laid out alongside one of the compound's walls. He handed us two tins of tuna fish and a flask of tea. As darkness fell, the air cooled off somewhat. The sky became a screen, shot through with pin-pricked stars. Beneath it, I felt small and lost.

Over near the lean-to, I could see the soldier boys lolling around. They were listening to a silver battery-operated boom box that was tuned to the BBC Somali Service. A male newscaster's voice blared, speaking Somali, delivering what I assumed was news of the war. Then, with bizarre clarity, I heard him say the words *Shamo Hotel.*

The words caused a stir. The soldiers were sitting up and beginning to talk. Ali waved at us excitedly, pointing toward the radio. The newscaster said *Canadian* and then *Australian.* My eyes met Nigel's. The story was about us. The feeling was devastating. It was confirmation that our troubles were both real and deep.

I know now that kidnappings for ransom happen more frequently than most of us would think. They happen in Mexico, Nigeria, and Iraq. They happen in India, Pakistan, Algeria, China, Colombia, and plenty of other places. Sometimes the motivation is political or personal, but most often it's about money. Hostage taking is a business, a speculative one, fueled by people like me—the wandering targets, the fish out of water, the comparatively rich moving against a backdrop of poor. The stories pop up in the news and then often disappear: An American traveler is grabbed in Benin. A Dutch consultant is held for ransom in Johannesburg. A British tourist is dragged from a bus in Turkey.

Families are phoned; governments are contacted. A certain machinery quietly goes into gear. Nobody would ever call these situations common, but they happen enough that there are procedures in place, a standard way things go.

The first call to my family from Somalia came on August 24, a day after we were taken. A rumbly voice surfaced on my father's voice mail, the man named Adam saying, "Hello, we have your daughter." He said he would call again to talk about money and then hung up.

By nightfall, three agents from the Royal Canadian Mounted Police (RCMP) arrived at my father's home in Sylvan Lake, several hours' drive north of Calgary, and were sitting around the dining-room table, along with my mother, who had arrived from her home in British Columbia. The agents listened several times to Adam's message. They requested permission to tap my parents' phones and offered talking points for what to say when Adam called again. When it came to money, they were to tell the truth: they had none, and the government wouldn't pay a ransom either.

Kidnappings happened, my parents were told, but they also

ended. The RCMP agents then offered a bit of hard comfort: Nigel and I were now commodities. We were worth money. If our captors killed us, it would be their loss, too.

In Somalia, of course, we knew none of this. The hours crawled. Our hopes sagged. A day became a week and then a month. The kidnappers moved us several times, hiding us in vacant buildings surrounded by high walls and in tucked-away desert villages, where all of us—Nigel, me, the three Somali captives, plus the eight young men and one middle-aged captain who guarded us—remained invisible. When they moved us, it was anxiously and usually in the quietest hours of night. Riding in the back seat of a Suzuki station wagon belonging to one of the group's leaders, I saw mosques and night markets strung with lights and men leading camels and groups of boisterous teenagers, some of them holding machine guns, clustered around bonfires along the road.

Each time we arrived at a new place, the captain shuffled through his set of keys. The boys, as we called our young guards, rushed in with their guns and found a room to shut us inside. Then they staked out their places to rest, to pray, to eat. Sometimes they went outside and wrestled with one another in the yard. The leaders of the group—Adam and three other men who wore expensive clothes and spoke a polished English—all lived offsite, visiting us once or twice a week, sometimes bringing supplies.

Our captors practiced a fundamentalist form of Islam, interpreting the words of the Koran in the most literal way possible. Most of the boys, we learned, had gone to insurgent training camps in rural areas. They were part of a loosely organized movement that was fighting their country's own faltering transitional government and Ethiopian troops, who were sent over the border in 2006 to support Somalia's attempts at democracy. They described this fight as their jihad. Nigel and I came from what they termed "bad countries." We belonged to the Western world, which to them was inscrutable and immodest and ruled over by Satan. Presumably, some portion of any ransom money they got for us would go to support the larger cause.

Every day I worked to make myself—to make us—harder to kill, by being friendly and remaining neutral on politics. If we could bore our captors without frustrating them, I figured, maybe they would deliver us back to the Shamo, like two boxes that had spent a month uselessly collecting dust in a warehouse.

When the leaders weren't around, the boys often loitered nearby. The air around us hummed with what I can only describe as male energy, a buzzy mix of repression and young strength. I felt it when they came to deliver food, when their eyes fell on me and then quickly moved away, as if the sight of me, or whatever thought that followed, was shameful. A number of them seemed curious about us, though, and eager to practice what little English they knew. We spoke most often with a guard named Jamal. He sat on the floor of our room, cross-legged, in a T-shirt and a pair of tan dress slacks with cuffs that rode high over his skinny dark ankles. He was 18, a clear work in progress, with long spindly legs and narrow shoulders that sloped forward, as if he were trying to shed some of his considerable height. On his chin, he had a few sprouting hairs, the very beginnings of a beard. He told us that his father had been killed by Ethiopian soldiers. The memory of it was fresh enough that it caused his eyes to water. "For me, this was start of jihad," he said.

Before jihad, we learned, Adam worked as a teacher. The captain was a farmer. Before jihad, some of the younger boys went to school. Now they were paid to guard us, though it wasn't much.

Jamal was openly interested in me and Nigel, asking questions and smiling at the ground as he heard our answers. Where did we live? What did we think of Somalia? Did we own cars? He brimmed with plans for his life after the kidnapping. He was engaged to marry a girl named Hamdi. He also wanted to study information technology in India, because he had heard there were many universities there.

His closest friend in the house was a young man his age named Abdullah, who was more heavily built and somber. Abdullah sometimes carried in our twice-daily meals—a couple of tins of tuna, several buns, a flask of sweet tea, and a mango or a few soft bananas. Unlike Jamal, he seemed stuck on the war. One day I asked him what he was going to do later in life. He gave me a fierce look, mimed the act of putting on a jacket, and made the sound of an explosion.

It took me a second. "Suicide bomber?"

Abdullah nodded. He believed that at the gates to paradise, soldiers in God's army got to enter through a special doorway.

Jamal, sitting nearby, shook his head as if to say no, no, no. "I don't want him to die," he explained. "He is my friend."

In early October—roughly six weeks after we were taken—they moved us into a concrete building where we sometimes heard gun-fire between warring militias outside our windows and sometimes a mother singing nearby to her child, her voice low and sweet. The sound of it filled me with longing. The three Somali men who were kidnapped with us were put into a room down the hallway, their shoes lined up outside the door. Abdi, the freelance camera-man, occasionally sat on the threshold, reading the Koran in the light from the hall. A few times I peered out and flashed him the hand sign for "okay," as in "You okay?" Each time he shook his head, looking forlorn.

Our room was large and unfurnished. Nigel and I lived like a two-person family, doing what we could to fight off depression, to distract ourselves from the gnawing hunger. I poured the tea, and Nigel washed our clothes. Our captors had given us basic sup-plies—two tubes of toothpaste, some Q-tips, nail clippers, a packet of acetaminophen tablets as large as horse pills. I received a cloak-like dress and headscarf, both made from red polyester. Nigel was given a couple of collared shirts. Between us, we had two tin plates and a single spoon. With what little food we were given, we made menus, eating our meals on a table-size square of brown linoleum the boys had tossed in our room. Some days we ate the buns fol-lowed by the tuna; other days it was tuna followed by the buns.

To pass the time we tracked insects as they climbed the iron window grates. Once, looking outside, we saw a fat brown snake, maybe eight feet long, rippling through the sand in the alleyway behind the house. Otherwise, there was little to see.

Nigel fashioned a small backgammon game, crafting playing pieces from our Q-tips—one of us using the cotton nubs, the other using pieces of the plastic handles, which he clipped with a pair of beard-trimming scissors. On a sheet from a notebook we received, he drew two rows of triangles and then, using a couple of acet-aminophen tablets and the scissors, carved a set of dice, itty-bitty white cubes with tiny numbers written on the sides in pen.

We played for hours. We played for days. He won. I won. We played rapid-fire and without much conversation or commentary, like two monkeys in some sort of deprivation experiment. If we heard footsteps in the hallway, we quickly slid everything under my mattress. Games, like so many other things that might divert us from religion, were forbidden, *haram*.

Early on, Nigel and I told our captors that we wanted to convert to Islam. It was a survival move and not a spiritual one, made in the hope that it might garner us better treatment. Five times a day now, prodded by the craggy voice of a muezzin calling from a nearby mosque, we went through the motions of prayer. We each received English translations of the Koran. A few of the boys spent time teaching us how to memorize verses in Arabic, so we could gain favor with Allah. In the evenings, the group of them sat on the patio, chanting Koranic verses.

Back at home, my mother had become the de facto negotiator for both my family and Nigel's. I was allowed to speak with her a handful of times. Our phone calls were quick, conducted over faulty cell-phone connections, and wrenching every time. It felt as if the two of us were swimming between enormous ocean waves, shouting into walls of water. She told me that she loved me, that people at home were praying for us. Our captors were demanding $3 million for the two of us. She told me they were trying to get some money together. Those were the words she used, "get some money together." What that meant, given their financial circumstances, I couldn't imagine.

Any time I thought of my parents, I was overcome with guilt. My one hope was that our captors would simply get tired of waiting and let us go. Each night, as we were getting ready to sleep, I would turn and say to Nigel, "Now we are one day closer to being free."

Then one morning late in October, several of the boys stormed our room, surprising us as we sat eating breakfast on the floor. They dragged away Nigel's foam mat and unhooked his mosquito netting from the wall. A few minutes later, they returned for Nigel, guns leveled at his chest, motioning him toward the door. There was no explanation, no dialogue. I watched the back of his shirt as it moved away from me. There was no goodbye or anything. He was just gone.

They put him in a small, bare room right next to the one we had shared. We'd peeked into it plenty of times before, as we came and went from the bathroom down the hall. We were worried from the start that they would separate us, because in traditional Islam, unmarried men and women were not supposed to consort. I couldn't guess why they chose that particular day to finally do it. Perhaps it had something to do with the fact that it had been eight weeks since we were taken from the road, and there was no sign of a ransom payment.

The boys' anger seemed to be percolating. There were days when nobody spoke to me at all—when Jamal said nothing as he delivered food, when Abdullah, the would-be suicide bomber, hovered menacingly in my doorway. The isolation put me in a cistern, dark and deep. The leaders of the group holding us mostly stayed away, though every so often one would arrive at the house and pose a question sent from home, breaking my solitude with a query flung over continents, evoking something both intimate and concrete.

"What award did Dad win recently?" Communities in Bloom, for his gardening.

"Where does Oma keep her candy?" In a pumpkin-shaped jar.

My answers were to furnish proof to my family that I was alive. To me, the questions also felt like gifts, an invitation to pass an afternoon conjuring my grandmother's tidy house or the quivering dahlias in my father's backyard.

Sometimes I was despairing, but other times I felt my mind beginning to carry me. I didn't know if it was a survival tool or the first flutter of lunacy, but I began to feel as if my thoughts held new power. One morning I ate a tin of tuna and then sat for an hour holding the spoon in front of me, trying to see if I could bend it with my mind. I couldn't, not even a little, but still, the idea seemed less crazy, more possible, than it once had.

During the hottest hours of the day, the boys dozed in the shade of the veranda outside, while one of them stayed awake for guard duty. Usually in the afternoons, it was Abdullah on patrol. He often opened my door without warning. He didn't say anything, clutching his gun, keeping his gaze on me for several full minutes without moving. Sometimes, he searched my room, noisily rooting through my belongings, throwing things against the wall. I realized later that he was just testing the waters—seeing what he could get away with as the others slept outside.

One day he showed up and closed the door behind him. He

leaned his gun against the wall. I knew right away what was happening. It didn't matter that I had worried about this. It didn't matter that I tried desperately to fight him off as he forced himself on me. In less than three minutes it was over, three impossibly long minutes.

I felt as if I had been evicted from my body, as if I no longer fit in my own skin. My mind ticked through every mistake I ever made. Why had I come to Somalia? What had I done? Every fear I ever had came back to me—darkness was scary, noises were scary. I felt like a child. I hated facing the uncertainty of every afternoon, not knowing whether Abdullah was coming or not.

Eventually, to ease my own agony, I began to walk circles. I did one lap around the room and then another. Soon, I was walking six or seven hours a day in my bare feet. A dirty pathway took shape on the floor, a miniature one-lane track. In motion, I told myself things, the words resonating right down through my legs: I will get out of here. I will be okay.

When I wasn't walking, I spent time standing at one of the two windows in my room, feeling the outside air float through the grilles that covered it. One afternoon, a light rain began to dapple the concrete wall across the alleyway from my window. The sky darkened to a powdery gray. A wind gusted, rushing through trees I couldn't see, causing the rain to spray sideways on the wall.

"God, it's beautiful," a voice said, clear as day, articulating my exact thought at the exact moment I had it.

The voice wasn't mine. But it was a voice I knew. "Nige?"

The voice said, "Trout?" Trout was a nickname I'd had since high school.

For a shocked second, we were both silent. He was maybe 10 feet away from me at the window in his room. Because the alleyway was narrow and the tin roof of our house overlapped slightly with that of the house behind it, the acoustics were perfect. Our voices carried clearly, sheltered by the rooftops. It was a little miracle of physics. We had gone weeks without figuring this out, but now we had.

Standing at our windows, Nigel and I spoke each day for hours on end, keeping our voices low and our Korans open on our sills in case anyone walked in. We ran through old stories, adding new details every time. We discussed our nighttime dreams, our inter-actions with the boys. I started one day to tell him about Abdul-lah, but then stopped myself: It didn't seem fair to involve him in something he could do nothing about. Instead, we made guesses about what was happening with ransom negotiations. We talked about the future as if it were arriving at any minute. When Christ-mas came, marking the end of our fourth month as hostages, we quietly sang carols together.

On January 14, a Wednesday, I stepped into the hallway, headed toward the shower, and noticed a new stillness in the house. The shoes belonging to our Somali colleagues—Abdi, Mahad, and Marwali—had disappeared, all three pairs. A while later, I was able to ask Abdullah where they went. He didn't hesitate. Seem-ing pleased with himself, he lifted a finger and made an emphatic throat-slitting gesture. My stomach churned. Before we were cap-tured, Abdi had proudly shown me pictures of his children—two boys and a girl, smiling little kids in school uniforms, who it now seemed, thanks to me, had no father. If our captors had killed their fellow Somalis, Muslim brothers all three, it didn't bode well for me and Nigel.

Was there some way out? There had to be. Nigel told me he had been studying the window in the bathroom we shared and thought we could climb through it. I, too, had looked at that window plenty of times, seeing no option there. About eight feet off the bathroom floor, recessed far back in the thick wall up near the ceiling, was a ledge maybe two feet deep, almost like an alcove. But what was at the end of it hardly counted as a window. It was rather a screen made of decorative bricks with a few gaps, serving as ventilation holes for the bathroom. The bricks were cemented together. And then, as if that weren't enough, laid horizontally in front of the bricks was a series of five metal bars anchored into the window frame.

"Are you crazy?" I said to Nigel. "It's impossible. How would we get out?"

"You should crawl up there," he said. "I've been looking at the bricks. The mortar is crumbling. We could dig it out."

"Yeah, but the bars . . ."

"I think I could pull them loose. They're not that secure. I don't know," he said, sounding not entirely confident, "but I think it could work."

It took some effort to pull myself up to the window in the bathroom. I had to stand with one foot planted on either side of the toilet seat, reaching up past my shoulders to boost myself up, as if levering my way out of a swimming pool.

With my face up close to the window, I could see that Nigel was right. The bricks covering the opening were only loosely cemented. The mortar between them crumbled at my touch, coming away in small cascades of white dust. I had brought my nail clippers, and using them, I was able to reach between the metal bars and poke into the cement between the bricks. With some diligent chipping, it seemed possible that we could remove a few rows of bricks.

The metal bars were another matter. They were about three feet long and appeared to be sunk deep into the walls on either side of the window, though Nigel had already managed to loosen one of them from its anchor points. He swore to me earlier that he could muscle at least one more out of its hold. Feeling elated, I dropped back to the bathroom floor, covered in grit and cobwebs. I hurried to my room, for the first time in months not thinking about danger or hunger or worry, consumed instead by the idea that we could make a hole to the outside, a body-size hole, and slip through it.

Standing at our windows, we began to work on a plan. What time of day would we go? What would we bring? Which direction would we run? Who would we seek out, and what would we say? The considerations were enormous.

All the while, we traded shifts in the bathroom, hauling ourselves onto the ledge with fingernail clippers in hand, chiseling at the mortar in hurried 5- and 10-minute bursts. The work was gratifying, like digging for gold. Sometimes I got dust; other times, with some careful prying, I managed to extract a nice little slab of fully intact cement.

Because my door was in easy sight of the veranda where the boys spent their time, I had to be cautious—knocking for permission to leave my room, never staying too long in the bathroom. I was also frail. The muscles in my arms had become wasted and wobbly, my elbows often buckling when I tried to pull myself up to the window ledge.

Given where his room was located, Nigel was in a better position than I to make undetected trips to the bathroom and to stay there longer. He worked methodically, but there was no hiding the mess we made, the skewed bricks and mounds of loose mortar sitting on the sill. I tried to take solace in the knowledge that the boys walked into our bathroom only once or twice a week—mainly to take the oversize bucket we used for water and refill it at a tap outside. The risk still felt huge.

On the start of the third day, Nigel announced that he had carved out the final brick. He then had to contend with the metal bars, but the first one was already loose, and he said it would take only one more to create enough space to pass through.

We decided that we should make our break that same night, slipping out the window around 8 P.M., just after the evening's final prayer. We were banking on that night being like every other night in the house, governed by the mind-numbing clockwork routine—prayer followed by dinner, followed by prayer, followed by bedtime for everyone but the two boys on guard duty, who would sit outside, talking idly in the darkness.

I was startled, then, when Jamal arrived in my room with dinner a full hour ahead of when the meal usually came.

"*Asalaamu Alikum,*" he said with a slow smile. Peace be upon you.

My thoughts spun. Did they suspect something? What was happening?

Jamal waved for me to pull out my tin plate and lay it on the floor. He then opened a plastic bag and slid something onto it—a slender piece of deep-fried fish, golden brown and glistening with oil. From his pocket, he pulled out two small limes and set them next to the fish.

It was protein, a gift. It seemed that he was worried about my diet. "You like?" Jamal said, pointing at the fish.

We stood for a few seconds, regarding each other. I gave myself an internal kick. Snap out of it. "Oh, Jamal," I said, lifting the plate, "this is so nice of you." I smiled at him, feeling a touch of guilt. I hoped the leaders wouldn't punish him too badly after I was gone.

Following the day's last prayer, I rapped on my door and pushed it open slightly to see who responded. It was Abdullah who peered down the hallway, which meant that he was on nighttime guard duty. My heart sank. Abdullah liked to roam.

"*Mukuusha,*" I said in Somali, pointing at my stomach. Bathroom. "I am feeling sick. Very sick."

Abdullah snapped his fingers to indicate that I could go.

Slowly and coolly, I left my room and walked down the hallway in the direction of the bathroom. Earlier in the evening, I'd smuggled my backpack to the bathroom and left it on the window ledge. Inside it, I had put a headscarf and the heavy black abaya I wore the day we were kidnapped, so that once outside, I could better blend in. Nigel stood waiting for me at his doorway. He had done some advance work in the bathroom, wrenching two bars out of the walls, then putting them back in place, propped up precariously with chunks of loose cement.

Up in the alcove, Nigel removed the two bars and next began gingerly unstacking the bricks from the window frame. I could hear him panting. One brick came away, then two, then three, then four. When they were all out, he jumped back to the floor and motioned that we were ready. After I put on my abaya, Nigel lifted me toward the window and the 18-inch gap that was now there.

I looked through that hole for no longer than two seconds, but it was enough to see everything. I could see the alleyway beneath, and the darkness of a village with no lights and everything uncertain beyond. We had worried about breaking our ankles in the drop. We had worried about so many things, and as I stared at the gap in the window, every one of those things felt there, right on the other side, along with our freedom. I turned around and started to back my way through the remaining window bars, sliding both feet through the gap—with two of the remaining bars above me and one bar beneath—lowering myself slowly into the air outside. I could feel a breeze on my ankles. It worked until it didn't: I pushed myself back and felt my rear end jam up against one of the bars still in the window. The gap was too small. If I couldn't fit, Nigel never would.

"Go, go, come on," Nigel whispered from below.

"I can't. It's not working." I thrust again at the bar to show him my predicament. He looked distraught, his forehead slick with sweat. I said, "Can you take out another bar?"

"Not now," he said, almost hissing. "It makes too much noise."

Nigel waved a hand, telling me to climb down. "Get back to your room," he said. "Quickly. I'll try to fix this up."

I walked to my room as casually as I could and closed the door noisily, to let Abdullah know I had returned. I lay on my mattress in the dark, trying to muster one calm thought. I knew it was only a matter of time before our plan was discovered—before one of our captors spotted the jury-rigged pile of bricks and bent bars that comprised the bathroom window or just read the whole stupid plotline in my eyes.

After dawn broke and the boy named Hassam came to open our window shutters before prayer, Nigel and I stood at our sills, deciding that we had to leave immediately. Quickly, we redrew the outline of our plan. We knew from the calls of the muezzin that there was a mosque somewhere close by. It seemed like the one good option, a place to find a crowd. We waited for the midday prayer, for the heat to arrive and the boys to start nodding off. I knocked for the bathroom, and Nigel met me there, holding my backpack. Early that morning, he pulled out a third window bar. I waited while he quickly unstacked the bricks again. This time, I didn't hesitate. I got one leg out the window and then the second. I slid a few inches on my stomach to lessen the distance to the ground, holding on to one of the remaining window bars for support, and then I let myself drop.

We hit the ground one right after the other, me and then Nigel, two soft thumps in the sand. My heart lifted and crashed with the impact.

Things were bad. I knew it the instant I touched the soil. Nothing appeared the way I had imagined it. To the left was a sideways-leaning fence made of patchwork pieces of colored tin and old, flattened oil cans. To the right was a row of shanties, built from more tin and pieces of loose burlap. There wasn't a bit of vegetation in sight, beyond a few brambly thornbushes, low and leafless in the sand. More alarming was the emaciated child, a boy of maybe seven, standing only a few feet away from me, naked but for a pair of shorts, swaybacked and wide-eyed and looking like he might scream.

The boy took off at a sprint—heading, I was sure, toward the first adult he could find.

It was as if a starting gun had been shot, as if a seismic disturbance had unsettled the air, rippling over the rooftops to the patio where our captors lay in repose. Everything became instinctual then. Nigel and I didn't even look at each other. We just started, madly, to run.

Every strategy we plotted at our windowsills flew out of our heads. Every bit of reason lifted away as we dashed down the alleyway.

At the end of the alley was a rutted sand road, and on the road there were shacks and some market stalls, and the land beyond was a flat brown. Nigel was yelling at nobody and everyone, screaming *"I caawi, I caawi,"* the Somali words for "Help me."

I saw it all in a high-speed panic, which is to say I barely saw it, or caught it only in flashes—a half-collapsed wall, a few nervous goats, a donkey lashed to a cart by two thin poles. We ran through it and past it, this landscape we had spent hours imagining, this place to which we were colossally mismatched, me behind Nigel, Nigel shouting, the heat warping the air around us, all of it with the unreality of a bad dream. People on the street spotted us and fled. Later, I would look back on it and realize that if you are running in a place like Somalia, everyone understands that you are running from danger. Which means that they, too, should run.

The mosque was tall and wide, painted green and white with a crescent moon on top and a short set of wooden steps leading to a wooden platform and an entrance. The platform was heaped with shoes, signaling that the place was full of people. Moving up the stairs behind Nigel, I felt the first trickle of relief, a feeling so unfamiliar that I almost couldn't identify it.

Just then, a lone person came skidding around the street corner. It was Hassam, one of the younger guards. His expression was one of disbelief and selfish terror. I saw Abdullah run up, just behind him.

I bolted forward into the mosque, forgetting to remove my shoes. What I saw first was a field of men—kneeling, sitting, milling about in small groups. There were prayer mats spread in lines across the floor. Heads turned. A few people stood up. The interior of the mosque was vast, a single room with a vaulted ceiling. I heard myself calling out Somali words and English words and also some Arabic, my brain blurry with distress. I shouted, "Help!" and "May the blessings of Allah be upon you!" and "I am Muslim!" Nigel, too, was yelling.

A crowd magnetized around us, men with puzzled faces, some showing alarm. And then Abdullah was upon me, having blasted through the door with Jamal right behind, both of them holding guns.

Abdullah lunged and I dodged, feeling his grasp slip off my shoulder. I ran to a far corner of the room, where another group of men sat on the floor. I said every Arabic word I could think of as they lifted their bearded faces toward me, dumbstruck. Off to the side, Jamal had corralled Nigel against a wall and was hitting him repeatedly in the head, pounding on him with a closed fist, beating him with every ounce of strength he had. Nigel, I could see, was trying to hit him back, all the while shouting, "Jamal! Jamal!" as if to remind him that, in a weird way, they were once friends.

My fear organized itself into speed. I ducked through a doorway leading out into the air. With Abdullah two paces behind me, I leapt over the three stairs that descended from the side door of the mosque, landing in heavy sand, shedding my flip-flops as I ran. A gunshot ripped overhead, hollowing out the air. I looked back to see Abdullah, who had stopped running long enough to fire at me. My mind circled back toward the mosque. Nigel was inside. Inside was safer than outside. Keeping my shoulders low, I did a high-speed 20-yard end run around Abdullah, throwing myself back up the stairs and into the mosque.

The scene inside was oddly calm. Nigel had managed to shed Jamal and was sitting, not quite placidly but pretend placidly, at the front of the mosque, in the semicircular area that served as the imam's pulpit, surrounded by a loose cluster of maybe 15 bearded men, most of them standing. I dropped to my knees next to Nigel, who was speaking English with some of the men, sounding like he was answering to some skepticism that he was Muslim.

Through a large, low window to one side of the pulpit, I could see a woman, sheathed entirely in black, peeking in at us, until one of the men strode to the window and slammed its metal shutters closed.

Abdullah had reentered the mosque. He was creeping his way into the group of bystanders, his gun canted loosely in my direction, sweat dripping through his hair and shining his cheeks. Nigel, meanwhile, was loudly reciting verses of the Koran like a schoolboy.

One of the men explained to us that someone was phoning

the local imam, who was in the next village but would come to hear our story and give his judgment. "*Inshallah,* everything will be fine," he said, indicating that we should remain seated on the floor. "*Inshallah,* maybe fifteen minutes."

I felt relieved by this. An imam, I figured, would want to help us. I could hear Abdullah and Jamal arguing—politely—with some of the men.

Abruptly, a woman parted the quarreling crowd, elbowing her way past the men with the guns. I recognized her as the woman who had been looking through the window. She wore a black abaya and full hijab, including a niqab draped over her nose and mouth, covering everything but her eyes. Every man in the place was staring at her. The woman noticed no one. She came right over to me, kneeling down at my side without a word. Automatically, I reached for her hand. Her fingers wrapped around mine. I felt, for a second, safer than I'd felt in ages.

Her eyes were brown and somehow so familiar that it was as if I knew them from somewhere. The tops of her hands were painted with delicate, tendril patterns of rust-colored henna, the sort of ornament that one woman draws painstakingly on another. She was speaking in Somali to the men around us. I watched her, my nerves firing. I couldn't understand what she was saying. I knew she was helping me somehow. I heard distress in her voice. When she looked at me, her eyes swam with emotion.

Without thinking, I reached out and brushed my fingers over her face, feeling the warmth of her cheek beneath the fabric.

I said, "Do you speak English?"

"A little," she said, moving closer. "You are a Muslim?"

"Yes, from Canada."

"You are my sister," she said. "From Canada."

She reached out both arms, and I let myself fall. I sank my face into the pillows of her body. Her arms fit snugly around me. I felt the edges of my vigilance soften, the domino fall of my defenses. I began to cry. As men jabbered around us, the woman tightened her hold on me. She was the first woman I'd interacted with in five months. Lifting my head to find her eyes again, I told her I had been a prisoner, that I wanted to go home. My voice rose and fell unevenly. Uttering the word *home* caused me to sob. I pointed toward Abdullah, who was scowling at us, probably 10 feet away.

"He is abusing me," I said, suddenly desperate. To be sure she understood, I used my fingers to mimic the mechanics of sex.

I watched the woman's eyes get wide. "Oh, *haram*," she said. *"Haram, haram."* She looked up to the crowd, her expression ferocious, and shouted a few agitated Somali words.

But before anyone could respond, the dynamic in the room changed suddenly. Two of the leaders of the kidnappers had marched into the mosque, looking disheveled and furious, with the captain next to them, waving a pistol.

One of them—a man called Ahmed—located me and pointed a finger. "You!" he shouted. "You have made a big problem!" The air in the mosque had grown stuffy and uncertain, filled with noise. Then came a loud, concussive crack, a gun going off somewhere inside the room.

The sound of it broke the spell, the holding pattern. I saw Abdullah pushing through the crowd in my direction, his head lowered like a bull's. I screamed as he dove at me. He caught my feet with his hands and began dragging me in the direction of the side door. I clawed at the ground as he pulled. I don't remember any of the onlookers trying to stop him.

It was only the woman who tried.

She clamped on to my arms and pulled me back, using her weight for leverage, letting loose a torrent of Somali. For a few minutes, my body was strung between them, with Abdullah yanking my legs while the Somali woman proved herself a stubborn anchor. We were being towed along—the two of us, linked like train cars—inch by inch across the floor of the mosque. My shoulder sockets ached to the point where I thought they would pop.

Finally, she could hang on no longer. I managed to lift my head and look back to see her sprawled on the floor and weeping openly. Her headscarf and niqab had been torn off in the struggle, leaving her exposed. I could see that she was my mother's age, in her early 50s, with a gentle plump face and high forehead. Her hair had been braided in tiny cornrows over her head. She still had one arm outstretched in my direction. Three men with guns now surrounded her.

Someone lifted my shoulders, maneuvering me roughly over the stairs outside the mosque and into a courtyard. My abaya had ridden up over my waist. My jeans, which were already baggy because I had lost so much weight, were slipping toward my ankles as Abdullah jerked me forward, holding my legs on either side of his chest as if pulling a cart. As we moved over the courtyard, my body skimming the dirt, I felt my frayed underwear sliding off as well. I was naked, basically, stomach to knees.

I felt something wet hit my stomach and realized I had been spit on. We were moving through a crowd, past a metal gatepost marking the edge of the courtyard and the entry to the road. I reached out and caught the post, latching on to it with both hands.

Abdullah turned to see what had stopped his progress. Beyond him and through the gate, I could see a blue truck waiting with its engine running. Another gunshot echoed from inside the mosque. Nigel, I thought. They've killed Nigel. The thought was like a suck hole, a thing that could kill me. I spotted a woman's narrow face looking down at me from the crowd, her expression unreadable. I screamed at her in English: "Why won't you help me?"

She looked stricken. "I don't speak English," she said in perfect English.

Suddenly, the knuckles on one of my hands exploded in pain. Someone had kicked it to loosen my grip on the pole. I howled and let go. Then I was being pushed to my feet and toward the truck. I saw two other men hauling Nigel through the door of the mosque and in our direction. The sight of him brought a wash of solace and a hammer blow of anxiety. It had been all of 45 minutes since we'd slipped through the window. We'd made it out but not truly out. We'd crossed the river only halfway. Things would get worse from here. Everything that followed would be aftermath, punishment.

Nigel and I would remain hostages for another 10 months. We were freed, finally, on November 25, 2009, 460 days after we were taken, and only after our families managed to raise just over $1 million for a ransom and the services of a private security company. They held fundraisers, accepted other donations, and borrowed where they could. (Later, we learned, to our relief, that the three Somali men who were kidnapped with us had not been killed, but rather released unharmed.)

For a while, I kept track of my freedom, counting the days and the weeks and eventually the months that separated me from my captivity, sliding them like beads on an abacus, hoping that at some point one thing would feel stronger, more significant, than the other. But it doesn't work that way, exactly. What I've learned is that freedom can't fully overtake its absence. Once lost, a part stays lost forever.

I live with what happened. Memories leap the border between then and now. One sensation abruptly rivets itself to another—hot sand, the smell of an overripe banana, the rattling of a diesel truck—and tosses me, with a pounding heart, into the past. But that day, in particular, stays with me. The sweaty paranoia of slipping through the window, the frenzied dash into the mosque, the confusion that followed. All of it sits locked in my mind, surreal and forever vivid. I don't know what happened to the woman in the mosque, the stranger whose name I never knew, who fought until I was dragged out of her arms. But I recall the elemental comfort of her embrace and all the terror and sadness she seemed to be beating back with it.

During the rest of my captivity, the memory of the escape became a sustaining one. It held an electrical charge, a force. We had been hopeful for how long? Ten minutes? Twelve? Whatever it was, in the context of the dark months to come, the feeling turned out to be vital. I craved it, just one hit of lung-clearing, odds-stacked-against-us, nearly impossible possibility. And when I most needed it, I found I could summon it—that mad, dim hope. It was like bending a spoon with my mind.

Clear-Eyed in Calcutta

FROM *World Hum*

I BLINKED. I MISSED IT. Instinctively, I had closed my eyes. The black goat's head had been pressed down between two small stone pillars, then held in place by a thin metal bar. Swiftly the machete was drawn up into the air—and with no pomp in an otherwise elaborate ceremony, came whooshing down toward the taut, thin neck of the bleating goat. When I opened my eyes after no more than an instant, the two men holding the four legs of the now decapitated animal were flinging the carcass back, away from the altar. The body bounced up against the wall behind them, then slid back a few feet into a pool of water and blood that was gushing from the angry artery of the goat's neck. The legs were still twitching. People, mostly women in colorful dress, rushed in and dipped their fingers into the blood, dabbing their foreheads, and then the foreheads of their children. The small horned head of the sacrificed goat was tossed beside its recently separated torso. All the while, the tongue was protruding, then retracting, as if the animal were gasping for breath it would no longer need. The eyes still appeared to contain life. My recollection is that the goat was still bleating, but that can't be correct.

I had been up in the hill country of West Bengal, in the soft climate of Darjeeling in the Lesser Himalayas, sipping delicate teas and hiking through crisp air over steep trails, before descending into the plains and humid chaos of Kolkata—although everyone I met who lived in the city of 14 million still called it Calcutta.

Little about Darjeeling's charming provincial decay prepared me for Calcutta's assault. Yet in truth, the cacophony and filth and poverty I found on the streets did not approach the squalor I'd always conjured in my imagination whenever I'd heard the word *Calcutta* before I ever saw the place. Only occasionally during my visit, when I would come upon a horribly disfigured small child, or a family of four living in a doorway, did the profundity of human degradation take me so wholly off-guard as to stop me in my tracks or make me gasp.

Like any place that exists with death hovering in such open proximity, Calcutta throbbed with life. The City of Joy's natural condition struck me as one of openhearted generosity.

At the Victoria Memorial, the monumental shrine to the queen left behind by the British, I wondered why the Indians hadn't ripped it down. Sipping tepid, watered-down coffee through a straw, I engaged in a passionate discussion on nuclear weapons and pop music with a few of the local intelligentsia, one flight above the street in the smoky College Street Coffee House. I woke early and got lost among the millions of carnations being strung together for wedding celebrations at the flower market, then walked across Howrah Bridge, one of 6 million people a day who do the same. I attended a raucous and joyful cricket match. I also visited Mother Teresa's Mission of Hope, as well as her Kalighat Home for the Sick and Dying, then her orphanage—I came away with a decidedly mixed feeling about the diminutive nun who was so invested in suffering, and who seemed to me all too human in her love of the spotlight.

But most memorably I walked amid crushing crowds—rarely with a tangible destination. Wholly, thrillingly anonymous, a singular cell pulsing through a giant throbbing organism, I was carried along for hours, relieved of individuality. Smells—cumin and excrement, frying grease, jasmine and human sweat—registered and dissipated without consequence. Images—perilously thin men squatting atop idle rickshaws, naked children peeing in the gutter, stunning young women—all unfurled as I was swept onward. Thoughts slipped past without relevance—my mind rested. Decisions were unnecessary. Life amid so many was cheap. And imperative, the sensation made even stronger at night, when the heat would soften and the dim, straining streetlamps left Calcutta's darker corners to mystery while a gauzy mist hung in the air as people sought respite from overcrowded dwellings.

During the best of my travel, I've felt the relief of locating myself by losing all sense of the familiar. Nowhere did I experience that more than in those swollen masses of humanity.

An introvert by nature, I wasn't a born traveler. Rather, I took to the road as a path away from a natural timorousness—an active effort to move more fully into the world I knew I wanted to inhabit. So when a long-familiar timidity came sneaking back to reassert itself in the instant the machete came sweeping down toward the goat's vulnerable neck outside the Kali Temple, I knew that I would need to return to the site.

Just as years before I had coaxed myself to climb aboard a listing riverboat headed down the Amazon while fear seized me, and as I had marched on through the wheat fields of northern Spain when internal voices urged me to retreat, I was compelled to take one more step in a lifelong journey away from trepidation.

The following day I approached the enclosure behind the temple of the Hindu goddess of destruction. The area was riotous in preparation for the impending Kali Puja Festival. Throngs of the devout were lined up to gain entrance to the temple. Drums were pounded, chanting filled the air. Just as I arrived, a black goat was being led to slaughter.

It strutted confidently through the crowd at the end of a short rope. Between an old man with a long white beard and a black-haired woman in a bright sari, I stood just beyond the sacrificial area—a 10-square-foot pen with burning incense and flowers littering the ground beside the altar. The animal was taken in hand by two men in sweat-stained T-shirts. Its head was shoved down between the pillars, exactly as I had seen done the day before. The condemned goat bleated once. The crowd surged forward. The machete was raised, then quickly brought to bear. The head fell, the body was hurled aside. And people—as by now I knew they would—rushed in to anoint themselves with the sacrificial blood.

My eyes were wide open.

This Must Be the Place

FROM *The New York Times Magazine*

I.

THE A-1 NATIONAL HIGHWAY in Spain heads north from Madrid straight over the Guadarrama Mountains, the peaks jutting like jagged shark teeth that cut the rest of the world away. And then you're floating, up through one last ear-popping *puerta*, or pass, perched above the upper Meseta Central, the football-shaped highlands that cover most of the country's northern interior, the silted land below glinting with flecks of red, gold, and green.

In that moment, you're no longer American, or anything at all. It wouldn't be surprising to see the entire flow of history illuminate that stage: megaraptors skittering after prey; savage packs of prehumans hoarding meat; the Romans building their roads across Hispania, and the Visigoths plotting and conniving; and, after them, the marauding Moors and marauding Christians, pillaging in the name of Allah, God, or chivalry; and then the huge, undulating flocks of sheep, whose wool became a source of Spain's wealth in the 15th and 16th centuries, spurring the grand imperialistic designs of Isabella and Ferdinand that brought the first caravels to the New World . . . and so on.

Harsh and given to extreme weather, the meseta of Castile isn't exactly Tuscany or Provence. It doesn't welcome a traveler with the same fecundity and open arms. From a tourist's perspective, it's a little like visiting South Dakota. You can drive miles on the meseta wondering if you've landed on the most lonesome patch of flash-baked clay in the world—past an abandoned car in a field, past a single tree in an ocean of nothingness—and then from a far hill comes the outline of a church tower, the silhouette of a castle (the reason that this land is called Castile), the clustered homes packed tightly together against what the wild night might bring.

On my first visit to the area more than a decade ago, I spun off the highway at Aranda de Duero and headed northwest through vineyards and sunflower fields, looking for a village I'd only heard about—a place called Guzmán (population: 80). I asked for directions in one small town from a group of old men wearing black berets on a shaded bench, then proceeded lost for half an hour, eventually cloverleafing back to that same exact spot. Finally, I found a thin serpentine road that narrowed as I drove, leading upward again.

And suddenly: tiny Guzmán on its hill, its skyline a cubist jumble but for the bell tower of the church and the square turrets of the *palacio,* as the 17th-century manor house is known. Some of the houses were so decrepit they appeared split open, as if by the fist of a giant. You could see a strewn book, someone's bloomers, artifacts of a lost life. Let there be no doubt, time had had its way here. You might have looked upon this place—and its detritus—and moved right along.

But something happened to me. Even now, I'm not exactly sure what. I have a friend who once told me about the first time he ever took a ferry to an island off the coast of North Carolina, and how he knew, right there on the ferry—with the salt spray and the light off the ocean—that he'd come back to this same spot every year. He'd come to relive that feeling of leaving his old self behind. That annual renewal, the reacquaintance with the person he felt himself to be on that island, was something he wanted to organize his life around. Similarly, Guzmán instantly and improbably became *my place.* It made no sense, practically speaking. Even if I didn't live 3,000 miles away, or if I spoke Spanish, or didn't have a baby at home, it wouldn't have made sense. And that was part of its tug, too. I was certain this town had secrets to tell—and that maybe my best self was there to be found. Sometimes, travel is this elemental: the desire to replace the old molecules with new ones, familiarity with its opposite. To find the kingdom on the hill and stand in awe in its gold-paved streets, even if those streets are strewn, as Guzmán's were, with sheep poo.

II.

You may be reading this on a beach right now. Or in a cabin in the woods. You may be visiting at a friend's cottage. Or you've just returned from Montauk, the Adirondacks, Tuscany. Maybe you're packing to go, checking a list (bathing suits, fishing rods, novels), waiting to board a plane, anticipating what has been a year in the offing: your summer vacation.

It's possible you've found your "place," too, the one to which you return, however temporarily, however near or far. When I was a kid, my family made an annual August pilgrimage to Cape Cod, where we rented a cottage in a little colony that brought the same families back each year. For that week, sometimes two, my father didn't commute or wear a suit and tie to his job, didn't wash the cars or regrout the shower on weekends, or sit at his desk on Sunday afternoon, paying bills, listening to opera. My mother didn't have to pack lunches or crisscross the county with her four sons, ferrying us to practices and music lessons and school events.

Even at the time, I realized my parents were somehow different on vacation, airier and at ease, youthful in their goofiness and laughter, more attentive to us—and each other—for during that one time of year, we mostly had ourselves, without distraction.

There were familiar vacation rites, too: the Sunfish we rented, the board games we played, the custard stand we walked the sandy road to each night. During the day, my father sailed with us, played football on the beach with us, swam with us. We, his sons, would ride his back into the piling waves.

What I now realize as a parent myself is just how much was really at stake on those getaways. And what inordinate disappointment could be evoked if things went wrong. I understand now how desperate my parents, like all parents, really were to "get away," to hit Reset and slip into new skins again—and then bring those people back in the Ford LTD station wagon with us. They talked about their hopes. They read the Cape real estate flyers, dreaming of ownership. And it was sort of the same with us kids: we banded together, arguing less, wore sailor hats bought at some taffy shop, found ourselves jumping off the dunes with other kids from other families. And the picture taking was another cue: this was who we were on vacation—happy, absorbed, alive—lest anyone forget.

And then, it was over.

At the end of the vacation, on the last night, we always built the same UFO. Two thin pieces of wood nailed into an X, candles affixed to the crossbeams. A plastic dry-cleaning bag was attached at the four points of the X. The candles were lighted, filling the bag with hot air, and then the whole thing rose and was blown out to sea, all of us on shore watching it go.

Even the next day, as our packed station wagon followed the jammed highways home, I kept envisioning that UFO aloft, off the coast, over an island, alighting in some foreign country, England, maybe, where everyone wore Beefeater costumes and said, "Pip, pip!" I remember my childish defiance, and having a thought that would return to me over and over as an adult, though now that small loss was connected to a much larger one. The question was, Who says this has to end?

III.

How I came to touch down in Guzmán, Spain—and to think of it as the place where there would be no end—is, like all good travel stories, a tale of going in search of one thing and finding something else, of what happens when you become the UFO and allow yourself to float away.

In 1991, I picked up some part-time work proofreading a monthly newsletter at Zingerman's Delicatessen, an exalted foodie haven in Ann Arbor, Michigan, where the rabid clientele lined up early on football Saturdays to buy their corned beef and pastrami sandwiches. In that era before we could carry on deep conversations about the virtues of Humboldt Fog versus Pleasant Ridge Reserve cheese, the newsletter was a gourmand's playground—and an argonaut's, too. Ari Weinzweig, the author and one of the deli owners, spanned the globe finding unusual and delicious victuals—and the newsletter was packed with culinary stories and histories. October of that year turned out to be "Spanish celebration month" at the deli, and the newsletter sang the praises of various olive oils, sherry vinegars, and Sephardic Jewish cooking, but there was one entry that seemed most remarkable, about a unique, otherwise anonymous Spanish cheese called Páramo de Guzmán. Until that time, it was the most expensive cheese the deli had ever sold, a house cheese from Castile that tilted toward Manchego. "Rich, dense, intense," Weinzweig wrote. "The result is . . . sublime."

According to Weinzweig, it was entirely handmade from an old family recipe, by a farmer from the small village of Guzmán named Ambrosio Molinos. He produced the cheese from the milk of his herd of Churra sheep, in a stable across from the house in which he was born (and his father before that, and his father before that). Ambrosio cut the curd into very small pieces, a time-consuming process that increased the density of the cheese, then aged it in a cave for up to a year, eventually drenching it in olive oil. In keeping with its idiosyncratic, outsider status, the cheese came sealed in a white tin.

At that time, I was monastically broke, too broke in my mind to try even a smidgen of this cheese, but I did rip out and save that four-paragraph entry, and nearly a decade later, in the year 2000, working as a magazine writer, I carried that ripped piece of paper on assignment to Spain, where I went to profile the futurist chef Ferran Adrià, whose culinary innovations and 30-course meals, each new dish served in three-minute intervals, seemed to embody the digital speed of our times.

On that trip, I had Sunday off, so I flew from Barcelona to Madrid, then drove up the gut of Castile and back in time to the cheesemaker's village of Guzmán. It was a lark, perhaps, but it was also a pilgrimage of sorts, my adult self enacting a dream of my younger, poorer self, to try that fabled cheese in that little Castilian village. As I drove, the radio reported more Basque bombings, and the day was so hot, the car tires actually began to melt on the pavement.

I found Ambrosio in the cool of his family cave, or bodega, the place where he aged his cheese. In Guzmán, there existed two dozen or so caves burrowed in the hill that marked the village's northern boundary. Some of the bodegas were said to date back as far as the Roman occupation of Spain. In a time long past, the fruits of the harvest were brought to the caves and stored—grain, apples, and, in particular, cheese and wine, the latter transported in casks made from cured goat carcasses—to be accessed during the harsh winter and spring. Legend had it that a man would sit in a room built above the cave and itemize what went down into the cellars, to report it all back to the lord of the land. This room became known as *el contador,* or the counting room.

As the families in the village built or inherited bodegas, they also added to these counting rooms, sometimes sculpturing a foyer and perhaps stairs that led up to a cramped, cozy warren that included a fireplace. Soon, people gathered at the bodega to share meals around a table and pass the time. And as the centuries unfolded and the caves came to serve a purpose less utilitarian than social, the room took on the other definition of *contar,* "to tell." The *contador,* then, became a "telling room." It was the place where, on cold winter nights or endless summer days, drinking homemade red wine and eating chorizo, villagers traded their secrets, histories, and dreams. In this way, the bodega, with its telling room, became a mystical state of mind as much as a physical place, connecting the people here to their past.

At that first meeting in the telling room, over the course of eight hours, Ambrosio told me a fantastical story. He was a hulking man with mournful eyes. His voice rumbled along, seemingly without breath. Working closely with his mother, he claimed to have recovered the old family recipe (it hadn't been written anywhere, of course), and when the villagers first tried that Molinos cheese, they found it so good that they were transported back to their own mothers' kitchens. As the cheese was passed along, more and more people fell under its sway, until a cheesemonger from Madrid began to sell it in the capital. From there the legend grew: Páramo de Guzmán was sold at Harrods in London, won medals at cheese fairs, and later arrived at Zingerman's Deli in Ann Arbor. It was said to have been served to the Spanish and British royal families, to Ronald Reagan and Frank Sinatra. Julio Iglesias was a fan, and Fidel Castro liked it so much, he tried to buy Ambrosio's entire stock.

As the demand for Páramo de Guzmán increased, it was nearly impossible for Ambrosio to keep pace—milking, boiling, harping the curd, cutting it in fine pieces, etc.—and now there were complicated business concerns imposed on what had, at first, been a very simple act of creation. As Ambrosio unspooled the story that day in his telling room, he said he'd asked his best friend from childhood, a corporate lawyer named Julián Mateos, to help him with the logistical complications of a growing operation, and to help him finance a move to a new cheese factory in a nearby village. Somewhere in all of the expansion plans, Ambrosio, the bohemian creator, claimed (though I would later find out that this claim was contested by Julián with equal insistence) to have been duped, tricked into signing his name to a contract and relinquishing ownership of the company.

That is, he'd actually had his cheese stolen.

So, no, I wasn't going to get a chance to try it, Ambrosio said bitterly. Because he no longer made the cheese.

And then he said he was plotting to murder his best friend. For that seemed the only fitting thing to do.

IV.

There was more, of course. As compelling as the legend of the cheese was (had I really walked into the middle of a murder plot?), and despite the fact that my pilgrimage to eat Páramo de Guzmán had been stymied, I was riveted by something else, something that illuminated a deeper need I hadn't identified before. Ambrosio spoke with such authority, stood so stubbornly in opposition to the world I lived in, that I could feel him lifting me, however momentarily, from the unceasing current of my other life to the shore of his. His words were prophetic, aphoristic, instructive, bawdy, hilarious. He was an amazing storyteller. (I knew this because my friend Carlos had accompanied me there to help translate it all.)

I left and then came back again, three months later, having roped another friend into playing translator, to make sure Guzmán and Ambrosio were real. There was the village, in its worn, November splendor, the wide, empty fields stretching away in robes of ermine and gray—and Ambrosio was exactly as I'd found him the first time, salt of the Castilian earth, adding more axioms to what he called his *filosofía grandísima*.

"The problem with modern life is that nobody knows how to defecate anymore," he said. "This is the most important thing." Then he held forth on the topic for an hour.

"Divinity, not machines," he said at one point, referring to the need for people to raise their animals with care and love, instead of leaving it to the brutal regime of industrial meat farms.

"Pigs need to eat beautiful acorns," he said. "And you need to converse with your chickens." He talked about how the impersonal machinery of modernity had destroyed the values and sensitivities, the tenderness and powerful connection that came from living close to the earth.

I couldn't get enough of this. I returned to Guzmán again—and again—making excuses at home, cashing in frequent-flier miles, or using work as a way to jump the Atlantic, with a side trip to the village. And there I sat for any cluster of days I could get, up in the telling room, like a toadstool, passively absorbing every conversation. The more Ambrosio talked, the more I realized that perhaps I hadn't ever known what I really yearned for. He was sunk into the here and now, while I seemed to spend a great deal of time in my deadline life racing through airports, a processed-cream-cheese bagel in hand, trying to reach the future. But here in the telling room, I sat noticing everything, infused with mindfulness: the pallor of light, the still life of the smooth glass *porrón*—the device from which wine was drunk here—on the grooved wooden table, the oversize man sitting in his shadow, occasionally revealed at angles or by the rumble or ragged passion in his voice.

In Guzmán, where everyone was so welcoming, I didn't feel like a dope for taking the unironic view, or stopping to say hello to the old women who swept out their houses each morning, and then pantomiming the rest. I stood in the middle of a sunflower field at midnight, and it wasn't weird at all. I could hear the hum of stars under that huge Castilian sky, and located the sound of myself thinking. How long had it been since I'd had that kind of clarity or peace? Standing there, I had—call it what you will—a fibrillation of insight, or a crumb-size epiphany.

The intervening voice was simple, almost corny, for it felt so good: *Belong to this.* But to what—a sunflower patch? Or the silence of the Old World? And did I already belong, or was I supposed to belong, aspire to belong, change my life to belong?

Guzmán: The old people here walked so slowly, they seemed to move backward. Besides a handful who worked in the fields, it was hard to tell if anyone had jobs, or deadlines. There was only spotty cell coverage, so eventually I turned off my phone altogether. Besides a bar, there were no stores to speak of (except one bakery run out of Marcos and Elena's house), so money, at least in the town itself, was mostly useless. In conversation, the people constantly invoked the past, and so it was mashed up in and intertwined with the present.

Even the way they said goodbye here—"*Ta l'o,*" which was percussively short for *hasta luego,* and translated as "until later" or "see you later"—suggested timelessness, for it meant the following, all at once: hello . . . so long . . . howareyouagain? . . . untilwepass . . . wearepassingagain . . . oh, hello! . . . goodbye! . . . again? . . . again! . . . and round we go!

At first you might have thought everyone here had short-term memory loss, but it was a rat-a-tat adaptation that captured the circularity of life in a small village and a reminder that, though very much alone and seemingly shipwrecked in the world, these sun-scorched orphans of Castile could at least depend upon seeing one another one more time.

V.

On the wall of my office back home, I pinned a photograph of Ambrosio. Though I'd taken it myself, it looked as if it could have been from a hundred years ago. During our first visit, he led me down 13 steps beneath the earth, to a close, tight space, clean and dry and well ventilated, with PVC pipe running to the surface for air. The floor and walls were stone, and several electric bulbs hung from the ceiling. Along one wall was makeshift wooden shelving where his world-famous Páramo de Guzmán was once kept. Now the planks sat empty. Back in the left corner was a cubby with more rickety shelves where the family stored its homemade wine in unlabeled green bottles. Even as Ambrosio talked on and on, he ducked into the corner, rummaged a little, and returned with an old wooden box. A handgun perhaps, to kill his old friend? Bilbo's ring? He unclasped its hook, reached in, and lifted out something wrapped in chamois—one white tin emblazoned with the black script and gold medal of the original Páramo de Guzmán, all that remained of Ambrosio's grand cheese experiment, of the greatest thing he'd created in his life.

I asked if he'd let me take a picture. He pulled a wooden chair into the middle of the cave and sat, holding the tin in one hand and the oversize key to the bodega in the other. He gazed directly into the camera, conveying measures of pride and sadness, nonchalance and seriousness. In explaining the cave's former function as a storehouse, Ambrosio had conjured "the Old Castilian," the mythic figure in this land who planted and scythed wheat by hand, who endured hailstorms that, in a blink, might viciously erase a year's work in the vineyards. The Old Castilian was guided by a chivalrous code long past, never buckling under the failures heaped upon him by nature or relenting in the face of the enemy. He carried those heavy casks of wine up to the caves on his shoulders, singing a *jota*, where they were counted by the man in the telling room.

Meanwhile, there I sat in my attic, tallying—words on the page, hours until deadline, measly amounts in the college fund. I sat attached to my machines, typing to keep my editors at bay, forfeiting time, staring at the photograph of Ambrosio, day after day. How to explain what it made me feel? It went beyond yearning now. Was it discontentment, the creep of some low-level depression? It was 2002. The world was at war, and I pitched a book proposal about Ambrosio Molinos and his cheese—about betrayal and revenge and happiness—so I'd have a reason to go back to the village. When it sold, I did.

Instead of taking my kids to Disney World, I brought them to Guzmán. For my "job." Instead of meeting my mom in some bucket-list destination a mother has spent a life dreaming of, I made her come to Guzmán, too. Thankfully, my wife loved the place as much as I did. We had another baby, and in the summer of 2003, we rented a house there. Our little girl took her first steps in Guzmán, and uttered her first words, *agua* and *hola*. Our son, walking through the streets one day in the Yankees batting helmet he never took off, was surrounded by sheep heading out to graze on the *páramo*, and the look on his face in that sheep cloud—two parts astonishment, one part *Daaaaad?*—is one a father never forgets.

In the telling room, I heard the legends, about the great Castilian knight El Cid, and the Spanish Civil War, about the local scandals and triumphs and a man who actually flew over the village one night, called to flight by the bones of his grandfather. There was Fernando, neatly dressed in chinos and polo shirt, who stood beneath the tree across the street from the church and never uttered a word. There was Crees, the stonemason, who had vowed that if by the age of 40 he wasn't a millionaire, he'd only do the minimum work required to feed himself, spending his days sculpturing naked women from stone in his studio in the fields.

Was this a Gabriel García Márquez novel? Anything seemed possible in Guzmán, even that I'd get to eat that last tin of the real Páramo de Guzmán. Every visit became stranger, deeper, more real—until I imagined I belonged. When I asked the mayor in the village—a woman with her own stories—if it seemed weird that I kept coming back, she said, "No, we're honored."

Honored? At home, in a mêlée of diapers and tantrums, sweetness, then tossed-over dinners, no one ever said they were especially honored by my presence.

So who were these good people anyway? And how was it that I'd come to need them more than they would ever need me?

VI.

Every year we arrive at this, the season of Facebook travel trills and vacation photos. However envious, I will never say no to viewing my friends' vacation photos, primarily because one of our tacit promises when we travel is that we'll bring back a good story—of our heightened state of living and the exaggerated adventures that befell us—and hope to let others live vicariously through it.

In Guzmán, I wanted the story to last. I wanted to freeze my life inside of it—and that of my family—for as long as possible. No matter what the speed of our American days, no matter how quickly we grew and aged, we'd always have that out-of-time Castilian village on its hill.

As delusional as this false everlastingness was, it gave me unreasonable comfort for some reason. And I had help in prolonging things, from Ambrosio himself. After telling his story of the cheese, he became less interested in talking about the various complicated aspects of it. "Why would you want to ruin a perfectly good day by going over that again?" he asked.

Exactly! There was time to revisit the legend of Páramo de Guzmán some other day. But first, I was happy to follow him out to the fields where he irrigated the crops. Or to help him harvest the grapes. Or to cruise from bar to bar, and town to town, meeting his friends. Here was Pinto, who made the best *rabo estofado*, or oxtail stew, from his mother's old recipe—and the Cristóbal brothers, who served the best roast suckling lamb. Here was Luís, who created antique keys patterned after ones he'd dug out of ruins—of nickel and brass and gold plate, some jointed or with fantastically ornate handles—though they opened no doors, for the doors they might have opened were all gone, lost to history.

If Ambrosio's story was a Slow Food tale gone awry, then what I was doing was Slow Reporting, Slow Thinking, Slow Storytelling, Slow Living. I was doing, I believed, what we all want to do, which is find a way to capture things before they dissolve, to not lose our lives to the relentless pace that keeps us from knowing who we are and what we want.

Not everyone was so charmed by my embrace of the Slow.

I missed the contracted deadline for my book—and then, having been granted a two-year extension, I missed that one, too. Soon, I found myself like Pluto, downgraded from planet to icy rock, orbiting erratically, elliptically. I tried everyone's patience, even that of my wife, who never once doubted the necessity of Guzmán—as a place and an idea—in our lives. But now we'd had our third child, and the book advance had evaporated long ago. And she had a career, too.

At my lowest, I was full of self-chastisements: *Why did you ever believe any good might come from chasing a piece of cheese?* I couldn't quite square my incomplete attempts to bring Guzmán vividly to life on the page with my attempts at reimagining my own life.

I have another friend who begins his annual vacation in Kiawah with a flurry of text messages—a close-up of the sweating gin and tonic on the porch railing, a sunrise beach stretching to some infinity—including triumphal, goading lines like, "Still snowing in Maine?" or "You hit that deadline?" But then, after the first few days, something else begins to happen. The photos are no longer of, say, the perfectly grilled sea bass, or some other marker of his escape, but of his kids. His messages grow forlorn: "Three more days . . . might as well pack up now." "What am I doing with my life?" And always, from the airport before flying home: "I'm dying." It's a joke, of course, but the truth, too—and it's what I was feeling after my protracted time in Guzmán.

I fell into inertia and frustration. I was struck by a Slow Epiphany that the real hindrance to writing this book was that all books, like life, eventually have an end. There's a last sentence, concluding with the report of a bullet-hole period. And then we float into white space.

Somehow the one thing I hadn't considered was that when this story was fully told, then the trip would be over—and I would render myself locked out.

VII.

Which is sort of what happened. Though not entirely. The story got told, and Guzmán gave me more in that regard—stories to tell—than any place I've ever gone or, I imagine, will ever go. I continued to wish I could find any excuse to go there, to sit with Ambrosio in the telling room one more time. But it was harder to justify now. My kids were getting bigger. Life here was intervening. We went as a family one last time.

The Guzmán of all these years later was now a place where there were modern streetlights (gack!), a refurbished *palacio* with actual hotel rooms (but who would come?), a seasonal influx of foreign field hands (mostly Romanians and Moroccans) packed into a couple of houses, eating out of a place that had once been a bar. The bar itself had moved three times, for even a tiny village needed its bar, even if it had nothing else. Ambrosio's beloved father had died—and was buried in the cemetery, where he'd been laid to rest with his head to the south and feet to the north (as opposed to everyone else, who was buried east to west) so that he could keep his eye on the telling room and all the wine drunk there.

Part of coming to the end, then, was allowing it. And coming to an admission: Where the village of Guzmán had been disintegrating on its rise of land that surveyed the meseta, I had hearked upon it, Quixote-like, and saw a lush paradise on its witness hill. Where its inhabitants were all dying their own slow deaths—lung cancer from smoking, failed livers from drinking, bodies beaten by farm labor, psyches weighted with sin and grudges—I'd seen a compelling tableau: kindly old men wearing black berets, women cane-clomping with dignity, all concealing light-filled truths within their secret hearts. If someone coughed up half a lung, graphically cursed the Creator, and spit out some foamy substance at the side of the road, I conceived of it as a sentimental gesture full of hidden meaning. In this world I'd found dusty-booted Ambrosio and fallen in love with the ideal for which he—and his cheese—stood.

I was happy to believe in it, for this is what travel is, too: a kind of childlike wonder—and the sort of woozy love that doesn't contemplate loss—that, when pushed further, becomes life again. There you are, with all your familiar dreams and conflicts, the constant skirmishes between frustration and transcendence, your best and worst selves. However far you go, there you are, with your same fear of mortality, and this deep desire to hold on to your kids forever.

Anyway, I'd like to imagine that Guzmán was in us, that it was no longer only a physical place. Our children remained fondest of stories told out loud. So, our telling rooms were the car, the kitchen, the dinner table. They were the moments after turning out the lights, when we lay next to each other in bed, in whatever combination of parent and child, in tangles of arms and legs, and poured out the last tales of the day in a hush meant to coax sleep but that often provoked the admonition "One more—please?"

At least this was how it felt on the best days, that we could build this little fortress against the crummy things of the world. And I could tell myself that more than a decade spent chasing a piece of cheese had been for a good reason, too. That I'd brought back a new ethos, or an ancient one, and tried to make it work a little in our lives. I still could be seen running through airports with a processed-cream-cheese bagel in my hand, but on weekends, it gave me great pleasure to turn off my phone for a while, to be unreachable. At those times, on a soccer sideline, I was randomly struck by the idea that life was loss, there was no escaping it, and so the best I might do, though never with the same flourish as Ambrosio, was to try to plant myself in the here and now.

It was November when we came into the village just before twilight, the sun sinking beneath the ceiling of clouds to light the land, the thin green murk of day giving way to a brilliant golden glow. We drove to the *palacio*, where we were staying, and when we parked, the children went sprinting off in the direction of the fields, eager to explore and play soccer. My wife and I unloaded the bags and then went ambling along the road down to meet them, one we'd traveled many times that first summer long ago.

There was no one around for this particular homecoming. Not

a soul. And perhaps this was most fitting of all. The houses were shuttered, and not a single window was lighted from within. The air was cool and clean. The village was all ours, until we came to the track that led to the Molinos barn.

As we approached, a huge figure loomed over our youngest, talking rapid-fire in that gravelly baritone. Our boy was looking up at him, head cocked, laughing, uncertain what to make of the giant he'd just met in the twilight of a Castilian village thousands of miles from home.

Ambrosio did what he always does, then, afflicted as he is by that great Castilian generosity: he let us in again. He showed the kids his barn, let them drive the huge tractor. He ferried us up to the telling room, and then out in the fields, to his house there, for a late dinner. Driving us back to the *palacio*, at midnight, he veered to the edge of that serpentine road as it climbed to the village, and then he was out in a vineyard, waving for us to follow. He stood there under a bright moon, with his finger to his lip. "Shhhhh, listen," he said. "If you listen, the silence has a lot to say."

The kids were rapt as my wife and I tried to translate, but sinking together into that earth, I had a feeling I'd had at least a hundred times here. It was that feeling of being a child again, of watching the UFO, of being told the story that would never die. The kids stood clustered around Ambrosio, as he pointed up the hill to Guzmán.

"I think there's something a little bit magical about this place," he said, then drew in a deep breath, and we let it be.

Love in the Time of Coca

FROM *Outside*

WE'RE FLYING IN A CESSNA 180 over jungle so dense that it looks like broccoli. Every so often, the canopy breaks to reveal an emerald patch, which marks the remains of a coca farm. Many of them in this 33,000-square-mile region southeast of Bogotá, called Meta, were wiped out 10 years ago during Plan Colombia, a controversial U.S.-backed antinarcotic operation that included aerial eradication of thousands of acres. The fumigation killed the local campesinos' legitimate crops as well.

Out the window to our right is a flat-topped 8,000-foot mountain. A waterfall flows from top to bottom in such a voluminous cascade that we can see the rising mist from the plane. Like the peak, the waterfall has no name, although it's at the center of 2,430-square-mile Serranía de La Macarena, which became Colombia's first national reserve in 1948.

"All this used to be controlled by guerrillas," Hernan Acevedo, our 42-year-old guide and copilot, tells us through his headset. "So this is pretty much virgin territory."

It's also restricted airspace. Because there are still military operations against guerrillas and drug traffickers here, Acevedo had to get air force clearance. Our Cessna has a sticker on the tail that reads "National Police of Colombia Department of Antinarcotics." It's an essential decal for any pilot to certify that he isn't trafficking drugs.

"This is the first year I've ever flown up here," our pilot, Mauricio Becerra, a 43-year-old software entrepreneur from Bogotá, tells me. "After this trip, you are going to know more of Colombia than ninety percent of Colombians."

Acevedo estimates that he's seen 50 percent of his country. With soulful brown eyes and a subtle sense of humor, he's the son of a doctor-pilot who flew to remote villages to provide pro bono health care. Acevedo and Becerra now fly for Colombia's Civil Air Patrol, a volunteer medical group that recently served 1,584 patients in a village north of Medellín. Acevedo is up in the air so often that his previous girlfriend demanded he choose between her and the plane. (He chose the plane.) Now, as parts of Colombia start to open up after years of paralyzing violence, Acevedo and a handful of his adventurous friends, like Becerra, are eager to explore it all.

In the past few years, international headlines have celebrated Colombia's comeback—and for good reason. With 45 million people, 75 percent of whom live in the five major cities, Colombia is almost twice the size of Texas. It contains three mountain ranges, peaks topping 16,000 feet, some of the most biodiverse habitats in the world, and whole regions of untapped Amazon rain forest. Eleven percent of its territory is protected in national parks, and it's the only country in South America that borders both the Pacific and the Caribbean, with 2,000 miles of coastline. These geographic wonders have made Colombia a grail for adventurers eager to chart the world's last remaining unexplored spaces. They also make the country nearly impossible to connect by road and even more impossible to police.

In 2011, most of Colombia's 1.6 million foreign visitors didn't veer off the Gringo Trail: the colonial Caribbean charm of Cartagena, the Edenic splendor of the Coffee Triangle, and cities like Medellín and Bogotá. But the number of annual foreign tourists is projected to reach 4 million by 2014. Is the rest of the country ready for its close-up? I'm curious to find out.

Today we're starting with a hike to Caño Cristales, known as the River That Ran Away from Paradise. The waterway has reached near-mythic status because of a plant called *Macarenia clavigera*. At certain times of the year, when the plant is in full bloom and the water flows over its tiny flowers, the river turns hallucinogenic shades of blue, red, yellow, orange, and green.

We land in the village of La Macarena, where Consuelo Ramos, a 22-year-old farm girl with a flawless French manicure, greets us. She has spent the past few years studying to be a guide for the local tourism association and walks us through her town of 3,500 inhabitants, where we pass kids playing soccer in the square, soldiers wearing combat fatigues and walking in formation, and silver-haired men sipping coffee at a sidewalk café.

Founded in the 1980s by farmers fleeing violence in Caquetá province, La Macarena exists because it's where the farmers ran out of food. To survive, they picked fruit and carved out a life in the jungle. The Revolutionary Armed Forces of Colombia (FARC) quickly interrupted their peace.

Forty-nine years ago, the FARC started out as the self-proclaimed leftist voice of the poor. By most estimates, it has since become the largest drug cartel in Colombia. In 1998, to start peace negotiations with the group, then president Andrés Pastrana gave it a Switzerland-size piece of land, which included La Macarena, to create a zone that the Colombian army was prohibited from entering. The FARC settled in, recruited soldiers, and grew coca. In 2002, the military reclaimed the zone by force.

To get to the trailhead for Caño Cristales, we motor northeast for about a mile up the Guayabera River in a dugout canoe, then hop in a truck to drive a few miles over a rutted dirt road. When we arrive, I'm surprised to see a small convoy of vehicles, their drivers patiently waiting for visitors to return from the river. On the hike in, we pass a dozen Colombians on the sandy path and a swarm of yellow butterflies flitting in the direction of the Technicolor river. I count 25 vacationers splashing in the fresh pools and picnicking along the shore. Acevedo tells me that an average of 480 tourists per month, roughly 20 percent of them foreign, visit between June and November. Recently, the national airline, Satena, operated by the Colombian air force, started flying from Bogotá to La Macarena on weekends.

Given the area's troubled past, the whole scene is surreal. But La Macarena is a showcase of sorts, a zone in the Colombian outback that the government, with heavy military reinforcement, has designated as a haven of responsible tourism to prove to the world that the country is finally outgrowing its very bad reputation.

Ramos serves us a wrapped banana leaf filled with fried plantains, rice, chicken, and potatoes, and tart lemonade. Then we take a swim. From the looks of these laid-back revelers, Colombians' years of enforced solitude may finally be over.

"I'm not going to lie to you," Acevedo later tells me. "The problems are still here. But we are finally free to go almost anywhere."

In Colombia, however, freedom is a fickle concept.

In 1991, wooed by Gabriel García Márquez's *Love in the Time of Cholera* and the foolhardy antics of Jack T. Colton and Joan Wilder in *Romancing the Stone,* I signed up for a Spanish-language immersion program in Bogotá, unwittingly arriving at the apex of cocaine king Pablo Escobar's power.

By the time of my visit, Escobar had declared "total and absolute war" on the government, according to Mark Bowden in his book *Killing Pablo.* Two years earlier, Escobar had attempted to assassinate presidential hopeful César Gaviria by blowing up an Avianca airliner, killing all 110 passengers on board. (Gaviria was not on the flight.) In Escobar's hometown of Medellín, a sunny, mountainous metropolis that he turned into the most dangerous city on earth, Escobar paid local hit men $2,500 for each cop killed. He also blew up a Colombian police headquarters in Bogotá. In 1990, Escobar kidnapped Diana Turbay, a Bogotá TV news director and daughter of former president Julio César Turbay Ayala. (She was subsequently killed during a rescue operation.) Over the next two decades, abduction would become a primary political weapon and source of income and is still the most effective way for drug cartels and guerrillas to blackmail enemies.

I showed up in March of 1991. For seven weeks, I lived with a family in a gated middle-class Bogotá neighborhood, where an armed guard stood watch 24/7 at the end of the street. On weekdays I would hop a bus to class. On weekends my American and Colombian friends and I frequented mountainside discos, bused to outlying villages, and flew to the Caribbean beaches of Cartagena and Santa Marta. The violence was a bizarre abstraction; I knew it existed, but I never saw it. By the end of April, our professor, Mauricio Barreto, decided that it was too dangerous for us to remain in the country. I wasn't ready to leave. Colombia was mysterious and sensual, from its mist-covered peaks to Fernando Botero's fat sculptures to the sexy couples salsa dancing until dawn. On May 3, my last day in Bogotá, I wrote in my journal: "I know I'm coming back."

When most people think of Colombia today, they still think co-caine, kidnappings, and guerrillas. In 2011, Colombia produced 760,000 pounds of cocaine. Farmers can sell a paste made from coca leaves, which is later processed into cocaine, for roughly $63,500 per pound. Cacao, the source of chocolate and one of the best alternative crops to grow, sells for 75 cents per pound. This is the very simple reason why, as Becerra told me, "as long as there's a demand for drugs, there will be violence in Colombia."

Much of the violence involves armed factions—guerrillas, like the FARC and the National Liberation Army, paramilitaries, and even the Colombian military—terrorizing local farmers for their land. Since 1985, more than 3.5 million Colombians, about 10 percent of the population, have been internally displaced. That statistic surpasses Sudan.

After Escobar was finally gunned down in 1993 by the Colom-bian military—with help from shadowy U.S. forces—the FARC took over the drug trade. Álvaro Uribe, Colombia's president be-tween 2002 and 2010, made it his priority to defeat the guerrillas, funneling money into the military. Between 2002 and 2006, hom-icides decreased by 50 percent, and they've been on the decline ever since.

In 2010, Juan Manuel Santos, President Uribe's minister of de-fense, took office. With $5 billion in U.S. counterinsurgency aid, he pledged to finally end the five-decade conflict, pursuing peace talks with the FARC, whose numbers have dwindled from 17,000 in the 1990s to roughly 9,000 today. As of November, the first talks were held in Oslo, Norway. Every Colombian I spoke to was skep-tical about the outcome, and their caution is warranted. Despite its denials, the FARC still holds captive an estimated 400 civilians and, according to the Colombian attorney general's office, makes an estimated $2.4 billion to $5.5 billion annually from the drug trade and other illicit activities.

Still, 21 years after my first visit to Colombia, I decided that the time had come to return. There had been encouraging signs that the climate for travel had changed. In February 2012, the FARC posted a written statement online—albeit with machine-gun sounds embedded in the page—that it would no longer kid-nap civilians. In April, when Cartagena hosted the Summit of the Americas, Barack Obama became the first president in U.S. history to overnight in Colombia. Paul McCartney even played a sold-out show in Bogotá.

Unfortunately, soon after I booked my flight, the FARC broke its promise and kidnapped a French journalist. I called my former professor to ask whether he thought the situation was really improving. Barreto, now a consultant for Caracol Television, which produces the hit show *Pablo Escobar, Boss of Evil*, was philosophical.

"The moment you start believing what the FARC says, you are in trouble," Barreto told me. "The moment you start believing what the government says, you are in trouble. Always read between the lines in Colombia." He gave a thoughtful pause, then continued, "Right now, the problem traveling here is not the guerrillas. The problem traveling in Colombia is because our roads are terrible."

"There's something you have to know," Acevedo says, gunning his Subaru wagon to pass a gas truck as we begin the 425-mile drive from Bogotá to Medellín. "Colombians are crazy drivers. I'll try to drive as civilized as possible. And that smell in the car? You don't have to worry. I just put on new brakes."

If you want to go off the beaten path in Colombia, it's best to be with people you trust who have fresh information. It's a bonus if they have good brakes. Given these criteria, Acevedo is the man for the job. Armed with two iPhones at all times, he's in constant contact with friends and coworkers all over the country. Two years ago, he was hired as the incoming tourism manager for Voyage Colombia, a large operator, to bolster its eco- and adventure-travel itineraries targeting intrepid Dutch, German, Canadian, and Brazilian tourists. His new branch is one of only four or five outfits with countrywide coverage in Colombia.

"Ask any Colombian and they'll say La Macarena is dangerous," he tells me. "That's why we're looking for *adventure* travelers. But we only go to places the government guarantees there's not going to be a problem."

By the end of this 11-day journey via Cessna, horseback, tractor, Subaru, mountain bike, Twin Otter, and ocean outboard, Acevedo, photographer João Canziani, and I will have traveled a few thousand miles.

At the moment, we are climbing 11,000 feet over the Cordillera Central, then dropping into Armenia, the heart of Colombia's mountainous Coffee Triangle. We'll spend a night at Hotel Bambusa, a peaceful hacienda on a cacao plantation exquisitely renovated by its artist owner, Santiago Montoya. The next morning, we'll drive to Los Nevados National Park, where we'll hike in the Cocora Valley under 260-foot wax palm trees before driving to an evening tutorial in coffee making at Hacienda Venecia. The century-old coffee farm sits on 495 acres nestled in the volcanic hills below Manizales, home to some of the best mountain biking in Colombia. There's no time to ride, though: we're driving on to Medellín in pursuit of yet another incredible network of trails.

The next morning, we meet Acevedo's friend Alejandro Puerta, a 40-year-old production engineer, mountain biker, and, according to his friends, technology nerd. In the past few years, he's used Google Earth to scout an estimated 200 mountain-biking routes all over Colombia. His most epic ride topped out at 15,750 feet on the Nevado del Ruiz volcano.

"I try every week to never repeat the same path," Puerta says.

Today, Puerta, his 38-year-old girlfriend, Mildred Uribe, and friend Carlos Carvajal, a 42-year-old mechanical engineer who just finished circumnavigating South America by bike, are taking us mountain biking on a favorite 20-mile route that follows the Cauca River, north of Medellín, and will end with a feast in Santa Fe de Antioquia, a 16th-century whitewashed colonial town with red-tile roofs and seven churches. On our right are the dry peaks of the Cordillera Central, with the Cordillera Occidental to the left. The smooth single and double track passes fruit orchards and a cluster of expensive-looking vacation homes before passing over a 400-year-old colonial bridge.

"Ten years ago I couldn't do this trip," Puerta says. "We were completely kidnapped inside Medellín. It was terrible." He is speaking figuratively, but his family experienced horrific violence firsthand, and he dislikes discussing the past. "I don't want people to be afraid to come to Colombia," he says. "It's not all drugs. It's not all bad things."

The country's extreme makeover is especially evident in Medellín. In 1991, the city, with a population of 2 million, had a murder rate of 7,081. That same year New York City, with four times the population, had roughly 2,200 murders. Today, Medellín has grown to 3.8 million people; it isn't crime-free, but homicides were reduced to 1,528 in 2011. (By comparison, New York City had 515.) Plus, as Carvajal tells me, its potential for cycling and mountain biking is enormous. On the last Wednesday of every month, he arranges, via social media, La Fiesta de la Bici, a noncompetitive ride that draws an average of 5,000 cyclists.

That evening, as Acevedo accelerates around the curves on the hourlong ride back to Medellín, the moon illuminates the twinkling lights below. As we reach the outskirts of the city, we pass a strip of drive-in lodges with names like Motel Sensaciones and the famous Metrocable, one of two gondolas that provide transportation from the poorest hillside barrios to the city. This gondola, along with a 1,300-foot escalator up another mountain, is connected to a high-speed light-rail system, which allows people in the barrios a way to get to work, reducing crime by more than 50 percent.

Later in the week, we ride the Metrocable at 8 P.M. on a Friday. The city smells like roses and *mani,* sweet roasted peanuts sold by street vendors. It's the eve of the famous Fiesta de las Flores, an annual weeklong party where growers transform Medellín into a garden, erecting brilliant flowery sculptures in every public space available. I watch the Virgin Mary miraculously materialize out of carnations, her image seeming to soothe the country's slowly diminishing posttraumatic stress disorder.

After more than a week of nonstop travel, we're all ready for the *tranquilo* vibe of a beach. We're heading to the central Pacific coast, known to have the best surf in Colombia and also an excellent place to see migrating humpback whales.

"The conditions are so good for nature here that it grows everywhere," says Guillermo Gómez, co-owner of El Cantil Ecolodge, an Eden on the edge of Chocó, Colombia's poorest region.

A former businessman from Medellín, 45-year-old Gómez is wearing flip-flops, board shorts, and a Billabong baseball hat and has the ripped physique of a surfer. As the crow flies, his eco-lodge is 120 miles from Medellín. But because it's accessible only by boat and backs up to one of the thickest jungles in the world, El Cantil might as well be a million miles away. To arrive there we flew into Nuquí, a relaxed village with no roads to the outer world, founded by escaped slaves nearly 200 years ago. Then we motored an hour south down the Pacific coast in an outboard panga.

"The reason the slaves came here," Gómez says, "is that nobody was going to find them."

Drug cartels infiltrate the area for the same reason. Last July, Colombian police seized 388 pounds of cocaine at a covert lab near a beach in Ensenada de Utría National Park, less than 20 miles from El Cantil.

"The cartels aren't interested in making problems for tourists," Gómez reassures me. In the 20 years Gómez and his family have owned their property, they have had very few security problems. Gómez's lodge has such an impressive safety record that when Uribe was president, he called Gómez looking for trustworthy, on-the-ground advice.

To crack down on the cartels, Uribe sent army intelligence officers to infiltrate nearby villages and weed out locals who act as liaisons to the drug runners. These days the cartels keep to themselves, and curious travelers from all over the world are attracted to El Cantil by its stunning location, fresh Chocóan meals, and chic *palafitos*—clean, rustic, oceanside cottages lit by oil lamps and strung with hammocks. This week a high-level international-development worker from the U.S. and his 17-year-old son are here to surf; a Dutch real estate lawyer, his wife, and two teenage daughters came to watch migrating whales; a professor of Latin American history from New York City is here with her two kids to relax before school starts; and a young Australian mining executive and his Colombian girlfriend are taking a romantic break from Bogotá.

"It's actually nice to harbor the illusion that people shouldn't come here," the U.S. aid executive told me as he and his son played cards in the open-air dining room. "Six months ago, my security team told me, 'No, you can't go to Chocó.' I convinced them that if there's a problem, the local *commandante* knows I'm here. I'll just call the police. They know everything that's going on."

Once again, Colombia isn't living up to its deadly reputation. What I'm seeing in front of me is paradise—the turquoise Pacific, black-sand beaches, and so much greenery that even the volcanic boulders sticking out of the ocean are covered in ferns and sprouting palm trees.

What are the odds of a catastrophic mishap for a traveler veering off the beaten path? The answer depends on who you ask and where you are. Even the State Department travel warnings tend to flip-flop: "Security in Colombia has improved significantly in recent years," but "terrorist activity remains a threat throughout the country." An unexpected result of the violence, however, is that most Colombians, perhaps by psychological necessity, crave peace and go out of their way to ensure that foreigners experience it while on their soil.

"Pablo was a real monster, but I chose the right path for me faster because I saw that violence," Gómez told me at dinner one night. "What's going on with this country makes us go deeper."

To attract more tourists, Termales, a fishing village roughly three miles south of El Cantil, has capitalized on what is literally its hottest asset: a sulfur spring. Using government funds, the people of Termales built a jungle spa with mud baths, decks overlooking a river, and beautiful concrete pools. When we arrive, a group of 10 Germans in Speedos are soaking in the springs.

Back at El Cantil, guests gather for a lunch of fresh tuna, coconut rice, fried plantains, and frosty Aguila beers. I nap in the hammock, then borrow a stand-up paddleboard from Gómez's wife, Adriana. It's late afternoon, and the water is choppy. I fall headlong into the salty waves a few times before I sync up with the ocean. Finally, I find my balance and paddle toward the sunlight.

TONY PERROTTET

Birthplace of the American Vacation

FROM *Smithsonian*

ONE OF THE LITTLE-KNOWN turning points in the history of American travel occurred in the spring of 1869, when a handsome young preacher from Boston named William H. H. Murray published one of the first guidebooks to a wilderness area. In describing the Adirondack Mountains—a 9,000-square-mile expanse of lakes, forests, and rivers in upstate New York—Murray broached the then outrageous idea that an excursion into raw nature could actually be pleasurable. Before that date, most Americans considered the country's primeval landscapes only as obstacles to be conquered. But Murray's self-help opus, *Adventures in the Wilderness; or, Camp-Life in the Adirondacks*, suggested that hiking, canoeing, and fishing in unsullied nature were the ultimate health tonic for harried city dwellers whose constitutions were weakened by the demands of civilized life.

This radical notion had gained currency among Europeans since the Romantic age, but America was still building its leisured classes and the idea had not yet caught on with the general public. In 1869, after the horrors of the Civil War and amid the country's rapid industrialization, Murray's book became a surprise bestseller. Readers were enthralled by his vision of a pure, Edenic world in the Adirondacks, where hundreds of forest-swathed lakes were gleaming "like gems . . . amid the folds of emerald-colored velvet." Murray argued that American cities were disease-ridden and filled with pressures that created "an intense, unnatural and often fatal tension" in their unhappy denizens. The wilderness, by contrast, restored both the spirit and body. "No axe has sounded along its

mountainsides, or echoed across its peaceful waters," Murray en-
thused, so "the spruce, hemlock, balsam and pine . . . yield upon
the air, and especially at night, all their curative qualities." What's
more, Murray pointed out, a new train line that had opened the
year before meant this magical world was only 36 hours' travel
from New York City or Boston. The vision struck a deep chord,
and his book ran into 10 editions within four months.

That first summer of '69, the Adirondacks were inundated with
would-be adventurers, each clutching a copy of Murray's volume
(including a tourist's edition in waterproof yellow binding, with
fold-out train schedules and a map)—an influx that was dubbed
"Murray's Rush" by the press. It was a "human stampede," wrote
one modern historian with a florid turn of phrase that Murray
would have appreciated—"like hungry trout on a mayfly-feeding
frenzy." Unfortunately, it was also one of the wettest and coldest
summers in Adirondack history, ensuring that the region was not
quite the Arcadian idyll Murray had depicted. Many of his fol-
lowers arrived woefully unprepared, and as nervous in the wild
as Woody Allen characters today. These Gilded Age city slickers
got lost only a few yards from their camps, overturned their canoes, and became terrified by deer or bear tracks. A late winter
meant that black flies—a biting scourge in the Adirondacks every
June—persisted well into August, and clouds of mosquitoes turned
many campers into raw-skinned wretches. The few rustic inns in
the area, which had previously only catered to a few gentlemen
hunters, were overwhelmed. One hotel became so crowded that
the rapacious owner charged by the hour for guests to sleep on
the pool table. Locals with no experience hired themselves out
as guides to the city rubes, adding to the chaos by leading their
groups astray and camping in dismal swamps.

These pioneer nature lovers were soon derided in the press
as "Murray's Fools" (the book had come out around April Fools'
Day), and the author was denounced by angry readers for grossly
exaggerating the charm of the outdoors. Meanwhile, gentlemen
hunters complained that Murray was too democratic, flooding the
forests with hoi polloi, including, shockingly, women. The young
preacher had even taken his own wife on extended camping trips.
"Let the ladies keep out of the woods," fumed one critic.

Murray was forced to publicly defend himself in the *New York
Tribune*. In a long "Reply to His Calumniators," he pointed out that

he could hardly be held responsible for the dreary weather, including rains that were "ten fold thicker than was ever known." Many first-time campers had failed to heed his tips, he noted, arriving in the wilderness "dressed as for a promenade along Broadway, or a day's picnic." And he predicted that the Adirondacks would become America's "great Summer resort": "Hotels will multiply, cottages will be built along the shores of its lakes, white tents will gleam amid the pines which cover its islands, and hundreds of weary and overworked men will penetrate the Wildness to its innermost recesses, and find amid its solitude health and repose."

Of course, Murray was right, and the outrage over that first summer did not dent the growing popularity of the Adirondacks. When the season of 1870 arrived balmy and clear, the region surged ahead as the country's democratic playground, with Murray as its chief promoter. Now a wealthy celebrity author, he mixed his religious duties with lecture tours around the Northeast, making more than 500 appearances to an estimated half a million Americans in the next three years. His soaring oratory, rugged good looks, and powerful physique made him a huge success, as did his rags-to-riches life story. Raised as a poor farm boy in Guilford, Connecticut, he had started at Yale College wearing handmade clothes and with $4.68 in his pocket. He spent his first summers in the Adirondacks at the suggestion of a friend, and began writing stories about it for a local newspaper. His passion for the outdoors often raised eyebrows among New England congregations: on one occasion, he arrived to give a sermon while still wearing his shooting jacket and hunting breeches, and leaned his rifle against the pulpit.

"Murray was the right person, in the right place, with the right words, at the right time," says Steven Engelhart, executive director of Adirondack Architectural Heritage in Keeseville, New York. Although enlightened American writers like Henry David Thoreau and Ralph Waldo Emerson had argued for the spiritual value of nature as far back as the 1840s and '50s—Emerson even slept out with erudite friends in the Adirondacks, in the so-called Philosophers' Camp on Follensby Pond—their work reached only a relatively small, elite group of readers. But Murray's book, with its direct, straightforward "how-to" tips, mixed with a series of humorous short stories about wilderness camping, truly seized the public's imagination.

The Adirondacks were soon booming. By 1875, some 200 hotels and camps were operating in the mountains, with new stagecoach services rattling from the train stations and steamboats plying the lakes. By 1900, the Adirondacks' summer population had risen to around 25,000 from 3,000 in 1869. Attracted by the fishing and hunting but appalled by the crowds, the Vanderbilts, Rockefellers, Carnegies, Huntingtons, and other fabulously wealthy industrialists built their own spectacular "great camps," where they could disport with their families in private luxury. The American vacation was born—quite literally. The scions of New York City took to declaring that they would "vacate" their city homes for their lakeside summer retreats, and the term *vacation* replaced the British *holiday* in common parlance. As fellow Bostonian Wendell Phillips put it, Murray's book had "kindled a thousand campfires and taught a thousand pens how to write of nature."

Today, New Yorkers have no doubt about the pleasures of escaping the city in summer. Last season, as the canyons of Manhattan began to radiate heat like a pizza oven, I found an original 1869 edition of Murray's guidebook in the archives of the New York Public Library. Its brown leather binding was beaten and cracked, as if it had itself been on a few canoe trips around the St. Regis lakes, but the pages were still intact, and were illustrated with engravings of outdoor life. The abundance of practical advice ("The Wilderness: Why I Go There,—How I Get There,—What I Do There,—and What It Costs") offered a wealth of detail on Gilded Age travel. Murray advised his readers how much to pay a guide ($2.50 a day), how to budget for food ($2 a week), and what to pack ("one pair pliable buckskin gloves, with chamois-skin gauntlets tied or buttoned at the elbow," and, as an insect repellent, "a bottle of sweet oil and a vial of tar").

Sadly, his favorite guesthouses have vanished, including Mother Johnson's inn, where "you find such pancakes as are rarely met with." But the general message of the guidebook could not be more valid today. Within a day's drive for 60 million people lie vast swaths of wilderness, including some 3,000 lakes, that are now protected as part of the Adirondack Park—a sprawling 6.1 million acre reserve that is larger than Yellowstone, Yosemite, and Glacier National Parks combined. The park was created in 1892, as conservationists became concerned at the effects of logging and other industry in the area. The state legislature set aside an initial 680,000 acres to be "forever kept wild" and began purchasing private land as it became available. Today, the Adirondack Park contains a complex mixture of state and private property, with nine different categories of protection. But despite its scale, the park has lost its iconic status. When it comes to wilderness, most of us think first of the western parks.

With a photocopy of Murray's book in my pack, I decided to leave the big city and see how much of the Victorian solitude could be found via Highway 81. Even in 1869, Murray recommended that travelers venture into the genuinely pristine corners—a principle that is rarely observed today. Of the over 7 million visitors who enter the park every year, only a small fraction stray from their cars. "This area is still pretty rugged compared to the rest of the Northeast," says Hallie Bond, former curator at the Adirondack Museum in Blue Mountain Lake. "Instead of agricultural farmland, you're suddenly in dark and forbidding woods, which can be quite daunting. We get some people who arrive in Lake Placid or Lake George"—two crowded tourist centers, their streets lined with clothing chains and fast-food stores—"and think they've seen the Adirondacks."

So I quickly turned off the main roads into Murray's favorite part of the region, which boasted scenery, he wrote, "to rival Switzerland."

As dawn broke the next morning, I was in a kayak on the mirror-still waters of Sagamore Lake and already spotting loons. The sudden emptiness was startling: not a single structure could be seen in the forest, except for the distant form of Great Camp Sagamore, whose wooden façade blended soothingly into the surrounding trees. Dipping my paddle through the rising condensation felt like rowing through the clouds.

For travelers today, the most direct link to the genteel past is by staying in one of the surviving "great camps." These vernacular follies began to sprout across the remotest lakefronts in the 1880s, designed along a uniquely American style pioneered by William West Durant, whose intention it was to literally bring the outdoors inside. They were built from tree trunks with the bark left intact, and their interiors were decorated with local stones, furniture crafted from branches, animal skins, and hunting trophies. After the Great Depression, many of the camps fell into disrepair when their owners' fortunes dwindled. Some burned; others were leveled or imploded with neglect. Today, only about 35 survive, and most are in private hands. But in a democratic process that Murray would have applauded, several of the finest have become available to the public.

Built in 1897, Sagamore was originally one of the many Vanderbilt family estates. Guests arrived by horse-drawn carriage and were welcomed by bonfires and fireworks before adjourning to the rustic chic of their cabins. Descendant Alfred Vanderbilt III fondly likened Sagamore to the fantasy village Brigadoon that magically appeared from the mists. ("As the horses came to rest, the weary travelers knew they had reached heaven.") The decades of social merriment lured guests from Hollywood, including Gary Cooper, Howard Hughes, and Gene Tierney, often to enjoy the luxurious gambling room. The Vanderbilts left in 1954, and the camp was in danger of collapse when it was taken over in 1983 by the not-for-profit Sagamore Institute. Today, its 27 surviving structures have been stabilized and guests can still enjoy the porch of the Wigwam building, for example, with its railing of bark-covered logs, or the open-air bowling alley made entirely from polished timber.

Farther north, by Osgood Pond, White Pine Camp was rescued in the 1990s by a group of history-loving investors. Built in 1907 for the New York banker Archibald S. White, it became "the summer White House" when President Calvin Coolidge moved in for three months in 1926, spending most of his days fishing, often in the company of Herbert Hoover. Today, the olive-green cabins have been refitted with period furnishings, and a slender 300-foot wooden promenade still stretches across the pond to an islet crowned by a Japanese teahouse, an iconic image of the Adirondacks today.

But perhaps the most symbolic restoration story is Great Camp Santanoni, built in 1892 for a prominent Albany banker, Robert Pruyn, and his wife, Anna, whose devotion to nature verged on the mystical. It's the only camp free and open to the public year-round—that is, if you can get there. Cars are forbidden on the grounds, so after I parked at the imposing riverside gatehouse in the town of Newcomb, I set off on a mountain bike along five miles of rough dirt road, passing the remains of the Pruyns' private farm. At last, an enormous log structure loomed from the pine forest, in the final stages of renovation. A lone volunteer caretaker took me through vast empty chambers constructed from enormous logs, as Newcomb Lake shimmered below in the afternoon sun.

When Great Camp Santanoni became part of the state park in 1973, historic structures were simply allowed to decay, or were even deliberately destroyed, to keep the land "forever wild." "They were seen as interfering with the purity of the wilderness," Engelhart explains. In 1979, Great Camp Nehasane, a magnificent edifice by Lake Lila, was obtained by the state and burned by park rangers, at the request of the owners. The loss of such a nostalgic treasure helped galvanize preservationists, and Adirondack Architectural Heritage was formed in 1990 in part to save Santanoni. Visitors began to trickle to the site after it was acquired by the state. "People had no idea," Engelhart recalls. "They would say, 'Oh my God, look what's here!'" In 1983, a new state law was created to help preserve historic sites and granted permission for building repairs. "It was real pitiful at first," recalls local craftsman Michael Frenette, who has worked on Santanoni every summer since 1997. "There was nothing but porcupine scat and rotten lumber." The boathouse had collapsed and was restored from about 30 percent of the surviving structure. Today, visitors can camp, hike, and take free rowboats and canoes out onto the lake.

As I explored, I met another staff member, grad student Nina Caruso. "Robert Pruyn once wrote that 'there is independence, delight, and peace in the isolation,'" she said. "Santanoni still has that. You get a bit of your soul back when you come up here."

It was hard to imagine that anyone had ever thought of letting the elegant edifice vanish. "It's easy to judge, but the nineteen sixties and seventies were the low point of public awareness of the great camps," says Engelhart. "They really saw them as white elephants. But the public's attitude has evolved over time. Today, we see the camps as valuable, because they reflect a design ethic we have come to embrace."

In Murray's day, the remotest corners of the Adirondacks could be reached only by canoe, often along hauntingly beautiful streams and rivulets. It's still the same today. About 1 million acres, a sixth of the park's area, is designated wilderness, its highest level of protection, ensuring that no motorized boats or wheeled vehicles are permitted, not even bikes. The High Peaks region around Mount

Marcy offers the most dramatic topography, and I hiked in to overnight at Johns Brook Lodge, a base for long-distance treks that has been operated by the Adirondack Mountain Club since the 1920s.

But Murray was not a fan of foot travel. With few trails in the 1800s, progress over fallen trees was painfully slow. "Key to Murray's Adirondacks was the idea of hiring a guide and traveling by river," says Bond. Murray waxes lyrical about guides with nicknames like "Snake-Eye" and "Old Mountain," who were raised in tune with nature. His ideal was one John Plumbley, "the prince of guides"—"a man who knows the wilderness as a farmer knows his fields, whose instinct is never at fault, whose temper is never ruffled, whose paddle is silent as falling snow." The Gilded Age guides even designed their own type of canoe, the Adirondack guideboat, with a shallow draft suited to navigate the smallest creeks, and lightweight enough to be carried across land.

For a trip that Murray would have approved of, I headed to the remotest stretch of the park, along the Oswegatchie River near the Canadian border. There, I signed up with Rick Kovacs, the last guide based in the town of Wanakena. "A century ago, there were fifteen guides working this river, each one with his own fishing camp," Kovacs told me as we paddled along the ever-narrowing Oswegatchie, whose waters were a rich brown from the tannin of decaying leaves and branches. "Now we're barely holding on." Like many of the 137,000 year-round residents in the Adirondack Park, he and his family company, Packbasket Adventures Lodge and Guide Service, struggle to make ends meet when the summer season ends.

The river snaked back and forth upon itself in tighter coils, as we paddled beneath enormous half-fallen trees from recent storms. "Easy bends, slow bends, sharp bends, rapid bends, and just bends everywhere," wrote a traveler of his 1907 trip here. Robins swung low overhead, and raccoon tracks could be seen on the banks. At one point, we pulled the canoe over a beaver dam. By late afternoon, we set up camp at the Spring Hole Lean-to. When I dove into the river to cool off, it was like swimming in iced tea.

Not a soul passed us by, and it was easy to assume that little had changed since the 19th century. But nothing in the Adirondacks quite meets the eye.

"It looks like pure wilderness," said Kovacs. "But even back in Murray's day, a lot of the forest was being logged, clear-cut, and burned. In the early nineteen hundreds, a logging railroad even went right by this river. The biggest trees would have been three hundred to four hundred years old, and grown as high as one hundred fifty feet. Even though the logging stopped a century ago, it will take a couple of hundred years more to get back to its original state"—assuming that recent weather extremes, which are affecting the forest, do not take their toll, he adds.

To some, that history of recovery is itself a kind of triumph. "Yes, the vast majority of the Adirondacks was cutover," says Engelhart. "But the fact that we can treat it as wilderness is itself a human creation. We're not leaving a wild area alone—we're recreating a wild area by leaving it alone. To me, that's equally, if not more, beautiful as an idea than if it had always been wild. It shows how we've changed as a people. We agree that wilderness is not something to be exploited, but something to be valued."

There are no physical memorials to Murray in the Adirondacks, so as a final pilgrimage, I sought out his favorite spot. Today, a vintage-style ferry, the *W. W. Durant*, plies the sparkling waters of Raquette Lake, past strings of forested islands, including one named Osprey, which has a small jetty and a residence shrouded by trees. At the height of his celebrity in the early 1870s, Murray returned to this islet for weeks every summer to pitch his tent and entertain a multitude of friends and admirers. One enthusiastic guest, sportswriter Charles Hallock, was particularly taken by the author's "comely wife," who could be seen around the campsite wearing a hunting cap and a "mountain suit of red and crimson plaid. How jaunty she looked!" Another described the islet as "a scene from fairy land," with Murray "perfectly aglow with enthusiasm over the wilderness and its attendant sports." He was also enchanted by Murray's wife, whom he described as 'The Lady of the Lake.'"

William H. H. Murray's subsequent descent into obscurity was as sudden as his rise to celebrity. Tensions with his conservative Boston church led to his resignation in 1874. (He thought more should be done for the city's poor.) Five years later, after investing too deeply in horse breeding and spreading his assets thinly, his finances and his marriage both collapsed, and Murray left New England for the anonymity of rural Texas. He failed in several business ventures, started an oyster restaurant in Montreal, and made a cameo appearance in Buffalo Bill's Wild West show. In 1886, he revived his skills as an orator, narrating for New England audiences a heartwarming series of short stories about the Adirondacks that featured a heroic trapper named John Norton. (They are little read today, since he "mired himself in a kind of nostalgia and sentimentality," one critic notes.) He made enough to repurchase his family home in Guilford, Connecticut, where he died in 1904 at age 64.

Murray's writings were slowly forgotten except among specialist historians. For a few years, his beloved Osprey Island was commonly referred to as Murray's Island, but it eventually returned to its original name. Privately owned, it remains off-limits to the public today. His best memorial is, of course, the Adirondack Park—which, with its complex system of ownership and regulation, is rather like Murray the man, eccentric and imperfect. Despite his midlife wanderings, Murray remained a tireless advocate for the park, insisting on the value of public access. In 1902, two years before he died, he wrote in the outdoor magazine *Field & Stream* that even New York State was only holding the wild lands of the Adirondack Park in trust for future generations. "God made them and made them to stand for what money cannot buy," he declared.

Excuse Us While We Kiss the Sky

FROM *GQ*

AS SINGAPORE AIRLINES Flight 322 descended through the early-morning haze toward Heathrow, Bradley L. Garrett, PhD—just Brad to his research subjects—looked out over the gray sprawl of London spreading to a horizon streaked by sunrise. He was returning from a monthlong study project in Cambodia, and seeing his adopted city of London again, he thought about all the incomparably strange and wonderful things he had witnessed there over four years—all the dizzying heights and hidden depths.

The plane touched down and taxied, its passengers cramped and bleary after the 14-hour flight. But when the aircraft reached the gate, its doors didn't open. After several minutes, the pilot came on the intercom, and Garrett fired off a tweet: "Just landed at Heathrow and we are told the police are boarding our aircraft. Welcome home. x."

A group of officers from the British Transport Police (BTP) entered the plane and came down the aisle. They stopped at his seat, 42K. "Dr. Garrett?" "Yes?" "We need you to come with us." An officer gripped each arm, and they led him down the aisle, past scores of wide-eyed passengers. In first class, former British prime minister Gordon Brown was furious over the delay.

Garrett was handcuffed and led through passport control, where his ID was seized. Fingerprints, mug shots, and DNA swabs followed. He was eventually led to a holding cell and then an interrogation room. There he was told that he was being investigated for burglary and property destruction, among numerous other possible charges. He had been the subject of a lengthy manhunt by the BTP. His alleged crimes were a blatant affront to the image of a high-tech security state London had constructed for itself. And yet, at one point during his interrogation, Garrett said, an investigator leaned across the table and whispered: "Off the record, Bradley, I love the work that you do."

Despite his scholarly bona fides—his doctoral work in geography at Royal Holloway, University of London, had garnered wide acclaim—Garrett scarcely looks the part of an academic, neither tweedy nor fusty. Thirty-two years old, with a trimmed goatee and a mop of straight brown hair hanging over black plastic frames, he grew up in Southern California and ran a skate shop before deciding to pursue a doctorate. His face, which is frequently lit up in mischievous, eyebrow-raised delight, still bears the pocks of over a dozen piercings he dispensed with in the interest of maintaining some veneer of academic respectability.

But it was his doctoral research itself that was perhaps most punk rock. His dissertation in human geography, which he defended earlier in the year, was entitled "Place Hacking." The title came from his argument that physical space is coded just like the operating system of a computer network, and it could be hacked—explored, infiltrated, recoded—in precisely the same ways. He conducted a deep ethnographic study of a small crew of self-described "urban explorers" who over several years had infiltrated an astonishing array of off-limits sites above and below London and across Europe: abandoned Tube stations, uncompleted skyscrapers, Cold War nuclear bunkers, a derelict submarine. The London crew's objective, as much as any of them could agree on one, was to rediscover, reappropriate, and reimagine the urban landscape in what is perhaps the most highly surveilled and tightly controlled city on earth.

The catchall term for these space-invading activities is *urbex,* and in recent years it has grown as a global movement, from Melbourne to Minneapolis to Minsk. The urbex ethos is, in theory, low-impact: no vandalism, no theft, take only photographs; as one practitioner put it, "a victimless crime." Despite some initial skepticism about the legitimacy of the topic by his university advisers, urbex proved to be a rich avenue of inquiry for Garrett—far better than his initial plan to study modern-day Druids. But in the course of his research Garrett had gone native in a big way, acting as both a scientific observer of a fractious subculture and an active participant in its explorations. And he made no excuses for that. "The whole definition of ethnography is that it's participation," he told me. "You go out and you interact with people, and you live with them, and you understand their lives."

One of the risks of going native, of course, is becoming the public face of the movement you are documenting. Earlier in the year, Garrett's face was splashed across the British tabloid media as a de facto urbex spokesman when his crew (whom he also refers to as his "project participants" and "research subjects," depending on the context) released an astonishing series of photos taken high atop the unfinished superstructure of London's 1,016-foot Shard, the second-tallest building in Europe. People were amazed to see shots of black-masked explorers standing casually atop construction cranes, the city glittering below as if viewed from an airplane.

There was some dismay that a city investing well over $1 billion on security in the run-up to the Olympics would be caught offguard so easily. The specter of terrorism was invoked, though Garrett saw his group's role—like that of "white hat" computer hackers—as probing security flaws to expose them and even suggested, half seriously, that he and his crew should be hired as consultants. Garrett looked at exploration more as an act of playful subversion than outright revolution. To prove it, he had invited me to come along and see this hidden world for myself.

I arrived at Heathrow on a redeye from New York at the exact same time as Garrett was being detained. After waiting three hours for him in baggage, I took a cab to his flat in South London. There the mystery deepened. The door frame was splintered, and the shattered door was held shut by a pair of fist-size padlocks. A neighbor told me the police had smashed in the door at 6 A.M., just as Garrett was landing. Three other members of his crew—"research subjects" all—had been swept up in a series of simultaneous raids across London.

As it turned out, the police had not come after Garrett for the notorious Shard tower climb. They were interested in another hack: Garrett's foray into an old World War II bomb shelter. Hundreds of feet below the streets, the Clapham Common "deep shelter" had been mothballed for decades, until the government rented it out to an American secure-file storage company called Iron Mountain. Garrett had found a way in through a massive air shaft a few blocks from his house. A doorway was forced open; then he and several friends rappelled a hundred feet down into the darkness. A magnetic door alarm was disarmed with gaffer's tape, and the group spent an evening cheerfully rummaging through box after box of bank files and legal documents. In his 359-page dissertation, Garrett described exactly how the entire operation was carried out in minute detail, and during his interrogation, the investigators flipped through the phone-book-size tome for reference. There was even a picture of him, grinning impishly, next to a stack of secure-file storage boxes.

Garrett finally arrived at his apartment that evening, 12 hours after he'd been detained. The police had given him keys to the padlocks they'd attached, and the door swung open crookedly. "When they gave me the keys," he said, "I told them, 'I hope you locked my house up better than you lock up your Tube stations.'"

Swigging from the bottle of Jim Beam Black he'd asked me to pick up at duty-free, Garrett surveyed the damage. The police had hoped to find urbex paraphernalia like manhole keys, bolt cutters, lock picks, and high-visibility fluorescent vests used to pass oneself off as a utility worker. Even the curved underwire of a brassiere, which can be used to slip a latch from the outside, would have been considered evidence. But the police had found nothing when they arrived. Garrett had hoped to rent out his small studio on Craigslist while traveling, and the place had been left as empty and spotless as a hotel room.

In the accrued pile of mail on the floor, there was a letter from Oxford University, offering Garrett a paid research position in the coming academic year. He had only to bring his passport to fill out some forms.

"Fuck," he muttered, running his fingers through his hair. His passport, of course, was now in the hands of the British authorities. The Transport Police had interrogated Garrett for hours, asking dozens of questions about his activities and affiliations, all of which he answered with "No comment."

Garrett was understandably despondent, and given the world of shit he had just entered—arrest, police investigation, possible deportation—I assumed that he would wish to beg off on the extensive itinerary he had planned for my visit. I offered to leave him to deal with his problems.

"No way," he said, looking up from the wreckage around him with a grin. "I'm doubling down."

By midnight, five of us were cruising through the streets of South London in a cartoonishly tiny Renault Twingo dubbed the Twinkie, its GPS preprogrammed with the locations of dozens of manholes and Tube stations. I was crammed in with several visiting explorers: Luca, a 28-year-old intensive-care doctor from Italy with a penchant for subterranean exploration; a computer programmer from France named Marc who goes by the nom de urbex Explo; and Helen,* a strawberry-blond 23-year-old photographer from northeast England whose nickname is Urban Fox. Helen loved climbing bridges more than anything: her website showed a nighttime self-portrait, taken high atop the Manhattan Bridge, posed au naturel. Given that our first adventure was subterranean, the only obvious omission was the group's underground guru, Greg—nicknamed Otter after going headfirst into a sewer. He had been arrested in the sweep that nabbed Garrett and had a prior court order banning him from exploring in London.

"He hasn't been banned from exploring," clarified Explo, whose French-and-Cockney-inflected English lent itself well to one-liners. "He's been banned from getting caught."

Still, Otter had kindly traced out a route for us to cross London entirely underground, something Garrett insisted was "a first in human history." Before we set out, Otter had asked if I had ever been in a sewer, and I admitted that I had not.

"I wouldn't go so far as to say it's pleasant," he told me. "But you will be surprised to find how not as bad as you'd think it would be it actually is."

Reassuring. How about safety?

"As long as you time your route with the tides in the Thames," said Otter, "the chance of drowning will be very low."

I see. And will there be rats?

"Lots."

As we passed the hordes of lager louts and lasses lined up out-

---

* Names of some explorers have been changed.

side clubs and vomiting in garbage bins, Garrett expressed his dismay that his own activities were the ones considered inappropriate: "The primary hobby in England is getting absolutely fucked and getting into a fight." Why should an activity as wholesome as urbex be criminalized? He was convinced the authorities found it suspect precisely because it seemed pointless to them and fit no neat theory of social order.

Following Otter's directions, we parked near a railway overpass and quickly suited up in waders and headlamps, trying to look as casual as possible as Garrett and Explo argued over the entry's precise location. When they found it, Explo stage-whispered, "Action!" Garrett pulled out a T-shaped metal key and inserted it into a hatch in the sidewalk. It opened with a rusty shriek. "That's how you pop a lid," he said. In an instant we were piling down slippery rungs into a dank and pitch-black hole. Garrett descended last, and I heard the manhole cover slam shut with a funereal clang.

We walked for what seemed like hours along an eight-foot-high tunnel. The experience encompassed an almost laughable agglomeration of stock phobias—darkness, rats, germs, drowning—but Otter was right: It smelled merely musty, not toxic, like wading down an underground stream, and soon I was swept up in the general enthusiasm of the company. As we started sloshing north, the crew's whoops of delight reverberated—sounding almost Auto-Tuned in the strange acoustics. Garrett told me he had once brought an inflatable raft down here and drifted along with London's effluent flow.

I began to get an inkling of the "radical freedom" Garrett had described in urbex. In his dissertation, he wrote that London's 1,200-mile sewer system has a "noxious comfort." (The system was engineered after the Great Stink of 1858 by Joseph Bazalgette, who might be surprised that he's become an urbex hero, given the honorific J-Bizzle.) Garrett sees the sewers as a zone of total self-reliance and personal responsibility. It was true. In a city said to have 200,000 security cameras, we were unmonitored and completely alone. The compass app on my iPhone was utterly useless, spinning in disoriented circles.

Otter had originally calculated that our journey beneath London, well over 15 miles, would take about 30 hours. But we missed a crucial turn somewhere in the warren of tunnels and soon reached an impasse, our way blocked by a Dantean lake of sewage. Explo wanted to backtrack, and Helen wanted to sleep in the sewer, but logic and exhaustion won out. We popped out into the middle of a quiet side street as a rosy dawn broke over London. We had, by some space-time wormhole, emerged only a few blocks from Garrett's flat, and we stripped off our hip waders before crashing on his floor, filthy and beat, a chair wedged against the broken door.

We continued on, like caffeinated vampires, sleeping by day and exploring the city after dark. Midnight was the new noon. One night we popped a lid on Fleet Street, where London's largest subterranean river flowed beneath the city, and we descended into the Fleet chamber, a massive tidal gate and storm outflow with gorgeous cathedral arches of brick. Almost no Londoner would ever see it, or even be aware of its existence beneath their feet. I glanced nervously at my watch, as the journey was timed with the tide on the Thames. Garrett cracked a beer.

When we came out dripping from the underworld, a double-decker bus rolled past, but the driver paid no attention to our extremely conspicuous group emerging from a manhole at 2 A.M. We circled around the city again, Garrett, restless, looking for something. He spied a 10-story construction site surrounded by chain-link and scaffolding. There was a small gap in the fence, just big enough for Garrett to haul himself effortlessly through. Wary of security guards and cameras, I followed as silently and elegantly as a bear clambering into a Dumpster. We made our way up an internal stairwell to the roof and onto the ladder of a massive construction crane. Finally we were sitting right next to the control cabin 150 feet up, feet dangled over the void, London glittering to the horizon. Garrett pointed out landmarks, famous and less so: Big Ben, the Eye, the Shard, St. Paul's Cathedral, the Gherkin, King's Reach Tower. The names sounded like constellations or rock-climbing routes. In fact, he had summited most of them.

The risks were as real as in mountaineering, of course. Explo had nearly fallen from a church steeple when a rusty ladder rung broke off in his hands, and Otter had once broken his arm in a sewer. A few weeks earlier, there had been a rumor that a Russian explorer had died falling through a skylight while crossing a rooftop. Predictably, the explorers downplayed the risk. "The percentage of us who actually die is pretty low for what we do," said Explo. The urbex ethos precluded suing property owners over injuries, and Garrett described the acceptance of risk, and a sort of dance with it, with a term he'd appropriated from Hunter S. Thompson: *edgework.*

As if to demonstrate the concept, Garrett climbed out onto the 100-foot jib of the crane, angled like a fishing rod high above the city. There was no ladder, nothing between him and the black cabs cruising the street far below. His movements along the fog-slicked struts were as deliberate as a stalking cat's. Edgework.

For Garrett, the thrill of urbex is as much about metaphysical exploration as it is physical adventure. The theoretical DNA of much of his work traces back to the concept of "psychogeography," defined by the French situationist philosopher (and noted alcoholic) Guy Debord in 1955 as "the study of the precise laws and specific effects of the geographical environment . . . on the emotions and behavior of individuals." Debord encouraged a practice called *dérive* ("drift" in French), which entailed wandering through an urban landscape guided only by shifting feelings, unmoored from the duties and associations of daily life. This means of spacily rebooting the urban environment is taken to its logical extreme with urbex.

The canonical text of the urbex movement is a book called *Access All Areas,* a work that's meant as both a spiritual and practical guide to a hobby that counters a consumer culture filled with "safe and sanitized attractions that require an admission fee." Its pseudonymous author, Ninjalicious, was a 31-year-old Canadian named Jeff Chapman, who had first written about his exploits in the 1990s in a self-published zine called *Infiltration.* Chapman died of cancer in 2005, just weeks before his book was published, lending his life's work an aura of unimpeachable, almost Christ-like authenticity.

Garrett sees his work as restoring the true spirit of Ninjalicious, pushing the urbex boundaries beyond the trendy venues: derelict and abandoned buildings, which he considers easy prey. The urbex term for derelict structures is *derp,* exemplified by the postapocalyptic photography nicknamed ruin porn. "The roots of urban exploration are actually in infiltration, and we've forgotten that as a community," said Garrett. "We're bringing it back to its core. We're seizing it from those fucking ruin fetishists." Garrett calls for a more radical set of tactics for what he calls "live sites":

places in active use. He sees this kind of unsanctioned access as the best means to regain freedom in a society that is utterly cordoned and securitized. As a sort of calling card, he carries sheets of stickers that read EXPLORE EVERYTHING, which he affixes everywhere he goes.

Some cities are more suited to this go-anywhere philosophy than others. London's vast security apparatus, for instance, presents a set of challenges that could be described as Orwell Lite: ubiquitous cameras, by-the-book cops, and a passive-aggressively reinforced expectation of propriety. This can add to the thrill, of course, but when the State kicks in your door, it's always a bummer. Paris, on the other hand, is spoken of in the urbex scene in the way Okies might have invoked California. "In Paris, they don't give a shit," said Garrett. "The quality of life is so much higher there, because people let you get on with what you want to get on with. They're not in your face all the time about it."

Garrett had initially suggested we go there, but given the confiscation of his passport, it was out of the question. Britain had become a prison island for him, and he didn't want to risk hacking his way out and back in again. But Explo and Helen wanted me to see it, and Otter wanted to go somewhere he wasn't legally enjoined from exploring, so we packed our gear and contorted ourselves obstetrically into the Twinkie and made for the Chunnel.

The following midnight I found myself following Explo's command of *Action!*, climbing after him over a construction fence surrounding a half-built office tower named Carpe Diem in the central business district of Paris. We found the main stairwell and humped 38 stories up, legs burning, gasping for breath. There were a half dozen explorers in the group, including Patch, a 25-year-old Brit who was currently wanted in London on the same warrant for which Garrett had been arrested. Patch's most recent job was as a stock manager at a big-box store, but for now he was staying in a squat and planning to return to London in a few months when the heat was off.

We came out onto the darkened concrete roof and then scaled the metal stairs of a looming tower crane, sweat freezing in the now alpine air. In the sharp wind, the crane swiveled side to side like a giant weathervane. Paris flowed and pulsed 600 feet below us, but it was eerily quiet at that height. In the distance, the Eiffel

Tower erupted into a glittering laser-light spectacle to mark the hour. Several people crammed into the operator's cab of the crane, which—*quelle surprise!*—still had the keys in it. Someone scrolled through the crane's commands on its touch screen. I asked them to *stop touching the fucking buttons, please.*

Exiting the building site after the long walk down, Explo whispered in a mock video-game voice: "Level Two, complete."

It occurred to me then that Explo's cry of *Action!* at the beginning of each adventure had a double meaning. It was both a call to arms and a director's command in the fantasy movie of his own life, in which he was the auteur and hero both. The urbex life is at heart a form of play, a pressure valve to regulate the atmospheric crush of daily life. Explo, at his programming job, might daydream of a manhole in the floor of his cubicle, of some escape from the mundane requirements of society. Once you begin playing this game, the entire world becomes filled with secret doors.

Some doors hide better secrets than others. One afternoon as we weaved through chaotic traffic, Explo pulled up next to a middle-aged black man with long dreadlocks and an army jacket, sitting on a park bench. "*Ça va*, Dirty?" he called, sticking his head out the sunroof. They conversed rapidly in French, then Explo popped back down. "That's Dirty. He invited us to a party later. It's funny, I consider him a friend and yet I've never seen him more than ten meters from a manhole. He's a cataphile."

A cataphile is an aficionado of the vast network of catacombs, quarried over centuries from the soft limestone beneath the city. Nobody knows for sure how far they extend, but more than a hundred miles of tunnels have been charted, underlying a tenth of Paris—a city of darkness beneath the City of Light. Barely a mile of the catacombs is open to the public, but a wide subculture of the creative and clandestine have used the network for decades. Late that night we returned to the same spot where Explo had spotted Dirty. There was a steel hatch right on the sidewalk, and Explo pointed out the places where it had been repeatedly spot-welded shut by the police and subsequently broken open by the cataphiles. He glanced around, quickly pulled the lid open, and we descended a dark ladder.

From down a stone side passage came the sound of echoing

laughter, the smell of hash smoke, and the flickering yellow light of a carbide lantern. Dirty held court before a half dozen visitors, dripping candles affixed around the room. He told me he had come down for a party 62 days ago and just decided never to leave except to resupply and use the facilities. (There are no bathrooms belowground.) He warned me to "respect the catas." The tunnels were originally begun as quarries but have served over the years as smuggling routes and ossuaries. During World War II, the Nazis and the Resistance had neighboring catacomb bunkers, each unaware of the other's existence. Explo pointed to an inscription carved in a stone monument dedicated to the memory of Philibert Aspairt. Like J-Bizzle in the sewers of London, Aspairt is a legend of the catacombs. He went missing while exploring down here in 1793, but his body wasn't found until 1804. We were having a party in his tomb.

Dirty led us down a narrow tunnel, which opened up into a large gallery. The leave-no-trace ethic of place hacking doesn't exactly apply in the catacombs; rather, they are a vast work in progress, just like the city above. Graffiti pieces and stencils covered the walls. More ambitious artists had carved relief sculptures into the stone itself, and one had spent what must have been weeks installing a graffiti mosaic out of thousands of tiny tiles. There was a lending library stocked with moisture-swollen paperbacks and a huge lounge table carved from a block of stone. In places along the tunnel, side shafts had been dug, called *chatières*, literally "cat flaps," connecting branches or forming new chambers. All this work had been done in total darkness, 50 feet below the streets, all for the delight and edification of the relatively small group of adventurers who might find their way there.

After we made our way out, I sat in a sidewalk café in broad daylight, drinking a café au lait and eating a perfect *galette au chèvre*, refusing to acknowledge to gawkers that I was aware I was covered head to toe in beige catacomb mud. So much of urbex is an exquisitely crafted inside joke, done for its own beautifully pointless sake, like the explorer who put a necktie on a statue in the pediment of the Panthéon, 120 feet above the Latin Quarter. He did tag a photo of it on Flickr, of course.

That day we napped on the grass beneath the Eiffel Tower, its riveted latticework swooshing into the blue heavens. Surely it would be the greatest climb in all of Paris, I observed. Explo agreed, were it not for the heavily armed soldiers patrolling its base. But he said he knew somewhere else just as sublime.

At the stroke of one, the spotlights that bathed Notre Dame Cathedral in a noontime glare were finally flipped off, and a group of singing drunks gathered along the Left Bank brought out their congas. This provided excellent cover as Explo, Helen, Otter, and I crossed the Pont Saint-Louis to the Île de la Cité and clambered around a corona of iron spikes 40 feet above the Seine. We crossed a shaded park and scaled another spiked fence, careful not to snag backpacks heavy with camera equipment and enough mountaineering gear to assault the Matterhorn. We spoke in whispers as we pulled on climbing harnesses, and looked up through the darkness at the soaring Gothic buttresses and pinnacles of the irreplaceable monument of world heritage we were about to climb.

I felt a twinge of conscience. Or rather, something more than a twinge. They warn you in journalism school—or so I hear—about the risks of going too deep with the subjects of your work, of losing grasp of the dispassionate objectivity necessary to report a balanced story. Garrett had already dealt with this ethical quicksand by surfing gleefully across it, unashamed of his decision to "become a part of the culture under study," as he put it. I stood before the same quagmire. It wasn't really about breaking the law, as I'd already done that many times over in two different countries. Standing there at the base of the 850-year-old cathedral, I felt conflicted between my deep desire to climb it and my equally deep desire to not be splashed across the French tabloids as the idiot American who snapped off a gargoyle.

But Explo was already halfway up, and he soon anchored a climbing line to belay us from above. I let the tide of *Action!* bear me along and started up the rope using special spelunking ascenders attached to my harness. I promised Explo to omit a few salient details about our route from this narrative; suffice it to say, nothing was harmed in the climb. But the intimacy with the building was startling. I passed so closely by a carved gargoyle I could see the furrows of its brow. Atop the first roof, we found ourselves in a long gallery of flying buttresses, which spanned outward like the landing struts of some alien spacecraft. Each buttress framed a 50-foot arched stained-glass window, darkened from within, and as we climbed to the next level, I pulled myself up next to one. I spun slowly on the rope, and for a heart-stopping instant my shoulder rested gently against the glass. I was so close I could see the seams of lead that connected the thousands of pieces of colored glass, the end result of centuries of labor at the hands of nameless artisans. I felt in that moment I would rather fall than damage it.

Three hours and three pitches brought us to the peak of the south transept, 180 feet above the Seine, which flowed past inkily as the drunks still drummed on the far side. My hands were black from the lead roof tiles. Carved saints and angels and a demonic bestiary of gargoyles peered from every nook, and the central steeple pierced the night sky. I'm not a believer at all, but I felt something akin to what I'd always imagined to be the intended reaction to a great cathedral, some visceral mix of awe and fear.

Over by the bell towers, you could see the corralled viewing platform where the public is allowed. No doubt it's great. But as the urbex ethos has it, buying a ticket, and obediently going the way you are told, is the exact opposite of the point. So there we were, at 4 A.M., witness to a sublimity almost nobody else would ever know. As it happened, the French Resistance had rung the cathedral's bells this very night in 1944, to signal the liberation of Paris. It was not nearly the same scale of freedom, of course, but it sufficed. As the first glow of dawn began to fade out the stars, we rappelled down, scaling the fences and dropping back onto the waking street.

Returning to London, we found Garrett trying to bring some order to the chaos that had spun out of his life. He had gotten his door replaced, though it would likely be months before the State got around to compensating him for it. But his fate was far from clear. Since he couldn't leave the UK, he would likely have to cancel a talk he was scheduled to give for Google in Arizona (topic: "Exploring the World Around Us"), and his job offer from Oxford might be threatened by his tenuous legal status. For all he knew, he'd be deported after his court hearing in a few months. But his spirit, to all outward appearances, was unflagging.

Garrett wanted to show me one final site, the gargantuan art deco hulk of the Battersea Power Station, with its four chimneys reaching 340 feet. Battersea is the iconic structure on the cover of Pink Floyd's *Animals*, a great ruined dinosaur skeleton of industrial civilization. It's been derelict since the early '80s and the subject of an endless string of redevelopment boondoggles. Most recently it had served as a parking lot for hundreds of police vehicles during the Olympics.

Waiting for a security patrol to roll by, we squeezed through a hole in the fence, sprinted across a weedy no man's land, and clambered up stairwells through the pigeon-flapping blackness. The power station's control room was the size of a basketball court, a steampunk fever dream of endless dials and switches and levers, like an analog nerve center for the "city of tomorrow" of yesteryear. The sense of touching unsanitized history, of being able to measure time in the accumulation of dust, was enormously powerful. Garrett threw levers back and forth, flipping dead switches in some sort of *Doctor Who* fantasy. "This is what they won't let you do in museums," he said.

We climbed higher and emerged into the rainy night, onto the scaffolding surrounding one of the chimneys, and scaled it to its top, halfway up the southwest stack, which was big enough to swallow a double-decker bus. A wavering reflection of London slid by on the surface of the Thames several hundred feet below, and trains maneuvered by at tilt-shift scale. The city looked like a misty diorama.

But an explorer can never rest, least of all Bradley L. Garrett, PhD. "Everyone's bored here; everything's been done," he said, fretting that all London's mysteries had been plucked. "We're just sort of waiting for the next big thing."

People tend to age out of urbex, to get respectable and lose the spark of curiosity that called them to explore in the first place. There are very few people who do it after 40, he told me. He hoped he could avoid that fate. He looked forward to the 20-mile super-sewer project, scheduled to be finished by 2025, and to the Crossrail tunnel, both being dug beneath London. And even if he were deported, banished from this island that had offered him such incomparable visions, there were always other options, other places. He'd heard of a secret Soviet subway system beneath Moscow. And the colossal sewers of Tokyo. Or the Second Avenue subway line being dug beneath Manhattan. He had always fantasized about piloting a tunnel-boring machine. The world was full of hidden possibilities.

Dream Acres

FROM *Outside*

MY TWO BROTHERS and I, along with a buddy of ours named Dan Bogan, own a shack at a place called Saltery Cove on Southeast Alaska's Prince of Wales Island. The shack is about 36 feet long and 12 feet wide, with the warped shape and discoloration of a cardboard shoebox that's been soaked in the rain. A partially uprooted old-growth hemlock leans menacingly over the back corner, and the front deck sits about seven feet above the shoreline on wooden pilings that are in various stages of decay. The tidal fluctuations in this area are so wild that the shack might be 200 yards away from the water's edge in the morning and then be at risk of becoming oceanic debris by lunchtime. When friends come to visit, they often scrutinize the engineering as though reluctant to commit their full weight to the structure, let alone sleep inside it. While doing so, they're prone to asking questions like "What made you guys buy this place?" with a weird inflection that seems to betray a hint of pity.

My usual, flippant reply is that real estate cliché about location, location, location. The appeal of our shack isn't so much the structure itself, but rather the bare-bones nature of its locality. Surrounded largely by the Tongass National Forest, it's a place where black bears gnaw mussels from the rocks in what might be described as our yard and killer whales pass by so close that you can hear them even with the door closed. But in truth that's only half the answer. The other half is more difficult to explain and also a bit masochistic: Saltery Cove is a place where everything—the weather, the ocean, the mountains, the people, the trees, the animals, even the buildings—seems capable of kicking your ass in a very physical way. And in today's increasingly tame and virtual world, where our primary sensations tend to be delivered by our Wi-Fi connections, a good old-fashioned ass kicking is something worth paying for.

Another way in which the cabin kicks my ass is through my wife, Katie. She often regards my purchase of the shack with that eye-rolling sense of dismissal that people will use when confronted with the subject of their spouse's past girlfriends or boyfriends. Not that Katie, a publicity director for a high-profile publishing house in Manhattan, entirely disapproves. Rather, she just feels that the expense of maintaining our "second home" is grossly incommensurate with how much time we spend there. When I try to justify the costs to her, I point out that it's not so much a second home as a first shack, and also that it could someday prove to be a good investment. When those justifications fail, I hit below the belt and tell her that I'd intended for it to be my primary place of residence but had willfully sacrificed that dream in order to stay close to her—my true love. That usually does the trick.

The purchase occurred during my late 20s, well before I'd met Katie. It was a time when I was more or less aimlessly bouncing around the country with little or no responsibility. In 2003, this landed me on Prince of Wales Island. I went there with my brother Danny to fish salmon and halibut with one of Saltery Cove's eight full-time residents, Ron Leighton, a man of mixed Native Alaskan and Irish descent who'll tear your head off for tangling an anchor line and then send your kid a birthday present even though the nearest mailbox is an hour's boat ride from his house. Ron's résumé includes a tour of duty as a door gunner in Vietnam, a career as a detective with the police force in Ketchikan, Alaska, and a parallel career as a halibut long-liner. He and Danny originally met when Danny traveled to Saltery Cove to do some environmental survey work through his job as an ecologist at the University of Alaska. Ron offered to put him up and show him around during his stay, and they struck up an unlikely friendship. Then, about a year after my own initial visit (a trip that included meal upon meal of self-caught shrimp, crab, and halibut), Ron called Danny to tell him that the shack across the creek from his house had been put up for sale by its owner.

The price was $80,000, nonnegotiable. Danny recognized that this was a lot of money for one guy to pay, especially for a place that might get knocked into the water by a hemlock and float away. Twenty grand, on the other hand, seemed reasonable. All he had to do was find three other guys who felt the same way. He called me in Rhode Island, where I was living in a short-term rental that sat so close to the water, I could watch movies in my living room at night while holding a fishing rod baited for eels and cast into the bay. I'd just sold my first book for what seemed like a staggering sum of money, and since I was still a few years away from adult responsibility, I knew I'd end up blowing my windfall on outdoor gear and alcoholic beverages. That I could take permanent possession of a setup similar to the one I was now enjoying—albeit 3,000 miles away—was an irresistible notion. Our brother Matt and our buddy Dan were equally intrigued. The four of us mailed in our checks.

Danny and I were the first ones to plan a visit. To get there from his house in Anchorage, where I'd been staying for a couple of months, we ended up flying into Seattle and then transferring planes to Ketchikan, a town with an airport that happens to be on a different island from the town itself. We collected our bags and then dragged them down a long ramp toward a ferry dock. After crossing to Ketchikan, we dragged the bags up another ramp and waited in the rain for a cab. Since this was our only chance to stock up on provisions, we made the rounds to the grocery, hardware, and sporting-goods stores. By then it was too late to get a floatplane, so we booked a hotel and caught a shuttle to the docks at dawn. There we loaded our supplies into the plane and flew over Clarence Strait toward the jagged and serpentine coastline of Prince of Wales Island, a landmass half the size of Hawaii's Big Island but with three times as much coastline.

Danny and I will forever remember the month that followed as the summer of trash. When we climbed off the floatplane to behold our new treasure, we were greeted by a two-acre parcel of garbage to which we now held the deed. There were steel barrels of chemicals such as kerosene, water sealer, and gear oil made useless by the intrusion of rainwater that had dripped through rust-perforated lids. Dozens of empty barrels, concealed beneath layers of moss, gave the landscape a bumpy look that reminded me of a rash. Elsewhere we found Styrofoam blocks as big as bathtubs, a mound of fiberglass insulation the size of a car, enough rotted lumber to build a rotted house, and what would eventually turn out to be 150 gallons of crushed beer cans. Two sheds made of plastic sheeting had simply collapsed over time, burying piles of junked fishing gear, inoperable chainsaws, rusted hardware, busted-up shrimp and crab traps, and coils of cracked plastic hose. When we opened an outhouse toward the back of the property, near the national-forest border, we found that both the hole and the structure had been filled with household garbage.

The only thing more staggering than the volume and variety of the trash was the fact that it had all come in on boats and planes, presumably over the course of many decades. There was no economically feasible way for us to get it out of there and into a landfill, so we did the only thing that made sense. In a weird moment of clairvoyance, I had packed along my flame-retardant military flight suit, and this became my uniform for the next month as Danny and I built infernos of burning trash with smoke plumes rivaling those seen on news broadcasts dispatched from Kabul.

In the evenings, we worked on the much more pleasurable task of learning to navigate the labyrinthine networks of straits and fjords and islands that stretched for watery miles away from our place. Initially, we stayed inside an area known as Skowl Arm; we were afraid to cross into the treacherous waters beyond, known as Clarence Strait, because of a nautical chart that someone had nailed to the wall of the shack with the words *Do Not Go* written across the entrance to the strait in red marker. But of course our curiosity overrode our caution, and one night we found ourselves out there in a 16-foot open-bowed skiff with a stalled engine and no radio. We were drifting so fast on the outgoing tide that it felt like we could pull a skier. Just as I began calculating how long the 10-pound halibut in the bottom of the boat would stave off starvation as we drifted toward death on the open sea, the engine popped to life with a puff of black smoke and we beelined for the safety of sheltered water. At the end of that month, when the floatplane finally picked us up for the trip back to Ketchikan, we circled around and passed over the shack. I looked down at it like a rodeo rider might view a bull that had just bruised him up. He knows it's a lot of trouble and that it doesn't make a lick of sense, but he's already planning another ride.

*

When I started dating Katie, I would try to impress her with stories of the cabin. I promised to take her up there and get her hooked into a halibut that was so big we'd have to sink it with a harpoon in order to drag it into the boat. She now admits that the bravado kind of turned her on, though she has a hard time explaining how my stories resulted in her mistaken impression of the shack as some kind of classy Aspen-style retreat where you stroll out to the hot tub in a white robe with a wineglass dangling between your fingers.

In reality, the hot tub that we rigged up prior to Katie's first visit was a livestock watering tank that we had shipped up on a barge from Seattle and then set out on some rocks by the stream. It was powered by an ingenious woodstove that circulated water through a heating box by means of its own convection currents.

Other improvements over the years included an adjoining workshop to store boat engines and tools. This freed up space in the shack's sleeping area so that it could actually be used for sleeping. Also, we'd worked out the problems in our plumbing system, which meant you could more reliably take warm showers using water that was diverted from the creek and heated with a propane burner.

In fact, the place had gotten so comfortable that my two brothers figured it would be a perfect time to introduce their significant others to the shack as well—along with Danny's three-year-old daughter. And in case things weren't quite cozy enough with seven people sharing three bunk beds and well under 500 square feet of space, we extended an invitation to our friend Brandt and his new girlfriend.

I was a tad worried about the crowding issue, but in hindsight I should have been much more concerned that it was midwinter. The area gets an average of 160 inches of precipitation per year, about four times as much as Seattle, and the bulk of that seemed to fall during Katie's stay. On her trip out to the cabin, she got stuck in a Ketchikan hotel because of the weather. When it finally cleared enough for her to get to the shack, it promptly turned shitty again once she landed. For days, the wind howled and snow dumped. We got out in the boat only a few times. Once, when we took a ride to set crab traps and ran out of daylight about two miles from home, the engine hit a submerged log with such ferocity that the bow of the boat dipped below the surface and scooped out a wave's worth of water, which flooded through the vessel like a tsunami. We bailed it out with a solemnness that came from knowing that we were maybe just a few gallons away from a capsized boat and possible death by hypothermia.

Another outing in the boat occurred during a storm surge that pushed the high tide up over the porch, and we had to chase down all the gear and food that had been swept into the ocean. The surge also caused a temporary shutdown of what so far had been the trip's one salvation, the hot tub. Its creekside location offered scenic views plus a handy source for changing the water. But when the high tide backed up the creek, all you could see of the tub was the top of the chimney. When the tide fell we moved the tub to higher ground and filled it with water siphoned from the creek with a long hose. Then the improperly drained hose froze and ruptured, so we were unable to change the water when it became soiled with dirt and spruce needles and the general funk caused by nine human inhabitants and a spilled White Russian that gave the water a milky tint. The tub's popularity waned significantly after that, though not as badly as my own after announcing that I'd miscalculated the kerosene usage and we'd soon have no way to heat the shack.

One of the best things about life is that now and then, when we're lucky, the reality of a situation rises up to meet our hopeful expectations. I thought of this a couple of summers ago, when Danny and his significant other, Corrina, got married on a grassy beach across the cove from our shack under sunny summer skies. Well over a dozen friends and family were gathered for the celebration. Salmon rolled in the stream mouth and flashed spectacularly during the ceremony. A bear sow and her two young cubs appeared down the shore and seemed to pose, as though Steve Irwin had been resurrected as a wedding planner. In the evening we gathered on the deck, drinking beer and boiling crabs and expecting at any minute the deck to finally collapse beneath the weight of all our friends.

It held firm and was still standing strong in the morning as the guests packed up their sleeping bags and tents and boarded planes headed to Ketchikan. Later that day, I took Katie out on the water and fulfilled at least part of my seductive promise. Although the halibut she caught wasn't big enough to require a harpoon, it was her first nonetheless. That night, she glowed with pride as we grilled a fillet of the fish. I served it with leftover boxed wine poured from the liner bag that someone had thoughtfully pinned under a rock beneath the creek's surface. After dinner, we went down to the shoreline and watched the light fade. We'd been married a year at that point. Something about the experience—maybe the air, maybe the wine, maybe the residue of hopefulness left over from a day of fishing—caused her to say that she was ready to have a baby so long as I was up for it. We were leaning against the gunwale of a beached skiff, and we just stood there for a while in silence. There was a mountain empty of people behind us, an ocean full of fish in front of us, and at our side a cabin in the slow and steady process of accumulating memories. And in that moment I could see clearly why I'd bought a place that was so hard to get to: even if I had to leave right then, I couldn't.

Now We Are Five

FROM *The New Yorker*

IN LATE MAY of this year, a few weeks shy of her 50th birthday, my youngest sister, Tiffany, committed suicide. She was living in a room in a beat-up house on the hard side of Somerville, Massachusetts, and had been dead, the coroner guessed, for at least five days before her door was battered down. I was given the news over a white courtesy phone while at the Dallas airport. Then, because my plane to Baton Rouge was boarding and I wasn't sure what else to do, I got on it. The following morning, I boarded another plane, this one to Atlanta, and the day after that I flew to Nashville, thinking all the while about my ever-shrinking family. A person expects his parents to die. But a sibling? I felt I'd lost the identity I'd enjoyed since 1968, when my younger brother was born.

"Six kids!" people would say. "How do your poor folks manage?"

There were a lot of big families in the neighborhood I grew up in. Every other house was a fiefdom, so I never gave it much thought until I became an adult, and my friends started having children. One or two seemed reasonable, but anything beyond that struck me as outrageous. A couple Hugh and I knew in Normandy would occasionally come to dinner with their wrecking crew of three, and when they'd leave, several hours later, every last part of me would feel violated.

Take those kids, double them, and subtract the cable TV: that's what my parents had to deal with. Now, though, there weren't six, only five. "And you can't really say, 'There *used* to be six,'" I told my sister Lisa. "It just makes people uncomfortable."

I recalled a father and son I'd met in California a few years back. "So are there other children?" I asked.

"There are," the man said. "Three who are living and a daughter, Chloe, who died before she was born, eighteen years ago."

That's not fair, I remember thinking. Because, I mean, what's a person supposed to do with *that*?

Compared with most 49-year-olds, or even most 49-*month*-olds, Tiffany didn't have much. She did leave a will, though. In it, she decreed that we, her family, could not have her body or attend her memorial service.

"So put *that* in your pipe and smoke it," our mother would have said.

A few days after getting the news, my sister Amy drove to Somerville with a friend and collected two boxes of things from Tiffany's room: family photographs, many of which had been ripped into pieces, comment cards from a neighborhood grocery store, notebooks, receipts. The bed, a mattress on the floor, had been taken away and a large industrial fan had been set up. Amy snapped some pictures while she was there, and, individually and in groups, those of us left studied them for clues: a paper plate on a dresser that had several drawers missing, a phone number written on a wall, a collection of mop handles, each one a different color, arranged like cattails in a barrel painted green.

Six months before our sister killed herself, I made plans for us all to gather at a beach house on Emerald Isle, off the coast of North Carolina. My family used to vacation there every summer, but after my mother died we stopped going, not because we lost interest but because it was she who always made the arrangements and, more important, paid for it. The place I found with the help of my sister-in-law, Kathy, had six bedrooms and a small swimming pool. Our weeklong rental period began on Saturday, June 8, and we arrived to find a delivery woman standing in the driveway with seven pounds of seafood, a sympathy gift sent by friends. "They's slaw in there, too," she said, handing over the bags.

In the past, when my family rented a cottage my sisters and I would crowd the door like puppies around a food dish. Our father would unlock it, and we'd tear through the house claiming rooms.

I always picked the biggest one facing the ocean, and just as I'd start to unpack, my parents would enter and tell me that this was *theirs*. "I mean, just who the hell do you think you are?" my father would ask. He and my mother would move in, and I would get booted to what was called "the maid's room." It was always on the ground level, a kind of dank shed next to where the car was parked. There was never an interior stairway leading to the upper floor. Instead, I had to take the outside steps and, more often than not, knock on the locked front door, like a beggar hoping to be invited in.

"What do *you* want?" my sisters would ask.

"I want to come inside."

"That's funny," Lisa, the eldest, would say to the others, who were gathered like disciples around her. "Did you hear something, a little whining sound? What is it that makes a noise like that? A hermit crab? A little sea slug?" Normally, there was a social divide between the three eldest and the three youngest children in my family. Lisa, Gretchen, and I treated the others like servants and did very well for ourselves. At the beach, though, all bets were off, and it was just upstairs against downstairs, meaning everyone against me.

This time, because I was paying, I got to choose the best room. Amy moved in next door, and my brother, Paul, his wife, and their 10-year-old daughter, Maddy, took the spot next to her. That was it for oceanfront. The others arrived later and had to take the leftovers. Lisa's room faced the street, as did my father's. Gretchen's faced the street and was intended for someone who was paralyzed. Hanging from the ceiling were electric pulleys designed to lift a harnessed body into and out of bed.

Unlike the cottages of our youth, this one did not have a maid's room. It was too new and fancy for that, as were the homes that surrounded it. Traditionally, all the island houses were on stilts, but more and more often now the ground floors are filled in. They all have beachy names and are painted beachy colors, but most of those built after Hurricane Fran hit the coast, in 1996, are three stories tall and look almost suburban. This place was vast and airy. The kitchen table sat 12, and there were not one but *two* dishwashers. All the pictures were ocean-related: seascapes and lighthouses, all with the airborne Vs that are shorthand for seagull. A sampler on the living-room wall read *Old Shellers Never Die, They Simply Conch*

Out. On the round clock beside it, the numbers lay in an indecipherable heap, as if they'd come unglued. Just above them were printed the words *Who cares?*

This was what we found ourselves saying whenever anyone asked the time.

"Who cares?"

The day before we arrived at the beach, Tiffany's obituary ran in the *Raleigh News & Observer.* It was submitted by Gretchen, who stated that our sister had passed away peacefully at her home. This made it sound as if she were very old, and had a house. But what else could you do? People were leaving responses on the paper's website, and one fellow wrote that Tiffany used to come into the video store where he worked in Somerville. When his glasses broke, she offered him a pair she had found while foraging for art supplies in somebody's trash can. He said that she also gave him a *Playboy* magazine from the 1960s that included a photo spread titled "The Ass Menagerie."

This was fascinating, as we didn't really know our sister very well. Each of us had pulled away from the family at some point in our lives—we'd had to in order to forge our own identities, to go from being *a* Sedaris to being our own specific Sedaris. Tiffany, though, stayed away. She might promise to come home for Christmas, but at the last minute there'd always be some excuse: she missed her plane, she had to work. The same would happen with our summer vacations. "The rest of us managed to make it," I'd say, aware of how old and guilt-trippy I sounded.

All of us would be disappointed, though for different reasons. Even if you weren't getting along with Tiffany at the time, you couldn't deny the show she put on—the dramatic entrances, the nonstop, professional-grade insults, the chaos she'd inevitably leave in her wake. One day she'd throw a dish at you and the next she'd create a stunning mosaic made of the shards. When allegiances with one brother or sister flamed out, she'd take up with someone else. At no time did she get along with everybody, but there was always someone she was in contact with. Toward the end, it was Lisa, but before that we'd all had our turn.

The last time she joined us on Emerald Isle was in 1986. "And even then, she left after three days," Gretchen reminded us.

*

As kids, we spent our beach time swimming. Then we became teen-agers and devoted ourselves to tanning. There's a certain kind of talk that takes place when you're lying, dazed, in the sun, and I've always been partial to it. On the first afternoon of our most recent trip, we laid out one of the bedspreads we had as children, and arranged ourselves side by side on it, trading stories about Tiffany.

"What about the Halloween she spent on that army base?"

"And the time she showed up at Dad's birthday party with a black eye?"

"I remember this girl she met years ago at a party," I began, when my turn came. "She'd been talking about facial scars, and how terrible it would be to have one, so Tiffany said, 'I have a little scar on my face and I don't think it's so awful.'

"'Well,' the girl said, 'you would if you were pretty.'"

Amy laughed and rolled over onto her stomach. "Oh, that's a good line!"

I rearranged the towel I was using as a pillow. "Isn't it, though?" Coming from someone else, the story might have been upsetting, but not being pretty was never one of Tiffany's problems, espe-cially when she was in her 20s and 30s, and men tumbled helpless before her.

"Funny," I said, "but I don't remember a scar on her face."

I stayed in the sun too long that day and got a burn on my fore-head. That was basically it for me and the beach blanket. I made brief appearances for the rest of the week, stopping to dry off after a swim, but mainly I spent my days on a bike, cycling up and down the coast, and thinking about what had happened. While the rest of us seem to get along effortlessly, with Tiffany it always felt like work. She and I usually made up after arguing, but our last fight took it out of me, and at the time of her death we hadn't spoken in eight years. During that period, I regularly found myself near Somerville, and though I'd always toy with the idea of contacting her and spending a few hours together, I never did, despite my father's encouragement. Meanwhile, I'd get reports from him and Lisa: Tiffany had lost her apartment, had gone on disability, had moved into a room found for her by a social service agency. Per-haps she was more forthcoming with her friends, but her family got things only in bits and pieces. She didn't talk *with* us so much as *at* us, great blocks of speech that were by turns funny, astute, and so contradictory it was hard to connect the sentence you were hearing to the one that preceded it. Before we stopped speaking, I could always tell when she was on the phone. I'd walk into the house and hear Hugh say, "Uh-huh . . . uh-huh . . . uh-huh . . ."

In addition to the two boxes that Amy had filled in Somerville, she also brought down our sister's ninth-grade yearbook, from 1978. Among the messages inscribed by her classmates was the following, written by someone who had drawn a marijuana leaf beside her name:

> Tiffany. You are a one-of-a-kind girl so stay that way you unique ass. I'm only sorry we couldn't have partied more together. This school sux to hell. Stay
> - cool
> - stoned
> - drunk
> - fucked up
> Check your ass later.

Then, there's:

> Tiffany
> I'm looking forward to getting high with you this summer.

> Tiffany,
> Call me sometime this summer and we'll go out and get blitzed.

A few weeks after these messages were written, Tiffany ran away, and was subsequently sent to a disciplinary institution in Maine called Élan. According to what she told us later, it was a horrible place. She returned home in 1980, having spent two years there, and from that point on none of us can recall a conversation in which she did not mention it. She blamed the family for sending her off, but we, her siblings, had nothing to do with it. Paul, for instance, was 10 when she left. I was 21. For a year, I sent her monthly letters. Then she wrote and asked me to stop. As for my parents, there were only so many times they could apologize. "We had other kids," they said in their defense. "You think we could let the world stop on account of any one of you?"

We were at the beach for three days before Lisa and our father, who is now 90, joined us. Being on the island meant missing the spinning classes he takes in Raleigh, so I found a fitness center not far from the rental cottage, and every afternoon he and I would spend some time there. On the way over, we'd talk to each other, but as soon as we mounted our stationary bikes, we'd each retreat into our own thoughts. It was a small place, not very lively. A mute television oversaw the room, tuned to the Weather Channel and reminding us that there's always a catastrophe somewhere or other, always someone flooded from his home, or running for his life from a funnel-shaped cloud. Toward the end of the week, I came upon my father in Amy's room, sifting through the photographs that Tiffany had destroyed. In his hand was a fragment of my mother's head with a patch of blue sky behind her. Under what circumstances had this been ripped up? I wondered. It seemed such a melodramatic gesture, like throwing a glass against a wall. Something someone in a movie would do.

"Just awful," my father whispered. "A person's life reduced to one lousy box."

I put my hand on his shoulder. "Actually, there are two of them."

He corrected himself. "Two lousy boxes."

One afternoon on Emerald Isle, we all rode to the Food Lion for groceries. I was in the produce department, looking at red onions, when my brother sneaked up from behind and let loose with a loud *"Achoo,"* this while whipping a bouquet of wet parsley through the air. I felt the spray on the back of my neck and froze, thinking that a very sick stranger had just sneezed on me. It's a neat trick, but he also doused the Indian woman who was standing to my left. She was wearing a blood-colored sari, and so she got it on her bare arm as well as her neck and the lower part of her back.

"Sorry, man," Paul said when she turned around, horrified. "I was just playing a joke on my brother."

The woman had many thin bracelets on, and they jangled as she brushed her hand against the back of her head.

"You called her 'man,'" I said to him after she walked off.

"For real?" he asked.

Amy mimicked him perfectly. "For real?"

Over the phone, my brother, like me, is often mistaken for a woman. As we continued shopping, he told us that his van had recently broken down, and that when he called for a tow truck the dispatcher said, "We'll be right out, sweetie." He lowered a watermelon into the cart, and turned to his daughter: "Maddy's got a daddy who talks like a lady, but she don't care, do she?"

Giggling, she punched him in the stomach, and I was struck by how comfortable the two of them are with each other. Our father was a figure of authority, while Paul is more of a playmate.

When we went to the beach as children, on or about the fourth day our father would say, "Wouldn't it be nice to buy a cottage down here?" We'd get our hopes up, and then he would bring practical concerns into it. They weren't petty—buying a house that will eventually get blown away by a hurricane probably isn't the best way to spend your money—but still we wanted one desperately. I told myself when I was young that one day I would buy a beach house and that it would be everyone's, as long as they followed my draconian rules and never stopped thanking me for it. Thus it was that on Wednesday morning, midway through our vacation, Hugh and I contacted a real estate agent named Phyllis, who took us around to look at available properties. On Friday afternoon, we made an offer on an oceanfront cottage not far from the one we were renting, and before sunset our bid was accepted. I made the announcement at the dinner table and got the reaction I had expected.

"Now, wait a minute," my father said. "You need to think clearly here."

"I already have," I told him.

"Okay, then, how old is the roof? How many times has it been replaced in the last ten years?"

"When can we move in?" Gretchen asked.

Lisa wanted to know if she could bring her dogs, and Amy asked what the house was named.

"Right now it's called Fantastic Place," I told her, "but we're going to change it." I used to think the ideal name for a beach house was the Ship Shape. Now, though, I had a better idea. "We're going to call it the Sea Section."

My father put down his hamburger. "Oh, no, you're not."

"But it's perfect," I argued. "The name's supposed to be beachy, and if it's a pun, all the better."

I brought up a cottage we'd seen earlier in the day called Dune Our Thing, and my father winced. "How about naming it Tiffany?" he said.

Our silence translated to: *Let's pretend we didn't hear that.*

He picked his hamburger back up. "I think it's a great idea. The perfect way to pay our respects."

"If that's the case, we could name it after Mom," I told him. "Or half after Tiffany and half after Mom. But it's a house, not a tombstone, and it wouldn't fit in with the names of the other houses."

"Aw, baloney," my father said. "Fitting in—that's not who we are. That's not what we're about."

Paul interrupted to nominate the Conch Sucker.

Amy's suggestion had the word *seaman* in it, and Gretchen's was even dirtier.

"What's wrong with the name it already has?" Lisa asked.

"No, no, no," my father said, forgetting, I think, that this wasn't his decision. A few days later, after the buyer's remorse had kicked in, I'd wonder if I hadn't bought the house as a way of saying, See, it's just that easy. No hemming and hawing. No asking to look at the septic tank. Rather, you make your family happy and iron out the details later.

The cottage we bought is two stories tall and was built in 1978. It's on proper stilts and has two rear decks, one above the other, overlooking the ocean. It was rented to vacationers until late September, but Phyllis allowed us to drop by and show it to the family the following morning, after we checked out of the house we'd been staying in. A place always looks different—worse, most often—after you've made the commitment to buy it, so while the others raced up and down the stairs, claiming their future bedrooms, I held my nose to a vent and caught a whiff of mildew. The sale included the furniture, so I also made an inventory of the Barcaloungers and the massive TVs that I would eventually be getting rid of, along with the shell-patterned bedspreads and cushions with anchors on them. "For our beach house, I want to have a train theme," I announced. "Trains on the curtains, trains on the towels—we're going to go all out."

"Oh, brother," my father moaned.

We sketched a plan to return for Thanksgiving, and after saying goodbye to one another, my family splintered into groups and headed off to our respective homes. There had been a breeze at the beach house, but once we left the island the air grew still. As the heat intensified, so did the general feeling of depression.

Throughout the '60s and '70s, the road back to Raleigh took us past Smithfield, and a billboard on the outskirts of town that read, WELCOME TO KLAN COUNTRY. This time, we took a different route, one my brother recommended. Hugh drove, and my father sat beside him. I slumped down in the back seat, next to Amy, and every time I raised my head I'd see the same soybean field or low-slung cinderblock building we'd seemingly passed 20 minutes earlier.

We'd been on the road for a little more than an hour when we stopped at a farmers' market. Inside an open-air pavilion, a woman offered complimentary plates of hummus served with a corn-and-black-bean salad, so we each accepted one and took seats on a bench. Twenty years earlier, the most a place like this might have offered was fried okra. Now there was organic coffee and artisanal goat cheese. Above our heads hung a sign that read, WHISPERING DOVE RANCH, and just as I thought that we might be anywhere, I noticed that the music piped through the speakers was Christian—the new kind, which says that Jesus is awesome.

Hugh brought my father a plastic cup of water. "You okay, Lou?"

"Fine," my father answered.

"Why do you think she did it?" I asked as we stepped back into the sunlight. For that's all any of us were thinking, *had been* thinking since we got the news. Mustn't Tiffany have hoped that whatever pills she'd taken wouldn't be strong enough, and that her failed attempt would lead her back into our fold? How could anyone purposefully leave us, *us,* of all people? This is how I thought of it, for though I've often lost faith in myself, I've never lost it in my family, in my certainty that we are fundamentally better than everyone else. It's an archaic belief, one that I haven't seriously reconsidered since my late teens, but still I hold it. Ours is the only club I'd ever wanted to be a member of, so I couldn't imagine quitting. Backing off for a year or two was understandable, but to want out so badly that you'd take your own life?

"I don't know that it had anything to do with us," my father said. But how could it have not? Doesn't the blood of every suicide splash back on our faces?

At the far end of the parking lot was a stand selling reptiles. In giant tanks were two pythons, each as big around as a fire hose. The heat seemed to suit them, and I watched as they raised their heads, testing the screened ceilings. Beside the snakes was a low pen corralling an alligator with its mouth banded shut. It wasn't full grown, but perhaps an adolescent, around three feet long, and grumpy-looking. A girl had stuck her arm through the wire and was stroking the thing's back, while it glared, seething. "I'd like to buy everything here just so I could kill it," I said.

My father mopped his forehead with Kleenex. "I'm with you, brother."

When we were young and set off for the beach, I'd look out the window at all the landmarks we drove by—the Purina silo on the south side of Raleigh, the Klan billboard—knowing that when we passed them a week later I'd be miserable. Our vacation over, now there'd be nothing to live for until Christmas. My life is much fuller than it was back then, yet this return felt no different. "What time is it?" I asked Amy.

And instead of saying "Who cares?" she said, "You tell me. You're the one with a watch on."

At the airport a few hours later, I picked sand from my pockets and thought of our final moments at the beach house I'd bought. I was on the front porch with Phyllis, who had just locked the door, and we turned to see the others in the driveway below us. "So is that one of your sisters?" she asked, pointing to Gretchen.

"It is," I said. "And so are the two women standing on either side of her."

"Then you've got your brother," she observed. "That makes five—wow! Now, *that's* a big family."

I looked at the sunbaked cars we would soon be climbing into, furnaces every one of them, and said, "Yes. It certainly is."

PETER SELGIN

My New York

A Romance in Eight Parts

FROM *The Missouri Review*

> And with the awful realization that New York was a city after all
> and not a universe, the whole shining edifice that he had reared
> in his imagination came crashing to the ground.
> —F. Scott Fitzgerald, "My Lost City"

NOT LONG AGO, while lurching through cyberspace, I chanced upon a luncheon menu from Schrafft's, circa 1962. Especially among the city's working women, Schrafft's was once New York City's most popular restaurant chain. The menu is an arresting artifact, one that might have been concocted to certify an era's lost innocence—how else account for Jellied Tomato Bouillon, Browned Lamb Hash with Wax Beans, Deviled Tongue and Swiss Cheese Sandwich, Corn Soufflé, Minute Tapioca Pudding, Fresh Banana Stuffed with Fruit Salad, Green Apple Pie, and Grape-Juice Lemonade? Top center on the menu: "May We Suggest Bacardi Cocktail 70¢."

My eyes misted over. Here was the New York City I once fell hard for, the city of my childhood and young dreams. And though the menu belonged to a vanished time, still, it was real—as the Hotel Paris had been real, as the passenger ships lined up in their berths had been real. As my innocence, my ambitions, my disappointments, my failures, and a host of betrayals—mine, my father's, the city's—all had been real.

I. Love at First Sight

GAS HEATS BEST. They loomed: black, blocky letters on a yellow field painted on the side of a gargantuan corrugated hatbox. An ad for home heating fuel. But to my six-year-old eyes, it might have been God creating Adam in the firmament of the Sistine Chapel.

It was my first trip to New York with my father. His "business trips," he called them, though someday I would learn there was more to them than that. My twin brother, George, and I took turns, each of us going with him every other Friday. The trip took just a little over an hour, but as far as I was concerned, we might have been blasting off to Venus or Mars.

We rode in my father's Simca, an ivory wagon with whitewalls and a split tailgate. I watched him work the gearshift, a thin chrome rod with a pear-shaped knob—an object of fascination that I would secretly commandeer whenever Papa went into the post office or the bank, my vocal cords imitating the engine's winding RPMs, ignorant of such things as clutches. As Papa backed the Simca past the dying birch tree in the turnaround, I'd see my brother and my mother standing there, my mother waving, my twin crying—as I would cry a week later when it would be George's turn. Why our father took us separately I'm not sure. Maybe because we fought so much.

At the end of the driveway we'd take a right onto Wooster Street and head to Danbury, where we drove past the war memorial and the fairgrounds. On Old Route 6 we'd pass by the Dinosaur Gift & Mineral Shoppe with its pink stucco tyrannosaurus, headed toward Brewster. Interstate 684 had yet to be built, so we rode on what would today qualify as "back roads," past apple orchards, nurseries, and reservoirs, then down the Saw Mill River Parkway through exotically named places—Croton Falls, Katonah, Armonk, Chappaqua—tallying bridges and groundhogs.

While driving, my father hummed: "The Blue Danube," a Maurice Chevalier ditty, his cigarette dangling. He drove with an elbow out the window, preferring his arm to the car's turn signal. The Simca's glove compartment burst with road maps, but my father never consulted them. The city's outskirts were a tangle of parkways, thruways, expressways, and turnpikes. That my father could untangle them amazed me, but then they seemed to belong to him, all those highways, as did everything to do with the city.

We crossed over the Henry Hudson Bridge. At the tollbooth, Papa tossed a nickel into the yellow basket. We glided under the girders of the George Washington Bridge. Here the city began in earnest. We passed the Cloisters and Grant's Tomb. Among drab shapes in the distance I saw patches of bright color, the funnels of passenger ships in their berths. To our left as we drove on, a skyscraper garden flourished, the Empire State Building sprouting like a deco fountain at its center. Amid this profusion of architecture rose the fuel storage tank, the one proclaiming GAS HEATS BEST. This utilitarian structure was no less awe-inspiring to me then than the *Queen Elizabeth* or the Empire State Building, subjects I'd sketch again and again in Mrs. Decker's kindergarten class.

The elevated ended; the Simca descended into a shadowy jungle of bumpy cobblestone streets. Somewhere along Canal Street we parked. Gripping my hand, Papa led me from one industrial surplus store to another, foraging for plastic and other parts for his inventions, his rotary motors, his color coders, his thickness gauges and mercury switches. The sidewalks were crowded, yet somehow to me the people weren't real. They reminded me of the baubles on a Christmas tree, each with its particular charms and quirks but, unlike the buildings, insubstantial. There were no dogs and few children. New York City was a place for grownups.

From Canal Street we walked to Chinatown, where we ducked into shops packed with lacquered trays and jade carvings. Here the streets smelled of fish. In one of those shops, my father bought me a wooden box (I still have it; it sits on top of the bookcase by the desk where I write). In Chinatown the plethora of street signs, their messages transformed into adornments by virtue of being illegible, impressed me even more. The enigmatic characters clung to the air, butterflies caught in a web of utility lines and fire escapes.

Then to Greenwich Village, where we entered boutiques lush with beads and trinkets and suffused with the smell of incense, and where one shop window confronted us with a panoply of chessboards and pieces carved from rare woods and exotic minerals. Already I had begun to see the city as a colossal museum, with objects displayed in various galleries according to periods and styles. Beyond displaying its holdings, the city had no discernible purpose. It existed for roughly the same reason as the town park on Lake Candlewood or the Danbury State Fair: to amuse the likes of me.

We lunched at Schrafft's, then drove back uptown toward our hotel, stopping on the way at Manganaro's Italian import store, where my father bought a pound of Parmesan cheese—a jagged hunk broken off a great golden wheel. By then the air had dimmed, the better to display the lights of Times Square, where flashing neon signs advertised everything from Pepsi-Cola to Castro Convertibles and a giant man in a fedora exhaled smoke rings from a cigarette into the electrified dusk. Then up West End Avenue to the Hotel Paris.

Of all parts of the city, that hotel was my favorite, a wedding-cake-shaped fortress of garnet-colored bricks topped by a crenellated water tower, with a flagpole reaching even farther toward the sky. I recall a lobby of pink marble walls with a mirrored dining room adjacent and a caged, old-fashioned elevator attended by a colored lady (I use the term in keeping with the times), whose beehive of fire-engine-red hair was as imposing as she was diminutive. She let me man the controls, a courtesy for which I will never forget her. You had to pull back on the lever just so, or the elevator and the floors wouldn't line up properly. She put her brown hand on top of mine, her warm grip guiding me. At each floor the doors opened to different hallway carpeting, arabesques of blazing bright color that, in their inscrutable intricacies, mimicked the metropolis outdoors.

Like all the rooms in the Hotel Paris, ours was small. It stank of the last occupant's cigarettes, which was okay by me. I accepted the odor as part of the city—my father's city, it came to seem to me, as if he had laid every brick and cobblestone and erected every skyscraper. As he unpacked his suitcase on the bed, I watched, engrossed. A suit jacket, a pair of socks, two pairs of underwear, a can of athlete's-foot powder, his safety razor and battered shaving brush, a shoehorn, and a necktie.

The necktie fascinated me most. Though I'd seen it often before, hanging in his closet back home, here it took on a new aspect. With its yellow paisley drops against a maroon background, it was no longer just my papa's necktie; it was his New York City tie. At that moment, that necktie became the city for me, as the stale cigarette smell in that hotel room became the city, and the gaudy hallway carpeting, and the red-haired elevator operator, and the hunk of Parmesan cheese, and the passenger ships in their berths, and the GAS HEATS BEST sign, and the groundhogs digging holes in the lawns along the Saw Mill River Parkway. It was all my New York back then, courtesy of my father, who had invented it just for me.

II. Puppy Love

At 15, my friend Chris Rowland and I used to visit his neighbor Clara. A spry, matronly woman in her 80s, she lived across the street from the Rowlands in a white shingled cottage by the brook. Chris would bring a casserole his mother had made. Clara would thank him and put it away. Then we'd sit in her parlor, Clara in a thronelike wicker chair, eating cookies with cider while she sipped tea from a china cup. We thought it was tea.

New York City was Clara's favorite subject. She still kept her apartment there. She spoke of how, in her younger days, she and a friend had opened a teashop in Chelsea, and of the Broadway actors and actresses who had patronized it. "Oh, we had quite a time of it, quite a time," said Clara, fanning herself with a Japanese fan.

One day Clara gave us the keys to her apartment. Chris's father drove us to the station in Brewster. Through the green-tinted window—to the rhythmic clacking of train wheels—we watched the familiar world of houses, church steeples, and trees morph into a landscape of buildings, viaducts, and bridges. Then we plunged underground. For a while everything turned black. We stepped out of the train car to find ourselves in a grimy marble cathedral vaulted with sallow stars.

At the newspaper kiosk, Chris bought a box of Good & Plenty; I got a Bit-O-Honey bar. We both chipped in for the *Daily News* and a folding map of the city. We couldn't decide whether to walk to Clara's place or take the subway. Walking, we would see a lot more, but a subway ride would be thrilling. We took the subway.

It was late September, but the subway platform still hoarded the summer's heat. The station's dim lighting gleamed off the edges of its innumerable tiles. A man in a gray suit leaned against an iron pillar; others stooped impatiently over the tracks. None said a word. My friend and I obeyed the unwritten law by which New Yorkers pretend to ignore each other. A muffled roar and a fusty breeze heralded the subway train's arrival. The roar grew deafening as it squealed to a stop and its doors slid open.

We careened under the city, each of us clinging to a strap as the subterranean world rushed by, a murky blur punctuated by lustrous stations whose waiting passengers could only watch in envy as we roared past on express tracks: 34th Street . . . 28th Street . . . 23rd Street . . . At the place called Union Square, we jumped a set of iron teeth that stretched to fill the gap between subway and platform. Then up we bounded through a maze of latticed stairways and catwalks into a world of blinding sunshine.

To judge by our map, Clara's apartment was five blocks east on 18th Street. We passed a Chock full o'Nuts and a corner fruit stand. We carried our suitcases and walked fast, as if our arrival were not already accomplished—as if by walking any slower we'd dispel the magic of this dream, like those dreams in which you will yourself to fly. Now and then we faced each other to share a grin that said we'd gotten away with something, or were about to.

Clara's apartment was on the top floor of a tenement. We bounded up the three flights. An elaborate series of keys was required for entry. The apartment smelled of mothballs and musk. Should we open a window? Was that allowed? The walls were covered with framed photographs, theatrical posters, and quaint watercolors of Parisian street scenes. A bronze Laocoön graced the fireplace mantel. Even up there with the windows closed, we heard the traffic below, the impatient horns of trucks and taxis. While Chris unpacked, I studied the photographs, mostly of Clara and a friend, presumably the one with whom she had run the teashop. In one they both wore fur coats; in another they showed off identical plumed hats. It had never dawned on either of us that Clara might be lesbian. "Oh, I've had many, *many* beaux," she'd said to us more than once while sipping from her china cup. Even seeing the photographs, the thought didn't occur to me, as it didn't occur to me that someday I would live in the city, that I would engage my ambitions, inflame my desires, commit various acts of ignominy and treachery, and experience a multitude of triumphs, disappointments, sins, failures, and betrayals there.

By noon Chris and I were back out in the street, burdened no longer by our luggage, carrying only the folding map and an eager-

ness to see everything. Uptown or down? We went down. To the tip
of the Battery we walked, passing the still-unfinished towers of the
World Trade Center. We stood by a railing watching seagulls wheel
over the decks of a ferryboat taking tourists to the Statue of Lib-
erty. From there we walked uptown through the Chinatown I first
came to know with my father; its cagey streets seemed less magical
without him guiding me through them. Then up to Little Italy,
with its green-and-red pennants and flags, past the iron-fronted
buildings of the Bowery to the East Village, where, at the crowded
counter of a Ukrainian café, we slurped twin bowls of blood-red
borscht. As we were leaving, I gave a quarter to a panhandler.

"Don't spend it all in one place," I said, earning a disapproving
look from Chris.

Midtown. Rockefeller Center. Radio City. Central Park. The
Met. The names arrested me with their authority. At the Guggenheim we balked at the price of admission: $3.50 to penetrate a co-
lossal Carvel ice-cream cone. To hell with it! In the district known
as Harlem, the streets were in every sense browner, its buildings
slung low to accommodate a sky brought to its knees by dense,
ponderous clouds. We walked faster, the gusts flapping the lapels
of our Windbreakers, passing a building shaped like the parabolas
we'd learned to draw in algebra class. At every other block, a sudden whirlwind whipped grit into our eyes and made us grip our
jackets at our throats and hunch like old men.

We'd started across town, hungry for Broadway and humanity,
eager to arrive at the colossal pinball machine known as Times
Square, when the rain caught us. We carried no umbrellas. We'd
bought extra tokens, but there were no subways in sight. Taxicabs
were prohibitively expensive. Headlong and purblind, we plunged
into the monsoon. By the time a subway entrance arose out of
the tempest, we were soaked. We clutched our knees, laughing
and coughing as we caught our breath. The subway zoomed us
to Times Square, where we emerged into a sea of black umbrellas
backlit by blurred neon signs. At an establishment called Nedick's
we ordered two "frankfurters" apiece and large cups of orange
drink and ate while watching people hurry by in the rain. Even
soaking wet, New York was a great place, a wonderful, lewd, sexy,
forbidden place. Those trips with my papa had been mere flirtations, as chaste as my grandmother's kisses. Now I was a man, and
the city was mine to embrace less innocently.

By the time we left Nedick's, the rain had softened to a drizzle. We passed under a succession of marquees featuring slasher and porn films and peepshows for 25 cents, a Coney Island boardwalk of X-rated sex. Had Chris, whose parents were of New England Puritan stock, not been there to shame me, I'd have ducked into one of those seedy theaters. I'd have paid a quarter for a peepshow—or two. Or three. Two women in leopardskin miniskirts and high heels emerged from the shadows to offer us a good time. I showed interest; my friend didn't. I had started a conversation with them when, saying "We're already having a good time, thank you," Chris took my arm and kept us walking.

We got "home" after dark. What a strange feeling, having those apartment keys. "The keys to the city!" one of us joked as the door to Clara's apartment swung open. The musty smell was still there. So was the Laocoön. It wasn't even half past seven, but we were both beat. Though the rain had stopped, still, the city seemed less inviting by night, consisting only of bars and other forbidden and overpriced venues.

Instead we brewed a pot of tea and sat there, in Clara's living room, talking in hushed, tired voices to the murmurs of traffic until our eyelids grew heavy and we slouched to bed, proud of ourselves for having passed, to our own satisfaction, the city's audition. It was the first of many such trials, but I didn't know that then.

III. Romance

The rat was as big as a squirrel. It twitched in a trap next to the walk-in fridge. My boss, a retired New York City cop, kept his old service revolver in his office. He took aim, told me to stand back, and blew the thing to furry pink bits, which afterward I scooped into a metal dustpan and carried to the Dumpster.

It was my first job in New York. I'd hoped to be a bartender or a cook, but the owner of the Rozinante Tavern had different plans for me, so I spent most of my time there in the basement, peeling potatoes and cementing cracks in the concrete floor.

It wasn't long before I got a better job just two blocks south, in the oldest building in Soho, a former brothel with shuttered windows and a pitched roof. To work at the Broome Street Bar you had to be an artist: a painter, writer, architect, dancer, photographer—it didn't matter what kind. I told the owners that I was a Pratt student, but that failed to satisfy them. I had to show them some sketches before they hired me as a dishwasher.

The bar's owners were two diametrically opposed brothers named Kenn (two *n*'s) and Bob. Short, bowlegged, cigar-smoking Kenn wore blue jeans, cowboy shirts, and belts with enormous buckles. He saw himself as the rough-and-ready type. Bob, on the other hand, was a slender, soft-spoken, effete man with pale skin. Their love of artists was the one thing the two brothers shared. While Kenn held forth with the patrons upstairs, Bob spent most of his time at a desk he'd arranged by the prep kitchen, keying numbers into an adding machine and chain-smoking Parliaments. He'd take four puffs of a cigarette before snuffing it out, having read somewhere that the first four puffs contained less nicotine. The floor under his desk squirmed with partially smoked cigarettes.

The bar had an open kitchen, with the dishwasher's station facing one end of the bar. I liked washing dishes. I liked the hot, soapy water on my hands and the sense that I was doing something useful. Dishwashing is honorable work, I told myself as the busboys dumped their greasy loads and I flirted with any decent-looking woman who sat on the last stool at the bar.

The other workers in the kitchen slung omelets and burgers, sliced sandwiches, and cracked jokes. Jimmy, the salad chef, was an architect. Francis, the prep cook, wrote show tunes. Joe Hinkle was writing a novel. The waitresses were mostly actresses and dancers. The griddle chef, a guy in his 40s named Bentley, a painter in the manner of Kandinsky, was the funniest and most cynical of the bunch, with a mop of sandy hair that covered his eyes and that he would toss back while flipping his burgers. Somehow, despite his talking a mile a minute in a flat, nasal voice with which he cut to the quick anyone he disliked, the ash from Bentley's cigarette never fell onto his grill.

The bar was a magnet for artists. John and Yoko were patrons; so were Jasper Johns and Robert Rauschenberg. Among the regulars was a sculptor named Bob Bolles. He had a job there, doing what I'm not sure: something to do with plumbing or the beer taps. Mostly he hung out at the bar. Bolles's artistic claim to fame was on permanent (so we thought then) display at the "motorcycle triangle," an open space at the intersection of Broome and Watts, where bikers parked their crotch rockets and where, without permission from municipal authorities, Bolles's jagged iron creations sprouted like rusty weeds, providing windblown papers and coffee cups with crannies to wedge themselves into and neighborhood children with objects to skin knees on. A short guy with an Edgar Allan Poe forehead, Bolles wore hoop earrings and red bandannas and was as much of a fixture in Soho as its loading docks, its bay doors, its freight elevators, as the trucks that barreled over cobblestones to and from the Holland Tunnel. When Bolles died of AIDS in the '80s, the sculptures fell into ruin. Eventually, under the auspices of a zealous borough parks commissioner, the "dangerous, dilapidated, rusting, falling-apart litter magnets" were carted off to a storage facility on Randall's Island, making way for a public green space called Sunshine Park—pleas to rename it after the sculptor having fallen on deaf ears.

Looming over the motorcycle triangle, across the expanse of a windowless building, the words *I Am the Best Artist* were spray-painted and signed by "René." This early example of guerrilla art was, as far as I know, that artist's only creation, but for me it did the trick. To be the best artist—that was the main thing. It was why I had come to the city: to practice my own art but also to breathe in the atmosphere of artists, to size up and learn from the competition.

What sort of artist I wanted to be, I wasn't sure. I had a grandiosity of purpose but no clear vision to go with it. I knew only that I wanted to touch and impress others with my work so they would someday say of me, "He's the best artist."

It was an imperative, an obligation—as inevitable as that GAS HEATS BEST sign I'd first seem with my papa as a child. To impress myself on the city as it had impressed itself on me, that was what I wanted, what I yearned for.

Meanwhile, I washed dishes.

IV. Promiscuity

The Pratt dorm was in a high-rise on Willoughby Avenue, lording it over a neighborhood of tenements and gnarly trees. From there I took a share with a retired church organist named Fletcher on

Washington Avenue—or was it Clinton? After that came the sublet
on DeKalb and another off Flatbush, down the street from Junior's,
where, for the price of a cup of coffee, I'd fill my belly with speci-
mens from the sour-pickle dispenser. From there I took a one-year
sublet in the East Village, on Seventh Street, where the avenues
are alphabetized and the women wore orthopedic shoes and drab
scarves around their heads. Next came the loft on Broome Street,
the summer the lights went out throughout the city. By candlelight
at the corner tavern they dispensed free lukewarm beer and half-
melted ice cream. Then back to Brooklyn, a fifth-floor walkup two
blocks south of the Heights, one of those jobs with a clawfoot tub
squatting in the kitchen and cracked, sticky linoleum. Followed
by another share, this one in Stuyvesant Town, where they didn't
permit air conditioners (fans only) in the casement windows and
where, during the holidays, they strung colored lights around the
lampposts. Was this before or after I lived with that crazy woman
on Cornelia Street, the one who nicknamed me "Leonardo" and
vowed to make a star out of me? Through her I auditioned for
the singing waiter job on Third Avenue and the talent manager
in Hell's Kitchen—the one who, wearing a velvet robe in his living
room, by means of an exercise called "The Boy on the Mountain-
top," tried to get me over his knees. After the crazy lady threw my
things out the window, I moved into the office of the literary agent
for whom I'd been working and who, for a cut in my $100 a week
salary, let me sleep on his sofa. After that, for a while I left the city,
returning to housesit for a lady whose dog mauled me. Then the
railroad flat in the area adjoining Soho north of East Houston that
my songwriting partner (I was writing songs then) and I dubbed
"So What." The greasy exhaust fumes from the diner downstairs
made my partner sick, so he left the city and me. That was when
I broke my leg and moved into the Gramercy Hotel. There, lying
prone in bed, I could reach out and touch both walls while listening to bottles breaking in the air shaft. Then the Greek woman
who taught me typography offered to share her Astoria apartment,
a shag-carpeted, plastic-slipcovered efficiency over a garage a few
blocks from Ditmars Boulevard, where the cafés featured excessive
chrome and glistening mounds of baklava. After Ourania and I
split, I moved to Sunnyside, to a one-bedroom near Calvary Cemetery, in a neighborhood of dismal pubs with shamrocks on their
awnings. Shortly after this I met, proposed to, and moved into a

two-bedroom with Tara. The apartment had French doors. I'd step out of the bathroom or the kitchen and see Tara there, through the grid of glass panes, bent over her watercolor block, smoking. Tara's smoking put the kibosh on our engagement, so I told myself, when in truth I'd been ambivalent from the start. For a while I hung on in Queens until, with a journalist named Steven, I went in on a rental on 1st Avenue, off 14th. It was a one-bedroom; we put up a makeshift wall. We spent a lot of time on the roof there, Steven and I, drinking a brand of cheap red wine called Gato Negro and having aggressive philosophical conversations. I stayed there until Paulette, my new girlfriend, and I got tired of squeezing into my captain's bed. She and I rented a floor-through in a brownstone on 101st near West End. In its living room, in the presence of two witnesses, a gay Episcopal priest married us. Six months later we bought our own place, a foreclosure on 94th and Columbus in an art deco building with a sunken living room and built-in sconces. Though on the ground floor and dark, it had a nice view of the dogwood tree in the courtyard. I set up my studio in the master bedroom and decked the walls with paintings of passenger ships and the Empire State Building at night. In spite of the rap deejay living downstairs, we were happy there until one morning I woke up from a dream in which, instead of a dogwood tree, our window faced the wide, gray-green expanse of the Hudson River. That same morning I boarded a train from Grand Central to the Bronx. At a place called Spuyten Duyvil I got off. Nothing but weeds, trees, water. Water! How I'd missed it! We lived on an island but rarely saw the stuff. Overhead loomed the blue arc of the Henry Hudson Bridge—the same bridge my father and I had crossed into Manhattan in his Simca. Six months later, my wife and I bought a co-op there. We called it home for the next 12 years, until we divorced. I was 50 years old.

V. Dissolution

The dreams of my youth, where had they gone? At the midcentury mark, one is entitled to such inquiries. I'd struggled, worked hard, produced, yet there was the nagging sense that I'd wasted myself, that I'd poured my essence into the city only to see it washed away like so much scum down its storm grates and sewage drains. Another part of me wondered, was it my own damn fault? In abandoning the city (and as any New Yorker will tell you, when you say "the city" you most assuredly do not mean the outer boroughs), had I forsaken my dreams? Had I been as fickle with them as with apartments and women? Had my quest for artistic glory been nothing but one long flirtation—as feeble and hopeless as the flirtations I had engaged in from my dishwashing station at the Broome Street Bar? Had my romance with New York, New York, been no more than a prolonged, fruitless act of mutual seduction?

The city was a vast repository of passageways and doors, any one of which might lead me to my destiny. To choose one door was to slam all the others shut. I remember one day, back when I was still in my 30s, coming home from one of a series of assignations with a woman who lived in a basement apartment on the Lower East Side. As I walked, the streets seemed to stretch out ahead of me like a cartoon stretched on Silly Putty, growing longer and narrower. Four-thirty in the afternoon. Ruddy, low-pitched sunlight spilled over the tops of buildings that frowned down at me, their cornices furrowed like brows. It might have been my imagination, but the doors of all the buildings seemed to have big padlocks on them and red-and-yellow signs shouting KEEP OUT and SECURITY ZONE. The gates were down on the bodegas. I had to resist the urge to run—a flight toward, or away from, innocence? The woman's name was Greta. Her lobby buzzer didn't work. To gain entry I had to phone from the corner or stand there on the sidewalk, hoping she'd see me through the bars of her window. We'd met at a loft party, a gallery opening, a play or poetry reading, somewhere where bad wine and cheese cubes were served. With a pocket full of toothpicks I'd left with her for her place in a taxicab. Her pet cockatoo squawked in its gilded cage. A pachinko machine hung by a mandala poster over her bed. All this is grasping at the past. There was no Greta, or there were dozens of Gretas, each as insubstantial as photographs in someone else's album, one for every address where I'd lived and for every woman I had loved and ought to have been faithful to. But I was never faithful. I was too circumspect, too terrified of anything binding, to be faithful. By choosing not to choose, I expunged all choices.

There were times when, on a busy street corner, I'd stand there, frozen, unable to make up my mind which way to cross, other pe-

destrians jostling me, casting me annoyed looks, cursing me under
their breaths though still loud enough for me to hear. I'd learned
my way around the city only to find myself directionless there. This
lack of impetus led to awkward situations, like the time when the
English actor intercepted me on the corner of Eighth and University. He was with the Old Vic, he said, in town to do a production
of *Macbeth*. He looked like Richard Basehart, so I believed him.
I had no hair; I'd shaved it off down to the skull. This attracted
homosexual men. Macbeth wondered where "a bloke from out of
town could get a good drink." I was still living in Brooklyn at the
time and said so. This didn't dissuade him. We went to Chumley's
and from there to his place, the borrowed "flat" of some other
actor. Having mixed us each a screwdriver, Richard Basehart lay
on the floor fondling himself while reciting apt passages of one of
Henry Miller's more explicit books. He didn't seem to notice or
care as I stepped over him and out the door.

Another time, during a blizzard that fell on my 23rd birthday,
a former priest who'd taken me to dinner for my birthday invited
me to spend the night with him, which I did, gladly, having always
resented those midnight subway expeditions back to whichever
miserable borough I happened to be living in at the time. When
the ex-priest took me in his mouth, I pretended to be elsewhere,
with someone else, enjoying the dim ministrations of an altogether
different set of tongue and lips. In the morning my host was beside
himself with shame. Me, I couldn't have cared less. What did it
matter? Why should I have cared?

Back then I was subject to a recurrent dream, a nightmare that
parachuted me into the combat zone amid its vaporous lights and
alleyways. Always in the dream I'd end up in a movie theater, one
of those sordid theaters near Times Square, attached to an unde-
ployed regiment of hunched men in Burberry coats, and where
the naked bodies projected on the screen were always teasingly out
of focus, looking more like Cézanne's peaches than like figures
engaged in carnal Olympics. However, the soundtrack was always
clear: a moan is a moan is a moan. As if by my own tumescence,
I'd be lifted out of my seat and led toward a red sign glowing over
the door to the men's room, behind which ultimate depravities
lay in wait, tinted with ultraviolet light, perfumed with stale urine.
Debased by my own dreams.

VI. Falling Out

The City of New York had become my illicit lover—a woman of the night whose sordid charms I could not resist but to whom I could never entirely give myself. I thought of my papa and of his "business trips." Decades passed before I finally accepted that he'd kept a mistress in the city, maybe more than one, though a single name, Berenice (*Beh-reh-nee-chay*) stood out for me, having surfaced time and again in my parents' frequent fights, so those four syllables still send their chill up my spine. According to my mother, I once nearly drowned in the Hotel Paris swimming pool, my treacherous papa having left me there to attend to his courtesan upstairs. I refused to believe it. Anyway I never saw this woman, this *Berenice,* who to this day exists for me on roughly the same plane as Cleopatra or Attila the Hun. My father, too, was unfaithful. The city was his lure, his temptress, his domestic and moral undoing. For her sake he betrayed his own family. Though when all was said and done, my father chose us.

But then—as scorned mistresses will—the city avenged itself.

I remember one of the last times Papa visited me there, a year or so before the first of a series of strokes felled him. Paulette and I were still living on the Upper West Side, in the 94th Street deco apartment. My father and I lunched at a diner, where he ordered a bowl of vegetable soup. When I asked him how it was, he looked down at the soupspoon trembling in his fist and said, in a voice heavy with sorrow, "Not so hot." He had come to the city to see me but also to gain an audience with the literary agent to whom he had sent his latest opus, a book titled *Beyond Pragmatism,* by which he hoped to advance William James's psychological theories into the 21st century—a hope against hope for this obdurate eccentric inventor who rarely read books published after the Hague Peace Conference and whose own manifestoes were riddled with hyphenated *to-day*s and plastered with Ko-Rec-Type. The agent had not returned his calls. Having paid for our disappointing lunch, my father repaired to a telephone booth across the street, where, for the 10th time that day, he tried to reach her, only to lose a quarter to the out-of-service phone. With uncharacteristic fury he slammed the receiver down. A few blocks uptown we found another phone booth, this one occupied by a young African American man, prompting my father, until then the least bigoted person I'd known, to combine one garden-variety epithet with one racial slur. "Papa, take it easy," I said (or something to that effect). "What's the *matter*?" But I knew perfectly well. It was no longer my father's city, the one he'd invented for me, his son. It had become an unfamiliar, hostile place. As I led us away from that phone booth, in my father's murky pupils I read an accusation of betrayal, as if I'd let him down, and not the city or his agent.

Now here I was, a few years later, with my papa dead and I, his son, suffering from his ailments, his insomnia and indigestion, not to mention a hefty slice of his egocentricity and more than a few of his eccentricities, feeling no less betrayed by the city that had been our mistress. By then Paulette and I had completed our migration to the Bronx. Though our window faced the northern tip of Manhattan, and though Grand Central Terminal was but a 22-minute train ride away, we'd turned our backs on the real city. In the shallows across the turbid waters we watched a snowy egret—a feathered vase—do its slow-motion dance for fish. We kept a pair of binoculars handy. Like having one foot in the country, we told ourselves and the friends we had ditched downtown. They assumed that the move had been voluntary, but I knew better: I knew that the city had already forsaken me, that I had failed to live up to its promises. Not that we never enjoyed ourselves, my wife and I. We took regular trips to Europe, ate good meals, threw parties packed with Manhattanites who risked nosebleeds and blown eardrums to venture north of 14th Street. But an undercurrent of distress ran through my contentment. It was this undercurrent that often woke me in the middle of the night. I felt bloated with regrets, thinking we should never have left Manhattan, that we might as well have buried ourselves alive. I tried to reassure myself. I told myself I'd wanted light, air, sunshine, fewer car alarms and idling, poisonous-fume-spewing buses. If I never saw Upper Broadway—that ragtag tunnel of produce stands and baby strollers—again, it would be too soon. Besides, the city wasn't the city anymore. It had been co-opted by the sitcom crowd. The popularity of television shows like *Seinfeld* was commensurate with its cultural decline. How I missed seedy Times Square! How I longed for the days before the peepshows succumbed to Walt Disney! Such had been my logic, my excuse, for abandoning the city and the dreams of my youth, a move that would prompt me, on those sleepless nights, to stumble into the bathroom and demand of my no-longer-quite-so-young reflection in the medicine cabinet mirror, *What have you done to my dreams, fucker?*

From the bedroom my wife asks, "Peter, what are you doing?"

I'm a poor underdog, / But tonight I will bark . . . etc. "Brooding," I respond.

"For God's sake, come back to bed!"

Then I say to myself, Wait, it's not over. There's still time, you're still young, you can still do it. You know the meaning and worthiness of art, that it makes life bearable by translating experience, letting us see universals and particularities in a kind of flickering way, that every artist holds the potential to delight and heal others by touching them with something genuine and of deliberate beauty. New York hasn't forsaken you, I assure my reflection in the mirror. That's your sense of gloom talking. And you haven't forsaken it. You just needed some peace and quiet in which to create.

Here was hope springing eternal; here was my childhood innocence shining its bright, dimwitted light again—the same innocence that 44 years prior had turned an ad slogan on the side of a fuel storage tank into a divine revelation. Despite my grown-up sense of gloom, I was still a child, still besotted, still as prone to bad judgment in hope as ever, still as wide-eyed with curiosity, expectation, and optimism as a six-year-old. Still as eager and willing as ever to march headlong into the arms of the enemy, *Berenice,* my father's ex-mistress. As if by conquering her I might atone for his sins.

VII. *Ashes & Echoes*

I'd meant to spend that September at a writers' retreat but came home early to attend a gala at Lincoln Center (and to pick up some warmer clothes; I hadn't realized how cold it gets in the Adirondacks). That morning I tried on my tuxedo to discover it no longer fit. I was about to head downtown to rent one when the telephone rang. It was the woman who had invited me to the gala, calling to say it had been called off. I asked her why.

"Have you got a TV?" she said.

Like half of the country, I spent the next five hours sitting with my hand to my lips in front of a TV. The city that I'd loved, re-

sented, felt challenged and betrayed by, whose slushy sidewalks
and ovenlike summer subways I had cursed—this place where I
had been loved, mugged, produced, embarrassed, paid, exhibited,
that had made me proud and angry and excited and bitter and
tired and joyous and hungry and regretful, that had been the setting of so many youthful enthusiasms, where I'd walked arm in
arm with and courted and made love with women, where I had suffered, celebrated, laughed, cried, whose myriad streets I could navigate blindfolded or by smell, whose subway turnstiles I'd jumped,
whose taxi drivers and waiters and shoeblacks I'd tipped, whose
cafés and galleries and atriums I'd haunted, whose streets I'd jay-
walked, whose muffins and bagels I had ingested by the score,
whose store windows had sampled my evolving reflection, whose
landlords had charged me rent, whose employers had paid my
wages, whose supermarkets and delis had supplied me with milk
and pickled herring, whose water supply had kept me hydrated
and hygienic, whose sewage system had eliminated four decades'
worth of my excretions, whose thrift stores and flea markets had
provided me with furniture and clothing, and whose populace
had endowed me with friends, lovers, acquaintances, clients, and
occasional enemies—that this setting that had graced a hundred
charming *New Yorker* covers could be changed so suddenly into a
tragic place, a grim war memorial, a Pearl Harbor, a Waterloo, the
Alamo, a place to feel reflective and sad, made me wonder: What
would future six-year-olds make of that blazing skyline? Would they
look upon it with wonder and joy as I once had? Would they see
a city of dreams? Or would they see only the memory of a single
disastrous day, twin columns of air where a pair of skyscrapers had
once stood?

Was I feeling sorry for the city or for myself? Was there a difference?

Sometimes it takes a disaster to put us in touch with our innocence, to remind us of just how romantic our delusions have
been. Seeing her ravaged made me fall in love with the city all
over again, made me embrace her with fierce, protective pride.
Even the city's past calamities—the Black Tom explosion, the Triangle Shirtwaist factory fire, the Fraunces Tavern bombing, the
Kew Gardens train crash, tragedies quaint by comparison, were
caught in my embrace, as were the rumble of the El, tuberculosis
windows, horse walks, Horn & Hardart, those stately clocks along

Fifth Avenue, the sunken treasures under the swirling waters of
Hell Gate. In a fervor of indignation, I reclaimed my city, the one
I'd inherited from my father. Nothing—not even an army of ter-
rorists—would take her from me again.

VIII. Separation & Divorce & Reconciliation

In the end it wasn't terrorists or my own sense of failure that took
me from New York, but a tenure-track position at a good university.

It's been four years since I left the city. And though New York
has never entirely left my thoughts, this is the first occasion I've really had to look back. I live in an A-frame on a lake in central Georgia. Two paintings hang on the wall behind the desk where I write.
The top painting is an interior of a subway car rendered in muted
grays and browns, with passengers asleep or reading books or gripping subway straps, as my friend Chris and I did when we were
15. The painting underneath it is of the Empire State Building at
night, its rows of windows represented by daubs of yellow paint, a
full moon burning alongside its glowing blimp tower. From that
painting I only have to turn my head a few degrees clockwise to see
the lake through the slats of the venetian blinds of the doors that
open out to my deck, with the weather-beaten dock from which I
swim reaching out over it. As places go, none could seem farther
from New York.

From my dock I count 200 strokes to the other side of the inlet
and as many coming back. These days, that and a three-three university teaching load is all the ambition I need. Thanks to the lake,
I have plenty of water to supply it. Between stretches of work at
my computer I swim sometimes as often as three times a day. With
every stroke I push the past farther away, and with it my memories
of New York City.

Who am I kidding? I'll carry the city with me forever. It's in my
bones, my flesh, my DNA, my genes. It's the egg that my father fer-
tilized and that gave birth to me. With every stroke I swim deeper
and deeper into the teeming metropolis of my dreams.

Sun King

FROM *Outside*

WE EACH HAVE OUR DREAMS and if they are meant to mean
anything at all you hold tight and don't let them go. You can
dream of love or money or fame or something much more grand
than a fish, but if a fish swims into your imagination and never
swims out it will grow into an obsession and the obsession might
drag you anywhere, up to the metaphysical heights or down into
an ass-busting nightmare, and the quest for my dream fish—South
America's dorado—seems to run in both directions.

Of course the dream is never just about a fish but about a place
as well, an unknown landscape and its habitat of active wonders,
populated by creatures looming around the primal edges of our
civilized selves. A place like the ancestral homeland of the Guaraní Indians at the headwaters of the Río Paraná, near where Argentina, Brazil, and Paraguay come together. In the Guaraní language, *pirá* means "fish," and this fish, the legendary dorado, is
called *pirajú*, the affix meaning "yellow." In my dreams the *pirajú*
skyrockets out of its watery underworld, a piece of shrapnel from
a submerged sun, like a shank of gold an archaeologist might find
in the tomb of an Incan king.

After years of unrequited dorado lust, last spring I seized the
dream by the gills and finally took off for the Southern Hemisphere. I would be hooking up with a guide known worldwide as
the king of dorado, Noel Pollak, the best person wired into the
fish and its latitudes, the guarantor of the dream and your inser-
tion into its depths. Six months earlier we had schemed to meet in
Bolivia at a Pollak-discovered location that had become renowned

as dorado nirvana, but we had not been able to manage that trip, for reasons I'll get to in a moment. Instead, we were now connecting at the end of what should have been the fair-weather season somewhere in Argentina's Iberá Wetlands—an area almost seven times as large as Florida's Everglades—although the specifics of our rendezvous weren't exactly clear to me. *Get on a plane, find me.* Noel was frequently off in the bush, out on the water, and our communications had been last-minute, the logistics addressed in a manner all too breezy and cavalier.

But that's how dreams operate—you fling yourself into their spell and expect it will all work out. What you really must expect however is the strong possibility that such immoderate optimism will be sorely tested.

After a daylong flight from Miami, I land after dark in Buenos Aires and check into the Hub Porteño past midnight. No one at the hotel has heard of my final destination, Mercedes, Corrientes. Indeed, even the placard at the airport ticket counter the next morning doesn't identify it on the flight manifest. At our first stopover, everybody disembarks but me and a Chinese businessman, and an hour later we put down in the weather-beaten colonial town of Mercedes, which is probably like flying into Chicken Neck, Louisiana, in 1955. Descending, I can see curls and snakes and catchments of muddy water everywhere, a saturated landscape, a fishery run amok, and I imagine schools of dorado patrolling the floodwaters of the pampas like marauding tigers, gobbling up rabbits and lambs.

Someone named Ricardo has come to fetch me in his mud-encrusted pickup truck. Hello, I say, how do you say mud in Spanish? *Barro.* We drive through somnambulant streets to a two-lane highway and then onto a deeply rutted dirt track, its surface melted to goo. *Mucho barro,* I say to Ricardo, who struggles mightily with the steering wheel. Too much rain, *sí? Sí,* he nods. The fishing has been affected, *sí?* A little, says Ricardo. We pass through endless flat ranchland, small rivers swollen with floodwater, the pastures lapped with water, sheep and cattle crowded onto the high spots. The clouds roil overhead, looking ever more threatening, the truck sliding in and out of the ruts until we finally skate sideways off the roadbed, axle-deep into the slop.

It's midafternoon by the time we mud-surf into Pirá Lodge. Pirá is the first five-star lodge dedicated exclusively to dorado fishing, built in 2000 by an outfitter called Nervous Waters. The compound is quietly welcoming, an understated outback haven for one-percenters, although put me to bed in a cardboard box, for all I care—my idea of privilege is limited to landing a ferocity with fins.

Of the original team of hotshot guides at Pirá, only one was Argentine, a fish-crazed kid from the capital named Noel Pollak, a self-described "born fisherman" who looks like most of the sinewy, bantamweight rock climbers I've known. In 1987, when he was 13, Noel decided he was a fish geek and taught himself fly-fishing, practicing at a lake in a city park. At 21, he dropped out of university to become a professional sport fisherman. For him it wasn't a decision, it was beyond intelligence, it was a calling, like entering the priesthood in waders.

He started giving fly-fishing lessons to friends and writing fishing articles for a magazine, *Aventura.* Then Argentina's largest newspaper, *La Nación,* asked him to write a biweekly column. But after two years on the beat, Pollak was sick of it all, fed up with writing—actually, fed up with being edited—and he walked away from the job. Instead of buying a car with his savings, he bought a skiff and began guiding in the nearby Paraná delta, 45 minutes from downtown Buenos Aires. Then Pirá Lodge came into the picture. He guided at Pirá for 10 seasons; by the third he was promoted to head guide, eventually managing the place. Then in 2006 he took an off-season trip to Bolivia, where he would encounter both glory and betrayal.

Noel takes me directly to the boat dock, where the lodge's pair of Hell's Bay flats skiffs are tied up on a channel of swift, caramel-colored water, providing access to the marshes and lagoons and the headwaters of the Río Corriente, a tributary of the Paraná. Both the Paraná and the Río Uruguay farther to the east eventually merge north of Buenos Aires to form the Río de la Plata, the widest river in the world.

Standing on the dock, even a newcomer can see that conditions are not normal here. The channel has overflowed its banks, submerging the lower trunks of willow trees, sending water up the lawns of the lodge. Two days earlier, a low-pressure system over the Amazon basin descended into Argentina and dropped 20 inches of rain in 48 hours, resulting in the worst flooding in 10 years. Not to be deterred, Noel fished the downpour with his last stubborn client, Jimmy Carter, who had left the lodge that morning to dry out in BA.

My moment of truth has now arrived. I'm an agnostic, an unapologetic philistine, one devolution away from fishing with dynamite. Noel puts his gorgeous bamboo fly rod in my hands, wants me to feel its craftsmanship, wants me to love it, wants to see what I can do, but it might as well be a nine-foot piece of rebar in my clumsy grip, and so I show him just how graceless an otherwise competent man can be, stripping out line like an infirm monkey, noodling my cast up and up until it plummets ineffectually midway into the channel. Because he has teaching ingrained in his personality, Noel seems to think he can help me overcome my deficiencies, and he probably could, but there's too little time, and I have no intention of spending it feeling frustrated and dumb. "No one who is learning should ever feel stupid," Noel says, trying to console me, but honestly, screw it. For once the art is beside the point. I don't want to learn, I want to fish, and I know how to handle my spinning rod.

Noel, unlike the majority of fly-fishermen I know, is an easygoing, tolerant guy. He maintains his composure in the face of my blasphemy and we go fishing.

We blast down the esoteric maze of pathways through the marshlands, the channels no wider than a suburban sidewalk. Noel pilots the boat like a motocross driver at full throttle, slaloming through serpentine creeks, making hairpin turns, rocketing ahead across small lagoons into seemingly solid walls of vegetation, the fronds of the reeds whipping my face.

After 20 minutes, the marshes open up into bigger water, providing a clearer picture of why the Argentines call this region Mesopotamia, the land between the rivers. The horizons are tree lined, but out here vast clumps of floating islands composed of reeds and their root systems define the ecosystem. As the water gets deeper and as wide as the length of a football field, horses are suddenly everywhere in the stream, washed out of their range. Only their heads are visible, nostrils flared red, chased by swarthy gauchos in pirogues trying to herd them back to terra firma. Farther on, where the marshlands pinch in again at the headwaters of the Corriente, Noel cuts the motor and climbs atop the poling platform bolted onto the stern and we drift, El Maestro calling out advice and wisdom to me, poised in the bow.

To fish for dorado requires the hyper-accuracy of a marine sniper, every cast by necessity a bull's-eye or you're in the vegetation. Of course, as a marksman, Noel uses the equivalent of a bow and arrow, and I'm firing a rifle. His mantra is persistent but gentle — *Cast at that riffle, cast at that inlet, cast at that confluence.* After dozens of fruitless casts, I'm thinking, Fine, let's do dozens more. That old man Jimmy Carter bounced around out here in hard rain for two days and boated eight dorados.

Try over there, says Noel, pointing to an eddy line where a channel runs out of the reeds into the main current. *Kaboom* is the noise you don't hear but feel when a dorado strikes, and the next thing you know the beast is in the air, a solid-gold furious thrashing bolt of life, and the next thing you know after that is farewell, goodbye, it's gone, and you are inducted into the Hall of Jubilant Pain that is dorado fishing. The fish launches out of the water with a hook in its bony jaws and razor teeth and when it comes back down after a three-second dance it's perfectly free and you're bleeding internally, experiencing some pure form of defeat.

"If you love fishing you're going to fall in love with this fish," Noel declares. "But they make you suffer, hombre. Like the woman who you really fall in love with, they always keep you at the edge. I will admit it, I like the difficult fish." With the sun about to set, I conjure a second fish into the sky and lose it, too.

At breakfast Noel jokes that he'll wear his lucky hat today, "the one I was wearing when I discovered this place in Bolivia," but then again, Bolivia didn't turn out so well. We take off in the skiff down the channel into the marshlands but the flooding is now unprecedented; its surge has separated vast platforms of the vegetation, breaking apart floating islands and jamming together new ones. We finally plow our way out into the Corriente and pole and drift the edges, both of us fishing for three hours. Nothing. We try every possible combination of structures and depths. Nada. Shit. Noel has never seen these waters like this. The Paraná — a four-hour drive north — will be better, he promises. The drainage is different, the riparian geology less susceptible to the washout here in the marshes. We head back to the lodge, pack up, and hit the road.

Fishing guides are in many respects the most innocent people in the world, always believing in the best, believing in the next cast, another chance, embracing a type of aesthetics and idealism found most bracingly in nature. Fly-fishermen especially are dismayed by a cretinous mentality, unable to comprehend a certain type of laziness and a certain type of greed.

Noel and I go to the Paraná because we can't go to Bolivia, where he and his investors built what became a legendary dorado camp, the Tsimane Lodge, up in the jungled foothills of the eastern flank of the Andes. Days of walking through the jungle, days of shitty fishing, then a flight in a bush plane and days more being paddled upriver by bow-and-arrow Indians in a dugout canoe, until finally the murky water cleared, the air brightened, the river was beautiful, and Noel experienced the most amazing day of dorado fishing in his life. They were all giants, and they came to him one after another. "I almost want to cry, remembering this," he tells me.

Three years of discovery and development, three years of fabulously successful operations, and then the money disappeared, all the profits—even the staff's salaries—vanishing into a wormhole. Noel doesn't want to air the details, but suffice to say that his greatest success was also his greatest ass-kicking, a pattern that seems close to the essence of existence, dorado style. Back in Buenos Aires, he couldn't even lift himself out of his bed for months. But he had left Nervous Waters, the outfitters of Pirá Lodge and in his opinion the number one fly-fishing outfit in the world, on good terms, and when his depression lifted Noel and Nervous Waters hatched a scheme for a new partnership built around a dorado trifecta—day trips out of Buenos Aires to the delta, a future lodge elsewhere in South America, and the first dorado operation on the upper reaches of the Paraná. This new place, called the Alto Paraná Lodge, based out of a 100,000-acre estancia named San Gara, would open for business in October.

It's a tedious drive north through flat countryside from Pirá to the estancia, where we arrive long after dark and meet Christian, the son of the owner, and two of Noel's friends—Mariano and Alejandro. Beautiful guys—they have boats, we don't. We're fed beef with side dishes of more beef and shown to austere rooms in what seems to be a converted barracks for the resident gauchos—the

estancia runs 3,500 head of cattle and 300 horses. In the morning, I awake to a riot of obnoxious parrots who inhabit, by the
hundreds, the crowns of the palm trees clustered at the end of
the veranda. The four of us squeeze into Mariano's pickup truck
and tow his boat to the river, about five miles down flooded gravel
roads. Rheas dash across the road, foxes, the huge but rarely seen
swampland deer known as *ciervo de los pantanos,* flushed out to
higher ground. The upper Paraná has been victimized by the same
weather system—20 inches of rain, the river rising three feet out
of its normal banks. In fact, as bad as the Iberá marsh was, the
Paraná is worse.

The river is expansive, miles across, Paraguay out there somewhere on the eastern bank, separated from us by an archipelago
of midstream islands cloaked with impenetrable jungle. The water
is the color of dulce de leche, whipped by a steady breeze. We roar
away to known spots, to unknown spots, scouting and fishing and
roaring away again, all the familiar exposed sandbars and beaches
now underwater from the deluge.

Within an hour I have my first dorado, but it's minnow size,
four or maybe five pounds, and then I lose a second, bigger one.
I'm spin-casting a spoon off the bow and Alejandro's fast-stripping
a streamer from the stern, losing fish after fish. When Noel takes
his place, the story's much the same, although he boats a half
dozen *pirá pita,* a smaller fish with as much fight as a dorado, using
dry flies. After a couple hours of happy frustration, we head out to
the islands and their solid walls of jungle, the first line of trees and
bushes half submerged, the shorelines sculpted with minicoves
and overgrown inlets and gaps and twisting eddies. It would be
impossible to get out of the boat but unfortunately I find a way,
kneeling in the bow to retrieve Noel's fly, entangled in a branch
just out of my reach, and I fall slow-motion into the fucking water.
I'm only three feet offshore but there's no bottom to touch and
I swim to the stern of the skiff and am pulled back aboard by my
wide-eyed friends. As dips go it's pleasant enough, but with 12-foot
caimans and truck-size catfish throughout the river, I'm not keen
on getting back in the water around here.

The fishing is grueling. We're casting from about 80 feet offshore
into tiny pockets between the foliage, beneath the foliage, along-

side deadfalls, the trickiest shots imaginable. We're all expert marksmen, but nobody is perfect enough in the wind to stay out of the branches. Farther on into the jungle we can hear the eerie rumbling of colonies of monkeys, their vocalization like pigs, not squealing but a low persistent collective grunting. Noel picks up his rod again and now there are three of us fishing, perfectly synchronized, our casts each landing within a yard of one another in separate pockets along the bank at the same moment, and something wonderful happens. "A triple!" shouts Alejandro at the wheel. Three dorado simultaneously erupt into the air, looking like a jackpot lineup on a Vegas slot machine, then fall back into the current, gone, all three.

That night two of the Pirá Lodge guides, Augustin and Oliver, arrive from the south to join us on the Paraná. In the morning, as a river otter frolics in the shallows, we zoom off in two boats toward the islands. I'm daunted by the wind and the choppy, dirty water and ask Noel how hard he thinks it's blowing—15 knots? Twenty? That's not the scale I use, says Noel. My scale is Perfect, Nice, Shitty, Awful. This is between Shitty and Awful.

But the day has its rugged magic, at least a window into the magic. Augustin, in Mariano's boat, lands a 12-pound hunk of what one American magazine referred to as "gaucho gold," and on an assassin's shot between two downed trees I'm struck by lightning, so to speak. The strike is immediate, a nanosecond after my diving plug hits the surface, and like a Polaris missile launched from a submarine, up comes the dorado, 15 pounds, jumping into the air above our heads. Like orcas, a dorado will jump out of the water onto land a full yard to pursue its prey—in the dorado's case, *sabalo*, panicked baitfish. Somewhere in the sequence I can feel the release of the hook and the fish is free again but honestly it hardly matters; Noel and Alejandro are hooting and will talk about that fish with a thrill in their voices for the next two days—*Oh man, that fish*—because it was huge and magnificent and for a moment it was ours. When the two boats reunite, Augustin tells us Oliver has spent the day "harvesting the forest," which means he's been an inch or two too far in all his casts, but at least he hasn't gone swimming. Noel and Alejandro tell him about the monster I hooked and lost. "And then," Oliver, an Englishman, says to me, "you were left with your thoughts." But there wasn't a thought in my head. I was left with only heartbreak. Yet to have owned the fish for a few seconds, to see it in the air, suspended between outcomes, has to be enough.

La vida es sueño, the Latins say—life is a dream. I think of Noel and his struggle in Bolivia. This time it's not the fish but something much, much bigger, and it stays in the air for what seems like an eternity but in fact is only three years, and when it falls back to the water, it's gone, receded back to the dream; you thought you had it but you never did and its descent is a form of bittersweet devastation. Sometimes you can catch the big one but the result is pathos and tragedy. And you can lose the big one and yet it persists and remains, a triumphant vision, something to carry forward beyond the dream. There's clarity here—these fishermen, these lovely men, the spread and flow of big water, the dance of the big fish, the ascendant luminosity, a blazing star built of muscle and teeth and fury, the golden arc of sweetness and sorrow, possession and loss. That's what you discover in the marshes, what you bring home from the river. That, finally, is the meaning of the dream.

The next day on the Paraná is a screaming disaster. Noel and I fly back down to Buenos Aires to fish the delta. In the morning, we are greeted by squalls but head out anyway into shining moments of solitude and silence, autumn light and autumn colors and yes, *kaboom,* up a little creek one last bull's-eye next to a log. *Pirajú,* the Guaraní god of water, strains for the sun.

A week later, in the suburbs of the capital, scores of people will be swept away by the floods. Any dream has its limits, and this dream had breached its boundaries, waiting to be dreamed again, and better.

The Last of Eden

FROM *Vanity Fair*

THE WELCOMING COMMITTEE comes down from the village.
Three of the men have yellow crowns of toucan feathers, red tou-
can-feather bracelets on their upper arms, and red toucan down
dabbed on the tip of their foreskins, which are tied up with string.
They are carrying beautifully made longbows and arrows that come
to their shoulders. The tallest man is called Piraí. He sits on one
of the benches behind the Brazilian National Indian Foundation's
post of Juriti, where I am staying, and his wife, Pakoyaí, in a skirt
of finely woven tucum palm, sits next to him. Their son Iuwí is to
his right, and in the background is his father, Pirahá, who is also
married to Iuwí's sister, so Pirahá is both Iuwí's grandfather and
his brother-in-law. Pirahá has a big smile, which I recognize is the
smirk of someone with a sense of the absurd, who appreciates the
delicious ironies, the constant outrageous surprises of existence,
as people tend to do at the end of their lives. He is listening to a
bird in the nearby forest that is singing in triplets. Emaciated dogs,
little brown bags of bones, are snoozing and rolling in the dust. A
rooster is prancing on the path for the benefit of a dozen hens and
lesser males. Our gathering, on one of the last islands of intact rain
forest in the eastern Amazon, is taking place in the context of an
entire ecosystem. All these communications and interactions are
going on that our contingent from the modern world is dead to.

Piraí starts to speak in Portuguese, his voice full of gravitas and
emotion. "We are Awá," he says. "We don't succeed in living with
chickens and cows. We don't want to live in cities. We want to live
here. We have much courage, but we need you close to us. The

Ka'apor and Guajajara"—neighboring tribes the Awá have testy relationships with—"are selling their wood to the whites. We don't want their money and their motorcycles. We don't want anything from the whites but to live as we live and be who we are. We just want to be Awá."

Then Iuwí gives an impassioned speech in Awá, which none of us understand, but his words have such conviction and pride they bring tears to my eyes. Two courageous Awá men, father and son, in their prime—there are not many others here in their demographic, nowhere near enough to take on the *madeireiros,* the loggers who are killing their trees and their animals and are now within a few miles of here, and the thousands of other *invasores* who have illegally settled on their land and converted a third of their forest to pasture. I think of all the speeches like this given by brave natives in the Americas over the last 500 years, who were trying to save their people and way of life and world but were unable to stop the inevitable, brutal advance of the conqueror and his "progress," and how this is probably what is going to happen here, to this remnant tribe in its endgame.

The Awá are a distinctive-looking, diminutive forest people, smaller than any of the dozen other Amazon tribespeople I have met. Reduced size is adaptive in a rain forest. You can move around more easily and unobtrusively. Not only humans but other species are smaller in rain forests. The older Awá, like Pirahá, have long scruffy hair and broad grins. Despite all their vicissitudes, they seem to have a happy outlook—they're just glad to still be here, and what they can do for the others is to show it with their big smiles. Some of the women and kids have beautiful faces, long and narrow at the chin, their noses long and curved down at the end, their dark, almond-shaped eyes gleaming with interest. They are more like Ainu or Quechua, indigenous people from Japan or the Andes, than musclebound bruisers of Amazonia like the Xavante or Kayapo.

Some of the kids look a little inbred. There is a lot of marriage between close kin here, there being no one else to marry. And there being more men than women, some of the women have several husbands—polyandry, a rare marital arrangement, found most famously in Tibet. But some of the men have several wives, so there's polygyny, too. There seems to be a lot of flexibility in who sleeps with whom. In fact, an Awá woman is not thought to get pregnant from one man—she has to have sex with several men, generally three. Reproduction is a collective, cumulative effort, and all of the men who sleep with her are the father of her child: plural paternity, the first I've ever heard of this.

Two days earlier I had set out from São Luís, the capital of Maranhão, the easternmost state in the Brazilian Amazon, on the Atlantic coast of northern Brazil. After driving south, into the interior of the impoverished state for 300 miles on increasingly sketchy roads, and walking through glorious rain forest for a couple of miles, I reached the ethno-environmental protection post of Juriti, in the roughly 289,000-acre Território Indígena (TI) Awá. The Awá of Juriti are made up of three groups who were contacted for the first time in 1989, 1992, and 1996, and, with the children they've had since then, their population is up to 56. There are still 100 or so Awá who remain uncontacted. One of the three known isolated, or *isolado,* groups—there are probably more in the other last islands of Maranhão's rain forest—is closely related to Juriti's 1996 group, who had decided they had had enough of life on the run, which has been the Awá's survival strategy for nearly 200 years, and a successful one until now, with their forest shrinking and the modern world closing in, and there being nowhere else to go. The Awá of Juriti still go out in the forest and hunt every day and have the same basic outlook and beliefs that they did before they were contacted. Their only concessions to modernity are that they wear clothes most of the time, grow some crops, and hunt with guns, except for a few of the old men, who still prefer their bows.

The Awá are among Brazil's more than 800,000 "Indians," who belong to at least 239 different cultures and speak roughly 190 different languages, yet are only 0.4 percent of the country's 200 million people. Modern Brazil is a fractious, joyous mix of classes, races, and ethnically distinct regional subcultures, with a very rich 1 percent, a middle class that has been stuck in neutral since the global recession, and a dark-skinned proletariat, millions of whom have nothing—no home, no job, no land, no opportunities. So many realities at odds with each other, and most of the population under 25 and idealistic and anxious about what the future holds. This anxiety and the desire for real change and a decent government not riddled with corruption are what triggered the massive, spontaneous, countrywide demonstrations last June.

It is astonishing that there are still uncontacted native people in such a devastated part of the Amazon. The modern frontier, with its chainsaws, bulldozers, loggers, squatters, and cattle ranchers, has been eating away at the Awá's rain forest for 40 years. Illegal logging roads have penetrated to within a few miles of where one of the three known bands of *isolados* roams. Survival International, the tribal peoples' champion, has classified the Awá as the most endangered tribe on earth. FUNAI, Brazil's National Indian Foundation, has put the Awá in its most vulnerable "red alert" category.

Survival International reached out to the photographer Sebastião Salgado, and he invited me to join him on this expedition, whose purpose is to shine a global spotlight on the plight of the Awá and to persuade Brazil's Ministry of Justice to evict the *invasores* so the Awá and the forest they depend on can be left in peace. There is no time to lose. All the bureaucratic hoops seem to have been jumped, a process that began in the 1970s. In 2009, an expulsion decree was handed down by a federal judge in São Luís—who described the situation as "a real genocide"—but that was overturned. In 2011, Judge Jirair Aram Meguerian ruled that the Brazilian government had to evict the illegal loggers. But they are still there, an anarchic collection of families, some of them rich *fazendeiros,* or ranchers, with satellite dishes and solar panels on their roofs, but most of them *posseiros,* dirt-poor, landless, illiterate squatters living in mud huts with roofs of *babaçu*-palm fronds. The Ministry of Justice has to give the order for the eviction operation, which will be a joint endeavor involving police, army, FUNAI, and the Brazilian Institute of Environment and Renewable Natural Resources. The ministry is understandably reluctant to carry it out, because things could turn violent, and because many of the *invasores* are among the millions of homeless, jobless Brazilians, the very people the ruling Workers' Party is committed to improving the lot of. In addition, much of the land in Maranhão is owned by a small oligarchy of extremely wealthy ranchers who have their hands in much of the logging and are not sympathetic to the Indians.

It's been 10 years since TI Awá was demarcated, and 8 since it was officially deeded to the tribe, and 2 since the expulsion decree, and nothing has happened except that more *invasores* have arrived and more trees have been cut. There's already a 12-mile slice that's been taken out on the TI's southeastern border—I drove through it, and hardly a tree has been left standing—and it's going to be very hard to get the *invasores* out of there.

Carlos Travassos, FUNAI's chief of general coordination with uncontacted and recently contacted Indians, who is with us, tells me that of Brazil's roughly 239 tribes, the Awá *isolados* are one of only three who are still nomadic. They hunt with bows and arrows and gather fruit, nuts, and honey in the forest. They don't have villages or grow anything, and they don't want anything to do with the outside world, which they are aware of—their family members having been killed by its guns and diseases—but not to the extent that they know that they are living in a country called Brazil, or what a country is, or that they share a planet with 7 billion of us *kanai,* the Awá word for everyone who is not one of them.

Where the Isolados *Roam*

There are 66 uncontacted tribal groups in the Brazilian Amazon, according to FUNAI, and another 30 or so unconfirmed ones—more than anywhere else in the world—and Carlos Travassos is certain others will come to light as the last fastnesses of the rain forest are penetrated. FUNAI's *sertanistas*—backlands experts, as they were called—used to do the delicate and dangerous job of making contact with them, but its policy since 1987 has been to not initiate contact, to have nothing to do with the *isolados* unless absolutely necessary, and to intervene only if the tribespeople's well-being and ability to live their way of life are affected. Travassos, who is from São Paulo and did his first fieldwork in one of its favelas, or slums, is only 33 and full of energy, and he cares passionately about these people. From 2007 to 2009 he was stationed in the Javari Valley of Brazil and Peru, which has the greatest concentration of *isolados,* perhaps as many as 16 different peoples. He has a video on his laptop of some Korubo shouting from a riverbank in 2009. Four hundred Korubo, in three groups in the Javari Valley, are still uncontacted. The men are extremely muscular. Their weapon of choice is a seven-foot club. They have clubbed 7 FUNAI employees and 100 loggers and other *invasores* to death.

The Awá have killed a few invaders, most recently a logger they found on an illegal trail three miles from Juriti in 2008, but they are a gentle, unaggressive people, Travassos tells me. We talk about how *uncontacted* doesn't really convey the reality. Most of the uncontacted villages spotted from the air have banana plantations, and the banana was brought to the New World by the Portuguese, so there must have been some contact somewhere along the line. *Autonomous* and *stateless* have been suggested as alternatives, but there are millions of people in those categories who are at least marginally in the modern world, so those terms don't really work either.

Salgado and I agree that this is not only about the Awá. It is time for all the people in their situation—the Indians in Brazil's 688 Terras Indígenas, the 370 million indigenous people in the world, 40 percent of whom are tribal, who have been treated abominably for centuries on every continent by the Europeans who came, saw, and conquered—to be valued and cared about. This is their moment, and one hopes we can help, and the moment seems to have arrived in Brazil just as I did. In the days leading up to our trip, Terena Indians clashed with ranchers in Mato Grosso do Sul, south of Amazonia (the reason being that the Ministry of Justice took the land from the ranchers and gave it to the Indians, to whom it rightfully belonged, then gave it back to the ranchers), and some Terena set several of the ranchers' compounds on fire. The Federal Police were sent in and one of the Terena was shot dead. Simultaneously but unrelatedly, 30 Kaingang Indians, the demarcation of whose *terras* in the southern state of Paraná has been getting nowhere, took over the Workers' Party's headquarters, in Curitiba, and Kayapo and other tribespeople have occupied the site of the Belo Monte dam, on the Xingu River, an ill-conceived boondoggle that will put much of their homelands underwater. Recently, more than 100 Mundurucú Indians took over FUNAI's headquarters, in Brasília, Brazil's capital, where we met with its president two days earlier.

The minister of justice, José Eduardo Cardoza, says the Força Nacional will contain or put down these Indian revolts, and the ministry oversees the agency—FUNAI—that is supposed to be looking out for them. As Antônio Carlos Jobim put it, Brazil is not for beginners. A large segment of the population thinks the Indians are *malandros*—lazy good-for-nothings—who don't contribute anything to the society. Why should they, only 0.4 percent of the population, have 13 percent of Brazil's land surface when millions of Brazilians have no land at all? The *ruralistas,* the conservative ranchers, have a powerful lobby in the Congress in Brasília, and the mining and timber companies are dying to get onto the Indians' land. There is a bill to open the TIs to mining and logging "in consultation" with their Indian occupants but not giving them veto power, and another to take the responsibility for demarcating future TIs away from FUNAI and give it to Congress, and the *ruralistas* are pushing for the existing TIs to be re-demarcated and reduced.

To see what the Indians' lands would look like if the *ruralistas* get their way, we only had to look outside our pickup truck's window on the journey to Juriti. The Amazon rain forest used to cover the western half of Maranhão, but now 71 percent of that is gone, according to the latest satellite images, and more than half of what remains is in the TIs, which are altogether 13 percent deforested (TI Awá itself is more than 30 percent deforested). All day long we drove through thick, lush pasture, dotted with white, humped Nelore zebu cattle, grazing in what was once thick, lush rain forest.

Never Stand Under a Howling Guariba

During my 10-day stay in Juriti, I get into a routine of going out into the forest each morning with Patriolino Garreto, one of FUNAI's three rotating *chefes de posto,* and whatever Awá he can round up who are interested in joining us, which is only the teenagers. Patriolino is a local 58-year-old country boy who has been working at the Juriti post since 1994. He doesn't speak Awá or know much about their culture. *"Os mitos deles só eles que sabem,"* he tells me as we climb up to the ridge above the village—they are the only ones who know their myths.

"Paca, anta, queixada, veado, guariba"—Patriolino reels off the names of the Awá's main prey: agouti, tapir, peccary, deer, howler monkey. "Our forest in Maranhão is full of delicious meat," he says, "but so much of it is gone." Loud drilling directs us to a huge black woodpecker with a red crest and white cheeks tearing into a dead tree. We stop to watch a procession of 30 leaf-cutter ants, each carrying a vertical flake of leaf many times its size—mulch for their fungus gardens—enter one of the tunnels into their subterranean colony under a five-foot-square dome of bare earth. Soon afterward we find ourselves in a space maybe 100 yards square in

which eight or so male pihas are screaming their hearts out, hoping to entice nearby females who are looking for partners. These competitive-display gatherings are known as "leks." None of the pihas, small gray birds in the continga family, are visible in the dense jungle foliage, but the collective din of their piercing whistles is earsplitting. The pihas own the soundscape of the Amazon rain forest. One of the Awá boys does a perfect imitation of their two-note shrieks, which sound like greatly amplified catcalls. Even the birds are fooled, and thinking a new male has joined their lek, they answer him excitedly and even more shrilly.

The Awá are masterful mimics of the birds and the monkeys. This is an essential skill for people making their living in a rain forest. Patriolino says that when you hear a piha it means water is nearby, and, sure enough, we come to a *brejo*, a little swamp of *açai* palms, whose dark blue berries have antioxidant properties and are a big item in health food stores around the world. On the midslopes above the swamp, thick columns of magnificent, towering angelim trees—andira, one of the species the loggers are after—shoot up every couple of hundred feet, and on the ridge we find one that has been marked for cutting, probably by Guajajara working for the *madeireiros*. The barbarians are unquestionably at the gate.

The boys climb a vine way up into a flaring-buttressed sapopema tree, which is how they get honey, but we come to another towering sapopema in the middle of the forest that has been felled with a chainsaw. Patriolino explains that some of the Awá borrowed FUNAI's chainsaw and dropped the tree to get the honey in its crown so they wouldn't have to climb it. I ask Patriolino if an Awá hunter saw a mother tapir—a relative of the horse with a short, prehensile snout; it's the largest land mammal in the neotropics—and her calf, would they think, with the game getting so scarce, now that they are hunting with shotguns and the *madeireiros* are, too, maybe they should let them go? Do they have any concept of wildlife management? Patriolino says, "No. They don't think that way." A tapir feeds the entire village for a week.

A shotgun pops in the distance. Iuwí has shot a *guariba*, a howler monkey, the Awá's main source of protein. The boys also find the honey of some *tiuba* bees in the hole of an *inari* tree, scoop it out, wrap it up in one of the broad green leaves of the arums proliferating on the forest floor, cut a strip of *pauari* bark, which they use as a cord to tie the bundle up with, and one of them slings it over his shoulder. "The forest gives the Awá everything," Patriolino says.

Iuwí emerges from the forest with the carcass of the howler. Howlers are so important to the Awá that they give them a special classification, closer to humans than other monkeys are. Their howling bouts at dawn and the end of the day sound like wind rushing out of the portals of Hades. Patriolino says you never stand under a howling *guariba,* because it will shit on you.

Bands on the Run

The Awá were originally from Pará, the next state west, part of a wave of Tupí-Guaraní hunter-gatherers who came from south-central Amazonia sometime in the mists of prehistory and settled in the lower Tocantins Valley. When the Portuguese arrived on the scene, 500 years ago, the Awá had villages and plantations and were in a more or less constant state of war with their neighbors the Ka'apor. The Portuguese enslaved them and gave them smallpox, and perhaps fleeing a revolt on their subjugators' plantations between 1835 and 1840 called the Rebelião da Cabanagem, which took 20,000 to 30,000 lives, they fled east to Maranhão. Having learned how vulnerable they were as sedentary agriculturists, they became hunter-gatherers, who could break camp and take off in minutes. The first documentation of their presence in Maranhão was in 1853. By 1900 they had moved into the traditional space of the local people, the Guajajara, who are the largest tribe in Brazil, more than 20,000 strong, and have been in contact the longest, since some French came upon them in 1615. Being much less numerous, the Awá had to keep a low profile and melt into the forest. It was impossible for them to secure and defend land for growing crops. By the time the first Awá were contacted, in 1973, they had lost all their farming skills and interest in farming, and even the knowledge of how to make fire. But this was not cultural devolution, as has often been written about the peoples who had sophisticated cultures on the Amazon River itself and fled up to the headwaters of its tributaries and became hunter-gatherers. It was adaptation. And now the Awá are going to have to adapt again—to the modern world. The contacted ones already are.

In the 1940s, cotton became Maranhão's new crop, and a

wave of colonists flooded the interior. The Guajajara, Tembe, and Ka'apor—some of whom were indigenous, others of whom fled east when the Awá did—entered into relations with them, but the Awá stayed hidden from the national society. Many Awá died between 1960 and 1980, particularly after Brazil's military dictatorship took over, in 1964, and instituted a policy of "assimilating" the indigenous people that included exterminating the recalcitrant ones, those standing in the way of "progress" and national unification. The government dropped bombs on them and fed them sugar laced with arsenic. Many of the atrocities were exposed in the 7,000-page Figueiredo report, in 1967, which led to the dissolution of the Indian Protection Service, whose employees had committed many of them, and the founding of FUNAI as well as Survival International, which was started in 1969 by a group of Brits horrified by a story in the London *Sunday Times Magazine* about the genocide in the Brazilian Amazon. There are stories about Awá being massacred over the years: during the construction of two highways across the state in the '70s; by builders of the 550-mile-long railroad to the iron-ore mines in the Serra dos Carajás, in Pará, in the early '80s, and the settlers who poured in in its wake; by refugees from the drought in Piauí; by the *pistoleiros* of ranchers; and by loggers. Most recently, in 2011, an eight-year-old Awá girl from one of the *isolado* bands in another TI reportedly wandered into a logging camp and was tied to a tree and burned alive as an example to the others. But more Awá, according to Travassos, have died of colds and at the hands of their traditional enemies, the Ka'apor.

The Last Frontier

Back from our walk in the forest, we stop in the village. Several of the women are sitting in their hammocks, beading bracelets and necklaces. The village is really squalid, with discarded rags, decomposing garbage, and bones of old meals strewn all over the place. The Awá are not used to living in fixed settlements and haven't learned basic hygiene like sweeping the compound every morning. A number of infant wild animals, orphans of those shot by their husbands that the women have adopted almost as surrogate children—to the point of suckling them—are lashed to posts: two adorable golden-brown *quatis,* ring-tailed coatimundis; a bug-eyed little night monkey; and a mangy, deranged-looking black-bearded saki monkey.

The Awá are getting used to my being here. Takwaré, a teenager, gives me their Neymar-style haircut, cutting the sides close and leaving the hair on top and in the back. (The kids must have seen Neymar, Brazil's reigning soccer god, playing on television on a trip to the health clinic in Santa Inês, halfway between here and São Luís.) Every time I see him after that, he asks, *"Quem corto seu cabelo?"*—Who cut your hair?—and I shout, "Takwaré!" and he convulses with laughter. Awá humor is based on repetition. They're already being sucked in, subverted.

I visit Pirahá, who has a dozen arrows tucked under his *babaçu*-frond roof, each of which he spent days on and is a work of art. They are meticulously crafted of strong, dark brown bamboo called *tenkara* and have two kinds of points. One is like a spearpoint, but made of wood, with razor-sharp edges, and is for the big game—tapirs, peccaries, deer—while the other has a barbed point for monkeys, agouti, and birds. The young men are no longer hunting with bows, and in another generation the art of arrow making will be gone. The young Awá in the three other villages are 10 to 20 years farther down the road to "progress." So there's a sense of futility that I pick up after a while in some of the FUNAI people who are with us. "What are we doing here? What can we really do for these people?" one confides. "Why are we risking our lives when they're going to lose their culture anyway? Whenever I leave this place, I weep." On the porch there are three rifles and a stack of loaded clips in case *madeireiros* or *pistoleiros* decide to pay a surprise visit. The Amazon frontier is still very Wild West.

One afternoon, as I sit in my room at the post, Takwarenchia, one of the elders, appears at the window with a big grin. I show him the catalogue of a show on tribal people called *No Strangers* that was at the Annenberg Space for Photography, in Los Angeles, earlier this year, and Takwarenchia lets out an appreciative "Ahhh!" each time I turn the page to a new picture. Then we start teaching each other our languages. I point to my nose and say "Nose," and he watches how my mouth moves and says "Nose." Then he points to his nose and says *"Epiora."* In short order, Takwarenchia and I have 50 words in common.

*

I am not getting a particularly mystical or spiritual vibe from any of the Awá. This is another Western fantasy, like the noble savage and the idea that tribal people are great conservationists. Iuwí, Piraí's son, who spoke so movingly at our welcome and shot the howler monkey, has started to ask me for my Swiss Army knife, contradicting his father's statement that the Awá are not interested in anything we have. Every time I see him he asks, or rather states, "You are giving me that knife." This is only natural. You see these amazing things the *kanai* have, and you want them. But giving things to tribal people can create discord and a culture of dependence. It is one of the first things Carlos Travassos went over with us before we arrived. We were not even to share any of our food with the people at Juriti. I know all about this problem. Thirty years ago I went into a rain forest in Madagascar with a local young man who knew all the birds cold, which he had taught himself from their calls and glimpses of them in trees, and even knew their Latin names, while the people in his village farmed and rarely went into the forest. He was a natural-born naturalist and a sterling young man. When I was leaving I gave him my little Nikon binoculars. Years later I read that he had been killed by the villagers, who were envious that he was getting so many things from the tourists.

Cosmic Famine

Pigs have been found. Wild pigs — *queixada*. The village takes to the forest. Uirá Garcia, a 36-year-old anthropologist at the University of Campinas, who speaks Awá and spent 13 months here researching their hunting, kinship, and cosmology, has flown up to help us understand them. Uirá is a light-skinned black man from Rio. The Awá classify him as "another kind of *branco* [white person]." He and I join two men, two women, and three of their pet *quatis*, whom they have unleashed from the posts. They're the size of large kittens but have no trouble keeping up with us on our daylong, eight-mile slog through the forest. We cross a log bridge over the 20-foot-wide Rio Carú, which runs below the post and the village. A huge morpho butterfly, flashing creamy white and blowtorch blue, melts into the dappled shadows ahead of us. "The forest is alive for the Awá," Uirá explains. "They know exactly where they are at all times. Everywhere there is a story.

'This is where I killed a *paca.*' 'This is the tree I found honey in.'"
He shows me a map of their trails that he made with some of the
hunters. There are dozens of trails, each with a different purpose.
Some are only used seasonally. One goes to a place two days away
where there are many *copaçu* trees. They take it only when the
copaçu is in fruit.

We sit on a log, the first resting place, where they always stop, 45
minutes out. The men have gone on ahead to find the pigs, while
the women are amusing themselves with the little *quatis,* who have
boundless curiosity and nervous energy. One has poked its long
snout and its entire body except for its elevated, excitedly twitching tail into my backpack. The women keep flinging the *quatis* into
the forest with peals of laughter, and they keep coming back for
more. "The *quati* is most intelligent," Uirá says. "If you let it go
days from the village, it finds its way back. It follows the human
scent. When it gets big, it becomes too aggressive to keep and goes
back to the forest and joins a band. The hunters recognize the
ones that are former pets and don't kill them."

One of the women imitates the call of a *macaco prego,* a capu-
chin monkey, which she hears in the distance: the same note
seven times. But it is not a monkey—it's her husband, trying to
locate her. Uirá starts to explain the Awá's extraordinary take on
their forest universe, the intricate web of correspondences and
reciprocities they have with the plants and animals. "Every Awá is
named for a plant or animal," he explains, "with whom he has a
special relationship for the rest of his life. Every species of tree has
an animal that is its owner. The *araras,* parrots, are owners of the
araucaria trees. The *guaribas,* the howlers, are the owners of the
uwariwa trees. The other animals that eat the fruits of these trees
have to ask permission of the parrots and the howlers, and the
whole forest is structured this way [*a floresta é todo demarcado deste
jeito*]. There is an underworld of ex-humans—ancestors of their
enemies, the Guajajara, who fell through since-covered holes and
are still living—and a heaven with magnificent beings called the
Karawara, who come down to earth to hunt and get water and
honey. With the game disappearing, there will be a cosmic famine,
because it won't be the end of just the Awá but the Karawara, too.
The end of the forest will be the end of the cosmos. There will be
a famine on earth and in heaven."

We hit the trail, which becomes fainter until finally, after a couple of miles, we are bushwhacking, slashing through *mata de cipò*—vine-infested jungle—with machetes. The men appear. They have shot one of the capuchins and a *quati,* which they leave with the women, and they go off again to keep looking for the pigs. We reach a beautiful spot on a little stream and stretch out on its banks. One of the women bathes, sitting in the water with her curvy back turned to us, like a Gauguin. There really is an emerald forest, and we are in it. But as we are basking in what is left of the afternoon, Uirá is stung by four wasps, and one gets me on my left thumb, which quickly swells. A hundred different things can get you in the emerald forest. The Awá are most afraid of the ghosts of the dead—the bad part of you that doesn't go to heaven, the anger that you have to have to be able to hunt and kill your brothers and sisters the animals—who are drifting around in the forest and making otherwise unexplainable noises and are responsible for all illness, misfortune, and death.

Muito Irritados

I want to visit Tiracambu and Awá, two of the other, more acculturated Awá villages, but the already barely negotiable road through the invaded part of the TI is washed out, so I take a skiff with a two-horsepower engine down the Rio Carú, the skiff that brought Augustin do Violão to spell Patriolino as *chefe de posto* last night. Another reason I want to go to Tiracambu is to meet Karapiru, the most famous Awá, the poster boy of Survival International's campaign. His family was attacked by some ranchers in 1991. His wife and son were killed, another son captured, and he was shot in the lower back but managed to escape and spent the next 10 years alone on the run, until a farmer found him in Bahia, 400 miles south. An interpreter was brought in to persuade him that he would be better off letting FUNAI take care of him—he would eat much better, and his health needs would be taken care of—and the interpreter turned out to be his son, who had survived the assault and recognized his father from the bullet scar in his back. Travassos says Karapiru is a stand-up guy, *uma ótima pessôa,* super-calm and unassuming. Now in his 60s, he still hunts every day, with his bow.

*

The river snakes east, describing the border of TI Awá, on the left, and TI Carú, on the right, another reserve, created primarily for the Guajajara, more than 8,000 of whom live there, but also several hundred Awá, including one of the uncontacted bands. The milky river is full of stingrays, caimans, anacondas, and piranhas. TI Awá ends, and the left bank becomes the domain of the *caboclos,* the mestizo river people who live on the Amazon's thousands of tributaries. My driver, 20-year-old Jessel, is a *caboclo,* but he looks completely Indian. I ask him which tribe he is descended from, and he says, defensively, *"Sou Brasileiro"*—I'm Brazilian. He tells me that the *caboclos* have nothing to do with the Guajajara, who are good-for-nothing *malandros.* They have big plantations of marijuana, which came from escaped slaves in the 18th century, and smoke it ritually, to make contact with the spirits.

After two more hours Jessel pulls up to a dock, and we say hello to Jessel's aunt, whom we find in the kitchen of her mud *babaçu*-thatch hut. It's a cozy scene; apart from kerosene lamps and flashlights, a jug for filtering water, and a radio, a step away from the Indians, like a sod-roofed homestead on the American plains 150 years ago. The aunt serves us *cafezinhos,* little cups of sweet black coffee, and delicious little pink bananas. She radiates the kindness and unflappable calm of the *gente humilde,* Brazil's poor people. It is the country's transcendent quality. You find it even in the urban slums.

Back on the river, every 500 yards there is a stack of *maçaranduba*—Brazilian redwood—on the *caboclo* side, waiting to be picked up and taken to the buyers downstream. After three more hours we pass, on the Guajajara side, a dozen long, freshly milled and squared pieces of wood, roughly 20 feet by 30 inches by 30 inches. These must be destined for a more high-end customer, maybe in the States. The trafficking of Maranhão's timber is going on right in the open, and nothing is being done about it. This is the reality. Logging is the mainstay here, and no one has come up with an economic alternative. The majority of the mayors of the state's municipalities are *madeireiros,* and the only trees that are left are in the TIs. This is why the expulsion of the *invasores* from TI Awá has been taking so long. There is no political will to carry it out.

A few minutes later, we reach São João do Carú, the municipal seat and regional trading center, which is only 19 years old. Before that it was the *hakwa,* or hunting territory, of one of the

Awá's clans. The settlement of this region was very rapid. Teenagers cruise the main drag on dirt bikes.

I spend the night at a flophouse for ranch hands, and in the morning Cicero Sousa, who runs people and supplies to FUNAI's posts around the state, shows up in the same spanking-new silver Mitsubishi with unreal off-road capabilities that he drove me down from São Luís in, and we set off for Tiracambu with João Operador, the third of Juriti's rotating *chefes de posto,* who is coming along to replace a broken grindstone. After hours of nothing but pasture and cows—and Cicero at one point saving our lives with a last-minute swerve that avoids a head-on collision with a huge truck barreling around a blind curve on the single-lane paved road—we reach the Rio Pindaré, which describes the southern border of TI Carú. The 550-mile railroad to the Carajás iron mines runs along it through what was Awá land. Survival International prevailed on the World Bank and the European Union, which were lending more than $1 billion to Vale do Rio Doce, the company that was building the railroad and developing the mines, to make it a condition that all indigenous tribes' land in the Carajás railway corridor be demarcated. This resulted in the creation in the early 1980s of the half-million-acre TI Carú and the million-and-a-half-acre TI Alto Turiaçu, to the northwest, which some 50 Awá share with the Ka'apor and the Tembe. Carú and Alto Turiaçu were not contiguous. Between them was what eventually, in 2005, became TI Awá, whose creation was fought every step of the way and dragged on for 20 years. It was at various times going to be about 500,000 acres, then around 130,000, and finally ended up being about 289,000, by which time much of it was devastated.

Every couple of miles there is a little *povoado,* a town along a railroad that sprang up as people who worked on the tracks brought their families, and then others came, too. A lot of Awá were killed by these settlers. Now the *povoados* have streets and houses and stores with electricity and running water. We stop at one so I can buy ammo for the Awá of Tiracambu, which I have to do because Cicero and João Operador can't. This is one criticism I have of FUNAI. It converts the Indians from bows to guns, which makes hunting much easier, but then the game gets depleted, and after a few years the hunters have to make, in the case of the Awá of Juriti, a day's lope from the village before they can find a tapir or a peccary. Equally insidiously—and in the long run of dubious benefit—the conversion forces them into the cash economy, because they have to have ammo. FUNAI provided the Indians with ammo until last year, when, perhaps fearing their increasing militancy, or to save money, the Brazilian legislature enacted the Indigenous Peoples Disarmament Act. The Indians can keep their guns, but they have to buy their own ammo, and the only way they can do this is by selling their trees to the *madeireiros*, in the process selling themselves down the river. Putting the Indians in this situation does not seem to have been very well thought out, or humane, or in the best interests of the people FUNAI is supposed to be there for. It brings them into the economy, which they were doing fine—even better—without, then it leaves them high and dry. This is why I have to spring for the ammo, a prerequisite for any visitor. I had to buy some for the Juriti Awá, too, so they can kill more animals and continue to upset the equilibrium they had with their ecosystem when they used bows. But to ask the Awá to go back to bows is no more realistic than asking people in the modern world to give up their cell phones.

A few settlements later, Cicero turns onto a path that goes through the bush down to the river. Tiracambu's *chefe de posto*, José Ribamar Silva Rocha, is waiting on a sandbar with a skiff to pole us across. We walk up a ways to the *posto*, which has electricity from a line across the river. The modern world is right on the other side: every hour on the hour, 24 hours a day, a two-mile-long train whose cars are heaped with iron ore destined for Europe and China passes. It is a terrible, grating noise. The Awá call it "the Train of Fear" because it has scared all the animals away.

José has an old-time European face and in his black Wellingtons and with his hair in a little ponytail he looks like a character in a Thomas Hardy novel. He tells us that for three years two brothers, Aoréh and Aoráh, lived up the hill. Nobody knew what tribe they belonged to. They spoke *uma lingua desconhecida*—an unknown language. Maybe they were *isolados* from around Paragominas. There were several groups until the ranchers wiped out all the forest. Aoréh died in São Luís of cancer of the stomach, and Aoráh is up in Awá Guajá, the Awá village in TI Alto Turiaçu.

After dinner Tiracambu's leadership, half a dozen young men and a few girls in their late teens and early 20s, come from the village, and Cicero tells them why we are here. I am a journalist from a place very far away called America—it would take at least two years to walk there—and would like to meet Karapiru. And João Operador has brought a new grindstone for the rice huller, the machine that takes the chaff off the grains of dry rice these Awá grow.

Several of the young leaders have three horizontal black lines from the juice of the genipap tree painted on their cheeks, Guajajara warrior lines, which many of the young Brazilians who have taken to the streets are wearing, except that they are green. These slashes apparently migrated from the Guajajara to the national society and have been the insignia of Brazilian protests since 1992.

In the morning, João Operador tries to change the grindstone and discovers it's the wrong size. The young leadership comes from the village with the answer to our petition. We gather on the porch of the *posto,* and one of them, who is wearing a monkey-claw necklace over his T-shirt, says no visiting *brancos* will be allowed into their village or to talk to Karapiru until we talk to Soteiro. Hélio Soteiro, who also came with us to Juriti, is the FUNAI officer in charge of the four Awá settlements and the three *isolado* groups. He answers to Travassos—he's Cicero's boss—and is based in São Luís. Cicero says he has conjunctivitis, which is very contagious to the Indians, so he can't come to see them until it clears up. Plus he is in charge of the operation to expel the *invasores* from TI Awá—his main preoccupation at the moment.

"We are going to sell our rifles," the leader tells us. "What good are they? Because we don't have ammunition and we don't want to sell our trees like the Guajajara are doing." I show them the three boxes of shotgun shells I have brought for them. They are the wrong caliber. These Awá have 12-gauge shotguns, and the Juriti hunters have 20-gauge ones. So my offering does not sway them. The leader continues to enumerate their grievances. They don't have gas for their chainsaw and generator, and there are six more things. So that's that. "They were *muito irritados,*" Cicero says as we head out in the truck.

These Awá boys have been learning about militancy and activism from the Guajajara. FUNAI's popularity in Tiracambu is clearly not high at the moment. Already the young leadership has thrown out the Catholic missionaries of CIMI, the Indigenous Missionary Council, after deciding that their presence was, all in all, not good for the Awá—the services its missionaries were providing had a hidden agenda, to get them to renounce their animism and their own big guy in the sky, Maira, and to come to the Lord and be saved from eternal hellfire.

FUNAI's popularity is even lower in the other village, Awá. The young leadership there is even more *irritado*. A few days ago a woman in the village died of visceral leishmaniasis, which is fatal unless treated promptly and properly, and it wasn't. So they have taken one of FUNAI's vehicles as compensation for her preventable death. Cicero thinks there's no point in schlepping over to Awá, because it would be like walking into a hornets' nest. According to Uirá Garcia, the village's 150 inhabitants are divided into the progressives, who are militant and fighting for their rights, and the traditionalists, who are even more traditional than the Awá of Juriti. They go off into the forest for two or three months at a time.

While we are pondering our next step, Cicero gets a call from Soteiro and announces that the mission is aborted. We have to return to the *posto de vigilância* immediately. The *posto de vigilância* was built six months ago at the entrance to TI Awá and is where the expulsion operation, if it ever happens, will be run out of. Things are heating up. Four truckloads of *invasores* have gone to São Luís to protest to their *deputado* about their impending eviction. They're asking that 8 of the 12 miles they've invaded be given to them—there's nothing left of the forest, so what good would they be to the Indians?—claiming that where they are isn't in the TI anyway, and demanding that the whole thing be resurveyed. This is what happened in 2011 when the government issued the decree to dismantle their houses, fences, roads, and other works: the *invasores* made a lot of noise and threatened violence, and the government backed off. We have to go back because there are only two people at the *posto,* and Cicero has to supervise the repairing of the road so Salgado—who is on a tight schedule and can't take the river—can get out.

I was hoping to interview some of the *invasores,* but Cicero doesn't think this is the moment. It could be dangerous because they are *superirritados*. It sounds like I've reached the point of diminishing returns, and another Amazon adventure has concluded. Cicero drops me off at a place where I catch a van to São Luís, and from there I fly down to Rio, my 10 days among the Awá already seeming like a dream—but an unforgettable one.

Cult of Progress

My thoughts keep returning to the *isolados*. How unified are they in their resolve to have nothing to do with the modern world? Do they have arguments about what to do? Their conversations, their campfire stories, must be very interesting.

In March, a FUNAI team went up the Igarapé Mão de Onça to check on the *isolados* there for the first time since 1997, when there were nine of them, and found evidence—a recent fire and a lean-to with fresh *babaçu* fronds—suggesting they were still there. In June, the team went back and could find no sign of them, but discovered new logging trails only a few miles away. Leonardo Lenin, the leader of the FUNAI team, fears the worst.

Back in Brasília, there are encouraging signs that Justice Minister Cardozo may enforce the expulsion decree. In June, 300 soldiers and 46 vehicles were brought in to shut down the *madeireiros* in TI Alto Turiaçu. Seven illegal sawmills were decommissioned, and thousands of logs were destroyed. Cardozo says the soldiers will next be moved to TI Awá and reinforced with the troops who carried out the long-delayed and only partially successful expulsion of the *invasores* from the Xavante's territory last year. Operation Awá, the eviction of the 1,500 families, will be carried out by the end of the year.

I hope so. I would love to come back and learn more about the Awá's amazing cosmology and record the birds and the monkeys and their flawless imitations of them. Brazil can't afford to lose the Awá. Mankind can't let any of these last tribal people who live off the bounty of their forest, reef, or desert and are an integral part of their ecosystems, along with all the other species, disappear. These last 350 Awá are precious. As Octavio Paz observed, "The ideal of a single civilization for everyone, implicit in the cult of progress, impoverishes and mutilates us. Every view of the world that becomes extinct, every culture that disappears, diminishes a possibility of life."

GARY SHTEYNGART

Maximum Bombay

FROM *Travel + Leisure*

IT'S 5:41 A.M. and I'm headed from the airport into the city
formerly known as Bombay. In the next two weeks I will hear its
current name, Mumbai, spoken exactly zero times, so I'm going
to stick to Bombay. Bleary-eyed and tired after 15 hours aboard
Kuwait's intriguing and completely dry national airline, I am staring at the ramshackle temple by the side of the road with these
beguiling words stretched across its façade: *Never be afraid to trust
an unknown future to a known god.*

What the hell does that mean?

We are puttering down a series of dying streets and highways
in a tiny, ancient Fiat that would have made an East German Tra-
bant look sturdy, dodging an obstacle course of mopeds, fellow
Fiats, and the occasional resigned-looking bullock. Suddenly I am
feeling spiritual. My usual liberal arts agnosticism is difficult at a
time like this. I want to trust in a *known god* for the duration of
my stay in the city. In short order, we pass by the Status Refine
Gourmet, the Palais Royale skyscraper, and the Happy Home &
School for the Blind. A sign instructing the reader of THE SYMP-
TOMS OF MALNUTRITION ("If your child complains of constant
lethargy perhaps malnutrition is to blame") hangs next to a gleaming Porsche dealership. I am silent, and a little stunned. My driver
is honking every other second, as is everyone around him. But it
feels less like a plea to get out of the way than an affirmation of
one's existence. The honking says *I'm here!* Which is what everyone
in this impossible, ridiculous, and addictive city wants you to know.
They're here! And they're coming right at you.

I've come to Bombay because of a book written by a friend. Ounce for ounce, Suketu Mehta's *Maximum City: Bombay Lost and Found* is, in my opinion, not just the best book on Bombay, but the best book on anywhere in the world right now. *Maximum City*, a Pulitzer Prize finalist, has been rightly compared to Dickens's and Balzac's 19th-century treatments of London and Paris, and it gives Bombay the same immortal sense of flowing, unabated, tragicomic life. You close Suketu's book thinking that Bombay is not just a snapshot of the world, it is the world. Or at least the entry level to the world. It's where you get off the train from your village and join the path that leads eventually to London or Palo Alto or, as I see from the grimy window of my Fiat, to a gated community in the suburbs built exclusively FOR ARISTOCRATS.

I forgot to mention that it's also a very funny book. And Bombay is a very funny city. At one point during this trip, as Suketu's taxi idles at a red light, a 14-year-old kid tries to sell him a pirated paperback copy of *Maximum City*. Suketu asks him what the book is about.

"Oh, all of Bombay is in this book!" the young street salesman says.

"Well, how much do you want?" Suketu asks.

"Six hundred rupees!" the kid says—about $9.

"Six hundred? Do you know I've written it?"

"Fine," the kid shrugs. "If you've written it, you can have it for four hundred."

Which is to say, if you want to trust your unknown future to a known god in Bombay, he might as well be Suketu.

What's it like to be a lonely person in Bombay? I guess I'll never find out. People talk to me even when it's clear that I don't understand Marathi, Gujarati, or Hindi. To not talk to someone here, to keep your opinions to yourself, is seen as mildly offensive. I meet Suketu at the best place for talking, the Press Club. Suketu's journalist buddies are gathered on the club's rooftop, which overlooks the cricket field of the Azad Maidan. This is part of the greenbelt in the center of South Bombay that leads to the Victorian Gothic skyline of the famous Oval Maidan (the Rajabai Clock Tower is a fearsome answer to Big Ben). We munch pappadum and deep-fried tapioca balls, smoothing their crunchy passage with a combination of Thums Up, a beloved local Coca-Cola impostor, and Old

Monk, a beloved local rum impostor. After the worldwide coverage of the horrific rape and murder of a young woman in Delhi, I get the immediate sense that the country is wounded. One of the journalists says, "They'll talk about rape for now, the way they used to talk about corruption, and then nothing will change." It's hard to argue with this brain trust, most of whom seem to have written at least one book about their country. But I take note that on our busy rooftop, there are only three women in a sea of men, and all of them are at our table. One of them is a young journalist named Nishita Jha who covers gender violence and pop culture for *Tehelka*, "India's most fearless weekly." Everyone chimes in to tell me that Bombay is far more cosmopolitan than Delhi and far safer for women. (After the recent gang rape of a female photojournalist in Bombay, I'm not as sure about the second part.)

I am introduced to Naresh Fernandes, a delightfully bearlike, shaved-headed journalist. "Naresh is the gangster of Bombay," Nishita says, affectionately. "He runs everything." Naresh has an "alcoholic's license," allowing him to buy 12 units of whiskey a week, as a way around Bombay's draconian booze laws. He was also part of the *Wall Street Journal* staff and has a facsimile of one of the paper's Pulitzer Prizes hanging proudly above the toilet in his apartment. But Naresh, the author of *Taj Mahal Foxtrot: The Story of Bombay's Jazz Age*, is no cynic when it comes to this city's past.

The next day he takes me and Suketu to the Chhatrapati Shivaji Terminus, better known by its former name, the Victoria Terminus, and still better known to all Bombay natives as VT. Naresh is excited because this truly stunning structure—supposedly the second most photographed in India, after the Taj Mahal—has just opened a so-called Heritage Gallery, allowing visitors a guided tour of the building's innards, whose scale and detail have no earthly equivalents. "Exotically Gothic" is what our guide calls this mix of Gothic Revival and Mughal architecture. The railway station easily puts New York's Grand Central to shame with its solid-granite columns, Italian marble, carved-wood ceilings, an open cantilevered staircase beneath the octagonal dome, and stained-glass windows that light up the structure like a veritable Duomo of the rails. There are bas-reliefs of the different ethnicities of India, along with a sculptural riot of squirrels, dragons, crocodiles, monkeys, birds, and foxes. Only Queen Victoria is missing from her central niche.

The state of the trains departing VT is not quite as stunning.

Even the first-class cars are like a prison on wheels, the beige color scheme and the barred windows perfectly complementing the maximum-security motif. There is a compartment FOR LADIES ONLY and another car reserved for people with disabilities and cancer patients, the last represented by a drawing of a crab. The done thing for the millions of passengers who commute from the far-flung suburbs to the city every day is to jump out of the moving carriage while the train is still slowing down at VT. In my attempt to look cool before the Bombay natives, I nearly kill myself when I try this, my arms windmilling to gain balance as I stumble across the platform, the wind of the still-passing train against my back, along with the sound of laughter. I end up on my knees, palms on the ground, in a near-universal position of prayer, pain coursing up my shoulders and thighs.

Naresh and Suketu take me as far away from the Press Club and my hotel in relatively tony South Bombay as one can go, to the slums abutting the railroad tracks near the Bandra station, which is north of Bombay proper. The iconic Taj Mahal Palace hotel, where I am staying, has a "destiny planner," or in-house astrologer, but we decide to consult a white-clad, bearded man sitting by the railroad tracks with his parrot. The parrot picks out cards from a deck and the man interprets his little green friend's advice. "Saturday is not a good day for you," the parrot tells me through his master. "Do not conduct business on a Saturday." I am stunned by the parrot's ability to identify my ethnicity. Do I really look *that* Jewish? The parrot and I lock eyes, and beaks, for a while. "Your wife is smarter than you," the man interprets for the parrot, which is also true. He asks me my name. "Gary is not your birth name," the parrot tells me. Which is correct as well: my birth name is Igor. *Never be afraid to trust an unknown future to a known god,* I think. The dusty parrot by the railroad tracks knows all.

Naresh walks me over to a hunger strike conducted by a gathering of slum dwellers, sitting beneath banners for L'Oréal Paris. In the distance, the shimmering locus of their anger—the ugly, shoddily built apartment buildings, the so-called transition housing to which they will soon be shunted. Six months after being built, these six-story tombstones look like ruins, and the locals tell us they're infested with bugs. It is one of Bombay's paradoxes: sometimes it is preferable to live in a slum. "This is an epic land grab," Suketu says.

On the other side of the train tracks we pass the series of century-old heritage bungalows that comprise the Catholic Willingdon Colony. Naresh tells me a crooked developer has bought up all of them and is going to tear them down to make way for something called Orchard Elegance or Elegant Orchard, another high-rise. Even as he is saying this, a group of thugs in khakis and dress shoes, lean and menacing, confront us in the lush passageways of the colony. The thugs begin screaming at us. Naresh shows his press pass. I can almost sense the violence about to start, and Suketu braces for impact. I can suddenly feel every bit of the humidity, the breezes of the Arabian Sea too far away. A fat-bellied police officer approaches and we ask him to intervene, but the constable is clearly on the side of the thugs. The cop and the gangsters decide to give us a good lesson in Bombay's municipal civics. *"Bhagao! Bhagao!"* they shout in unison.

"Get out! Get out!"

And so we run.

That evening I am glad to be back at the Taj hotel, where the staff still speak in hushed tones about "the unfortunate events" of the 2008 terrorist attacks. That tragedy notwithstanding, the Taj does a preposterously good job of tuning out the steamy world outside, the parrot astrologers and khaki-clad thugs. When you're looking down the stairs at the sublime pink Escher-scape of its infinite staircase or swimming below the fantastic Victorian cupola of the hotel, a congregation of pigeons above you, the world feels better than it should. The Taj's butler staff (each of the club rooms has its own butler) may have given me the nicest treatment I've ever had in my life outside of marriage. Need a horrific stain magically rubbed off your suede shoes? Samrat, the butler, makes everything right in less than half an hour. Then there are the joys of a sunny Parsi breakfast of *akuri* (spiced scrambled eggs) on toast at the Sea Lounge, the boats bobbing by the triumphalist British bulk of the Gateway of India, a line of tankers coming into port. Which brings me to the food.

Within my ghee-covered pages of *Maximum City* lies a veritable larder of India's many cuisines, Suketu's subjects constantly munching on street snacks. There is a two-page disquisition on the *vada pav* (the spicy deep-fried potato patty) alone. Back at the Press Club I meet Roshni Bajaj Sanghvi, a food columnist for a website called Mumbai Boss. The lovely Roshni has a Bombay native's wonderful sense of nostalgia, and during our drive through the city yells out things like "They used to sell popcorn over there!" or "I lived behind Shroff's eye clinic!" More poignantly, as we pass the green expanse of the Horniman Circle Garden, she says, "I used to go to the study corner in the park, because my family was too noisy and I couldn't concentrate." The next day, I stop by the park's little study corner, tucked away within the greenery, and find a small enclave of schoolboys and girls with monstrous backpacks poring over numbers and figures. Some of the kids look barely high school age but are already elbow-deep into *Marketing and Human Resource Management.* Far more than the land grabs and the headlines about crime, this is India.

Roshni takes me to Highway Gomantak, a restaurant off a service road in the unfashionable Bandra East neighborhood (I'll get to Bandra proper shortly). It's a working-class family place, with writing on the walls attesting to Krishna's many names. The food is coastal Maharashtrian and Goan, all of it heaped before you in great waves of fried sublimity. There's an elegant fried version of the lizardlike "Bombay duck," an intensely ugly fish that is beautiful on the inside. There's a pomfret curry with coconut milk and tons of turmeric and green chiles and coriander seeds. Roshni tells me that the dish has at least a dozen ingredients, but it's the coconut that gives it such a nice, sweet balance. The fish in my stomach makes way for hot clams, swimming in spices and bearing a sharp kick of cinnamon and cloves that manages to overwhelm even the 220-volt current of chile. "These are spices that will wake you up from the dead," Roshni says.

As we drive back to South Bombay we pass the infamous new Antilia building on upscale Altamount Road. The 27-story, reportedly $1 billion tower is home to a family of five who, rumor has it, delayed moving in because the megahome conflicts with Vastu Shastra, an ancient Indian architectural doctrine (disobeying it brings bad luck to a home's inhabitants). The world's most expensive private residence is owned by one Mukesh Ambani, India's richest person, who is worth an estimated $21.5 billion. The tower apparently has three helipads and a series of floating gardens.

"Ambani built a special snow room for his mother," Suketu tells me that night. "His mother once got caught in a snowstorm in Boston and she enjoyed it quite a bit. So he built her a room that produces artificial snow. She looks out on the hot Arabian Sea beneath a Massachusetts snowstorm."

We're at the Café Marina, the rooftop bar at the Sea Palace Hotel. In addition to the sea, the hotel looks out to the fabled dome of the Taj Mahal Palace hotel and the Gateway of India beyond. I can practically see my room from here. I'm talking to Kitu Gidwani, a friend of Suketu's and star of TV and indie Bollywood. "The lifespan of a Bollywood star," the brilliant actress tells me, "is from fourteen to thirty-five." She has crossed the latter date, but looks as beautiful as ever.

As the sea breezes sweep the rooftop and I down another vodka tonic, the conversation turns to tango and psychoanalysis. The mass spread of psychoanalysis would suit this city well: there are few places in the world where people talk as much, as eloquently and passionately and randomly.

The next day I head north to Bandra. Once a suburb of the great metropolis, this former farming and fishing village has been transformed into a rival of the densely settled South Bombay. Comparisons with Brooklyn have been drawn, although Bandra's relative tranquillity, and its proximity to Bollywood studios, make it feel a little more like Santa Monica. Bandra is aspirational in a cute way. The American Express cleaners are right next door to the American Express bakery.

The party center of Bandra used to be the Olive Bar & Kitchen. The whitewashed Mediterranean place is still known for its profusion of cleavage on Thursday nights, when the DJ really lets loose. On other nights, it serves fatty duck, foie gras, and all the contemporary classics of the big-belly set. I watch a suitably large man set two BlackBerrys down on the bar next to a woman in power stilettos. "Drink, boss," he says to the bartender, who wordlessly answers with some tall, icy concoction.

I meet Suketu and Naresh, who is a resident of Bandra, at the recently opened Pali Bhavan restaurant. The atmosphere is laid-back, with old sepia-toned studio photographs of Indian families, a corrugated-steel ceiling, and a back window that, according to Naresh, is sealed "because it looks out on a slum." After a week in Bombay, the proximity of poverty to luxury no longer surprises. I bite into the *galouti* kebab, which, according to the menu, was "created for the leisure loving nobles who preferred not to chew."

The food at Pali Bhavan ranges from the country's north to south without missing a beat. Next, we travel back to the common man's *vada pav,* the fried potato patties that are a proud vegetarian answer to the burger. The Pali Bhavan version is amazing, filled with peanuts and garlic and served with a vibrant *ghati masala.* Even the presentation is simple and beautiful—five perfect sliders lined up on your plate. The juicy char-grilled corn on the cob, another street favorite, is a gratifying snack. Then there's *bharwan karela,* stuffed bitter gourd in pumpkin gravy. Indian children endure their karela the way ours do broccoli, but at Pali it is an eye-opening combination of bitter and sweet.

The next day, I follow Roshni's advice and head to the Café Military, in the Fort neighborhood, smack in the center of South Bombay. Military, despite its name, is a friendly, open-window kind of place with beer-drinking locals and excellent Parsi food. The *keema salli* is a snack-perfect dish of crunchy potato sticks with savory minced meat. With the cheerful staccato of the ceiling fan and the old brown cabinetry, Military is timeless and fun, like a cool *boteco* in Ipanema.

I would be remiss if I didn't also mention the Mi Maratha restaurant, in Lower Parel, a spare white room where locals from the enormous corporate park nearby graze on hot-and-sour fish curry and the spice bomb that is chicken *sukha,* filled with bony morsels, slurped up with the aid of many chapatis. The *jhinga thali* with dried shrimp and jumbo prawns is alone worth the trip to this neighborhood in progress.

One of the last chapters in Suketu's *Maximum City,* "Good-bye World," concerns a wealthy family who give up their riches to become Jain monks and nuns, wandering around the countryside, living under brutal and basic conditions, trying to reclaim something they had lost amid the frenzy of Bombay. I've only been here for 10 days, but I have been chased out of a housing colony by gangsters, charmed by psychoanalyzed Bollywood stars, banged up after jumping out of a moving train, and eternally convinced of the prescience and wisdom of railroad parrots. I end my journey at one of the holiest Hindu places in the city, the Banganga Tank, on Malabar Hill.

The holy lake was originally built in the 12th century and, according to legend, flows straight from India's holiest river, the Ganges. Flanked by the laundry sprouting off apartment buildings, the greenish holy water accepts worshippers in saris and dhotis. Ducks and geese take to it as well, the only place in the city where the car honks are exchanged for goose honks. Everything smells of cooking and family life, and children play cricket on what may well be the world's smallest pitch. The eyes are dazzled by the pastel colors, the rising stupas of nearby temples, the kites launched by gaggles of kids.

I walk around and sample the continuous call-and-response of religious chants, and then, during a sudden interval between prayers, I hear that Bombay rarity, the impossibility you can enjoy only in the "snow room" of your 27-story personal skyscraper perched high above the slums: silence.

THOMAS SWICK

A Moving Experience

FROM *The Morning News*

TRAVEL IS MOSTLY BOREDOM—and if you're not bored, you're pretty sure that everyone else is having more fun. For professional travel writers, the feeling's not just true, but considerably worse.

Travel suffers from false advertising. Tour operators, vacation companies, cruise lines, hotel chains, bad travel writers depict it as something "adventurous," "exciting," "romantic." Though disingenuous, it's understandable: they're in the business of travel, and their job is to sell it to consumers.

As a result of this hype, people who travel often experience disappointment. Friends will tell you of their wonderful trips, and much of the time they're being mostly honest. But they conveniently leave out the train they missed due to miscommunications, and the town that was shut tight for a holiday no one told them about. Travel, like football, is best in highlight form.

And people will gleefully tell you about their vacations from hell. The worst trips, travel writers love to say, make the best stories; everybody loves a good tale of woe.

Travel stories are divided, rather religiously, between paradise—a word used promiscuously by travel magazines—and inferno. Those about so-called heavenly places predominate, at least in written form (since most publications are dependent on advertising, and many feel the need to be promotional), while tales of the hellish generally belong to the oral tradition, though they sometimes make it into books, like the excellent anthology *Bad Trips*. But there is very little middle ground. You not only don't read, you rarely hear someone say: "The trip was so-so." Or: "Something was missing." Or: "I left feeling a little unsatisfied."

Readers sometimes say to me, You always meet the most interesting people when you travel. I tell them, Not really, I just write about it when I do. Most of the time I'm wandering around lonely and aimless. In my own way, I am as guilty as the cliché mongers of perpetuating the idea of travel as a continuously fascinating activity—though all writers shape their experiences into an unrepresentative series of highlights; otherwise our stories would be too boring to read.

Condé Nast Traveler has never printed the "Top Ten Places Where You Won't Feel a Thing."

But in *Reading Chekhov: A Critical Journey,* Janet Malcolm writes about her trip to Russia, in the course of which she lost her luggage. The effort to be reunited with her belongings propelled her out of her tourist shell, required her to deal with the locals, introduced a small drama into her journey. She came to the conclusion that "travel itself is a low-key emotional experience, a pallid affair in comparison to ordinary life." Most tourists, she noted, are not doing anything adventurous or exciting or romantic; they are passive observers, visiting landmarks, looking at paintings, and are less engaged in life than they are on a typical Monday at home. It is only when something happens on our journeys—which is, frequently, something going wrong—that we are able to break through the surface of a place.

I read Malcolm's observation with the shock of recognition. It was so true and yet so unacknowledged. When we travel, particularly those who go alone, which is most travel writers, we take ourselves out of our lives for a while. We're capable of enjoying most of travel's gifts—the welcome break from routine, the glorious novelty, the invaluable lessons—but we're frequently left emotionally flat.

One October in Genoa I walked the streets as darkness fell and offices emptied. Perhaps because the scene was one I never get in Florida—crowded sidewalks, a chill in the air, a charged twilight—I thought back to the years I spent in Warsaw, walking with my wife on autumn evenings. I peered into the faces of women as they passed close and totally oblivious to me on their way home to dinners and lovers.

Wistfulness is not the most enjoyable emotion, but for a traveler it's one of the most common.

Travel has been called the saddest pleasure. Sometimes it's sad because of what we see: poverty, misery, hopelessness. Kate Simon, writing in *Mexico: Places and Pleasures* of some of the capital's less reputable ones, ends the section on a philosophical note: "There is no playfulness in it, nor even much energy, just restlessness and several kinds of desperation and, if the night is cold and damp, the sight will depress you, which you may deserve or even want, if you've come this far."

Often, though, travel is sad because what we see doesn't include us. Much of a travel writer's life, I once wrote, is spent watching other people have fun. Everyone who travels has the same experience; we're all outsiders, excluded from the action. Being left out is never pleasant, but in travel it's even more frustrating because a few days ago you were not just part of a group, of friends or family; you were the envied and celebrated member, the one heading off, as the travel brochures put it, for exciting adventures in exotic lands.

There are people who don't need people. David Foster Wallace spent his last days aboard the MV *Zenith* in his cabin, traumatized by the orchestrated "fun" of cruising. The resulting story—"Shipping Out," published in *Harper's* in 1996—is a recognized masterpiece in the "bad trips, great stories" school. John Steinbeck, in *Travels with Charley,* drove coast to coast and back again with surprisingly few encounters and—as was revealed not too long ago—even fewer real ones. Bill Bryson, the most popular travel writer of the last few decades, has admitted he doesn't enjoy talking to strangers.

Of course, writers of any kind are never the norm; those of us who write about travel are different from the start, since we usually head out alone. The reason cited most often is freedom from distraction; when you're by yourself, you're more attuned to your surroundings. Less discussed, but just as important, is the fact that, alone, you're also more sensitive. You not only notice your surroundings more clearly; you respond to them more deeply. Smiles and small kindnesses mean more to the unattached traveler than they do to a happy couple. A merchant in Fethiye adds a few extra sweets to my purchase and I'm extremely touched, in part because no one has paid any attention to me in days. If I'd been there chatting with my wife, I wouldn't have been so moved; I may not have even been aware. And the merchant quite possibly would not have been inspired like he was by my lonely presence.

Once on a trip I went days without having a conversation with anyone other than myself, which resulted in dangerously low levels of self-esteem. Everyone around me was talking, gesturing, laughing. What was wrong with me? One morning I headed toward a building with sliding glass doors and the doors refused to open. They seemed to confirm my suspicion that I had ceased to exist.

A lot of travel is a search for solitude. A love of nature propels travelers away from crowded cities to forests, rivers, deserts, oceans, mountains. There is a subgenre of travel book—from Peter Matthiessen's *The Snow Leopard* to Joe Kane's *Running the Amazon*, to Jon Krakauer's *Into Thin Air*—that treats travel as an expedition (some more meditative than others), occasionally a test.

A friend and fellow travel writer once told me that he can appreciate a beautiful landscape but doesn't feel the urge to immerse himself in it the way he does when he sees a great city. With nature, it's enough for him to stand back and admire.

As a mostly urban traveler, I understood him perfectly. Driving around Arizona I was mesmerized by the mountains, the way their colors changed depending on the time of day, but I was content to see them from afar (often through a windshield).

Years earlier, on the south rim of the Grand Canyon, I drove from one observation point to another, not just for the views, but for the reactions of visitors. Almost as fascinating as the great hole, for me, was its effect on the people who stood at its edge—everyone from the Japanese schoolgirls desirous of a photograph with me (or any handy American) to the retired Ohioan reciting Robert Service's "The Ballad of the Northern Lights." I needed a story, and suspected that my uninformed thoughts on the geological marvel wouldn't be enough. Also, unaccustomed to the power of nature, I was curious about its influence on others.

A few years later, at Glacier National Park, I took a hike and saw a grizzly foraging on a distant mountainside. On another walk I encountered a family of mountain goats. An easterner on my first trip to the Northwest, I was more elated than I'd been at the Grand Canyon, probably because I'd found furry, animate nature.

True nature lovers aren't so fussy. A ranger at Everglades National Park once told me that sometimes after work she drives home, changes out of her uniform, then comes back to the park—to enjoy it in the evening. This in a place that, while possessing a subtle beauty, has none of the dramatic scenery, or adorable animals, of western parks. The ranger loved everything about the Everglades, though, even the mosquitoes; their relative absence during our hike distressed her slightly, as she wanted me to see their impressive swarms. She showed me the best place, the next time I came at night, to gaze up at the stars. She had fashioned a life in which she didn't need to travel to be transported by landscape. In fact, all she needed to do was to go to work. She seemed the most grounded person in South Florida.

Evelyn Waugh, in "A Pleasure Cruise in 1929," wrote: "I do not think I shall ever forget the sight of Etna at sunset." He described the pink light mixing with gray pastels and confessed: "Nothing I have ever seen in Art or Nature was quite so revolting." Judging by their photographs, many travelers are taken by sunsets. Scenic towns built next to water, like Oia on Santorini, fill with crowds for the daily dropping of the orb into the sea. Key West has turned the event into a communal celebration, complete with buskers. It's a big deal at the Grand Canyon, too, though there people turn their backs to the sun, to watch the play of light on the rocks. They do the same at Uluru in Australia, where the high-end tourists enjoy the show with the help of sumptuous tailgate spreads.

Music, more than food, works on our emotions, usually in a positive way. Often it's the music you stumble upon that makes the biggest impression. You enter a St. Petersburg church where a choir on the balcony sings vespers, and your listless spirit, overdosed on sights, instantly lifts. In Latvia I attended a midday organ concert in Riga Cathedral—no emcee, no introduction, no visible musician—just a sudden eruption of pipes followed by a cascade of baroque. It was pure refreshment, in a country where I didn't speak a word, and it brought a feeling of peace that was the perfect antidote to the traveler's confusion.

Growing up in New Jersey, I visited New York City frequently, but it took me years to get into the Guggenheim and MoMA because I couldn't pull myself away from the shows on the sidewalks. New York gave me my love of walking city streets, even though for years

I never made it out of midtown. But those dense blocks alone provided endless visual stimulation: the prostitutes who greeted me with soft hisses and defeated faces as soon as I exited Port Authority, the camel-haired lawyers strolling Park Avenue, the yarmulked merchants chatting in the Diamond District, the liveried doormen facing Central Park, which, like the museums, I never entered because of my fear of missing out. I roamed Manhattan hunting for sights I couldn't forget.

I've traveled the world in much the same way, walking and observing. "Grin like a dog and run about through the city," as Jan Morris has described the activity, appropriating a line from the 59th Psalm. You never know when you'll find gold. "I am a camera," Christopher Isherwood declared in prewar Berlin, eight decades before the age when everybody *has* a camera. But how many of us see the way Isherwood did?

One of my loveliest memories of Mexico dates back to my first trip there in the early '90s. My last evening in Mexico City I walked the huge Zócalo and noticed an animated crowd at one end. Approaching, I saw that it was made up mostly of children, who were throwing parachuted figures high above a subway grate. Dozens of toy soldiers rose with an updraft, sailed gracefully through the air (backdropped by the cathedral), then landed on the pavement a few yards away, where they were instantly scooped up and hurriedly carried back for their next mission. It was all so ingenious—child's play out of a public work—and incongruous—a simple pleasure in a monumental space—and the joy was so infectious that it planted in me an affection for Mexico that, after two subsequent visits, has only increased.

Sometimes you can be moved by making yourself part of a tableau vivant: wearing a costume and dancing through the streets of Port of Spain at Carnival—get close enough to the trucks carrying the speakers and the vibrations will literally shake your heart—or entering, after weeks on the *camino,* the cathedral city of Santiago de Compostela.

In the summer of 1982 I was coming to the end of two years in Warsaw, where I'd married and worked as an English teacher. As a fitting final act, I decided to walk the nine-day pilgrimage to the shrine of the Black Madonna in Częstochowa. A popular August event, that year's promised to be even more so, as martial law was

still in effect after the outlawing of Solidarity, and the imprison-
ment of its leaders, back in December.

The pilgrimage drew thousands, a two-headed beast—religious rite and political rally—making its way through the heart
of Poland. The weather was hot and sunny until we arrived into
Częstochowa, where we walked under a low, sullen sky. Crowds
lined the streets for our entry, just as they had in Warsaw for our
exit, making me feel, once again, as if I were part of a liberating
army. As a foreigner, I felt unworthy to be the recipient of so much
adulation—a boy handed me a bottle of soda, a man presented
me with flowers—but on a personal level it seemed a kind of recognition not so much of my walking 150 miles but of my spending
two years in Poland, suffering through the winters, standing in the
queues, learning the language (its own kind of torment), living
with Poles through the ordeals of their history. And of course marrying one of them, the light of my life. Many Americans have lived
and married abroad, but few have received such a loving and public valediction.

Being a resident, I had earned the points toward this reward,
but to redeem them I had to become a traveler. (A pilgrim, one of
the most venerable types.) The second identity strengthened my
already ineradicable ties to the country.

When I started traveling professionally, I was surprised and delighted to find that I could still make emotional connections to
places. I discovered this for the first time in Portugal, where—after having schlepped around Spain—I met a young Dutch woman
who introduced me to her friend, a colorful poet, who invited me
to dinner (this after weeks of solitary meals) and then took me to
a dive to hear men singing fado. It was in Lisbon that I discovered
the secret of travel writing, which is also the secret of memorable
travel: you approximate, as best you can, in the short time allotted
you, the life of a local. Once back home and writing, I stumbled
upon another secret: the *best* trips make the best stories. Though I
had known this in theory from books like Patrick Leigh Fermor's
A Time of Gifts and *Between the Woods and the Water,* which are nearly
as crammed with friends as they are with learning.

I divide places I visit into two types: those I like okay (a part
of one's critical skills is an ability to find what's attractive), write
about, and don't think about much, and those that, in some fun-

damental way, touch me, and continue to haunt. This group, in order of appearance in my life, is made up of Alsace, Poland—both
places I lived and worked—Portugal, Mexico, Vietnam, Turkey,
Lithuania, and Brazil.

For someone who travels for a living, it might appear to be a surprisingly short list. Its size would seem to support Malcolm's theory
of the "low-key emotional experience" of travel; its content, for
the most part, my belief that the less-visited places often produce
the most meaningful trips. In Spain I toured the guidebook cities—Madrid, Barcelona, Seville—where, not surprisingly, no one
was particularly curious about foreigners. Many of the residents,
you got the feeling, had had quite enough of us. Lisbon, off to the
side, on the lower edge of the continent, was not besieged and,
subsequently, was much more welcoming. Among other things,
the Portuguese speak the best English in southern Europe (outside of Gibraltar and Malta). Sevillaños made me feel like a tourist;
Lisboners made me feel like a guest.

Like most everybody who's been there, I love Italy. I've visited
seven times, and every time I arrive in the country I feel happy,
even when taking a train from France, a country I lived in and
whose language I speak. The French, André Gide said, are Ital-
ians in a bad mood. (Alsatians are different, at least the farmers
I worked with, who had little of the Gallic discontent.) I've had
wonderful experiences in Italy, like most people who've been
there; I've met good people and, with some of them, I've become
friends. Yet I've never felt the emotional bond with Italy that I feel
with Vietnam—possibly because there are so many people vying
for her affections. She is the most popular girl in the school. I love
Italy, but I've never gotten the feeling that Italy loves me back.

Loving the unloved, you assume the feeling is mutual. You may
be wrong, as travelers often are. But it doesn't change the nature
of your affection, or your relationship with the people you get talking to at the post office who invite you to their home, cook you
dinner, and refill your glass and tell you stories of life under a
dictatorship. At the end of the night, they insist on escorting you
back to your hotel, where you exchange phone numbers and e-
mail addresses. At that moment the place stops being just the site
of your vacation; it becomes the home of your friends. It takes on
a significance, and enters your heart.

Born on the 9th of July

FROM *Outside*

DAY ONE IS THURSDAY, and we roll out of Juba, South Sudan, in the ambassador's official ride, a Toyota Land Cruiser in spotless white. The driver's door is showered with gold stars across a familiar sky-blue flag and the words *L'Union Européenne*, the heraldry of someone who matters in this vast, imperiled infant of a nation.

The someone is Sven Kühn von Burgsdorff, a lean, 55-year-old German, and ambassador, who is not the German ambassador. Sven actually holds an obscure but equivalent title, commissioner, and represents the European Union as a whole. That makes him a kind of supranational diplomat for 27 nations, with a major say in the spending of $395 million in European aid to South Sudan over the next two years. A former commando, he once toughened his feet by running barefoot in the snows of Lower Saxony and jumps out of airplanes to relax. I personally will hear him speak five languages before this trip is over. Also in the Land Cruiser are Italian photographer Marco Di Lauro and Sven's son David, a bushy-headed 26-year-old surfer and International Medical Corps programs officer already hardened by years of rolling around Africa chasing big waves.

The ambassador has a paraglider in the back of the Land Cruiser, crammed in with camping gear, food, and bottled water. We are headed out of the dismal capital, driving south for four hours toward the Imatong Mountains, where we hope to find and summit Mount Kinyeti, at 10,456 feet the highest peak in the country. The ambassador wants to tour the south of South Sudan, get some exercise, and then fling himself off the peak in his paraglider, avoiding a crash landing in the central African jungles while claiming some fun distinction like First Unpowered Descent from a Place No One Has Heard Of. The only problem as we leave town late Thursday: von Burgsdorff mentions that he has to be back in Juba on Sunday afternoon, which leaves us just Friday and Saturday to make a hike that should take three days.

But what are schedules out here? Only 15 minutes outside Juba we're held up by a potential land mine, one of untold numbers believed to be scattered around South Sudan after the 22 years of civil war that led to its independence from Sudan. A cluster of cars is pulled to the side, the passengers sitting under a tree, and down the road are a pair of armored bulldozers operated by remote control.

Ambassador Sven spends the break speed-reading a thick report on a typical messy dilemma in South Sudan: how to join the International Criminal Court without destroying relations with the nation's neighbor and former overlord, Sudanese president Omar al-Bashir, an indicted war criminal who holds the key to negotiating an oil deal. Sven makes neat marks in the margins and then fires up his satellite phone. With the thoughtless ease of a Type A *Übermensch,* he rocks four of his five languages in a couple of minutes: French with a colleague, English when reading back text, German to his son, and then, calling out the window to ask about the land mine, some Juba Arabic, a common dialect among soldiers and policemen here.

The robot bulldozers soon flatten whatever it is they've uncovered. There is no explosion. The road opens, and we start crawling forward again.

The newest country in the world is physically large—240,000 square miles, the size of France—and catastrophically ungoverned. It is a featureless grassland for most of its open, landlocked run. South Sudan is a landscape without clear divisions or functioning borders, touching Sudan and the Arab world to the north and the troubled Democratic Republic of the Congo and Central African Republic to the west, with East Africa pressing up from below. The waters of the Nile and thick seasonal rains drive a wedge of green grass across plains teeming with animals. National Geographic explorer Mike Fay made global headlines in 2007 when he completed the first aerial survey in 25 years and estimated that there were 1.3 million animals flowing across it, a great migratory river of white-eared kob and other antelope and gazelles dotted with a stash of elephants and a handful of species—including beisa oryx and Nile lechwe antelope—existing nowhere else on earth. Finding this many unknown animals anywhere was like finding El Dorado, Fay said at the time; finding them in war-torn Africa was even better.

Though no one has counted in decades, there might be 10 million people, too. South Sudan is quilted internally by some 60 tribes, many of them nomadic herders with long-standing antagonisms. But a year before my visit, on July 9, 2011, the Dinka, Nuer, Bari, Azande, and dozens of others came together to declare independence and raise the tricolor flag—black, red, and green—of a new nation. The president, a Dinka and former military officer named Salva Kiir, favors black cowboy hats and lives in hotels. A disorganized parliament struggles to create a host of new ministries out of empty buildings, and the national archives are a pile of crumbling documents on the floor of a tent.

Independence has added innumerable corrupt factions, including newly enriched local businessmen from the Tribe of Hummers. South Sudan is not a society in recovery: there never was any real infrastructure, government, civil society, rules, laws, or rule of law here, so there is nothing to recover. Instead it's a scratch country, invented as a solution to an insoluble problem of semipermanent war and defined by what it lacks. There is no electrical grid, no mail service, almost no roads even of the dirt kind, and perhaps a few hundred miles of asphalt if you count every paved block in Juba. The have-nots have a lot of not: barely a smidgen of schools, almost no health care, a population living on zero dollars per day in a subsistence-farming economy where cattle are traded like currency. There are more guns than people who can read; refugee camps are more common than towns; snow would be easier to find than a road sign.

South Sudan was carved from the much larger, Arab-dominated country of Sudan, the last in a series of remote governments, from ancient Egypt through the Ottoman Empire, which viewed the south chiefly as a source of converts or slaves. In the 19th century, British explorers traced the routes of the Blue and White Niles but left little impression on the land and evacuated in 1956, leaving the northerners—typically pale-skinned Arabs from Sudan's capital, Khartoum—in charge. The vast open spaces became a kind of formless border between the Middle East and Africa, with Muslims in the north and black Africans, often Christian or animist, in the south.

When people talk about the war here, they have several to choose from. They might mean the anti-British struggle of the 1950s or the coups and countercoups of the 1970s, but they probably mean the south-versus-north war that broke out in 1983 and lasted 22 years. In general, all the wars have pitted central authority in Khartoum against the margins, including the Darfur genocide that began in 2003 in Sudan's far west. The war in the south featured the same genocidal tactics as in Darfur but ran longer, immobilizing the region for decades.

Unlike Darfur, which still lingers under Sudan's rule, the southerners actually won. Hiding in the countryside, they wore out the Khartoum regime, which agreed to a peace treaty in 2005. More than five years later, a massive deployment by the UN helped midwife a truly independent South Sudan, and former U.S. secretary of state Hillary Clinton and current ambassador Susan Page both pushed hard to make the peace deal stick. In 2011, USAID and other agencies spent more than $100 million on everything from schools to refugee camps, including an impressive array of road-building projects. That's only a quarter of the money promised by the U.S., but this year's budget calls for $244 million, easily the largest aid package in South Sudan, and Sven's European Union is also investing heavily in rural development and "capacity building," the euphemism for helping the South Sudanese construct a government that isn't corrupt.

Good luck with that. President Kiir recently sent a pleading letter to his ministers asking for the return of $4 billion that he said had gone missing. Oil will be as much curse as blessing: some 75 percent of the old Sudan's oil fields are just inside the southern territory, while the only two pipelines go north, through Khartoum to the Red Sea. Since independence, relations between Sudan and South Sudan have declined rapidly, the north withholding payments for southern oil, the south retaliating by withholding the oil itself. (South Sudan lost 98 percent of its government revenues; the north was hurt almost as badly.) Meanwhile, continuing outbreaks of violence have threatened to ruin everything, and despite a new deal to restart the flow of oil and cash, neither was moving

during my visit in late 2012. South Sudan had the desperate, in-
flated feel of a wartime country dependent on charities and aid,
with Chinese contractors waiting in the wings for their turn.

Maybe the fighting will stop. Maybe the oil will start. But no
matter what happens, almost anything will be an improvement.

Day two and the air is wet and warm, the voice of Africa a low
rumble of water from a deep cleft. Somewhere down below the flat
acacia trees, hidden in thick green bush, is Imatong Falls. South
Sudan's other great resource is water, pouring copiously out of the
high southern hills toward the northern deserts. We catch only
a brief glimpse of the heavy, rushing cascade along with our first
peek at the steep and jagged mountains overlooking the tree-filled
valleys. Then we move on without pause. Sven is setting the pace
and it is fast. No time for soaking our toes or for anything but
walking.

The day before, in the Land Cruiser, the von Burgsdorffs engaged in what diplomats would call a frank discussion about the
extent of paved roads in South Sudan.

"One thousand kilometers," Sven said.

"No, Papa! No!"

"Yes, for sure. Minimum."

"No, Papa. A thousand? You're crazy. It's like a hundred."

Sven began naming towns with a few paved blocks here and
there. "He's counting every sidewalk!" David shouted from the
back. They could go at each other like this five times an hour,
merciless, relentless, and still laughing. Sven takes pride in his
son—even more in walking him into the ground and eating
weirder things. If David surfs with great whites in Cape Town, Sven
parachutes off a high cliff above Juba into the arms of waiting policemen (actual story). Somewhere between the dismal reality (a
hundred kilometers of asphalt) and the diplomatic optimism (a
thousand) is the real South Sudan, the one that matters.

It was night by the time we plunged down the final miles of the
road south, passing the town of Torit and arriving in a small village
called Kitere at the very end of the road ruts. We woke up on the
dirt floor of a hut in darkness. "The adventure starts where the
road ends," Sven offered, and nothing was a cliché at 5:40 A.M.

Once we've gathered a guide and a few porters from Kitere—a
biblically named crew called Daniel, David, Simon, John, and

Joseph—we start ascending steeply up through fields of 10-foot-tall sorghum on a muddy path no wider than a single man. Even this begins to fade quickly, and after passing a few final primitive huts and cornfields, we climb an ever narrower track, slippery clay sending us crashing down repeatedly. Sunrise makes it clear that our route to Mount Kinyeti—about 31 miles round-trip, by Sven's calculation—will be painful. Impenetrable brush closes over the trail, which is soon reduced to a hunters' trace used by outsiders only about once a year. Daniel says he's brought five previous groups to the mountain since 2005.

We cross five streams the first morning: the first two are bridged, after a fashion, the logs wet with the spray of tumbling whitewater. The next streams aren't bridged at all. The guides, sure-footed in sandals or rubber boots, leap from rock to rock; I fall in once and use all three pairs of my socks on the first morning. Marco takes the cautious approach, crossing barefoot while swearing, "I'm never going to work with you again!"

The fact is, we're out of our league. Sven is a fitness freak and sets a pace that even the hardened Africans have trouble keeping. Back in Juba, I talked with Peter Meredith, a famed South African kayaker who is trying to launch the first commercial rafting trips in South Sudan, to take expats from the capital on floats down the White Nile. Meredith suggested doing the hike to Kinyeti in three or more days, but with Sven's meeting in Juba, we must travel 31 miles, get up to 10,000 feet, and be back at the road in a little over 48 hours.

Ferns enclose the trail, and the dramatic views of the pale green Imatongs are extinguished by triple-canopy jungle, a chaotic world of switchbacks amid stinging fireweed and stands of mint and wild cannabis. Eight hours pass this way, until we finally collapse at 7,500 feet next to a crude lean-to. We fumble into sleeping bags and tents; the disciples curl up on the ground under their jackets.

"On stone, on water," Joseph tells me, "we sleep."

Getting any view of South Sudan as a whole is tough. Juba is located well enough, sitting where the powerful White Nile drops out of the central African lakes, the mother water rolling northward past the city at running speed before it splits into meanders to form the vast, 11,500-square-mile Sudd wetland, among Africa's largest. Eventually, the waters regather, joining the Blue Nile in Sudan proper and pushing past Khartoum and on to Egypt.

But Juba is more encampment than city, a sprawling settlement of homely huts and instant apartments whose population has swelled to more than a million as waves of returning exiles and rural people have moved in. Many thousands of foreigners have come here as well, riding around in white Land Cruisers during the twice-a-day traffic jams that are a mark of pride for locals. The most common signage is anything beginning with the letters *UN*, and a trip across town uses reference points like "Go past WHO" and "Turn left at WFP." Diplomats from the U.S., Europe, Africa, and China have set up shop, as well as hundreds of foreign NGOs, everyone from the Red Cross and Norwegian Church relief to War Child and—it's all about cattle here—Veterinarians Without Borders. In a place where hotel rooms are made from empty shipping containers and everything from gasoline to rice is imported on the back of a truck from Kenya, inflation has skyrocketed: a taxi across Juba costs twice as much as in New York, hastily built apartments are priced as if in central Rome, and locals can afford nothing but *asida*, or corn mush. Many foreigners are sweating out their lives in the northern refugee camps, healing and organizing, but in Juba the expat tone is that of a lunar colony with pool parties and endless paperwork.

In a two-story white building I meet Cirino Hiteng, one of the young country's rotating cast of ministers and its most dashing defender of wildlife. He wears a Nairobi-style short-sleeved suit in gray, topped with a narrow-brim trilby and accessorized with a South Sudanese flag pin, a flashy watch, two rings, and a Livestrong-style yellow bracelet reading HOPE FAITH LOVE. Hiteng may look like the minister of hip-hop, but his affection for animals is deep.

"I love nature," he says plainly. "I have a spiritual connection. Every year I fly five hours up and down looking for animals. Elephants, oryx, ostrich, elands. I spotted a cheetah this year. I always spot the most."

Hiteng is from a peasant family in Torit, near Mount Kinyeti, and he recalls walking to school ("Nine miles there, nine miles back") to write his first letters in the sand with a stick. He got to Catholic school and eventually earned a PhD in international relations from the University of Kent, in Canterbury, England. A South

Sudanese with an advanced degree is a rare thing, and Hiteng has rotated through an array of posts, serving as chief of staff to the president and now minister of what is called Culture, Youth, and Sports.

He tolls off the positives in South Sudan. There are, in theory, 12 game reserves and 6 national parks, and the annual antelope migration through the most famous, Boma National Park, is probably the second largest on the planet. There are dramatic rapids on the Nile and long stretches appropriate for the whitewater rafting that has become popular in Uganda. He thinks the Imatong Mountains will develop as a tourist destination and helicoptered to Kinyeti's summit with a UN team. "I planted the flag of South Sudan," he says. "I tell the local people, Don't cut down the forest; it will bring the *mzunga*, the foreigner. Did you see Imatong Falls? Imagine if you put some cottages there. You have breathed the air of God."

One moment Hiteng deflates his own enthusiasm ("It's too early! Even the backpackers are not here!") and the next he's rapturing onward ("We could put some floating hotels in the Sudd; enjoy the birds. That would be amazing!")

Still, Hiteng is well aware of South Sudan's problems. The parks, many of them dating back to British rule, have almost no staff funding, training, equipment, or infrastructure, and animals are constantly poached for meat. Giraffes — slow-moving and hard to miss — are shot first, and there are organized raids by horsemen from Sudan, who massacre elephants and carry the tusks hundreds of miles back to Omdurman, where artisans carve them and export them to China. The Chinese themselves are also here, building roads and hoping to invest, like Europeans and Americans, in the oil industry. The common denominator in all this, Hiteng concludes, is lack of infrastructure. "Roads!" he cries. "South Sudan is a huge land. It is almost impossible to travel across it." Better roads will bring medical care and tourist dollars to the isolated tribal cultures that define both the glory and problems of South Sudan. They'll also open up more areas to poaching and illegal logging.

That afternoon I visit another minister, Gabriel Changson, the head of Wildlife Conservation and Tourism, crossing Juba on the back of a *boda boda,* the euphonious name for a motorcycle taxi. Changson is not as flamboyant as Hiteng — he sits calmly behind a desk the size of a lifeboat, wearing a pressed dress shirt. But, like Hiteng, he is well educated. A Nuer from near the border with

Ethiopia, he has a background in banking and a master's in economics from Duke. ("Go Blue Devils!" he says.)

Changson doesn't know his own age ("About sixty," he guesses), but he knows tourism will protect the animals of South Sudan. Like Hiteng, he talks about Kenyan-style eco-lodges, tent safaris, bird watchers in the Sudd swamp, and the need to train South Sudan's 14,000 wildlife rangers, army conscripts without equipment or skills. The country's paper parks are roadless and so large—Boma is 8,800 square miles, and the Zefah Game Reserve, in the Sudd, is 3,700—that they can't be patrolled.

"A hungry man will not listen to our rules," Changson says, "but if we offer an alternative livelihood, they will pick it up." His conservation agenda starts with humans: tribespeople need boreholes for clean drinking water, health centers, basic schools, and model villages. Then they will consider ecotourism. Until there is security, Changson candidly admits, "nobody will come."

Right now nobody is coming. In two weeks I meet one tourist: a Japanese woman literally checking off a list of African countries. There is currently nothing for a tourist to do. I sign up for a safari to Boma, but it's canceled amid late-season rains and shifting paperwork. Meredith, the kayaker, says his hopes for a rafting business were curtailed when NGOs and embassies, out of security concerns, banned their Juba staffs from leaving the city on weekends.

The country has perhaps five years to transform itself into a conservation nation, American biologist Paul Elkan, country director for the Wildlife Conservation Society (WCS), says. "What's important in South Sudan is intact ecosystems. Big blocks of wilderness. Some of the last great wilderness in Africa. The largest intact savanna in East Africa."

There are many bright spots—more than a million if you count those migrating antelope. And the WCS has been able to count thousands of elephants in South Sudan, collaring 34 with satellite transmitters and tracking them daily. But the country's situation is changing rapidly, and for animals and ecosystems, Elkan says, "the pressures are higher," as peace allows people to start moving around, exploiting resources. Several of those WCS-tagged elephants, in fact, have already been poached.

Keeping the animals alive will depend on law and order in the countryside, schools and boreholes, tourism of the right kind, legal and regulatory advances, training for rangers, and an infrastructure of roads, lodges, and spotting planes, all within five years. Without that seismic shift, the elephants will be wiped out, the hartebeests turned into bushmeat.

"It's a fixer-upper," Elkan says.

Day three turns out to be surprisingly easy, for the simple reason that Marco and I never make it up the mountain. By the end of day two, we had reached the flanks of Kinyeti, the barren summit visible just once through the thicket of vegetation. But the slopes are steep and the journalists weak.

We huddle around a campfire well before first light, chilled and wet after a night on the ground. Daniel calculates that it will take the Germans 4 hours to ascend the last few miles, on a switchbacking trail that climbs 2,500 feet in thick forest before bursting into the clear. But Marco and I—Daniel calls us *la marwani,* the old men—will need 5 hours to summit, and that's before the hike back out to the road. All in all, we're looking at a 12-hour haul.

While we sulk in our tents, Sven and David storm the peak. They make it up in less than 4 hours, Sven hauling the 30-pound paraglider himself. On the misty top, they hold out South Sudan and European union flags in a snapping, cold wind. Too much wind: the glider stays in its pack. The von Burgsdorffs march back down and collect the shamefaced journalists for the hike out. Elapsed time: 7 hours.

So my cowardly day three is only this: a half dozen miles crashing down wet trails in dense brush, leaping rock to rock, pounding up and down spurs of mountain in a frantic effort to keep Sven in sight. Patient, merciful Daniel paces me for a while at the back of the column, pointing out the dangerous fireweed, whose hairy edges sting like coals, and a vine that coagulates wounds. When we're attacked by safari ants—stubborn black biters that crawl up inside our pant legs—he shows me how to find and kill them under the fabric. The disciples pause to scrape "honey" from a dark hole in a eucalyptus tree, actually a sweet sap loaded with crunchy insects. The forest gives up its secrets.

In the late afternoon we encounter two hunters, giddy young men running in circles, frantically searching for a slim, straight tree. Using machetes, they chop down something the thickness of an arm, cut it to 10 feet, and jog off into the bush, inviting us to follow.

Not far away, they've caught a boar. The pig is in a wire snare and has raged against the jungle for hours, clawing a circle of black dirt in the exact radius of its leash. Daniel warns me to climb up onto something: "If he comes for you, he will kill you." Indeed, I can see the animal's three-inch incisors when it snarls.

The Imatongs are remote and untroubled, so this is one of the only places in South Sudan where no one carries a gun. The hunters have already fired an arrow into the pig's throat, with no effect. Now they set about beating it to death with their 10-foot pole. The men then swiftly bleed the carcass, truss it on the same pole, and lead us up and over a forest and down into a swamp where they've built a smoky fire. They devour a big pot of *asida* as the pork cooks. Later I hear that these men are poachers, but there are no rangers, no signs, no evidence of laws and rules, only hungry men of the bush crawling forward.

We move uphill onto dry ground in the last moments of light and pitch our tents under magnificent, ash-white eucalyptus, which climb 200 feet or more into the air. You don't normally see tall trees like these in South Sudan, but here is more evidence of what war has preserved. The trees grow in perfect rows—the area was a British plantation at the time of Sudan's independence in 1956 but has been neglected ever since.

Sven is looking everywhere for the future. Around the fire he outlines development ideas. There's potential for an eco-lodge at Imatong Falls. And down in Daniel's village, Kitere, they could form a cooperative and harvest some of these trees to pay for schools or farming equipment. Eventually they might start a sawmill, like in the old days, and have a small, sustainable business. All it will take is clearing the old British logging road, which is blocked with dead trees but otherwise in fine shape.

"Why don't you clear the road?" he asks Daniel.

"The problem is the government," Daniel answers.

Maybe Daniel is right—nothing happens until a big man gives his blessing. But Sven is frustrated by this kind of routine passivity. "Always," he says bitterly, a rare crack in his diplomatic reserve. "It's always the government's fault."

The wind sweeps the high branches back and forth, flakes of papery bark raining down on us like snow.

We make it out in the morning, hopping all the streams again at double speed, busting our humps to make it back to Juba on time.

But then the Land Cruiser breaks down. After all that, Sven has to miss his meeting. He takes it well, sitting in the hot shade of Torit all afternoon, drinking tea, finally at rest.

Like the great migrations and towering eucalyptus, South Sudan's human cultures have endured because war immobilized the country decade after decade, paralyzing progress. Questions about the survival of animals and habitat are not separate from the survival of man himself, and tribes here have persisted to a surprising degree, especially in the country's cattle camps. These *laagers*, island-like villages that appear like beaten-down brown circles in the immense green of the savanna, form wherever seminomadic groups settle to let their cows graze.

In Juba, Marco and I hire a car and driver ($500 a day) and head north before dawn, hoping to find such a camp. After only an hour of bad-road driving, we spot a herd of Watusi cows, white beasts with great curved horns, scattered in the bush. A few hundred yards of walking brings us to a cattle camp, a dozen half-naked men and women gathered beside a smoldering dung fire. They're Mundari, native to this region and known by the ash smeared on their bodies and the three Vs of ritual scarring across their foreheads.

They greet us with indifference (mostly) and wild threats (the largest man). A towering, ash-covered warrior wearing only a blanket, he immediately challenges me to a fight, but then calms down and allows us to settle in around the fire. The Mundari have blankets, a few plastic sheets for sheltering infants against the rain, and wooden goads, the short prods used to move cows. There are two cell phones in the camp, neither working. A couple of immensely tall women sit on blankets, steadily shaking gourds back and forth, churning the milk of the cows into a fermented, alcohol-like drink.

Cattle are bank account and social status—a hedge against hunger, an investment, and the key to getting married. (With some tribes, paying a dowry in cattle has become a human rights concern, as girls as young as 12 are traded as child brides.) Cattle raids—organized stealing expeditions—are endorsed by both culture and economics here. In 2011, more than 1,000 people were killed during a cattle war between the Nuer and Murle, on the outskirts of Boma National Park. A hundred thousand cows were stolen, along with hundreds of women and children.

The men paint my face with dung ash, roaring with laughter at the result. Then Marco and I head off, passing a town—a few roadside kiosks selling gasoline in soda bottles alongside an empty refugee camp—before moving deeper into nothing. During a pee break, I'm zipping up by the roadside when three naked men walk out of the tall grass.

They aren't here to herd cattle. Their scarring is Mundari, but they carry burnished cow-leather shields and carved fighting sticks, not normal goads. Their skinny, hard bodies are naked and oiled, as if for a wrestling match, but they're in a good mood. We stare at each other for a while until we are interrupted by a tense hiss. They fall quiet, squinting. I follow their gaze back down the road. Another file of men, also naked, also prepared for fighting, has appeared in the distance.

Our guys wave a pennant in the air, a colorful homemade flag, and their guys break into song, jogging quickly forward. Moments later, all the men embrace and laugh. In the middle of the dirt road—it's not like there's any traffic—they break into new songs and put on a display of stick fighting, blows rattling the shields, their shiny bodies staging scenes straight from an Attic vase. The driver—a Ugandan—cowers in the car, saying, "I have never seen anything like this in my whole life!" If you want a romantic encounter with ancient Africa and don't mind land mines, South Sudan is the place.

On the last day of my trip, rising for another East African dawn, I meet Paul Elkan at the WCS's little compound near the airport. In the past seven years, Elkan has logged more than 1,000 hours flying over the plains of South Sudan, many of them with National Geographic's Mike Fay, and has seen a genocidal civil war turn into a cold peace. Like many NGOs, the WCS is trying to build something from nothing, scraping together training programs and keeping two airplanes aloft. After some puttering around with the Cessna, the motor finally catches, and we're off to see the biggest secret in South Sudan.

First, however, a charity traffic jam. In an almost roadless country, air transport is king, and there are more than 60 planes parked at the airport, mostly small grasshoppers from the UN, NGOs, and missionary groups. We taxi toward the runway but are edged out by an Ilyushin 76, a container ship to our rowboat. Elkan has to

hold back the throttle as the cargo plane—marked WORLD FOOD
PROGRAM—idles on the runway. "Juba Tango Charley," Elkan
calls, hoping to nip in ahead of the jet, "holding short and ready."
But there's no answer from the tower, and after five minutes the
Ilyushin finally lumbers into the sky with a reek of jet fuel and a
searing roar that could jump-start a migration.

We pop up quickly, sailing over the tiny precincts of Juba at
1,000 feet, and then, still climbing, across the meandering Nile,
leaving behind the charcoal smoke, the glitter of round tin roofs,
the chaotic yards containing donkeys. Right there, we enter
3,900-square-mile Bandingilo National Park, which hosts huge migrations of antelope twice a year but is otherwise empty, without
even the trace of red dirt that marks a walking trail. The plane
buzzes along at 2,000 feet, rattling like a '68 Beetle with wings, but
Elkan is affectionate, praising the Cessna. ("All good planes come
from one place," he says. "Wichita.")

We've put in an hour like this, pleasant and cool, the only easy
travel in South Sudan, when Elkan points to patterns in the grass
below. The vast plain—a flat horizon in every direction—is now
touched with a few dark lines where antelope have moved northward. Animals follow the grass, which follows the rain; at the end
of the dry season, that means migrating north, toward the retreat-
ing edge of the Sudd wetland. Elkan flings the plane over onto a
wingtip, circling down on the first antelope. These are white-eared
kob, the most common and the easiest to spot, thanks to white
flashes on the males' necks and ears. There are dozens, then hundreds, but it isn't the time of year for dense gatherings, and we
aren't flying to see antelope. Elkan levels out the plane, climbs
back to 2,000 feet, and heads . . . Well, I can't say where he heads.
For another hour he follows a GPS signal toward a part of South
Sudan that is seldom seen, one more vast wilderness in this land of
empty spaces. The location is secret because of what is there: one
of the last great elephant stands in East Africa. To poachers, every
elephant herd is simply a collection of millions of dollars of ivory
waiting to be shipped to China.

Two hours out from Juba, we drop back down to 300 feet. The
grass shows patterns again, not the tiny depressions left by passing
antelope but dark, wet zigs and zags, diamond patterns gathering
tighter, trails crossing trails.

We probably could have found this herd just by looking for

those shapes in the grass, but Elkan is running down the satellite trackers and knows they were, yesterday at least, just ahead of us. The grass turns to a beaten black mat, crushed flat in the bright sun, and then, against a splash of water, there are elephants. Ten. Then 20. Then 50. Then hundreds.

"Four hundred," Elkan estimates.

That's just one particular herd. There are thousands of elephants out here, beyond the reach of poachers, another secret of this hidden-in-plain-sight land. Here's hoping some things are never found.

JEFFREY TAYLER

In the Abode of the Gods

FROM *World Hum*

THEIR SACRED PLEAS released by winds to the heavens so near, swallow-tailed prayer flags of white, green, and royal blue, inscribed with the black curlicues of Buddhist scripture in Tibetan, fluttered against the clouds grazing the pass high above the Mekong River. I stood beneath them sweaty, panting from the altitude, peering down into Himalayan canyons with plunging forested slopes. With my Tibetan guides, Tenzin and his wife, Anadorma, I had just spent three hours ascending a punishing switchback trail from Yongzhi (their home village, at an altitude of 8,130 feet) on the Mekong's stony banks. They paused briefly, exchanged hurried remarks in Tibetan, and, with sharp cries of "Yiip! Yaaas! Gaaa!" prodded ahead the two mules carrying our gear and supplies.

This was no time to rest. Just after dawn we had set out from Yongzhi on a 15-day, 200-mile pilgrimage trek around the third holiest mountain in the Tibetan Buddhist cosmogony, the 22,107-foot-high Kawa Karpo, in northwestern Yunnan Province. For Tibetan Buddhists, only Mounts Kailash and Nanja Bawa are more sacred. Tibetan lay Buddhists and lamas perform the pilgrimage to put themselves in good standing with Samsara, the deity who, depicted on their temples' murals as clawed, fiendish, fanged, and red, turns the Wheel of Life and determines their next reincarnations on the basis of acquired *sonam,* or spiritual merit. (Otherwise in Buddhism samsara denotes a soul's endless wandering through repeated deaths and rebirths, a fatiguing cycle ending only for the enlightened few, with the attainment of Nirvana.) Earn enough merit, Buddhists say, and your next reincarnation will be an auspicious one, as a human, and not, say, as a lowly scorpion or snake.

Tibetans hold that the deities Kawa Karpo and his wife, Metsmo, inhabit the mountain's summit, while a host of lesser divinities haunt the vales below. Such beliefs have no real place in the godless philosophy of compassion, nonviolence, and renunciation taught by the Buddha in northern India, in the sixth century B.C. There Buddhism flourished, providing the downtrodden with a refuge from the caste system and winning over kings, but eventually Hinduism largely subsumed it (though it still draws Dalit converts). But when Buddhism reached Tibet a thousand years later, it changed, fusing with the indigenous Bon religion, an ancient animist faith that hallows nature and populates the landscape with gods, and still enjoys the loyalty of 10 percent of Tibetans. Bon influence, in fact, is what makes Tibetan Buddhism "Tibetan," and the Dalai Lama himself has recognized Bon as one of the key religions of Tibet. We might expect him to: the concept of continuously reincarnated Dalai Lamas with a divine mandate to rule is a vestige of Bon.

If Kawa Karpo's ridges rise and fall like the spine of a *Tyrannosaurus rex* ready to pounce, its summit stands in northwestern Yunnan Province, and not in the adjacent Tibet Autonomous Region (through which the pilgrimage route loops). This makes sense: along with parts of Sichuan, Qinghai, and Gansu Provinces, northwestern Yunnan belongs to historical Tibet (that is, Tibet at its most geographically expansive, before the Chinese occupied it in 1950 and redrew its boundaries), and is ethnically Tibetan. Yunnan is, in fact, the least "Chinese" region of China, and is home to 28 of China's officially recognized minority peoples. Twelve hundred miles southwest of Beijing, Yunnan only became part of China in the 13th century, when Kublai Khan, founder of the Yuan dynasty, annexed it. From its pristine heights, two of Asia's greatest rivers, the Mekong and the Salween, cascade south into Burma, Laos, and Cambodia. The province's remoteness and natural beauty have of late served as a cash asset: in 2002 the Chinese government grandiosely renamed it *Shangri-La* (from James Hilton's 1933 novel, *Lost Horizon*) to promote tourism as a source of income following the abolition of commercial logging.

Long enamored of Buddhism and the compassion, nonviolence, and transcendence of desire and suffering it espouses,

I decided to embark on the Kawa Karpo pilgrimage—an enact-
ment of the allegory that life is a journey as steep and circuitous as
those depicted in paintings in Buddhist (and Hindu) temples. If I
could not bring myself to believe in reincarnation, I nevertheless
relished the prospect of passing 15 days communing with a wilderness redolent of Buddhism and conducive to contemplating its
enlightening doctrines. I've come to believe that these doctrines,
with their stress on universal tolerance and renunciation, might
offer us a way out of our current planetwide crisis of diminishing
resources, relentless consumerism, and terrorist violence.

Tibetan pilgrims have trekked the route since times as imme-
morial as the origins of Bon. The first Westerner to undertake it
did so only 80 years ago, and foreigners are still a rare sight. In
fact, people of any sort would be few when I chose to go—at the
end of the (summer) typhoon season. Tibetans usually head to
Kawa Karpo in the drier months of autumn, after the harvests are
in. But I preferred the uncrowded time, the better to appreciate
the wilds.

There would be risks. The route consists mostly of precipitous,
avalanche-prone mountain trails, many of them above 13,000 feet,
and marked, if at all, by piles of mantram-inscribed prayer stones
in the lower reaches, or by prayer flags at the passes. Of their perils
I had heard much sobering talk when I arrived in Zhongdian, the
nearest town. In the previous year alone on Kawa Karpo, a Japanese hiker had died in a landslide, and two British travelers had
succumbed in a snowstorm. Nuoji Zhaxi, the local entrepreneur
who helped me arrange my pilgrimage, also told me of four Chinese crushed recently in a rockfall near the village of Yubeng, and,
most infamously, of the party of 17 Japanese mountaineers who, in
1992, died in an avalanche with their two local guides while trying
to scale the peak itself.

"The gods want us to worship Kawa Karpo," Nuoji told me
gravely, "but not to touch it. Those who touch it die."

Kawa Karpo remains unscaled. So dangerous are trails near its
summit that some devout Buddhists attempt them in the hopes of
accelerating their passage into the next life. Suicide pilgrimages
on the mountain are a tradition—one of which I hoped not to par-
take. So I took care to outfit myself properly and arranged for experienced guides, Tenzin and Anadorma, both 36, who for most of
the year are small-time farmers of Yongzhi's scant arable land. Ten-

zin, an eight-time pilgrim, was tall, bony, and stoop-shouldered, with a frequently pained expression on his otherwise benevolent face; Anadorma, a veteran of five tours, was tirelessly cheerful and agile, and kept her long black hair bundled beneath a baseball cap turned backward. They had loaded their two mules, white Hujya and brown Ramo, with provisions (rice, salted pork, green peppers, and tea, bought in the base-camp village of Deqin, a six-hour cliffside drive and hike from Yongzhi), utensils, and even dried corn for the high passes, where fodder for our pack animals would be scarce. Our common language would be spoken Mandarin, of which I have a working knowledge.

The trek would involve no technical climbs, so my equipment and garb would be basic: a tent, a lightweight sleeping bag and ground pad, trekking shoes, polarized sunglasses, and rain gear. A GPS module would let me check altitudes and distances; a pocket thermometer clipped to my expedition knife, temperatures. For spiritual sustenance I packed two key Buddhist texts, the Dhammapada, something like an extended Buddhist Sermon on the Mount, and the Bodhicaryavatara, a guide to enlightenment by the Indian monk of the eighth century Shantideva. The Dhammapada belongs to the ancient Indian canon; Shantideva's text holds sway in both Indian and Tibetan Buddhism.

Thus kitted out, we quit the pass above Yongzhi. We marched north, parting the clouds, along a mostly level, foot-wide trail. My heart and lungs pumped hard in the thin tepid air. But within an hour we were engaged in a loping descent through dewy grass toward a waterfall, a slit of froth and glitter tumbling from a cliff into the dark forest, with Kawa Karpo's massif on our right, across a ravine, lost in the clouds.

Downward we strode, our mules' bells ringing.

By noon we had descended to the Mekong's headwaters, which roared blue-white at trailside, and found ourselves penetrating a jungle, stepping over mossy ledges, marching through tunnels formed by giant arching ferns and lushly leaved trees draped with garlands of phosphorescent gossamer moss. The route's altitude varies from 6,000 feet to almost 16,000 feet, and cuts through three (of four) types of biogeographic terrain: humid tropical, humid temperate, and polar. The primeval forests of Yunnan, some of China's last, support 7,000 species of plants and 263 varieties of orchids, plus 450 kinds of birds, as well as snow leopards, bears, and the elusive Yunnan golden monkey. But just when it seemed we were most alone, wandering through enchanted domains, skirted women in pink tassled headdresses would cross our path, smiling and hailing us in Tibetan, shouldering baskets brimming with wild mushrooms (one of the few regional exports). Then they, like sylvan sprites, would scurry up a slope and into the foliage, and be gone.

That evening the skies cleared as we left the jungle and strode down the rocky path into Yonsiton, a sweeping, stone-dotted meadow overhung by jagged bluffs. Above the Mekong great trees rose like sentinels, silhouetted against drifting banks of fog. A pair of wizened cowherds in black boots, baggy brown jackets, and worn leather hats welcomed us with few words and radiant smiles. My guides put up in an abandoned herders' hut. I thought I would do so, too, but it was foul with dung. So I pitched my tent on a knoll just beyond it.

After we used chopsticks to down a meal of stir-fried pork and rice cooked over a campfire fueled with branches Anadorma collected, I retired. The sun sank behind the peaks, the azure empyrean flushed with lavender before darkening to star-studded cobalt. Gazing out through my tent's gauze door, I watched meteors flit and flash, until I drifted off to sleep.

Sometime after midnight rain began pattering down. The sun never rose; the sky at dawn just shaded from black to luminous gray.

"Dogela Pass, Dogela Pass," said Tenzin, standing over the campfire as we ate breakfast. "We must start now, because ahead, high above, is Dogela Pass."

We were soon on the move, hiking back into a jungle invaded by drizzle and billowing mists, always skirting the Mekong. Now, for me, the charms of the trek gave way to its inevitable discomforts: fatigue and aching thighs; sweat soaking through my clothes; and shortness of breath that increased with our gain in altitude.

Just past a clearing called Dokin Lata, we crossed a wooden footbridge festooned with prayer flags, and found ourselves at the base of a steep tumble of boulders and bamboo thickets riven by a waterfall plunging down over rocks from fog-obscured heights.

"Where's the trail?" I asked Tenzin.

He pointed to the waterfall.

"You're kidding."

"No. The rains flood the trail now. It's the typhoon season. Wait."

He unsheathed his knife, dipped into the bamboo grove, and hacked about. A few minutes later he emerged clutching a stalk. He cut off a four-foot segment, honed the bottom end into a sharp V, and sawed the upper end flat.

"Here," he said, "you need this to hike with, or it's not safe." He turned to the mules. "Yiip! Yaaass! Gaaa!"

"Yiip! Yaaass!" echoed Anadorma.

Following the mules, we began climbing from rock up to slippery rock, hoisting ourselves a foot or two higher with each precarious step. Water poured down and the fog thickened; bamboo groves hedged in over the stream. Within an hour my thighs ached and my gait grew unsteady, and my (modern, waterproof) boots slalomed over moss and into puddles. Tenzin and Anadorma climbed on methodically, never pausing. Whenever I felt like complaining, I glanced at their footwear: cheap Chinese sneakers and shreds of socks.

My eyes stung with perspiration. I glanced up the trail. Two streambed switchbacks above me labored the mules, their loads wobbling, their iron-shod hooves clacking and slipping on the boulders, causing Anadorma to gasp. All at once I imagined the mules losing their balance and crashing down on top of us—a real and potentially lethal possibility. I knew from bitter experience that laden mules, like people, could misstep in the mountains and fall.

I dragged myself upward, wondering how I was to experience the spiritual on a pilgrimage that might end up mostly a workout for the body. Then I remembered the Buddha's words from the Dhammapada: "The mantram is weak when not repeated; a house falls into ruin when not repaired; the body loses health when it is not exercised."

Spiritual, in other words, should not mean sweat-free.

Around one in the afternoon, with the waterfall now far below us, we were trudging above timberline beneath looming anvil peaks, on a path zigzagging up an ashen scree, heading for prayer flags that flapped madly in clouds blowing through a saddle of barren rock: Dogela Pass, at 14,384 feet. Winds now chilled the sweat covering me, and I took baby steps to save strength, feeling as though a fiendish Samsara had racked me all day on his infernal wheel.

Anadorma, in the lead and till then spry, suddenly staggered and halted. She bent over double. Tenzin took out a pack of cigarettes, of all things, and handed it to her. Then he came over to me and proffered the pack.

"What?" I asked. "Are you crazy? We're at 14,000 feet here! And anyway I don't smoke!"

Looking grave, he pressed the cigarettes on me. They turned out to be a box of Chinese medicine for people with heart trouble; he wanted to share his pills with me, in case I needed them. Anadorma looked pale. She popped one and swallowed.

"Oh my God," I asked her, "are you okay?"

Holding her hand to her heart and inhaling deeply, she averted her gaze. After a while she got up and started walking again.

A half-hour later we reached the prayer flags, a mess of ragged banners strung from poles leaning every which way, many collapsing. Wind-driven clouds poured through the pass like steam from a locomotive's smokestack. Anadorma's eyes had lost all their sparkle. She and Tenzin dropped to their knees and began erecting tiny huts from stone slabs—"for a dead person's soul to live in," explained Tenzin. Tibetans believe that after death, our spirits spend 49 days on earth before reincarnation, and so need a temporary dwelling place. The yak-butter candles the bereaved burn in Buddhist temples are meant to light their way.

Anadorma stood up, her hands trembling, swallowing hard and rubbing her eyes. Finished with his hut, Tenzin pulled a rope decorated with prayer flags from our white mule's side pack, and tied it to a stake. Anadorma did the same, driving her walking stick into the ground and attaching her own banner to it. As mists flooded over her, she turned and faced the pass. Tears gushed out and she began choking through a recitation of prayers. She then dropped to the ground and prostrated herself three times, touching her forehead to the earth.

Then she stood in silence, looking down.

"Are you okay?" I asked softly after a minute or two.

Her face screwed up. "Papa!" she cried out, her voice cracking, tears streaming anew down her red cheeks. "He died two years ago!" She sobbed and wiped her eyes again, and turned away.

We stood for a while longer saying nothing, and then made our way up over the pass and into Tibet. From here to the horizon, peaks of 19,000 to 20,000 feet rose like slumbering Titans of gunmetal rock, their heads hidden in clouds.

We spent the night at Tsisonton, a meadow at 12,200 feet, alpine and fresh with conifers, and traversed by the Salween River, our new aqueous trailside companion, one tamer and less voluminous than the Mekong.

Tending another meal of rice, spicy green peppers, and gristly pork, Anadorma sat by the cooking fire as its embers dwindled, her face drawn, and occasionally daubed away a tear. Even Buddhists as devout as she could, at times, find less-than-perfect solace in their faith.

Fog slunk down from the surrounding crags and enveloped us in a milky gloom that turned leaden as the light failed; and our breath puffed white as we huddled around the fire, saying nothing. Later, as I settled into my sleeping bag, now and again gasping for breath in the chill damp air, I could do nothing but wish for the morning.

"This place is called Kanuma," announced Tenzin in a hushed voice, dropping back from the mules and stopping under a canopy of dripping deciduous trees. He stared reverently at a stream bubbling out from a waist-high cave, at the mouth of which shiny rocks lay plastered with one-yuan notes. He pressed his palms together, bowed, and recited prayers. "The god Tsukya lives here. We must honor him as we pass his home." To ignore the deity might invite his wrath—not all Bon's gods are kindly—which we could not afford in this wilderness.

He drew a one-yuan bill from his pocket, dipped it in the stream, and smeared it on the rock; he cupped his hands and took a drink. He stepped aside to let me do the same. He then pressed his palms together and prayed. We grabbed our walking sticks to rejoin Anadorma up the trail.

With Kawa Karpo always a powerful presence mounting into the clouds, we traipsed on through jungled lowland ravines dank and dark, save for the glowing lime green of vine-draped boughs, or errant phantoms of fog pierced by solitary spears of sunlight. The forest teemed with hidden life, often signaled by rustlings from unseen corners, the cries of secreted birds, the chants of invisible insects. It was easy to see why the votaries of Bon populated these redoubts with deities: every rock and fallen log seemed alive, every dell the home of concealed beings espying our progress through their domain.

The trail worsened, degenerating into a swath of muck, ankle-deep puddles, and slippery stones; we stumbled upward, with Anadorma lashing ahead the frightened, often stumbling mules. Somewhere far beneath us the Salween boomed, growing mighty with tributaries rushing down the slopes and investing the trail. As we pressed through the foliage, fat black slugs affixed themselves to my bare hands and neck. It was hard for me to get a grip on their squishy, slimy, annulated bodies and remove them. Then I realized that they were leeches, capable of cutting a Y-shaped incision in skin with the razor-thin teeth of their sucker mouths. I scraped them off, disgusted with the sores they left behind.

We finally emerged beneath cliffs by the river, at a grassy clearing named Gaituchyeta (altitude 9,940 feet), and halted for lunch. Here we found five or six garrulously cheery, scruffy-haired pilgrims, strapping their provisions to their backs (no mules for them) in burlap bags, readying themselves to depart. They left behind no litter; most pilgrims are too poor to throw away anything.

We started a fire in a makeshift hearth of castaway stones. The sun flayed us with fierce yet welcome rays; a rainbow limned prismatic colors into the azure. But our mule Hujya, once divested of his load by Anadorma, was unimpressed. He promptly lay down, his belly distended. He showed no interest in all the succulent grass around.

"He's been overeating," said Tenzin. "I'll cure him."

From his bamboo walking stick he cut a stiletto sliver four inches long. Hujya took alarmed note and clambered to his feet, neighing as his masters approached. They grabbed his head and pried open his mouth, exposing teeth encrusted with yellowish green cud. Tenzin inserted his fingers between them and yanked out his bulbous, pink-gray tongue. He jabbed the stiletto into the tongue's underside. Hujya, to my astonishment, offered little resistance. At least the first time. The stiletto somehow went awry, so Tenzin had to jab once more, twice more, and twist it in hard. On the third try blood spurted out, Hujya bucked, and they released him. He loped away, dripping blood, shaking his head and snorting.

But within an hour he was standing by the Salween, tearing grass from the muddy sward and chewing. Tenzin's folk treatment had somehow cured him.

The subtropical damp seeped into everything we owned; a warm mist floated in the air, settling clammily on our skins. Surely this was 100 percent humidity: I huffed onto my camera lens and the moisture would not evaporate. It was therefore with consummate relief that, at noon on our fifth day, we stopped for lunch in a fire-heated tent kiosk of sorts that sold Pepsis and (un-Buddhist) beer and the usual buckets of instant Chinese noodles to pilgrims. A grizzled smiling elder, who, despite his age, had just fathered a son he kept swaddled floppily to his back, offered us his hearth to cook lunch over.

The fire lifted our spirits. I took the chance to dry socks I had washed two days ago. I draped them on my walking stick and hung them over the flames.

The elder sat back, his smile fading. Anadorma stopped stirring her pot and regarded me with cold eyes.

"Ah, what's wrong?" I asked.

Said Tenzin solemnly, "Please remove the socks from the fire. Fire is sacred to us, and may not be used to dry socks or underwear. It could offend the gods."

"Oh, I'm sorry!"

I did as I was told. Everyone smiled again. How alien Tibetan Buddhism was proving to be! The rational precepts I so admired took second place to Bon-inspired superstitions. My pilgrimage around this holy mountain was not enhancing my belief, strongly held, in Buddhism's possible role as a potentially saving (rational) ideology, but was rather driving home the fact that once in the hands of man, it had been encumbered with all the trappings of local religion and thus unsuited for universal application.

An hour later we slipped through a tangle of prayer flags and crossed over Nantulaka Pass, out of fog and into light. The sun straightaway burned off our sweat. Gone was the jungle. Dry pink gravel, not mud, now skid underfoot as we descended through groves of pines, looping down toward the village of Abe. The temperature rose into the 90s, wearying us, slowing us down. Ticks now replaced leeches, skittering toward us, hungry for blood, over the pebbly ground whenever we stopped.

Perched on a promontory jutting above the valley floor, Abe was all stone houses and cornfields occupying terraces of dry earth. As evening fell we marched in, covered with dust, and made for the pilgrims' shelter (a concrete veranda under a wooden roof) on the outskirts. Clamorous gangs of rag-clad children skipped by; women in chupas (traditional pink woolen shawls) and floral skirts trudged along, sweating under baskets of produce. Goats, sheep, and donkeys snooped through refuse heaps, prodded by toddlers scarcely udder-high.

Soon two Buddhist monks, smiling dusty fellows dressed in robes of burgundy and saffron, stopped and peered into our courtyard, studying me with amazement as I set up camp. I went out to greet them. Li Qi Zhaxi was 27; Zhaxi Jansu, 36. They belonged to a monastery of the Nyingmapa ("Old Order"), the Tantric school founded in Tibet in the eighth century by the Indian monk Padmasambhava (Guru Rinpoche, in Tibetan), who allegedly converted Bon's gods to Buddhism. Tantric Buddhists recite the Sanskrit mantram *Om mani padme hum,* or "Hail the jewel in the lotus," in meditation as a means to enlightenment, and to invoke the deity of compassion, Avalokiteshvara, the patron saint of Tibet.

Before the Chinese reoccupied the feudal theocracy of Tibet in 1950 (the current Dalai Lama was then its ruler, and remains the head of the government in exile, in India, to which he fled in 1959), an estimated 25 percent of Tibetans were monks, and monasteries numbered around 2,700. The Chinese, especially during the Cultural Revolution, destroyed large numbers of monasteries, perhaps leaving as few as eight (though many are now being restored). Li and Zhaxi told me that monks in their monastery outside Deqin numbered about a hundred, and everything there was fine. They buttressed the impression I had that at least in the remoter parts of historical Tibet, the authorities did little to interfere with traditional Tibetan life.

"We're doing this pilgrimage for the second time," Zhaxi said. "We've taken two months to get this far." He glanced at our mules. "We carry all we have on our backs."

Two months! Surely they traveled following the path laid out by Shantideva in the Bodhicaryavatara, "taking [their] rest and wandering as [they] please . . . a clay bowl [their] only luxury." With my pack animals and GPS, I felt like a profligate on a luxury tour.

"Are you begging for alms," I asked, "as Buddha's disciples did?"

"No, we're buying our food," said Zhaxi, showing me a wad of yuan.

I told them of my interest in Buddhism and queried them about their practices. Had they read the Dhammapada?

"The what?" both replied.

Neither had heard of it; they read the Nyingmapa texts. I sensed again how deeply the (Indian) Buddhism I studied differed from theirs. I felt an even deeper alienation when they pulled out their Pö Bas, thumb-size leaden statuettes of the Buddha on what looked like stout triangular knife blades. Good-luck charms, they said, asking me to show them mine. I had none, and told them I didn't believe in such things.

"What, you don't carry a Pö Ba?" said Li. "Aren't you worried on such a pilgrimage? With my Pö Ba, I know no harm will come to me!" Tenzin looked equally alarmed. What the heck was I doing out in these dangerous mountains without a Pö Ba?

We were picking our way along a narrow trail circumventing a wall of rock and packed earth. A drizzle was falling—bad news.

"Weixian!"—dangerous—Tenzin declared, slowing and pointing to cracks in the trail. Boulder-size stretches of it, sodden by rains, often broke free and slid down the mountain during the typhoon months, which were also avalanche season—that is, now.

The next morning had come on foggy but torrid. We had left Abe kicking up dust, following a tenuous, foot-wide path; one slippage of earth, and we would tumble hundreds of feet into the Salween below. Death could strike, in Shantideva's words, like "a shattering thunderbolt from nowhere."

Floods had washed out the pedestrian bridge we needed to cross, which compelled us to detour up along the Yakura (a river as frothy and violent as the Salween), our destination, I assumed, another bridge.

But no. Between steel fixtures on opposing banks, 50 yards apart, a pair of rusty cables hung over the water.

"We'll have to cross by pulley," Tenzin shouted above the current's roar. "I'm afraid now. This could scare the mules and hurt them."

The wild-haired pulley masters, a man and a boy as wiry as they were grimy, allowed for little ceremony. Anadorma presented herself at the cable first. The man swung the "saddle" (a loop of doubled-over canvas dangling on a chain hooked to the cable) around her behind. He grabbed a mess of weeds (to protect his hand), settled into his own saddle, embraced her tightly with his free arm, and kicked off. The two zinged down over the rapids—he controlled their speed with his weedy grip on the cable—and landed with a bounce on the other side. The boy transported our gear the same way. The man then zinged back over to us from the second, higher pole-and-cable arrangement.

"Bring on the mules!" he shouted, switching the cloth saddle with heavier tackle.

Tenzin led unsuspecting Ramo to the pulley master. Without ado, the man looped and locked him into the tackle, placed his foot on his flank, and shoved the poor beast bug-eyed over the edge. The mule, whinnying insanely, swung out three-quarters of the way and lost momentum, halting above the rapids, where he hung kicking and neighing in blind panic.

A frenzied exchange of shouts ensued, with the man issuing commands to the boy on the other bank; the lad strapped himself into his saddle and pulled himself along the cable, stopping well clear of the lethally flailing hooves. He swung a hooked cable that latched on to the mule's line, and then pulled himself and his terrified charge back to the other bank. He nearly caught a horseshoe in the face releasing him from bondage.

Hujya and Tenzin went next, leaving me last. "Cross the river bravely," said the Buddha, referring to the torrents of fear and desire one must ford to attain Nirvana. I managed to be brave enough, though the cable somehow scraped my shirt, shredding it and singeing my chest. But I alighted otherwise unharmed.

We set out to rejoin the Salween, traipsing through barrens where prickly pear cacti replaced pines, with the sun hot on our necks and the temperature rising into the 90s. Now and then Tenzin severed cactus leaves with his knife, split them, and offered me the icy, pulpy green fruit within—a cooling consolation as the heat mounted.

By late afternoon, caked in grit and mightily tuckered out, we reached the shepherds' huts of Wencuan, a clearing by the river at a mere 5,800 feet, where we would rest for a day—our seventh on the trail, and the halfway point in the pilgrimage.

*

The Salween eddied and seethed beyond our camp, which stood beneath tawny serrated cliffs, 15 or 20 feet from the water. After pitching my tent, feeling filthy after having taken only occasional bucket baths for a week, I grabbed my soap, shampoo, and towel, and climbed across boulders to a secluded cove, fed by a spring, where a depression of stone, ringed by ferns and flowers, formed a thigh-deep pool emptying through a tiny channel into the river.

I stripped and climbed down into the pool, expecting the shock of frigid water. But it was warm! (*Wencuan,* I later learned, means "warm springs.") Nothing could have raised my spirits more. I soaped and splashed, heated further by the bronzing afternoon sun, my aching joints soothed and loosening. A week's worth of dirt swirled away into the Salween. Bathing here seemed like a sacred ablution.

I finished and spread out to dry my clothes, money belt, and boots, all of which had been damp for days and smelled of mildew. Then I climbed up the main boulder and stretched out on its hot surface, to let the sun heal me further. Above me dangled prayer flags, and someone had carved Tibetan verse around a pair of open eyes etched into the rock wall above me, reminding me of the Buddha's words: "The disciples of [the Buddha] are wide-awake and vigilant, rejoicing in meditation day and night." Avoiding intoxicants, ever wary of desire's deceits, one strives purposely for Nirvana—the state of truth and bliss beyond self, passion, and cravings.

I meditated, my thoughts gradually disappearing into the river's entrancing roar, until I surrendered to the Void. Or, more succinctly, fell asleep.

Back at camp a while later I found that Tenzin and Anadorma had also bathed. They sat, spiffy and burnished, by the fire sipping cups of *bai jiu* (moonshine), enjoying the evening cool.

"Like some?" asked Tenzin.

"No thanks."

I wanted nothing to interfere with my senses' imbibing all such a healing evening had to offer.

The moon soon waxed; bats circled and dipped in the gloaming. We chatted, really relaxing for the first time, and stayed up late. (We were to rest the next day.) They told me about their daughter and how she has to study in another village because remote

Yongzhi has only a (poor) primary school. Though belonging to a minority people exempt from the one-child law, they found one child was enough—all they could afford, in fact. The politics of repression never came up. Villagers in remote areas such as theirs had little to do with the Chinese authorities.

Tenzin said, "I'm happy with my work. I get to make the pilgrimage over and over; the more times, the better." The merit he gained would return to him. He had chosen what the Buddha called the "right livelihood"—a prerequisite for enlightenment.

On a black stormy night two days later all notions of bliss had passed. We found ourselves beyond the village of Tsana, struggling up another splashing cataract-path, never having recovered from the previous day, when the sun broiled the mercury to a hundred degrees, the earth turned ashen and sterile, landslides had destroyed stretches of the trail, and not even servings of cactus fruit could quench our thirst. Trekking in the dark here was madness, for obvious reasons; but, having no Tibet permit (which Nuoji had lacked the time to arrange for me in Zhongdian), I could not afford to be seen by the Chinese authorities in Tsana. So we crossed through it after midnight, encountering no one.

Now we clambered up and up, slipping on the rocks. My headlamp cast enough light for me to see, but not, of course, for the mules, which often stumbled. Stone walls soon hemmed in the watery trail—we were, it seemed, cutting through a village. Finally, on hearing Tenzin's plan to forge ahead to Sondula Pass all night and all the next day, I objected. Tsana was behind us, and now we had to rest and wait for dawn.

He assented. We turned off the gutter and into a village home's courtyard. Relieved, I got careless. I took two steps and fell over a pile of firewood, landing on my hands. As I pulled myself up, my left hand burned with pain. I trained my lamp on it to discover I had dislocated my ring finger, knocking it out of joint at the main knuckle, leaving the last two phalanges nearly perpendicular to the first.

Tenzin and Anadorma gasped, aghast. Straightaway urgent thoughts assailed me: How could I go on like this for another week? How could I endure even the three-hour hike back to Tsana and whatever crude medical center they had, a hike that would probably end with my expulsion from Tibet and the failure of my pilgrimage?

I grabbed my finger and wrenched it back into joint.

I fell, dizzy, onto the logs, stars spinning before my rain-pelted eyes. A wave of nausea swept through me. I closed my eyes and tried to blank my mind.

Several minutes later, I timidly tried to flex my fingers. They all worked. I lay there panting for a while, under my guides' distressed gaze. Then I rose, and we set up camp. Until sunrise we slept.

A true pilgrimage must involve suffering, I reasoned, watching my finger swell and turn blue.

Three days later, in the shadow of soaring arrowhead peaks, we hobbled into Jaka (altitude 8,275 feet), a meadow where pilgrims rest before the last, grueling two-day ascent through alpine forest to confront Kawa Karpo at its closest near Shula Pass, the highest of the journey (at 15,764 feet). After this comes the descent to Meili, the terminus village back in Yunnan Province. Fatigued, still addled by the thin air, and my finger hurting and increasingly stiff, I felt in sore need of comfort. But Jaka was a mournful place. By the turgid Wei Chu River a deserted chorten, messily adorned with prayer flags, occupied a gravel courtyard scattered with yellowed leaves from a shaggy-branched tree; next to the temple stood a whitewashed stupa, emblazoned with protecting images of the snow lion (Tibet's symbol). Between the two structures prayer wheels, metallic cylinders embossed with mantrams, stood idle, their gilt exteriors catching the sun's expiring rays.

After hailing the disheveled caretaker, who had emerged from a stone hut across a fallow field to greet us, tugging at his gold earring, my guides set themselves up in his spare room. I pitched my tent by the chorten's barred entrance, noting, on its door frame and cornices, yellow and blue geometric designs, and pictures of the Buddha in his various manifestations seated in the lotus position.

About the shrine hung an air of loss and abandon, as if pilgrims would never again cheer this spot. The Buddhas, impassive in their portraiture, gazed down at me in the cooling air. The lapidary lines introducing the Heart Sutra in *A Buddhist Bible* sounded softly in my mind:

Everything changes, everything passes,
Things appearing, things disappearing,
But when all is over—everything having appeared and disappeared,
Being and extinction both transcended—
Still the basic emptiness and silence abides,
And that is blissful Peace.

Such cold solace! Buddhism posits the Void, boundless eons fore and aft, the continuous death and rebirth of worlds, worlds in which our presence is fleeting and, in effect, doomed—if we choose to perceive our own failings and successes, our self-made sound and fury, as lasting and meaningful. The way out is to transcend our concerns for self into compassion for the other.

But as the final sliver of orange sun slipped behind the mountains above, a plump-cheeked teenage herder ambled into Jaka, prodding her two cows with a switch. She saw me and raised her hands, palms pressed together, in a lively greeting, and smiled, instantly raising my spirits. She then skipped around the prayer wheels, spinning them (each squeaky rotation represents a mantram recited), thus invoking Avalokiteshvara, the deity of compassion, the "Glorious Gentle One" who watches over Tibet.

She waved goodbye to me and poked her cattle up the trail. From on high she looked back at me and, laughing, waved some more. Her laugh rescued me. I climbed into my tent and fell asleep listening to the Wei Chu's throaty riverine song. In the Void only compassion and human warmth provide relief.

"Kawa Karpo!" declared Tenzin and Anadorma reverently two evenings later, as we and our mules stumbled to a halt at the edge of a ledge. "Kawa Karpo!"

Across from us at Meiju Buguo (a cloud-level bluff at 13,751 feet) the "Great God Peak" towered 9,000 feet higher still, reaching into the stormy ether, its summit wreathed in churning cumulus, its tarry black slopes streaked with sugary snow and sliding down into an abyss of mist beneath us. Bon legend has it that Kawa Karpo was once a hydra-headed evil deity who reigned in terror over the Tibetans. The Buddha defeated him in battle, took him as a disciple, converted him to compassion, and, finally, gifted him with this mountain in reward for his transformation.

But as Zhaxi had warned, proximity to the godhead comes at a price. Deprived of oxygen, beset with chills, I collapsed on my haunches, my eyes trained upward. In this Tibetan world of rock and sky and ever-thinning air, I faced the awesome deity on his own lofty terrain, craving, for the first time, the intercession of the Glorious Gentle One.

Loving Las Vegas

FROM *Harper's Magazine*

I PITY PEOPLE who've never been to Vegas. Who dismiss the city without setting foot on its carpeted sidewalks. I recognized myself in the town the first time I laid eyes on it, during a cross-country trip the summer after college. My friend Darren had a gig writing for Let's Go, the student-produced series of travel guides. *Let's Go: USA, Let's Go: Europe, Let's Go: North Korea* (they always lost a few freshmen updating that one). The previous year his beat had been New York City. We'd spent the summer eating 50-cent hot dogs at Gray's Papaya for breakfast, lunch, and dinner and "research-ing" dive bars like Downtown Beirut and King Tut's Wah Wah Hut, which were beacons of pure, filthy truth in a city still years away from its Big Cleanup. This summer he was assigned the Southwest. The subways didn't run that far out, but his roommate Dan had a car, a brown '83 Toyota Tercel, and the idea was we'd hit the open road and split the writing duties and the money three ways.

It was 1991. We'd just been diagnosed as Generation X, and certainly we had all the symptoms, our designs and life plans as scrawny and undeveloped as our bodies. Sure, we had dreams. Dan had escaped college with a degree in visual arts, was a car-toonist en route to becoming an animator. Darren was an anthro major who'd turned to film, fancying himself a Lynchian auteur in those early days of the indie art-house wave. I considered my-self a writer but hadn't got much further than wearing black and smoking cigarettes. I wrote two 5-page short stories, two 5-page epics, to audition for my college's creative-writing workshops and was turned down both times. I was crushed, but in retrospect it was perfect training for being a writer. You can keep "Write what you know"—for a true apprenticeship, internalize the world's indifference and accept rejection and failure into your very soul.

First thing, Dan hooked up our ride with new speakers. We didn't have money or prospects, but we had our priorities straight. I couldn't drive. That spring I'd sworn I'd get my license so I could contribute my fair share, but no.

I promised to make it up to Dan and Darren by being a Faithful Navigator, wrestling with the Rand McNally and feeding the cassette deck with dub. Dub, Lee "Scratch" Perry, deep, deep cuts off side six of *Sandinista!*—let these be indicators of the stoner underpinnings of our trip out west. As if our eccentric route were not enough. From New York down to Lancaster, Pennsylvania, to visit a college pal. He took me to my first mall. Even then, I had a weakness for those prefab palaces. "I asked Andy why there were no security guards around," I wrote in my notebook. "He told me I had a New Yorker's mentality."

Then hundreds of miles to Chicago for a disappointing pilgrimage too complicated and inane to detail here. We bought two tiny replicas of the Sears Tower as consolation. Veered south, taking in the territory, cooking up plots. Inspiration: "discussing the plot of the movie Darren wants to write, about 7-Elevens that land in cornfields." Down to New Orleans, where we slept in a frat house, on mattresses still moldy and damp from the spring floods. One of Darren's childhood friends belonged to the frat. His brothers wanted to know why he was "bringing niggers and Jews" into their chill-space. We sure were seeing a lot of America on this trip.

Then west to tackle our Let's Go assignment proper. We wrote up the Grand Canyon and Lake Mead. Decided to keep driving so we could spend the night in Las Vegas, the camping thing not really taking. ("Hours of agony. Impossible to sleep. Bugs. A consistent feeling of itchiness.") Miles and miles of black hills and winding roads, and then at one crest it manifested, this smart white jellyfish flopping on the desert floor. We suited up in a cheap motel downtown. Anticipating all the sweaty, laundryless days and nights we'd spend in the Tercel, we'd hit Domsey's, the famous Brooklyn thrift store, before we left New York City. We required proper gear for our Vegas debut. Dead men's spats, ill-fitting acrylic slacks and blazers with stiff fibers sticking out of the joints and seams. Roll up the sleeves of the sports jacket to find the brown stains corresponding to the previous owner's track marks. We looked great.

The whole trip out I'd maintained that I wasn't going to gamble. Gambling was a weakness of the ignorant masses, the suckers inhabiting the Great American Middle we'd just driven through. I was an intellectual, see, could quote Beckett on the topic of the abyss, had a college degree and everything. I can't remember the name of our hotel—the place was long ago demolished to make way for the Fremont Street Experience. It wasn't a proper casino, just a grim box with rooms upstairs, but the first floor had rows of low-stakes gambling apparatuses to keep the reception desk company. On our way to check-in, we passed the geriatric zombies in tracksuits installed at the slots, empty coin buckets overturned on their oxygen tanks. These gray-skinned doomed tugged on the levers, blinked, tugged again. Blink. Tug. Blink.

Grisly. We were about to get our first glimpse of the hurly-burly of downtown Vegas. Before we pushed open the glass doors, what the heck, I dropped a nickel into a one-armed bandit and won $2.

In a dank utility room deep in the subbasements of my personality, a little man wiped his hands on his overalls and pulled the switch: *More*. Remembering it now, I hear a sizzling sound, like meat being thrown into a hot skillet. I didn't do risk, generally. So I thought. But I see now I'd been testing the House Rules the previous few years. I'd always been a goody-goody. Study hard, obey your parents, hut-hut-hut through the training exercises of decent society. Then, in college, now that no one was around, I started to push the boundaries, a little more each semester. I was an empty seat in lecture halls, slept late in a depressive funk, handed in term papers later and later to see how much I could get away with before the House swatted me down.

Push it some more. We go to casinos to tell the everyday world that we will not submit. There are rules and codes and institutions, yes, but for a few hours in this temple of pure chaos, of random cards and inscrutable dice, we are in control of our fates. My little gambles were a way of pretending that no one was the boss of me. I hadn't had time for driving lessons before our trip because I'd been too busy cramming a semester of work into exam period. It had been touch-and-go whether I'd graduate, as I'd barely shown up for my final semester's religion course. The last thing

I'd wanted to hear about was some sucker notion of the Divine. There's a man in the sky who watches over everything you do, as all-seeing as the thousands of security cameras embedded in casino ceilings. So what? Nothing escapes his attention, and nothing will move him to intervene.

After a few phone calls, the administration released me into the world with a D minus. What was it to them? My passive-aggressive rebellion against the system was meaningless. The House doesn't care if you piss away your chances, are draining the college fund, letting the plumber's bill slide until next month. Ruin yourself. The cameras above record it all, but you're just another sap passing in the night.

The nickels poured into the basin, sweet music. If it worked once, it will work again.

We hit the street.

Before we left town, we bought dozens of tiny plastic slot machines from a trinket shop. Pink, red, lime green. They joined the Museum of Where We'd Been. Everybody's a walking Museum of Where They've Been, but we decided to make it literal. We had serious epoxy. Each place we stopped, we picked up souvenirs and glued them to the Tercel. Two Sears Towers sticking up over the engine, a row of small turquoise stones just above the windshield, toy buffalo stampeding across the great brown plain of the hood. Bull's horns from Arizona, in case we needed to gore someone at ramming speed, you never know, and four refrigerator magnets with Elvis's face on the front grille, to repel ghosts. We dotted the hood with glue and stuck the slot machines on, the polyethylene totems marking us as goofball heathens.

Weeks later, we were in Berkeley, sleeping on a friend's floor. The friend was cat-sitting for a drug dealer, weed mostly. I didn't approve of the drug dealer's lifestyle choices—for vacation, he went camping. We wrote up our time in the land of Circus Circus and the El Cortez, the cheap steaks and watered-down drinks. Let's Go's previous correspondent had been a prissy little shit, filling his/her copy with snobby asides. ("But what do you *do* there?") He/she wrote:

> Forget Hollywood images of Las Vegas glamor, the city at base is nothing but a desert Disneyland. As a small, small world of mild, middle-aged debauchery, Vegas simply replaces Mickey and Minnie with overbright

neon marquees, monolithic hotel/casinos, besequinned Ziegfieldesque
[*sic*] entertainers, quickly marrying them in rococo wedding chapels.

Percy, where are my smelling salts?

And what's wrong with Disneyland? It brings joy to millions
of people and tutors children about the corporate, overbranded
world they've been born into. "It's a Small World" is a delightful
ditty, an ode to that quality of everyday existence by which the soul
is crushed, diminished, *made entirely small.* No need to denigrate it.
Better to worry about the lack of a clear antecedent for "them" in
that last sentence. I would protect Vegas. How about:

> The magic formula of this oasis of mild, middle-aged debauchery—of-
> fer everything but the gambling cheaply, and if you gild it, they will
> come—was hit upon by Bugsy Siegel in the 1940s. Das Kapital is wor-
> shipped here, and sacrifices from all major credit cards are happily ac-
> cepted.

Much more upbeat, although I apologize if some readers were
tricked into thinking the city is devoted to Karl Marx's book. I
think we were just trying to get fancy with *capital.*

Some of the classic joints we wrote about are gone now, and
we captured a time before Las Vegas made a science of demog-
raphy, but most of the basic observations in our Let's Go entry
remain solid. In between games of Risk (board-game version), we
cut up the previous year's text, discarded what we disliked, and
glued (more glue) what remained onto white paper alongside our
revisions and additions. "But remember that casinos function on
the basis of most tourists leaving considerably closer to the poverty line than when they arrived; don't bring more than you're
prepared to lose cheerfully" became "But always remember: *in
the long run, chances are you're going to lose money.* Don't bring more
than you're prepared to lose cheerfully." No, casinos are not out to
destroy you. The destroyed do not return to redeem reward-card
perks and lose more money. No one forces doom upon you, folks.
You need to seek it out.

We kept "Drinks in most casinos cost 75¢–$1, free to those who
look like they're playing" but added "Look like you're gambling;
acting skills will stretch your wallet, but don't forget to tip that
cocktail waitress in the interesting get-up." Out with the general
tsk-tsking and upper-middle-class disdain, in with "For best results,

put on your favorite loud outfit, bust out the cigar and pinky rings, and begin." You have been granted a few days' reprieve from who you are. Celebrate the gift of a place that allows you to be someone else for a time.

Then Darren wigged out and caught a plane home. He still had his childhood room. Dan was going to drive back east in August, maybe get a Eurail pass that autumn and check out some fucking castles or whatever. I was out of money when Dan set off, and I asked whether he had any room in the car, as the guy we'd been crashing with, the cat-sitter, was bailing out of California, too, and bringing all his stuff. After all, I was a good navigator. As luck would have it, they intended to stop off in Vegas on the way back.

No one laid a hand on the Museum when we were on the road. Odd, moon-faced kids—a motel owner's brood—gawked at it when we stopped at night but dared not touch. A cop pulled us over for speeding in Massachusetts the last day of our return trip. "What's all this?" We shrugged. What to say? He wrote us a ticket. The Museum lasted a few days in Cambridge before teenagers or disaffected housewives or whoever stripped everything. We'd made it home, and the spell had worn off.

We grew up. Our generational symptoms faded bit by bit. I got a job working for the books section of a newspaper. We ran fiction sometimes, mixed in with reviews. When the writing teacher who had rejected my work in college submitted a story, I passed on it. Not out of revenge; it just wasn't up to snuff. As in cards, it was business, not personal. I badgered one editor for an assignment, that assignment led to another, and soon enough I was paying my bills freelancing. Played poker at Dan's house every Sunday for a couple years, and one day we picked up hold'em. Dan got into computer animation and founded a visual-effects company, rendering animation for movies such as *Requiem for a Dream* and *Black Swan,* which Darren directed. We'd waited for cards, and then we played them.

Open Water

FROM *The New Yorker*

SHORTLY BEFORE DAWN, not so long ago, I stood in the stern of a small boat in the Venetian lagoon. I was rowing with a single oar, facing forward, heading west. Floodlights on the wharves of the mainland chemical plants, six miles away, glowed in front of me. I crossed a mile of shadowed, shallow, open water (dry — *secca* — is the name for such areas, accessible only by motorless, flat-bottomed boats) and entered a dredged-out channel called Canale Orfano, the Orphan Canal. It took me to the Graces, an island that measured 800 feet by 600 feet and was surrounded by a marble-topped brick wall that plunged into the water. Confined within the wall was a complex of tile-roofed buildings, sculptures, meadows, trees. In the 15th century, it was a monastery. More recently, it served as the site of an infectious-diseases hospital. Now it was abandoned. At the island's dock, a series of signs declared, WARNING ARMED GUARDS; BEWARE OF DOGS; WARNING VERY DANGEROUS DOGS; WARNING DANGER!!

I tied up and called, *"Ciao?"*

The yellow façade of an administrative building was penetrated by a breezeway leading to the island's interior. I saw green, wildness. I jumped ashore — silence — and took some tentative steps. Through a dusty window on the right side of the breezeway, a receptionist's desk held a touchtone telephone and a gray appointment book, covered in dust. Lined up on a low wall were discarded medical instruments: a speculum, a curette, a mysterious metal rod that ended in a nautilus whorl. Paths led off in three directions.

A shovel—long, wood-handled, sturdy—sat in a pile of rubble. I grabbed it to ward off the dogs.

Then I heard a motor. First commuter of the day. I spun and walked back to the dock. A big, fat-bellied, bargelike boat, known as a rat—*topo*—and used for hauling everything in the city, from trash to melons to cement, three men in it, burbled by. I leaned on my shovel and stared them down. Then I walked back through the breezeway and hooked to the right, down an overgrown path. I found an abandoned boathouse, a 12-person Carrara marble banquet table with a corner knocked off, a vegetable garden going to seed, a delicately carved Renaissance wellhead. An actual rat crossed in front of me, stopped, turned, and gave me a proprietorial glare.

This was my third day rowing the 212-square-mile Venetian lagoon—at high tide, a crescent-shaped mirror broken by bricks and trees that seem to float; at low tide, a series of multiacre puddles threaded with shipping channels—and camping on a selection of its many abandoned or semiabandoned islands. I'd lived in the city when I was younger, and had seen its identity steadily succumb to tourism. I wanted to find out if it was possible to have an unmediated experience of the place, to discover a Venice that was all my own. And so: the islands. Some are no larger than a gas station, while others contain villages, farms, cathedrals. Venice occupies the center point of its lagoon, which is 8 miles at the widest, and 30 miles long. This center is all that most visitors see today. But when the city was flourishing, between the 9th and the 18th centuries, its islands were used to grow its food, defend against invaders, provide respite for its rulers, and isolate the sick, the insane, the pious, the dead, and the hazardous (gunpowder; glass furnaces; unmarried women). The 19th-century poet and critic Luigi Carrer wrote of the islands, "It could be said that the marvelous city, falling from the sky and splintering apart, had scattered about itself these shards of beauty."

Now, on this particular shard, inside a quarantine ward, I wandered through dispensaries carpeted in glass. Rifled-through cabinetry spilled paper onto nurses' stations. Back outside, the sun was starting to burn off the morning fog. Butterflies—along with rats, the principal inhabitants of Venice's islands these days—were coming out. Three hundred feet to my left, in a grove of trees, a Doric capital was shining in the sunlight. I made for it, plunging waist-deep into brush and thorns, beating both back with the shovel. I found a large clearing in which two freestanding columns were connected by a rusted iron bar. An open meadow ran like an aisle between them, concluding at the island's southern perimeter wall, where a marble throne was built into the bricks. A sad, regal, teenage girl was sitting on it. She was opulently dressed, and tiny—three feet tall. Around her neck was a plastic necklace so oversize that it hung to her ankles. A wicked-looking little boy in a beret stood between her knees, tangled in it. He was staring right at me, pointing all his fingers, obviously modeled on some naughty, centuries-old Venetian child. I pulled off the necklace. And I could easily have removed Mary, Jesus, and the throne, and taken them with me. Instead, I put down the rosary and was hit with a strong feeling that I'd had my share of trespasser's good fortune.

I sprinted across the island, jumped back into my boat, and rowed off. I had just made it to the island's northern edge when two launches, bristling with armed police from the Division for the Protection of Cultural Patrimony, roared up to the dock. Men stormed the island, searching, I assumed, for a suspicious man with a shovel, recently sighted by a passing commuter. A Venetian-art expert in New York later described the Madonna as "late fourteenth century, although some parts of it already look forward to the early fifteenth century." I attempted a nonchalant stroke and did not turn around.

I first came to Venice as a prisoner. Twenty-one years earlier, a blue Fiat van crossed what was once the longest bridge in the world, over the western lagoon from the mainland, carrying six inmates of a reform school.

I had committed the ridiculous crime of stealing a Yamaha motor scooter. A potential felony—which wasn't ridiculous at all. This was in San Francisco, a few months before my 18th birthday. I blamed it on the fact that my wealthy, divorced parents had thrown me out of their homes and I'd had no money for the bus. My father, negotiating with a probation officer, hit upon a novel way to get me out of both jail and the country—a school for troubled youth in Tuscany, supported by Diane Guggenheim, who'd lived much of her life in Europe, like her cousin Peggy. Diane poured her family's money not into art but into a school that espoused the philosophy, as the headmaster told the *International Herald Tribune*, that "every child has his own Renaissance." The State of California agreed to release me. A trip to Venice was part of this rebirthing program.

Driving had removed the temptation for any of us to make a break for it on the train. Now we were hustled onto the No. 1 *vaporetto* (the word for ferry or waterbus). An hour later, we disembarked near the sea. It was January, and we were the only guests at our hotel.

That night, as we walked single file over a bridge, a splash and a creak made me turn. I saw a boy around my age getting into a 20-foot vessel I can now identify as a *mascareta*. Then a girl came out of the shadows behind him. He took a candle from his jacket pocket, impaled it on a metal spike attached to the bow, and, after a few flicks of a lighter, got it going and set a glass windshield in place. She sat on a crossbar. He picked up a long oar and started rowing—not poling but rowing, standing up and facing forward. His feet were positioned like a skateboarder's.

I was a skateboarder. This made stealing a motor scooter not just a crime but a betrayal; what true skateboarder stole something that eliminated the need for skateboarding? Italy, with its cobbled streets, was unskateable—Venice especially so. But as the *mascareta* moved through the water, the boy's glide and stance were so familiar that I felt I was looking at myself in some other life.

Nobody else noticed. The boat was silent as it navigated the dark canal, moving out of sight and then drawing close again, sliding around buildings before turning into the open lagoon.

Years later, as I prepared to return to Venice and explore the islands, I dug up a book, bound in marbled paper, entitled "The Private Journal of Sean Wilsey." It described my first visit: "I bought a *gondoliere* hat today and I am wearing it constantly. A man walked by me in the street and said, *'Gondoliere dove va?'*"—"Gondolier, where are you going?" The comment was doubly sarcastic, posed, as it was, in the formal tense, but I was too enthralled by the city to notice: "I will never be quite the same after Venice because it has shown me that man can create true beauty and that I believe is Man's purpose." I dipped my gondolier's hat in the Grand Canal "to season it."

On the obligatory gondola ride with my school group, out on

the open water in front of the Doge's Palace, I asked to switch places with the gondolier. He shrugged. Standing at the top of the boat's crescent-shaped hull added two feet to the view. But I could barely keep my footing. This was like riding a skateboard on a sheet of ice. Propulsion and control were arcane verging on impossible. We began to spin in a circle. I looked as far as I could across the water, at islands covered in trees and mysterious buildings, until the gondolier repossessed his oar. An entry in my journal reads, "I made a solemn vow to return to Venice and become a gondolier."

Post-reformation, my father called me at school, saying, "Maybe you should try six months as a gondolier. How is your singing in Italian? I'd hire you for a short trip." He suggested that I look up Gino Macropodio, who'd rowed him on his third honeymoon, with my mother. It seemed that Dad had taken note of my Venetian obsession, and figured out how to use it to avoid extending an invitation home. But this also struck me as a good way of reconciling the seeming irreconcilables of my situation. After two years in reform school, I was a naif who used to be a thief, an uneducated 20-year-old without a high school diploma. In *Death in Venice,* Thomas Mann described the "roguish solicitude" of a gondolier. This was something I could shoot for.

First, I called the gondoliers' union and asked for an apprenticeship. Someone there told me to learn the mechanics of rowing—no gondolier had the time to teach me—and put me in touch with a rowing club (a collection of dues-paying Venetians who convene to row traditional wooden boats). I was instructed to get off the *vaporetto* on the island of Giudecca, find the second-longest bridge, walk away from it to the south, and knock on the last door before the water. The sidewalk turned into a wooden gangway covered in guano and shellfish fragments. Behind the door, a heavyset man in his 50s invited me into an office where the red-and-gold banner of the Venetian Republic was displayed like a rebel flag. He took $24 off me, and held up a white V-neck T-shirt with burgundy trim, emblazoned front and back:

ASS. CANOTTIERI GIUDECCA

Gliding around with the word *ass* on your chest was very skaterly. I took it.

"But who will teach me to row?"

"Other members will help you. Just ask for lessons."

In the club's yard was a barn full of *sandoli, s'cioponi, mascarete, pupparini, sanpierote,* and *vipere,* flat-bottomed, slant-sided vessels—low, maneuverable, brightly painted, faster than a gondola, which presents too much freeboard to the wind. There were also a few gondola variants: a *gondola traghetto,* for carrying commuters (old, leaky, pink); a couple of narrow, fast, and impossible-to-control *gondolini;* and a *caorlina,* rowed by up to six men, and so big it was effectively a barge.

A sullen pensioner called Luciano sat next to a crane on the seawall, reading a communist newspaper. His job was to put craft in the water. But Venice was in a rowing recession. Oars were the province of the old. Hours passed without anyone coming to the club. I finally found a fat, shirtless man in mirrored sunglasses and asked him, "*Signore,* could I go out rowing with you?"

Not just silence but a complete refusal to acknowledge my presence. In the caste system of Venice, I was unnoticeable.

This went on for days. I came to the Ass., greeted Luciano—"*Ciao!*"; "Oh, *ciao* . . ."—and was ignored, until one afternoon, unexpectedly, he put down his newspaper, fetched a red-and-white *mascareta,* craned it into the water, and told me to climb down an iron ladder and get in. I rowed for 15 elated minutes, incompetently. Then a wiry and very tan old man showed up and agreed to take me out. He hollered, "Shonee! Your leg—*you've got it completely wrong!* You are not capable!" The next day. "Worse dun yesterday! You row from the *stomach* not the *balls.*" Soon I was being berated several hours a day.

Gino Macropodio, my father's gondolier, 60 years old, wore his shirts unbuttoned to the navel and a solid-gold Lion of St. Mark on a chain around his neck. Most days, he could be found at the gondoliers' station immediately in front of the Doge's Palace, or at the bar around the corner, which he called "my office." Twice a week, he partnered with a pair of young gondoliers, Roberto and Romano, to work shifts from a small wharf behind St. Mark's Basilica.

Gino possessed Mann's "roguish solicitude," but in combination with knowledge, effusiveness, and style. In conversation, he could veer from Venetian history to classical music to the wonders of combining alcohol with athleticism. (He'd once rowed three miles across the lagoon with six friends to drink 40 bottles of wine—"and then we rowed *back*.") He made statements like "I have a terrible defect—I like to see beauty." In response to my credulous admiration for Giacomo Casanova's escape, in 1756, from a cell beneath the lead roof of the Doge's Palace, an action so bold that the memoirist found himself "alone, and at open war with all the forces of the Republic," Gino was doubtful: "They let him go. Nobody escaped from there. It's fiction. He worked for the state. Really, Sean, reading is good. But you must try to look between words and see the point of view." I have never heard it put forward by any historian that Casanova went from Venice to Paris not as a fugitive but as a spy.

Gino's favorite composer was Wagner, "an immortal artist," who "died February 13, 1883, if I recall correctly. Maybe '82. But of the day I am certain. February thirteenth. And he was an autodidact."

"Like you."

"No. I'm nothing."

Silence.

"I'm a scoundrel of the canals of Venice."

The first time we met, I showed up unannounced, covered in sweat, hair matted in multiple directions, wearing the Ass. shirt. Gino shook my hand. He couldn't close his fingers completely—the result of 40-plus years of holding an oar—but looked at me hard with pinpoint pupils in eyes so shockingly blue that they seemed recently dredged. He bought me a coffee, and explained that the hunk of cast metal on the gondola's prow was the *ferro,* meaning "iron." It supposedly represents the elfin cap worn by doges in lieu of a crown, each of the six jutting teeth beneath it standing unromantically for one of the six administrative zones (*sestieri*) of the city. (I, romantically, considered getting it tattooed on the back of my neck.) The *ferri* on other Venetian boats look like ax heads, spears, shells.

Gino took me out rowing. All boats rowed with a single oar require a forward and a reverse stroke to execute a straight line. This is complicated by the fact that a Venetian oar is 14 feet long, and is held in place by a piece of carved walnut called a *forcola* (a bastardization of the word *fork*) that rises up from the right side of the aft gunwale. A little C-shaped incursion, called a bite (*morso*), is cut into the *forcola* and acts as a cradle for the oar. At the entrance to the bite, a nib, known as the little nose (*nasèlo*), takes the full power of the straight-course-keeping reverse stroke and, if you have no skill, fails to keep the oar from popping out. My oar popped out all the time. This was called "losing the *forcola*." When I lost the *forcola*, 14 feet of hardwood crashed onto the starboard freeboard, knocked me off balance, and needed to be lifted back into place as the vessel bobbed and pitched. It was weightlifting while surfing. When he saw how terrible I was, Gino said I should keep practicing and invited me to dinner. His policy: feed me, teach me about Venice, and see if I became a rower.

Gino loaned me a copy of *Life on the Lagoons,* by the Scottish historian Horatio Brown. Published in 1894, and dedicated to "my gondolier," the book stated that the "traditions and instincts of republican Venice endure with greatest tenacity among the gondoliers . . . They, more than any other institution of Venice, have successfully withstood the changes and chances of progress." As I got to know Gino, I realized that custodian of the past was a role he inhabited with seriousness. I once heard him express his esteem for a friend by saying, "He has never owned a motor."

Gino was only ever called Gino, making him an exception to the rule that all gondoliers have nicknames—when he was young, he was known as the Rooster, but nobody called him that anymore. His shift partners, Roberto (nickname: Nanoci—Little Giovanni) and Romano (nickname: Pullman—Bus), called me Che Qua e Che Eà. This was pronounced as a single (Hawaiian-sounding) word, "Kekquakeà," and meant "He Who Is Here and There." It seemed to encapsulate my efforts at self-reconciliation.

Most of the talented amateur rowers in Venice were training for regattas. My breakthrough came at the instigation of a female racer named Claudia Forcolin, who taught me the most important thing about rowing: not to think. She had blond hair (like most Venetian women), and when she took me out, she wore a bikini. This was overwhelming to Kekquakeà. I forgot how bad I was and started to get better. Then she said, "I think you're good enough to row in the back."

This allowed her to lounge in the prow. She seemed to love this. I definitely loved this. Claudia occupied some of the more spectacularly clueless passages of my journal: "She is quite attractive. She took off her clothes and rowed in her bathing suit which was distracting. Bikini. Madonna! We are friends, though, and I am in no way interested in her. She is really sweet and I made her smile *parecchio*"—a lot. I went on: "She said yes. I CAN ROW DA SOLO! I then went to San Marco to tell my Gondolier friends the good news. They bought me drinks like usual and I asked Gino if he would adopt me."

Claudia was the object of gondolier admiration. Perhaps there was more to Kekquakeà than at first there seemed? Or perhaps not. The nickname was uttered with a knowing smile and a slight handsome shake of the head. Not contempt. There was fondness in it. It was understood that there was something charming about me. But I was dimly aware that the phrase alluded to other, less flattering qualities. Roberto told me, "It doesn't really have a meaning." So I decided it just meant *me*. In the evening, I'd find myself crossing a bridge and hear it shouted by somebody rowing in the canal below: *"Oi! Kekquakeà!"* and then the person would drift around a corner and be gone. It was like a surfer's name. Like the big kahuna. Only 20 years later, at the start of my trip through the lagoon, did I learn that it was a phrase applied to misfits, and, among gondoliers, it was double-edged in its affections. An Italian friend alerted me to yet another connotation: "It's sort of a way of saying you're kind of a fag."

I began to venture out on my own. From the journal of Kekquakeà: "The wind was pretty difficult . . . I couldn't even get going and went backwards . . . Then I got pushed into a boat with two guys fishing. I said *Ciao,* how are you, I came to visit, and believe it or not they knew me. One of the guys was a gondolier."

"Kekquakeà," he said, and gave me a shove. "And from there on I handled it. I went out and circled a pole that I had chosen. I then drank my milk and came back."

I rowed the canals of Giudecca. I rowed a mile south to St. Clement's Island, known to locals as the Island of the Insane, for its female psychiatric ward. Gino described the inmates as "dangerously crazy women, not just moody ones." He added, "There's another one for those." I tried to cross the Canal of Giudecca to Venice but couldn't handle the waves kicked up by motorboat traffic. After a handful of solo outings, I came alongside the seawall and Luciano refused to lower the Ass.'s crane. The man who denied my existence (Gigi, I'd learned from the other rowers) appeared, accompanied by Claudia. He took off his shirt and handed it to her—I wanted to do that.

She smiled and said, "Good luck."

He climbed down into my boat, installed a second *forcola*, in the front, and put an oar in the bite, and we rowed into the lagoon. A few hundred feet out, he spoke to me for the first time.

"Turn the boat around."

Pulling a 180 is a simple maneuver if the vessel has any forward momentum: you slip your oar under the water, feather it, and press down. As I did so, I noticed that people had gathered on top of the wall to watch us. Gigi shouted, *"Via!"*—"Away!"

The *mascareta* lurched, and he'd already completed two strokes by the time I regained my balance. Then two more. I suddenly understood that I was supposed to do what any Venetian could do: use the leverage of my position in the back to overpower him and turn us away from the wall. It was a battle—a tug of war—in which I had the advantages of youth and physics.

My oar popped out of the *forcola*. I slammed it back in and rowed a stroke. He completed two more in the time it took me to get back in position for another. We were going straight for the wall. I put in one more hard stroke, applying so much force to the *forcola* that it threatened to shatter. I heard cheers from the wall. Then I lost the *forcola* again, said "Fuck!" in English, felt the boat turn his way, slammed the oar back in, threw my whole body into the next stroke, hit the water with the wrong part of the blade, and sent a curtain of spray over us both.

Someone shouted, "Go, go, Sean!"

I fell to a knee. We began to turn in his direction. I got up, socketed the oar, and put in two decent strokes, and we were straight again.

I matched him stroke for stroke for the next 10 strokes. Everyone on the wall was screaming now. We headed straight for the bricks and the noise, fast, neither of us stopping, 50, 30, 10 feet, and I was still giving it everything, no longer flailing, the spear tip of the boat's *ferro* shaking back and forth: his way, my way. Just before we crashed, he snapped his oar out of the *forcola* and stabbed it into the lagoon. The boat turned and slapped the wall sideways.

Everybody whistled and shouted: "Gigiiiii! Shoneeee!"

He pointed to himself, and said, *"Sessantaquattro"*—sixty-four.

Youth is full of prohibitions. Stealing that Yamaha in San Francisco was a gesture of autonomy. Once I was cleansed of my criminality, naiveté became my way forward. Kekquakeà's way—to deny even the existence of prohibitions. And returning at the age of 40 to row the parts of the lagoon that I'd never been able to reach was an attempt to reclaim my independence *and* my naiveté (both long gone). When I left Venice, the old man who'd told me to row from the stomach had said, "You can't *go;* you're a Venetian now." But I'd known just enough to be certain of how little I knew. Now I thought I was ready. It was a midlife-crisis kind of readiness—I figured that I wasn't going to do it when *I* was 64. But I also sensed a possibility of balancing between two places and getting to some long-desired third. And what better place to balance than in a row-boat on the waves?

In Manhattan, where I'd lived for 18 years, I talked to Dean Poll, the holder of the concession to run Central Park's boathouse, and the custodian of the gondola *La Fia di Venezia* (subsequently rechristened *Dry Martini*)—a gift to the Central Park Conservancy from a Venice-loving philanthropist. Poll gave me permission to go out on the lake, after specifying, "Any money you make with that you gotta split with me." The official gondolier, Andrés García-Peña, an Italian Colombian painter, took me on as his apprentice after I promised I wasn't out to steal his job.

The only customers I ever rowed were a pair of 11-year-old Latino kids, Alex and Benny, who shouted from the shore, "How much for a ride?" I quoted the base rate, $30, and they replied, "Can we just sit in it?" I took them out anyway. Afterward, they declared, "You got *mad* skills!" and insisted on paying me a dollar. Like any good scoundrel of the canals, I kept Dean Poll's 50 cents.

I contacted the Venice City Hall, got permission to visit the is-lands (many of them are barred to visitors), asked Gino Macro-podio if he could help me find a boat—and if he would come with me.

"No," he said. "I've put down the oar. And don't try and do it in a gondola. Gondolas aren't made for the wind. You need an outboard motor to be safe."

"No way. I'm doing this with my own strength."

"But not in a gondola."

So he found me a wooden racing *sandolo* owned by a rowing club on a littoral island between the Adriatic and the lagoon. Af-ter I'd passed a rowing exam, I was given the boat—sky-blue and bright yellow, 24 feet long—and warned of numerous dangers.

There was a crime wave in the lagoon. Albanians were running guns and stashing them on deserted islands. Mosquitoes carried West Nile virus. Certain gondoliers were fighting certain taxi drivers for the city's cocaine trade, so taxi drivers were capsizing rowboats.

Aside from encountering a woman sunbathing nude on the deck of a runabout, and some inquisitive monks on an island that had been given to an Armenian, in 1717, to establish a religious order (one asked if I'd discovered "the nymphs, the sirens, the women who live under the water"), I found that my first two days were uneventful. On the third day, on fire with adrenaline from my close encounter with the police, I rowed two miles, hard, for Bailer Island, where, out of sight, I tied my *sandolo* up to a navigational piling and fell asleep.

Nobody came to arrest me. Waking, an hour later, I rowed a couple more miles in the wind (barely easier than swimming), and wound up on St. George in the Seaweed, where, in the 1850s, John Ruskin was captivated by "the kind of scenes which were daily set before the eyes of . . . Titian." A monastery had been founded there in the 11th century, and in the early 1400s St. Lorenzo Giustiniani, the first patriarch of Venice, after renouncing his wealthy family ("Christ died on a cross and you want me to die on a feather bed?"), lived there in seclusion, as did the young Pope Eugene IV. The monastery contained a library of rare manuscripts and paintings by Bellini, which were destroyed in a fire in 1716. Before the completion of a railroad bridge from the mainland, in 1846, St. George was the first piece of Venice that travelers encountered when arriving from the west, and it was the site of grand receptions intended to impress them. Eugenio Miozzi, the renowned Venetian bridge engineer, described the treaties hammered out in the seaweed as "anticipating by eight centuries the role of the League of Nations."

I rowed for all that, aiming for the western side of the island. But the tide had shifted and was heading out fast. Whitewater broadsided the boat. I lost the *forcola*. Finally, I gave in and rode the current, like a surfer, to the east side.

The wind died as I rounded a corner and entered a canal-cum-driveway that led into the island's walled interior. A boathouse at the end had collapsed—rammed, it looked like, by a huge *topo,* which was still sitting there. I spied a mooring spot, tied up, jumped ashore, and immediately stumbled upon a matching pair of bronze door handles, scaled in rust, sitting in a pile of bricks, bottles, seaweed. They were heavy, and when I scratched them, dull gold shone beneath the corrosion. I stashed them in my boat. The way onto the island was blocked by the wreck, which had been turned on its side by whatever wind, current, or drunk had brought it here. I pulled myself aboard, balanced along the vessel's gunwales, and then dropped to the other side. I was in a room at the bottom of a stone staircase that clung to a wall with no visible means of support. Everything was powdered with flaked plaster. Vaulted ceilings were punctured by sunlit holes.

I decided to climb the unsupported staircase. Before I could reconsider this plan, I was 40 feet up in the air. I hugged the wall as I went, sidestepping pieces of fallen ceiling, and tiptoed, imagining that silence would make me lighter. On the top level of the building, the floor had collapsed in sections 10 feet wide. The wind blew hard through empty windows. It was a monumentally stupid place to go alone. But here was a pope's-eye view.

I tiptoed back downstairs, thinking that I would row east, to the former insane asylum. Now it was a five-star hotel. I'd find the concierge, ask if I could camp on the lawn, spend the evening at the hotel bar.

But I'd been enchanted by the stillness. Leaving the island's protected canal was like entering the jet stream sideways. The wind and the current had picked up, and I got snapped around a full circle and a half—like a skateboard trick. When I tried to flee back to St. George, I was hauled 200 feet to the Fusina Canal, the last dredged channel before the mainland. I began to row as I'd done with shirtless Gigi 20 years before, imagining that spirits were punishing me for taking the corroded door handles from the island. Door handles that saints and popes had grasped. I wanted to throw them overboard but couldn't take a hand off the oar.

I gave six hard pushes, came alongside a navigational piling, and grabbed—almost hugged—it. I'd been blown a quarter mile and could see the long bridge to the mainland. I turned on my cell phone for the first time in days. Crouching to get out of the wind, I called Gino. He didn't answer. And what was I going to ask him? When he was 12, he'd brandished a disastrous report card and told his mother, "The undersigned is *done with this.*" She'd told him, "Go work." He'd lied about his age, got a construction job, saved enough money to buy a gondola, and became the fifth in a line of Macropodios to take up the profession. He never married or had children. He never joined the gondoliers' union. He never needed anyone's help. I lay in the boat, and an hour later called again.

He said, "Good idea tying yourself to the piling."

"Yeah. But, Gino, how much longer is this wind going to last?"

"Who can say? It's the wind. It'll last till it's over. And now you see it's no joke out there in the lagoon. I told you you should have got a motor. Aren't you glad you didn't go in a gondola?"

"Yes."

"Well, anyway, I'm going to move my car right now. Which is good luck for you, as it's in the parking lot on Little Trunk." In the distance, I could see this island, which was devoted entirely to parking facilities.

"If you can meet me there, come meet me," Gino said.

"I'll try. The wind seems favorable."

Before I could change my mind, I started out, and as the white-caps of broadsiding waves sloshed in, rowed not so much with my muscles as with my bones. A wave hit so hard I thought my arm might break. The car ferries and big ships and heavy commercial traffic that frequent a shipping lane grew closer. I was in serious danger here. If I lost control, I'd get swept away to the impassable margin between water and land which Venetians call the Dead Lagoon, or drift into the path of a tanker. Yet I managed to cross the Canal of Giudecca—clogged with intersecting wakes and metal hulls, which I'd failed to cross 20 years before—aimed for an empty slip at a *vaporetto* depot, barely dodged a car ferry, and banged into the dock. I tied up and lay down. I was on the floor of a maritime bus station.

"And now?" Gino asked, when we found each other. "What are you going to do? Don't you have a plan? This lagoon is very treacherous."

Getting to Little Trunk had taken all my strength and ability. I needed Gino to help me. He was 80 and hadn't picked up an oar in 14 years. Whenever I asked him if he missed rowing, he said, "I've done my part."

He looked at the *sandolo*. "You made it here by yourself. Nobody towed you?"

"No."

"But you can't stay here."

I pointed to a methane plant on Braid Island, 500 feet from where we stood. "I could make it to that. Or try and go under the bridge and camp on Second"—a trashy-looking island that I'd regarded with pity every time I'd crossed by road or rail into Venice. "Mostly, I'd rather sleep on a clean island, where there aren't any rats, and I don't think Second is a very clean island."

"No. It's not so clean."

We both started laughing. He put a hand on my shoulder. "The north lagoon is calmer. And, if you make it through the night up there, then row to Venice in the morning. Find a rowing club along the edge of the city, and ask them to keep your boat so you can meet me for lunch. I'll be in St. Mark's Square at noon."

I steered for one of the mainland bridge's arches and slipped in. There were gray-white stalactites hanging from the ceiling, and gallery upon gallery of arched darkness. A sloppy concrete seam joined the newer automobile section to the old train trestle. The cold, damp air smelled ratty. I rowed out fast, and as I emerged by the squalid Second, littered with plastic detritus in medicinal shades of green and pink, I saw another island, about a mile away, its rolling, sunlit meadows rising, miragelike, from the water.

It was unwalled, and at the point of my *ferro*'s spear was a floating dock and a red *sandolo* with two men standing beside it. I saw them see me as I approached. I waved, taking one hand off the oar. Spooked, the men untied and rowed off in a needlessly wide arc. I pulled up and took their place. Then I heard low voices. Tucked away in a slot of water behind the dock were two more men, dressed in black, in a red-and-black speedboat. One had silver teeth and a nose ring. Both had buzzcuts.

I said, *"Ciao."*

Silence. I turned away. The strong smell of pot followed me.

I looked at my map. I was on the island of High Field—a natural location for drug dealers. The rowers in the red *sandolo* had probably left with such haste because they'd seen my boat's colors and feared exposure by a rival rowing society. Hoping to appear Venetian, I lay low.

Then I heard a motor. A stocky teenage girl was hunched at the tiller of a purple-and-white speedboat, prow out of the water and bearing aloft its name (in purple script): *Baby Fragola*. She came in fast, blasting techno, holding the collar of a huge Presa Canario war dog. A clean-cut boy in a white speedboat followed. They tied up and went ashore into a grove of trees. Ten minutes later, they returned and both climbed into *Baby Fragola*. Behind them came a man with spiked hair, arms banded in tribal tattoos. The buzzcuts jumped to their feet. Slurred words drifted my way.

Spike: "I threw him off a bridge near St. Mark's."

Buzzcut No. 1: "I smoked it."

Spike: "Then I took my clothes off."

A small wooden rat powered by a big American outboard arrived. A middle-aged man in a white T-shirt and khakis looked suspiciously at the island's inhabitants before coming ashore, followed by a salt-and-pepper Shih Tzu.

Spike asked for the time, and a buzzcut responded, "Five to eight." Dinner. They started up their engine and jetted off toward Venice. I jumped onto the dock and walked up through the trees. In the middle of a large, open meadow, the mirage I'd seen from afar, I found the man and his dog.

I asked, "Is this a safe place to camp? With the drugs and all?"

He said, "The smokers are harmless. But this is a place where people come to fight." He took a boxer's stance. "Looking for fights."

Aside from Piazza San Marco, all of Venice's squares are called fields (*campi*). They used to be covered in grass, and served as arenas for boxing. In 1574, Henri III, before being seen off by a ceremonial artillery salvo from St. George in the Seaweed, watched a staged brawl that he described as "too small to be a real war and too cruel to be a game."

"You're a foreigner?"

"Yes."

"If fighters come, just say you're not from here. They'll probably decide to leave you alone. Now let me show you where the good fruit is."

He led me down a slope to a tree bearing cherry-size plums, plucked one, and said, "No pesticides—delicious."

I ate one and immediately grabbed another.

"Don't gorge yourself. Eat too many and you'll get the shits." He squatted to mime this.

After he left, I had High Field to myself. It was ringed by trees, the high, open namesake meadow like a monk's tonsured scalp in the center. I discovered a handful of stone houses—an abandoned village—in a thick copse of trees.

At the top of the meadow, some benches had been set up under an open-sided shelter. The bleachers for battles. Nearby was a fire pit big enough to cook an ox. On a piece of planking were two competing graffiti:

Respect this sacred place.
Eat my penis you with your canoes of shit.

I lit a fire, simmered tomatoes and beans in a pan, undressed, and bathed with water that I'd brought in a huge rubber bag that doubled as ballast. A large, bright green grasshopper watched me from the graffitied plank. Then I put on pajamas, grabbed the pan and a spork, and looked out at the domes and bell towers of the city. Kekquakeà: a pajama-clad foreigner with a pot of beans and a pet grasshopper. He had found himself in the heart of Venice, alone.

By nine the next morning, I was back on the water, rowing toward lunch with Gino. The tide was out and the *secca* so extreme that I could submerge only half a blade. But a *sandolo* is designed to go anywhere. I quickly made it to the Canal of New Foundations, Venice's West Side Highway. I jay-rowed across six lanes of heavy traffic, threading like a skateboarder between a cab and a bus, and claimed a lane right up against a stone embankment. I got rocked hard, without interruption. Buses passed. Taxis. Runabouts. Rats ranging in comparative size from pickup to semi. Endless moped-like skiffs. *Vaporetti* filled with tourists came one after the other, backing up at the floating docks and jamming me into pockets of churning foam, stone and metal on all sides. I began to tread water with the oar, hovering in place, something I'd seen gondoliers do but didn't know I could do. On my right was a city canal called the Stream of Beggars. A taxi cut me off and I rocked through its wake into the stillness.

A couple of hundred feet of easy water and I saw a white-haired man standing on the dock of a rowing club. I held out my hand. Without hesitation, he took it and pulled me in. I told him my name.

"Tony," he replied.

"You must be a rowing club."

"Yes. We're the Generals."

On land, I started sorting through my gear and talking expansively about the previous night. "The fruit trees. The grass. The moon. The view. The friendly grasshopper. It was incredible. The best night I've ever spent anywhere."

Tony said, "It used to be a garbage dump. They closed it when it caught fire."

I took a long shower in the club's locker room, dressed in the cowboy boots and suit jacket I'd been hauling around in a dry bag all week, and walked across town. In St. Mark's Square, surrounded by tourists, Gino shook my hand and said, "You made it."

Before I left Venice 20 years earlier, Gino had let me row his boat for the first time with paying passengers. Two German girls, blond, twins, looked up at me in what I imagined was awe as I rowed them down the Stream of Lead. I rowed without speaking or splashing—preserving the silence in order to amplify the moment when we'd burst into the Grand Canal.

Then I one-handed my oar, pointed over their heads, and shouted, "Ponte Rialto!"

The girls performed an ungainly swivel, which rocked the boat and made me stumble. Simultaneously, the No. 2 express *vaporetto* came powering through the canal's sharpest bend, arced under the bridge, and bore down on us. We were going to be rammed. My adrenaline surged—but I had no idea how to move my 36-foot skateboard out of the way. A strong hand pushed me down into a crouch and wrested the oar from my grip.

Gino had been watching, poised to take over, noting criticisms and whispering warnings. Now I stayed low as he detailed my many mistakes.

"You let go of the oar just now for what reason?"

"To point out the sights."

"Never let go of the oar."

"Okay."

"Talk about history; don't point at it."

"Yes."

"And what did you think you were doing with that wall you almost ran into? Do you know how much it costs to buy a new *ferro*?"

Gino had kept the oar. I'd crouched, embarrassed. Then a

quick glance showed that the twins were enraptured. Fifteen minutes later, their parents handed over a hundred dollars in cash for the near drowning I'd provided.

"May we please have a photograph?" they asked me in perfect English.

After delivering a halting English response, "It's. No. Problem," I placed a daughter under each arm and Gino took the picture. I imagine I'm still in a family album, somewhere in Germany, as a gondolier's son.

Contributors' Notes
Notable Travel Writing of 2013

Contributors' Notes

Elif Batuman is the author of *The Possessed: Adventures with Russian Books and the People Who Read Them.* She is a staff writer for *The New Yorker* and writer in residence at Koç University in Istanbul. In 2007, she was the recipient of a Rona Jaffe Foundation Writers' Award.

Julia Cooke is the author of *The Other Side of Paradise: Life in the New Cuba* (2014). She is a frequent contributor to *VQR* and *Condé Nast Traveler,* and her writing has also appeared in *Guernica, Departures, Metropolis,* and the *Village Voice,* among others. She has lived in Mexico City and Havana and now calls New York City, where she teaches at the New School, home.

Janine di Giovanni has reported on war for nearly a quarter of a century, working in some of the world's most violent places. Her trademark has always been to write about the human costs of war and to single out individuals to recount the cost of conflict and human rights abuses. She is the author of five books, and her recent TED talk "What I Saw in the War" has gotten more than 600,000 YouTube hits. She is currently Middle East editor of *Newsweek,* a consultant on the Syria crisis for UNHCR, and a contributing editor at *Vanity Fair.* Her *Vanity Fair* article "Madness Visible" won the National Magazine Award and was later expanded into a book. She has also won Britain's Foreign Correspondent of the Year, two Amnesty International awards, a Nation Institute grant, and Spear's Memoir of the Year for her book *Ghosts by Daylight.* She has taught and lectured on human rights around the world, including at Sciences Po in Paris. In 2010, she was the president of the jury of the Prix Bayeux-Calvados for war correspondents. A member of the Council on Foreign Relations, she lives in Paris with her son, Luca. She is currently writing a book on Syria.

A. A. Gill, a contributing editor at *Vanity Fair*, is a features writer for the *Sunday Times* (London). He is the author of several books, including *To America with Love*, *AA Gill Is Away*, and *Here & There: Collected Travel Writing*. He lives in London.

Arnon Grunberg was born in Amsterdam in 1971 and works as a novelist and reporter. His work has been translated into 27 languages.

Harrison Scott Key is the author of the memoir *The World's Largest Man*, due out in 2015. His humor and nonfiction have appeared in *Oxford American*, *Creative Nonfiction*, *The Pinch*, *Reader's Digest*, the *Chronicle of Higher Education*, *Swink*, and elsewhere, and his work has been adapted for the stage by Chicago's Neo-Futurists in their show *Too Much Light Makes the Baby Go Blind* and others. He teaches at SCAD in Savannah, Georgia. On Twitter, he's @HarrisonKey.

Peter LaSalle is the author of several books of fiction, most recently the short story collection *What I Found Out About Her* and a novel, *Mariposa's Song*. A collection of his essays on literary travel, *The City at Three P.M.: Writing, Reading, and Traveling*, is forthcoming in 2015 and includes pieces from magazines such as *Tin House*, *WorldView*, *The Nation*, *Creative Nonfiction*, *Agni*, *Profils Américains* (France), and *Memoir Journal*, as well as *The Best American Travel Writing 2010*. He divides his time between Austin, Texas—where he teaches creative writing at the University of Texas—and Narragansett in his native Rhode Island, while also continuing to travel as much as he can to explore the various places where his favorite literature is set.

Amanda Lindhout and **Sara Corbett** are authors of the book *A House in the Sky*. Lindhout is the founder of the Global Enrichment Foundation, a nonprofit that works with women in Somalia and Kenya. Sara Corbett is a contributing writer for the *New York Times Magazine*.

Andrew McCarthy is the author of the *New York Times* best-selling travel memoir *The Longest Way Home*. He is an editor-at-large at *National Geographic Traveler*. He has written for the *New York Times*, *The Atlantic*, and numerous other publications. McCarthy is also an actor and director.

Michael Paterniti is the *New York Times* best-selling author of *Driving Mr. Albert: A Trip Across America with Einstein's Brain* and most recently of *The Telling Room: A Tale of Love, Betrayal, Revenge, and the World's Greatest Piece of Cheese*. His writing has appeared in many publications, including the *New York Times Magazine*, *National Geographic*, *Harper's Magazine*, *Outside*, *Esquire*, and *GQ*, where he works as a correspondent. Paterniti has been nominated eight times for a National Magazine Award and has been the recipient of an NEA grant and two MacDowell Fellowships. He is the cofounder of a children's storytelling center in Portland, Maine, where he lives with his wife and their three children.

Stephanie Pearson is a freelance journalist and contributing editor to *Outside* magazine. Her work has appeared in *Outside, O: The Oprah Magazine, National Geographic Traveler, Men's Journal, Popular Photography*, and the Lonely Planet Great Escapes book series, among others. She splits her time between northern Minnesota and Santa Fe, New Mexico.

Tony Perrottet was born in Australia and was a denizen of the East Village of Manhattan for many years. He is a contributing writer at *Smithsonian* magazine and a regular at *the New York Times, Wall Street Journal Magazine, Condé Nast Traveler,* and other publications. He is the author of five books, most recently *Napoleon's Privates: 2,500 Years of History Unzipped* and *The Sinner's Grand Tour: A Journey Through the Historical Underbelly of Europe.* He is currently working on a book about travel in ancient China.

Matthew Power was a contributing editor at *Harper's Magazine* and wrote for *GQ,* the *New York Times, Outside,* and *Men's Journal.* His work has been anthologized in *The Best American Travel Writing, The Best American Spiritual Writing, The Best American Science and Nature Writing,* and *The Best American Nonrequired Reading.* He was a three-time finalist for the Livingston Award for Young Journalists in international reporting. Power was the recipient of the 2005 Society of American Travel Writers Lowell Thomas Travel Journalism Gold Award for Best Land Travel Article and the 2008 Bronze Award for Best Adventure Travel Article, and he was a 2004 nonfiction scholar at the Bread Loaf Writers' Conference. He died in March, while on assignment in Uganda.

Steven Rinella is the author of *The Scavenger's Guide to Haute Cuisine* and *American Buffalo: In Search of a Lost Icon.* His writing has appeared in many publications, including *Outside, Field & Stream, Men's Journal,* the *New York Times, Glamour,* and *Bowhunter.*

David Sedaris is the author of the books *Let's Explore Diabetes with Owls, Squirrel Seeks Chipmunk, When You Are Engulfed in Flames, Dress Your Family in Corduroy and Denim, Me Talk Pretty One Day, Holidays on Ice, Naked,* and *Barrel Fever.* He is a regular contributor to *The New Yorker* and BBC Radio 4. He lives in England.

Peter Selgin's *Drowning Lessons* won the 2008 Flannery O'Connor Award. He has also written a novel and two books on fiction craft. His memoir, *Confessions of a Left-Handed Man,* was shortlisted for the William Saroyan

Prize. He teaches at Antioch University and is assistant professor of creative writing at Georgia College & State University.

Bob Shacochis is the National Book Award–winning author of seven books and countless magazine pieces. His most recent novel, *The Woman Who Lost Her Soul,* was a finalist for the Pulitzer Prize in 2014.

Alex Shoumatoff has 10 published books and since 2001 has been the editor of a website, Dispatches from the Vanishing World. He was a staff writer for *The New Yorker* from 1978 to 1987 and a founding contributing editor of *Outside* and *Condé Nast Traveler.* He is a senior contributing editor to *Vanity Fair.*

Gary Shteyngart was born in Leningrad in 1972 and came to the United States seven years later. His debut novel, *The Russian Debutante's Handbook,* won the Stephen Crane Award for First Fiction and the National Jewish Book Award for Fiction. His second novel, *Absurdistan,* was named one of the 10 Best Books of the Year by the *New York Times Book Review,* as well as a best book of the year by *Time,* the *Washington Post's* "Book World" section, the *San Francisco Chronicle,* the *Chicago Tribune,* and many other publications. He has been selected for *Granta's* Best of Young American Novelists list. His work has appeared in *The New Yorker, Esquire, GQ,* and *Travel + Leisure,* and his books have been translated into more than 20 languages. He lives in New York City. His most recent work is the memoir *Little Failure.*

Thomas Swick is the author of a travel memoir, *Unquiet Days: At Home in Poland,* and a collection of travel stories, *A Way to See the World: From Texas to Transylvania with a Maverick Traveler.* He has written for the *Missouri Review, American Scholar, North American Review, Oxford American, Wilson Quarterly, Ploughshares, Boulevard, Smithsonian,* and *Afar.* This is his sixth appearance in *The Best American Travel Writing.*

Patrick Symmes is a journalist who has published more than 30 articles in *Outside* magazine. He is the author of *Chasing Che* and *The Boys from Dolores,* both of which treat the revolutionary history of Latin America.

Jeffrey Tayler is a contributing editor at *The Atlantic* and has also written for *National Geographic, Condé Nast Traveler, Smithsonian, Foreign Policy, American Scholar,* and *Harper's Magazine,* among other publications. He is the author of many critically acclaimed books, including *Facing the Congo* and *River of No Reprieve.* His seventh book, *Topless Jihadis: Inside Femen, the World's Most Provocative Activist Group,* is out now as an e-book. "In the Abode of the Gods" is his fifth story selected for inclusion in *The Best American Travel Writing*. Since 1993, he has lived in Moscow.

Colson Whitehead was born in New York City in 1969. His writing has appeared in the *New York Times*, *New York* magazine, *Harper's Magazine*, and *Salon*. He is the author of several books: *The Intuitionist, John Henry Days, The Colossus of New York, Apex Hides the Hurt,* and *Sag Harbor*. His most recent novel, *Zone One*, was published in 2011. His newest book is a work of nonfiction, *The Noble Hustle: Poker, Beef Jerky and Death,* published in 2014. Whitehead was a 2002 MacArthur Fellow.

Sean Wilsey is the author of the memoir *Oh the Glory of It All* and coeditor, with Matt Weiland, of *State by State: A Panoramic View of America*. He currently serves as editor-at-large for *McSweeney's*.

Notable Travel Writing of 2013

SELECTED BY JASON WILSON

PAUL SALOPEK
  Out of Eden. *National Geographic,* December.
  A Stroll Around the World. *New York Times,* November 24.
DAVID SEDARIS
  Long Way Home. *The New Yorker,* April 1.
NOAH GALLAGHER SHANNON
  To Land Unknown. *New York Times Magazine,* May 19.
JESSE SMITH
  Florida's Promise. *Smart Set,* March 26.
THOMAS SWICK
  Warsaw, Liberated. *National Geographic Traveler,* August/September.

THOMAS CHATTERTON WILLIAMS
  How Hipsters Ruined Paris. *New York Times,* November 10.
ALEX WILSON
  At the Crossroads. *Surfer,* July.

THE BEST AMERICAN SERIES®

FIRST, BEST, AND BEST-SELLING

The Best American series is the premier annual showcase for the country's finest short fiction and nonfiction. Each volume's series editor selects notable works from hundreds of magazines, journals, and websites. A special guest editor, a leading writer in the field, then chooses the best twenty or so pieces to publish. This unique system has made the Best American series the most respected — and most popular — of its kind.

Look for these best-selling titles in the Best American series:

The Best American Comics

The Best American Essays

The Best American Infographics

The Best American Mystery Stories

The Best American Nonrequired Reading

The Best American Science and Nature Writing

The Best American Short Stories

The Best American Sports Writing

The Best American Travel Writing

Available in print and e-book wherever books are sold.
Visit our website: *www.hmhbooks.com/hmh/site/bas*